GREENING INTERNATIONAL INSTITUTIONS

The Law and Sustainable Development Series

Edited by Philippe Sands, Foundation for International Environmental Law and Development (FIELD), School of Oriental and African Studies (SOAS), London University

'Global environmental problems demand global, cooperative solutions. That means rethinking international law. Building on their formidable international experience, Philippe Sands and his colleagues have launched us into that rethink. A legal parallel to the Blueprint series: welcome, timely and provocative.' David Pearce

UNCED called for the 'further development of international law in the field of sustainable development'. A new area of law is now evolving to take into account issues of environment, development and social justice. The books in this series aim to address and define the main legal issues involved and to contribute to the progressive development of law.

Other titles, all available from Earthscan, include

Greening International Law
Edited by Philippe Sands

Improving Compliance with International Environmental Law
Edited by James Cameron, Jacob Werksman and Peter Roderick

Interpreting the Precautionary Principle
Edited by Tim O'Riordan and James Cameron

Property Rights in the Defence of Nature
Elizabeth Brubaker

GREENING INTERNATIONAL INSTITUTIONS

Edited by Jacob Werksman

earthscan
from Routledge

First published by Earthscan in the UK and USA in 1996

This edition published 2013 by Earthscan

For a full list of publications please contact:

Earthscan
2 Park Square, Milton Park, Abingdon, Oxon OX14 4RN
Simultaneously published in the USA and Canada by Earthscan
711 Third Avenue, New York, NY 10017

*Earthscan is an imprint of the Taylor & Francis Group,
an informa business*

A catalogue record for this book is available from the British Library

ISBN: 978-1-85383-244-4 (pbk)

Typesetting by JS Typesetting, Wellingborough, Northants.

CONTENTS

ACKNOWLEDGEMENTS

The editor would like to thank the contributors, the publishers and his colleagues at FIELD for their patience, and their understanding of the many logistical challenges that were faced in completing this volume. Special thanks go to Maria Adebowale at FIELD and Rowan Davies at Earthscan for their perseverance and assistance.

None of this work would have been possible without the help of FIELD's funders, including the Ford Foundation, the W Alton Jones Foundation, the Rockefeller Brothers Fund, the John Merck Foundation, the Conservation, Food & Health Foundation, and the German Marshall Fund, which have enabled FIELD to continue to work to challenge, support, criticize and reform many of the international institutions described in this volume.

LIST OF CONTRIBUTORS

Mehmet Arda is Chief, Environmental Issues Section, Commodities Division, UNCTAD, Geneva. After obtaining a BA in Economics from Dartmouth College and a PhD from the University of California, Berkeley, he taught at Ankara University. He joined UNCTAD in 1982 and his current interests include internalization of environmental costs, environmental policies and economic instruments in developing countries, and international trade in environmentally friendly natural products.

Mark Berman, BA, LLB (Saskatchewan), LLM in Public International Law (London) is currently working as a Legal Officer and Special Assistant to UNEP's Assistant Executive Director, Division of Policy and External Relations. He has previously worked as a Legal Officer with the International Legal Instruments Branch of UNEP's ELI/PAC. Prior to joining UNEP he served in a number of capacities with the Canadian Federal Department of the Environment.

Kyle Danish is a Master of Public Affairs candidate, 1996, at the Woodrow Wilson School of Public and International Affairs, Princeton University, and a Juris Doctor candidate, 1997, at Temple University School of Law.

Donald Fitzpatrick, MA LLB, University of Aberdeen, specializes in environmental and international law and has served internships at FIELD and at the United Nations Economic Commission for Europe.

Hilary French is a graduate in history from Dartmouth College, and holds a Masters degree from the Fletcher School of Law and Diplomacy of Tufts University. She is a Senior Researcher at the Worldwatch Institute, a Washington, DC based non-profit research organization which analyzes global environmental and development issues. Her research and writing focus on reforming international institutions to protect the environment and to promote sustainable development, as well as the linkages between international trade and environmental policy. She has lectured and published widely. She represented Worldwatch during the UNCED process.

Vanessa C J Goad, BA (Hons) English and German Law, University of Kent at Canterbury/Philipps-Universtat, Marburg is a qualified solicitor specializing in maritime law at the law firm of Watson, Farley and Williams in Piraeus, Greece. She formerly worked as Recent Developments Editor of the *Review of European Community and International Environmental Law* at FIELD.

Korinna Horta is an environmental economist at the Environmental Defense Fund, a non-profit organization in Washington, DC. Horta, who is European and fluent in six languages, works with non-governmental organizations and grass roots groups in developing countries to promote public policy changes in international financial institutions and related private sector investments.

Wayne King is the Managing Director of Island Wide Services Ltd, located in Rarotonga, Cook Islands, an environmental consulting company specializing in sustainable development and environmental management issues in small island states and non-industrialized countries. He is the former Executive Officer of the Cook Islands Environment Service, and represented his government during the UNCED process, and at the meetings of the UN Conference on the Sustainable Development of Small Island Developing States, and the Climate Change and Biological Diversity Conventions.

Martti Koskenniemi is Professor of International Law, University of Helsinki. He is Former Counsellor (legal affairs), Ministry for Foreign Affairs of Finland.

Aradhana Kumar is an attorney with Milbank, Tweed, Hadley and McCloy in Washington, DC. She did her LLM at Washington College of Law, and has a law degree from India and a Masters degree in International Relations. She worked for the Environmental Defense Fund after graduating from law school.

Zen Mackuch, (BA, LLB, MSc, LLM) is a barrister and solicitor qualified in Canada and England. He is a Lecturer in Environmental Law at Imperial College, University of London, and a member of the Denton Hall Environmental Law and Management Group. He specializes in international, EC and comparative environmental law and international trade law, and has provided advice in these fields to fifteen governments.

Chris Mensah is Legal Adviser to the International Civil Aviation Organization (ICAO). Before joining ICAO he acted as legal adviser to the Permanent Mission of the Republic of Vanuatu to the UN, and served on the Vanuatu delegation during the UNCED negotiations and at the Earth Summit.

Jean Milner received her undergraduate and law degrees from the University of Cape Town in South Africa. In 1995, she completed an LLM in international and environmental law at The American University, in Washington, DC, and was recently admitted as a member of the New York State Bar.

Annie Petsonk is International Counsel for the Environmental Defense Fund. Prior to coming to the EDF, she was a trial attorney at the Environment and Natural Resources Division of the US Department of Justice, and worked at UNEP's Environmental Law Unit. She is an Adjunct Professor at the George Washington University and University of Maryland law schools. Her particular interests include extraterritoriality, and economic incentive approaches to international environmental law.

Philippe Sands is a Lecturer in law at the London University School of African and Oriental Studies (SOAS) and Director of Studies at FIELD. He is also Visiting Professor of International Law at New York University and a practising barrister. He has acted as Counsel for several cases before the International Court of Justice and European Court of Justice.

Helen Sjöberg is currently Assistant Professor at the Department of Environmental and Energy Systems, University of Lund, Sweden, and a Research Associate at the Natural Resource Management Institute of Stockholm University, Sweden. Her educational background is in the fields of biology and international affairs. She has worked for a variety of international organizations including the Global Environment Facility, the Global Environment Fund, the World Bank, and the Carnegie Council for Ethics and International Affairs.

Han Somsen is a Lecturer in law at Warwick University. He is case editor of the *European Environmental Law Review* (Graham & Trotman) and European Advisor to *Water Law* (Wiley). He has edited *Protecting the European Environment: the Enforcement of EC Environmental Law* (Edward Elgar) and published widely in various journals on issues related to European environmental law.

Alexander Timoshenko, Doctor of Juridical Sciences, is Chief, International Legal Instruments Unit at UNEP's Environmental Law and Institutions Programme and Activity Centre. He is an international legal scholar and former Director of the Department of Environmental Law at the Institute of State and Law of the USSR Academy of Sciences. In his previous positions he has collaborated extensively with UNEP, the UN Economic Commission for Europe, the Brundtland Commission, the World Conservation Union (IUCN) and other international bodies.

Jacob Werksman is Programme Director at FIELD, and a Visiting Lecturer in International Economic Law at SOAS, University of London. At FIELD, he had provided legal advice and assistance to developing country governments and intergovernmental and non-governmental organizations, on the institutional and financial aspects of the design and implementation of international environmental and economic agreements.

INTRODUCTION

by Jacob Werksman

OVERVIEW

This book was commissioned to mark the 50th anniversaries of the conferences that established the United Nations and the Bretton Woods institutions (the World Bank and the International Monetary Fund), and to anticipate the approach of the fifth anniversary of the United Nations Conference on Environment and Development (UNCED, or the Earth Summit).

The San Francisco[1] and Bretton Woods[2] conferences launched history's most prolific period of international institution building. Held towards the end of second world war, these conferences created a role for international institutions as critically important fora for the development and coordination of international efforts at resolving armed conflicts, preserving peace and promoting social and economic development.

The 1992 Earth Summit took the concept of global governance a stage further, by seeking to resolve emerging conflicts between the development aspirations of humankind and the need to preserve the earth's finite natural resources. Large parts of UNCED's agenda for 'sustainable development' were also entrusted to existing and new international institutions.

50 years after San Francisco and five years after Rio, the authors of the chapters that follow have been asked to contribute to an intensifying process of intergovernmental review, by assessing the extent to which the trust of the international community in these institutions has been justified. The authors draw upon a variety of backgrounds and disciplines. Some have decades of experience, others are at the outset of their careers; some have studied the opportunities for progress from an academic distance, others have worked directly, from the inside and the outside, with the institutions they have been asked to describe.

The result is a diverse collection of pieces, from which common themes emerge. The reader can draw from each chapter an understanding of the shape and function of each institution, of the scope of the activities with which it has been entrusted, and of the niche it seeks to occupy in the larger system. What emerges is a pattern of organization that has grown and contracted, erratically and organically in response to the competing demands, concerns and resources of the states and constituencies it serves.

WHAT IS AN INTERNATIONAL INSTITUTION?

All of the institutions described in this book (with the exception of Chapter 15) are 'international' in that they are created by states. States create institutions as a means of achieving collective objectives that could not be accomplished by acting individually. Either directly through international agreement, or through the act of an existing international institution, states establish a new institution's purpose, the scope of its powers and the shape and functions of its organs.

In doing so, states devolve to the institution an aspect of their sovereign power, vesting the institution with an independence and will of its own. The extent of this devolution may, in turn, determine the ability of the institution to influence the behaviour of states. Thus, a theme running through the chapters that follow is an assessment of the powers that have been vested in the institution by its member states, and the effectiveness with which it has been able to exercise those powers.

Today, international institutions occur in great variety. The two main academic disciplines that study them – lawyers and political scientists – have tended to analyze, define and categorize international institutions differently. One of the more sophisticated taxonomies of international institutions identifies a 'sliding scale' in the formality of international institutionalization. At one end of the scale are institutions that merely provide fora for international cooperation; at the other end are organizations with powers and characteristics distinct from the states that created them.[3]

Lawyers tend to concentrate their attentions on the formal end of the scale, on international institutions that are known as 'international organizations'. Schermers and Blokker define international organizations as:

> forms of cooperation founded on an international agreement creating at least one organ with a will of its own, established under international law[4]

The definitions and taxonomies of the political scientist, on the other hand, take us away from legal formalities. Haas, Keohane and Levy, for example, make a point of focusing their definition of an institution on the extent to which it effects state behaviour rather than the formal legal structure of the institutions. Thus they define institutions, which can include international organizations, as:

> persistent and connected sets of rules and practices that prescribe behavioral roles, constrain activity, and shape expectations. They may take the form of bureaucratic organisations, regimes (rule-structures that do not necessarily have organizations attached), or conventions (informal practices).[5]

This volume, commissioned and edited by a lawyer, and tied to an agenda of reform of the international organizations that make up the United Nations and Bretton Woods systems, selects from the more formal end of the institutional spectrum. The authors, many of whom are also lawyers, are, however, interested in the full range of the 'sets rules and practices', from the formal to the informal, that accrete to each institution and that seek to influence, prescribe, constrain and shape state behaviour. Thus, the contributions that follow are less concerned with definition and taxonomy, legal or otherwise, and instead focus on what the institutions do, and how their roles have developed in response to UNCED's call for sustainable development.

WHAT CAN OR DOES AN INTERNATIONAL INSTITUTION DO?

International institutions can engage in the challenge of environmental protection and sustainable development on a variety of levels. Although UNCED was an international process, driven to a large extent by perceived threats to the global environment, much of the text of Agenda 21 focuses on local environmental issues, such as land use, drinking water and air pollution. International institutions can play a role in responding to challenges at both the local and the global level, whenever international cooperation is required.

Generally, international institutions have taken up environmental issues in response to challenges related to:

- threats to the global commons and the allocation of shared resources;
- transboundary spill-overs and externalities; and
- disparities in financial and technical capacity.

Nearly every chapter in this volume touches to some extent on issues related to the global commons or shared resources, including, for example, biological diversity, the ozone layer, the climate system, and high seas fisheries. Because the activities of all states can affect or be affected by threats to these resources, international institutions at the regional and global level have helped governments to develop strategic responses based on the exchange of information, common goals and shared burdens.

Pollutants, and the laws that seek to regulate pollutants, can spill over boundaries, and have impacts on the environmental and economic interests of other states. International institutions can seek to intervene to prevent environmental and economic damage. The sections in this volume on dispute avoidance and settlement, and those chapters that deal with regional and global trading regimes, describe attempts by international institutions to ensure a harmonization of environmental standards that both afford protection and avoid interference with legitimate economic interests.

As all states seek to move towards a higher level of protection of the local and global environment, international institutions can seek to redress the great disparities in the capacity of nations at different levels of economic development to share in this effort. Financial and technological resources can be pooled and developed through the activities of institutions described in this volume, such as the World Bank, GEF and NEFs, and UNDP. International institutions such as UNCTAD and UNEP, through research and capacity building, also provide intellectual and technical resources to developing countries.

Thus, international institutions can play what Boyle has described as a 'fiduciary role in protecting the environment'.[6] A range of interrelated functions should be kept in mind when reading the accounts of the institutions contained in this volume. These functions include:

- awareness raising and agenda setting;
- collecting, processing and disseminating information.;
- setting international standards and regulations;
- capacity building, and providing financial and technical assistance; and
- avoiding and settling disputes.

Awareness raising and agenda setting

While each of the institutions discussed in this volume plays some role in focusing the attention of states on environmental issues, Agenda 21 recognized the UN General Assembly as 'the supreme policy-making forum that would provide overall guidance to Governments, the United Nations system and relevant treaty bodies'.[7]

With the highest profile of any global institution, high expectations often attach to the work of the UNGA. Fitzpatrick's study in Chapter 1 provides the reader with a feeling for the extent to which the structure and the powers of an institution facilitate and constrain its work. The General Assembly's universal membership and extremely broad mandate has allowed it to take up many issues of global concern. Yet it is constrained by powers which are limited to making recommendations that are not binding on its Member States.

The effectiveness with which the UNGA has been able to promote environmental objectives has had to rely upon subtler stuff, primarily the sensitivity of Member States to the hortatory character of its pronouncements, and the publicity that can attend its debates. Accordingly, states have relied on UNGA to gather or to legitimize the consensus of the international community.[8]

Mensah's analysis of the Commission on Sustainable Development (CSD), in Chapter 2, reveals a similar approach to institutional design. The choices states made in designing the CSD, which has a wide mandate and limited powers, demonstrate a continued reliance on soft approaches to environmental policy making. Thus, Mensah concludes, the strength of the CSD will be its ability to serve as a high-level focal point for representatives of states, sectors of the economy and political movements with an interest in environment and development, providing them with the opportunity to report on their progress in implementing Agenda 21, and debating their concerns. If the CSD seeks to apply too much pressure on its Member States, too quickly, Mensah warns that they will simply lose interest.

Collecting, processing and disseminating information

The development and enforcement of environmental policy depends heavily on comprehensive and reliable scientific and technical information. Policy makers' assessments of levels of risk to the environment, and the appropriate means for responding to those risks, must be based on data gathered without regard to national boundaries and that can be synthesised and verified through cooperative efforts.

The more focused the institution's mandate, the greater its need for precise information from its members states. Institutions created by international environmental treaties, explored in Chapter 4, are often focused on specific environmental objectives, and require precise and verifiable data on, for example, emissions of particular pollutants or catch levels for species of fish.

Koskenniemi's contribution on implementation control and reaction (Chapter 14) demonstrates that such data is essential not just for setting and adjusting environmental standards, but also in building the confidence of parties and non-parties that all states are meeting their commitments.

The analysis and assessment of information requires the establishment of institutional machinery in addition to intergovernmental fora. Accordingly, international institutions create bodies to provide them with scientific and technical advice, and require administrative support in the form of international civil servants to process information in a neutral and expert manner. The secretariats and advisory bodies of international environmental treaties can provide this function for their parties. Somsen notes, in Chapter 11, that the work of the European Commission has been essential to maintaining the momentum of environmental regulation in the European Union. The United Nations Environment Programme (UNEP), as described by Timoshenko and Berman in Chapter 3, seeks to offer these services as a catalyst for environmental change throughout the UN system.

Arda's contribution (Chapter 5) on the United Nations Conference on Trade and Development (UNCTAD) identifies the importance that internationally sponsored research and analysis can have in boosting the capacity and confidence of developing countries in international negotiations. 'Persuasion through sound analysis' Arda suggests, can make a contribution to the shaping of state behaviour and the advancement of sustainable development objectives at least as valuable as the design and enforcement of new standards and regulations.

Setting international standards and regulations

International institutions have produced environmental standards and regulations that range from non-binding guidelines and hortatory resolutions to programmes of action, and finally, to legally binding rules. For a number of the contributors, the legal character of the standards an institution is empowered to generate is the most important factor for assessing the ability of an institution to influence state behaviour.

Though generalizations are difficult to make across such a varied set of institutions, a number of basic observations are possible. States' willingness to grant legislative powers to an international institution will increase with the level of economic and political integration between member states, as is clearly demonstrated in Somsen's treatment of the European Union. It may also be said that a shared sense of urgency, as was the case for the Montreal Protocol (discussed in Chapter 4) will lead states to grant greater legislative powers to an international institution.

The Organization for Economic Cooperation and Development, (OECD), explored briefly in Somsen's contribution, is often criticized in light of its limited ability to produce binding standards. As Somsen points out, the OECD has nevertheless had a considerable influence on domestic environmental legislation by developing guiding principles based on the best practice of the world's leading industrialized countries. Furthermore, membership of the OECD has, since it was founded, represented a nation's economic coming of age. While the institution itself is not demanding in terms of the legal obligations it imposes, it creates high expectations and considerable pressures on countries that join it to improve their environmental standards.

Capacity building, and providing financial and technical assistance

This book devotes a section to institutions that are designed to provide financial and technical resources to build the capacity of developing countries. While the largest share of these resources are channelled through the Bretton Woods institutions described in Horta's Chapter 8, it is important to keep in mind, as Timoshenko and Berman point out, that the UN system also provides a significant amount of resources for capacity building.

Financial assistance through international institutions has long provided a mechanism for influencing development policy in poorer countries. A number of the mechanisms discussed in this volume, including the GEF, NEFs, and the financial mechanisms for international environmental treaties, earmark funds specifically for environmental objectives. These resources are, however, greatly outweighed by the funds available through the regular lending and grant portfolios of the traditional international financial institutions, such as the World Bank.

Horta's analysis exposes many complexities in a system for the transfer of resources which, from a distance, would appear benign in its intent and its effect. The short term macroeconomic trade and investment policies pursued by developing countries at the insistence of the World Bank and IMF can conflict with the longer term sustainable development objectives.

Assistance from donor countries need not, however, come only in the form of direct financial and technical support. Regional cooperation of the type described in King and Goad's contribution on the South Pacific region (Chapter 12) describes how donor supported international institutions can provide a mechanism for bringing back together cultures flung apart by geographical separation and the intervention of diverse colonial rulers.

Avoiding and settling disputes

The absence of institutions empowered to enforce international obligations by compulsorily settling disputes between states has often been cited as the Achilles' heel of the international legal system. Contributions from Sands, on the International and European Courts of Justice (Chapter 13), and from Koskenniemi describe how existing dispute settlement and avoidance procedures can, nonetheless, contribute to the effective development and implementation of environmental norms.

Although most international tribunals formally restrict the effect of their decisions to the states involved in the dispute, examples drawn from a number of the contributions demonstrate that the rulings of judicial and quasi-judicial bodies quickly come to influence the way in which standards set by institutions are interpreted.

The analyses that follow confirm, however, that states' collective willingness to adopt rules for environmental protection has far outpaced their readiness to subject themselves to institutions and procedures that have the power to enforce those rules.

The inevitable overlap between Sands' discussion of the European Court of Justice and Somsen's treatment of the European Union demonstrates the absolute centrality of a compulsory adjudicatory system to any highly developed body of law. Koskenniemi, on other hand, cautions that softer approaches to enforcement, such as the non-compliance regimes being developed under a number of international environmental treaties, could lead to a softening of the legal character of the rules themselves.

Conflicts may also arise between standards set in one institution and those set by another. The trend, marked in Koskenniemi's chapter, to develop specialized compliance mechanisms within distinct regimes raises the chances for conflicts between as well as within institutions. The absence of a single overarching court of appeal in the international system may allow the institution with the more rigorous dispute settlement procedures to determine the outcome of a particular dispute. Makuch's contribution on the World Trade Organization (WTO), at Chapter 6, anticipates that the great threat of the WTO to the environmentalist agenda may lie in the ability of its new Dispute Settlement Procedure to seize and resolve disputes between free trade policies and environmental protection.

The reader should not overlook the other international institutions and mechanisms for avoiding and settling environmental disputes scattered throughout this volume. In addition to the Makuch's treatment of the WTO Dispute Settlement Procedure, Fitzpatrick highlights the adjudicatory role of the Security Council in establishing a mechanism for providing compensation for damage to the environment resulting from the Gulf War. The World Bank Inspection Panel, described in Horta's contribution, provides exciting new opportunities for non-governmental organizations to challenge Bank activities that may threaten the environment. Kumar, Milner and Petsonk, in Chapter 7 on the North American Free Trade Association (NAFTA), note parallel developments within that regime.

AGENDA 21'S PRINCIPLES FOR INSTITUTIONAL DESIGN

The catholic scope of Rio's sustainable development agenda required policy makers to rethink the entire web of relationships that connects humans with their environment, and, in turn, with their local, national, regional and international institutions. It is, therefore, not surprising that Agenda 21, the massive framework document adopted at Rio to guide policy makers into the 21st century, devotes an entire chapter (Chapter 38) to 'International Institutional Arrangements'.[9]

Through Chapter 38, states agree to seek 'the integration of environment and development issues at national, subregional, regional and international levels, including in the United Nations system institutional arrangements.' Many of the contributors choose to use Chapter 38's general principles, aimed at all relevant institutions, or its express directives, targeted at specific institutions, to guide their assessments. Chapter 38 provides that:

> In the spirit of reform and revitalization of the United Nations system, implementation of Agenda 21 and other conclusions of the Conference shall be based on an action- and result-oriented approach and consistent with the principles of universality, democracy, transparency, cost-effectiveness and accountability.[10]

The reader will recognize many of the contributors using this pattern of institutional design principles to guide their assessments. 'Action' and 'results' are certainly useful goals for any institution to aim at. But universality, democracy, transparency, cost-effectiveness and accountability are more complex and politically loaded concepts. It is hoped that the contributions to this volume will provide the reader with a fuller understanding of what these principles can mean when applied to the reform of specific institutions, and how these general principles relate to the specific goals of sustainable development.

Universality and democracy

Universality and democracy describe the openness of an institution to the membership of the entire community of states, and the right of each state to participate as a sovereign equal in the functioning of that institution. These principles recognize that all nations are affected by, and have a right and a responsibility to participate in, policy making for sustainable development. As will be seen, however, universality does not necessarily mean that all international bodies must include the over 180 members of the United Nations. Indeed, as Mensah's chapter on the Commission on Sustainable Development and Sjöberg's Chapter 9 on the Global Environment Facility demonstrates, even the institutions formed directly as a result of UNCED rely on constituency systems to design representative, but smaller and more effective, bodies.

While democratic institutions may acknowledge, as a basic principle, the sovereign equality of states, sustainable development objectives may also require subtle variations on that principle. Democratic systems that allow for majority voting rather than unanimous decision making can empower a majority of states acting through an international institution to bind a minority of states to new rules they might have voted against. Developments described within the European Union, in Somsen's contribution, and in the chapter on international environmental treaties, demonstrate that the pressing nature of environmental issues can lead states to accept decisions that become binding on all parties on the basis of a majority vote.

A more subtle variation on democracy is seen in Sjöberg's Chapter on the GEF, which allows each donor country a vote that is weighted more heavily than the vote of a recipient country. Such weightings have been rationalized on the basis of a conception of democracy that allows taxpayers in donor countries to have a greater say, through their government representatives, in the way in which their tax dollars are spent. Only such weightings, it is argued, will give donors the confidence to give generously the 'new and additional' funds that have been deemed essential for sustainable development. Counterbalanced against these arguments are the institutions described in Danish's contribution on national environmental funds (Chapter 10). These funds devolve decision making power downward towards the recipient country governments and other 'stakeholders' that will be directly affected by the programmes and projects purchased with the resources.

Horta's chapter on the World Bank and IMF; Kumar, Milner and Petsonk's on NAFTA; and French's on NGOs; each demonstrates that UNCED's principle of democracy should extend beyond state-to-state relations. The involvement of non-state actors in the work of international institutions appears to be proving essential to ensuring that decisions made at the intergovernmental level are based on the full range of information, expertise and depth of conviction that many now acknowledge only NGOs can provide. Some, however, feel that the trend towards a greater acceptance of NGO participation poses a direct challenge to democratic governance and that it has outpaced the system's ability to assess who or what these groups represent, and on what they base their claims to speak on behalf of peoples, ecosystems or ideas.

Transparency and accountability

Transparency and accountability are institutional principles that go hand in hand to support procedures that allow those inside and outside international institutions to influence decisions, to understand how decisions are made, and to hold the institution responsible for the impacts of decisions. This requires the transparent flow of information into and out of decision making fora. Special attention should be paid to Horta's and French's contributions for explorations of these principles in the context of both the Bretton Woods and the UN systems.

Cost effectiveness

Each of the preceding principles undoubtedly entails additional costs, at least initially. Involving more voices, opening up processes and disseminating more information burdens administration and necessarily slows the decision making process. The principle of cost effectiveness requires an assessment of whether these additional costs can be justified by more effective outcomes. Five years onward these costs are adding strain to a UN budget already in crisis. Delegates and observers whose ranks have swollen at UN meetings find themselves being asked to keep careful track of their documents, as additional copies will not be provided. Extrabudgetary trust funds established to sponsor the attendance at UN meetings of developing country delegations are being depleted as quickly as they are replenished. Project funding cycles in the Global Environment Facility have slowed to a snail's pace, in part to accommodate new mechanisms for consultation between states, agencies and NGOs. It is, however, perhaps too soon to assess whether the application of these principles has improved the quality of the policies and activities of the international institutions that have begun to implement them.

INSTITUTIONS AND STATE INTERESTS

While international institutions provide a forum for cooperation, they can also become an outlet for ideological divisions between their member states. Because the structure of an international institution will define the power relationship between states on the issues that the institution covers, debates over institutional design were amongst the most contentious in the UNCED process.

In particular, tensions between developed and developing countries have surfaced in debates within and between institutions. Conflicts over the respective roles of institutions with overlapping and competing agendas, between the UN and the Bretton Woods institutions over socioeconomic policy, between UNCTAD and the WTO over terms of trade, and between the UNDP, UNEP and the World Bank over the design of the GEF, have often broken out down along North–South lines.

Recent reviews of the UN system from policy makers at opposite ends of the development spectrum – the Group of 77 developing countries, and the Group of 7 major industrialized democracies – have allowed political and economic tensions to be expressed in institutional terms. The North can be seen as supporting the principle of cost effectiveness[11] that favours weighted voting and constituency systems, and the South can be described as pressing for greater universality and democracy.[12]

Mensah's chapter serves extremely well to unmask the substantive issues that underlie this debate about institutional design and hierarchy. UNCED's attempt to resolve the false dichotomy between environment and development often dissolved into conflicts between developed and developing countries, with industrialized countries seen as pressing for higher environmental standards, and developing countries arguing for the primacy of the goals of poverty eradication and economic development.

Institutions become symbols for the underlying issues, and discussions for institutional rationalization and reform provoke interest groups to rally behind the institutions they feel best represent their cause. A glance backwards at Mensah's chapter on the CSD, and forwards to Makuch's WTO contribution, will demonstrate how trade and environment issues, for example, can exacerbate North–South tensions. At their respective stages of economic development developing countries are extremely sensitive to the role that environmental measures and standards can play in closing lucrative Northern markets to Southern products.

As a result many developing countries fear that:

> [D]iscussions and decision-making on economic and trade issues are increasingly being moved from the United Nations to the Bretton Woods Institutions or to GATT, in which negotiations are made unequal by the structure of these institutions and where even in principle there is no democracy in the decision-making process.[13]

As a result they rally around UNCTAD arguing, as does Arda, the new powers and broader agenda of the WTO demonstrate an even greater need for UNCTAD to continue to provide intellectual support for developing country economic interests.

The reader will note how the two institutions designed as a result of the UNCED process have sought to resolve the North–South issue in strikingly different ways. For a variety of reasons, Mensah's CSD fell back on existing formulas to design an institution based largely on familiar UN structures. Sjöberg's GEF, on the other hand, struck out for new territory, designing a rough hybrid of the UN and Bretton Woods structures and forcing agencies from each family of institutions into a new cooperative relationship.

RATIONALIZING GLOBAL ENVIRONMENTAL GOVERNANCE[14]

The great diversity and considerable overlap in competence of the institutions described in this volume may prompt the reader to ask whether the entire system of global environmental governance might not somehow be rationalized. While UNCED recognized the central importance of international institutions in performing the functions outlined above, it also emphasized that:

- there was a considerable institutional capacity and experience in the system already;

- few states were willing to bear the expense of creating new institutions; and
- the concept of sustainable development required not just increased institutional capacity, but also that existing institutions would have to change the way they were already operating.

Similar observations have led to a number of far-reaching proposals for rationalizing global environmental governance. The proposals reviewed here tend to emphasize the need to centralize functions, either through the creation of a new institution or the strengthening of an existing one. They seek to generate vertical, 'top–down' integration, whereby an overarching authority fills gaps, and either assumes the responsibilities of existing institutions or directs their coordination from above.

A New Institution

Sir Geoffrey Palmer, in 1991, proposed the creation of 'a proper international environmental agency within the United Nations system that has real power and authority.'[15] The structural details of Palmer's proposal are based primarily on the model of the International Labour Organization (ILO).[16] His International Environmental Organization (IEO) would perform both a legislative and a implementation function. An 'advanced supertreaty system' could take decisions setting international environmental standards by a two-thirds majority, demand reports from member countries, and take measures to 'secure compliance' with the regime's provisions.

The power and authority that Palmer seeks to vest in this institution, to take decisions other than by consensus and to enforce compliance, looks forward to a time when states have reached a broad and common understanding with regard to environmental issues. As Palmer notes, in areas like the protection of the ozone layer, where there is already a degree of political consensus, more progressive systems of rule-making appear to be taking root. However, as is pointed out in the Chapter 4 of this volume, this is not the case for most international environmental issues.

Similar proposals have emerged from reviews of the United Nations and Bretton Woods organizations, provoked by their 50th anniversaries. The Commission of Global Governance, an independent group of 28 world leaders, called for the establishment of an 'apex body', an Economic Security Council (ESC) that would, among other things, provide leadership in economic, social, and environmental fields.[17] The Commission proposes that the ESC would be established within the UN system, but intentionally avoids the legal details of its structure. Membership of the ESC would be limited, would be representative of the world's largest economies and, through a constituency system, would reflect regional interests. Unlike Palmer, the Commission recommends that the ESC's decisions always be taken by consensus, and that its powers should not extend to making legally binding decisions. Under the Commission's proposal matters related specifically to the global commons would be referred to a restructured UN Trusteeship Council (see below).[18]

A further recent iteration of a model for a new international environmental organization seeks to anticipate growing conflicts within the trade and environment nexus, where the hegemonic nature of the Uruguay Round agreements and the establishment of a more powerful World Trade Organization have led to calls for the creation of a counterbalancing Global Environmental Organization (GEO).[19] Dan Esty proposes an organization built upon a set of cardinal principles that could develop, over time, to perform legislative and adjudicative functions, developing international environmental norms, and settling disputes of an environmental character. While the GEO would focus on global environmental problems or 'transboundary pollution spillovers', its ambitions to harmonize environmental standards suggest that its scope could include environmental problems of a domestic nature as well.

UN Trusteeship Council

As its role in the post-colonial world dwindled, a number of institutional reformers set their sites on the existing institutional structure of the United Nations Trusteeship Council, originally established to supervise non-independent states emerging from colonial rule. With the movement of Palau to self-governing status, the Council has completed its work.[20] Maurice Strong, then the President of the World Federation of United Nations Associations, noted the close relationship between the global stewardship principles of the Council and the need for careful management of 'the global commons, the oceans, the atmosphere, and outer space.'[20] He suggested that the Council could act as a 'forum within which the nations of the world exercise their trusteeship for the integrity of the planetary systems . . . as well as for the global commons.'[21] The proposal has since been elaborated by the Commission on Global Governance, which proposes the Trusteeship Council would become the 'chief forum' on global environmental and related matters.[22] The Council would subsume the roles of the Conferences of the Parties, but only for those IEAs such as 'climate change, biodiversity, outer space, and the Law of the Sea,' that govern areas related to the 'global commons.'

Recommendations to reconstruct the Trusteeship council, for all their poetical attractions, have not yet been taken up. This is in part due to difficulties in amending of the UN Charter,[23] and in part because the momentum for the establishment of a high-level UN body to coordinate policy on environment and development issues was absorbed by the efforts to create the Commission on Sustainable Development (see below).

A strengthened UNEP

The United Nations Environment Programme[24], as Timoshenko and Berman point out in Chapter 3, has played an important role in stimulating the negotiation of environmental treaties and provides an institutional base for number of major environmental regimes. At first glance UNEP provides an attractive candidate to help unify international environmental lawmaking and implementation.

UNEP's ability to take a leading role in global environmental governance has, however, been severely limited by a number of factors including the narrow mandate provided by its constituent instrument,[25] its modest and declining budget, and by negative perceptions of its effectiveness. The same chapter of Agenda 21 that endorsed UNEP's role as a catalyst and information gatherer undermined the potential of its Governing Council to provide intergovernmental policy direction by establishing the Commission on Sustainable Development.

Hilary French, writing elsewhere, has recently recommended that these obstacles could and should be overcome by 'transforming UNEP into an operational UN Environment Agency' that would 'consolidate, and not merely supplement, existing environmental efforts.' French suggests that UNEP's current role as catalyst and forum for elaborating 'common minimum international environmental standards,' be strengthened, and that it serve as an 'umbrella organisation' for existing IEAs.[26] While French's proposal, like Palmer, calls for an institutional restructuring of UNEP along the lines of the ILO, it appears she would not have the revitalized agency take on the more ambitious legislative function described for Palmer's IEO.

The Commission on Sustainable Development[27]

The role of providing high-level policy direction toward global environmental governance could have been taken up by the Commission on Sustainable Development (CSD), created by the UNGA to ensure the effective follow up of UNCED. As Mensah's analysis indicates in Chapter 2, the Commission's powers are limited to receiving and considering reports from governmental, inter-governmental and non-governmental sources and to providing appropriate recommendations to the General Assembly. Thus far, overwhelmed by the broad scope of its mandate, and hobbled by the narrow scope of its powers, the Commission does not seem likely to fulfil more visionary ambitions for an over-arching international environmental organization.[28]

A web of relationships

A less ambitious but more pragmatic approach to reconceptualizing global environmental governance seeks to acknowledge and build upon the modular design that has characterized international environmental law making over the past twenty years. Such an approach recognizes the strengths and the practicalities of the existing system which has grown organically, gathering constituencies and functions in response to specific environmental issues. Until such time as international relations allow for more unitary forms of global governance, coordination and integration can take place horizontally between existing and emerging regimes as the need and opportunity arises.

Lee Kimball, who has written extensively on the institutional challenges of sustainable development, has begun to articulate a methodological framework for building a 'web of relationships' between disparate environmental regimes. Like the preceding commentators, she seeks to inform the design of an 'institutional setting for environmental management in the twenty-first century'.[29] Kimball suggests that broader issues raised by sustainable development are best handled in a high-level 'institutional setting' while more detailed tasks may be separable into 'logical management units' based on either substantive or geographic relationships.[30]

What emerges are several institutional tiers, with the role of coordinating and directing policy being played at the highest level by an institution like the Commission on Sustainable Development. Beneath that tier lie the specialized regimes of the IEAs which have the ability to draw together just those states with interests in areas covered by the regime. Within each regime are likely to be found scientific and technical fora that use their specialized expertise to direct policy-makers. Finally, at the national level are the institutions responsible for implementing the regimes within each country.[31] Each of these tiers, or building blocks, is or should be held together by a 'web of relationships' that can 'create an inter-locking network of obligations'.[32]

Sjöberg's analysis of the GEF in Chapter 9 leads to a similar conclusion. The roles of existing institutions can best be rationalized through a process of 'differentiation according to function' followed by an 'integration at the level of operations'. Attempts to coordinate from above, she suggests, are unlikely to succeed.

CONCLUSION: INSTITUTIONS AND LEARNING

Each author's review of the extent to which the institution described in this volume is making process towards an agenda for sustainable development involves what Paul Szasz has called an assessment of 'institutional learning'.[33] Two institutional characteristics Szasz identifies as barriers to institutional learning have been discussed above: constitutional and legal restrictions, and the tensions or differences in the agendas of major participants.

Szasz also describes a phenomenon more difficult to identify or address directly: cultural inertia.

> Organizations, like organisms, strive to maintain their existence, seek to perpetuate themselves, [and] are territorial and aggressive when their immediate environment is threatened.[34]

The General Assembly's 1997 review of progress on the implementation of Agenda 21, coming, as it does, in the context of a broader debate on UN reform, presents precisely the type of challenge to which institutions are culturally conditioned to respond. Many of the institutions reviewed in this volume have swallowed whole with relative ease the rhetoric of the now familiar UNCED principles. It is hoped that this volume will help take the process of assessment and reform a level deeper, and raise questions as to whether the demands of sustainable development require a more fundamental push against the inertia of institutional culture.

NOTES AND REFERENCES

1   On 25 June 1945 delegates representing 50 nations met in San Francisco at the United Nations Conference on International Organisation and unanimously adopted the Charter of the United Nations.
2   The Articles of Agreement of the International Monetary Fund and of the International Bank for Reconstruction and Development (the World Bank) were drawn up at the United Nations Monetary and Financial Conference held at Bretton Woods, New Hampshire in July 1944.
3   H Schermers & N Blokker, *International Institutional Law*, (3rd ed 1995).
4   *Ibid*, at sec 33.
5   R Keohane, P Haas, and M Levy, eds, *Institutions for the Earth: Sources of Effective International Environmental Protection* (1993) p 4–5.
6   A Boyle, "Saving the World? Implementation and Enforcement of International Environmental Law through International Institutions," (1991) 3 *Journal of Environmental Law* at 229.

7   United Nations Conference on Environment and Development, Agenda 21, UN Doc A/Conf.151/26/Rev.1 (1993) [hereinafter Agenda 21]. Chapter 38.1.

8   UNGA's recent role in the context of the entry into force of the UN Convention on the Law of the Sea was recently described as fostering '[a]n agreement reached in such a way [as to] truly represent the opinion of mankind' L Sohn 'International Law Implications of the 1994 Agreement' *American Journal of International Law*, 88:687 October 1994.

9   See Appendix 1 to this volume.

10 Agenda 21, Chapter 38.2.

11 Economic Communique of the Heads of State and Governments of the Seven Major Industrialized Democracies and the President of the European Commission, Lyon, June 27–29, 1996.

12 J Nyerere, 'Reforming the United Nations: A View from the South', address to the Forum on the Future of the United Nations System by Mwalimu Julius K Nyerere, Chairman of the South Centre, Vienna, 1 March 1995. See also The South Centre, *Facing the Challenge: Responses to the Report of the South Commission*, (1993).

13 *Ibid.*

14 Large parts of this analysis are drawn from J Werksman, 'Consolidating Governance of the Global Commons: Insights from the Global Environment Facility' 6 *Yearbook of International Environmental Law* (1995).

15 G Palmer, 'New Ways to Make International Environmental Law' 86 *AJIL* 259 [hereinafter Palmer] at 262.

16 DW Bowett, *The Law of International Institutions* (4th ed. 1982) 108–157 [hereinafter Bowett]. See, eg, V-Y Ghebali, *The International Labour Organization: A Case Study on the Evolution of United Nations Specialised Agencies* (1989); E Haas, *Beyond the Nation-state, Functionalism and International Organisation* (1964).

17 The Commission on Global Governance, *Our Global Neighbourhood* (1995) at 153–162.

18 *Our Global Neighbourhood*, p 252.

19 D Esty, *Greening the Gatt* (1994) p 75–83.

20 *See* Charter of the United Nations, Chapter XIII; Bowett 80–84.

21 M Strong, 'The United Nations in an Interdependent World' *International Affairs*, January 1989, at 20. See also D Zaelke and J Cameron, 'Global Warming and Climate Change: An Overview of the International Legal Process' 5:2 *American University Journal of International Law and Policy* 249 (1990) at 208.

22 *Our Global Neighbourhood*, p 251–253. Mr Strong was a member of the Commission.

23 For a close discussion of the legal implications of changing the Trusteeship Council's mandate, see P Szasz, 'Restructuring the International Organisational Framework', in E Brown-Weiss, ed, *Environmental Change and International Law* (1992) at 362 [hereinafter Szasz].

24 UNEP is a 'programme' created by the United Nations General Assembly, operating under the auspices of the Economic and Social Council (ECOSOC). UNGA Resolution 2997 on Institutional and Financial Arrangements for International Environmental Cooperation, 15 December 1972. Its legal character falls 'somewhere between the normal categories of [the United Nations'] subsidiary organs and [its] specialised agencies'. It does, however, have many of the characteristics of an independent international institution, with its own governing council, composed of representatives of 58 member states, a budget financed by direct, voluntary contributions, and its own secretariat. See Bowett at 58.

25 The limitations of UNEP's mandate led Palmer to conclude, in 1991, that '[g]iven the nature of UNEP's constitution, its achievements are substantial, but it is not an adequate international organisation for protecting the world's environment'. Palmer at 261. The Commission on Global Governance mentioned UNEP only once in a substantive way, in the context of its role as a GEF implementing agency. *Our Global Neighbourhood*, at 272.

26 H French, *Partnership for the Planet: An Environmental Agenda for the United Nations,* Worldwatch Paper 126 (1995) p 39.

27 Established by UN General Assembly Resolution 47/191 on the Institutional Arrangements to Follow UNCED, 22 December 1992, following Chapter 38 of Agenda 21, and in accordance with Article 68 of the UN Charter.

28 The future of the Commission will be determined, in part, by the fifth anniversary review of the implementation of Agenda 21 scheduled for the 1997 session of the General Assembly. This review, running parallel to broader debates on UN institutional reform, will provide an opportunity to renew or change the CSD's structure and mandate.

29 See, eg, L Kimball and W Boyd 'International Institutional Arrangements for Environment and Development: A Post-Rio Assessment' 1:3 *RECIEL* 295; L Kimball *Forging International Agreement: Strengthening Intergovernmental Institutions for Environment and Development*; and Kimball, Lee 'Toward Global Environmental Management: The Institutional Setting' 3 *YIEL* 18.

30 Kimball notes that the 'institutional setting is more conducive to high-level political involvement that can stimulate commitments to action than are narrow, specialised regimes'. L Kimball, 'Toward Global Environmental Management: The Institutional Setting' 3 *YIEL* 18 at 34.

31 *Ibid*, at 34–35.

32 *Ibid.*

33 Szasz, at 377.

34 *Ibid.*

PART I

Policy-making

1 THE UNITED NATIONS GENERAL ASSEMBLY AND THE SECURITY COUNCIL

Donald Fitzpatrick

INTRODUCTION

When the United Nations (UN) Charter was drafted 50 years ago, the protection of the environment was not an issue of global concern. Thus the Charter does not expressly give the organization competence over environmental matters. Despite the absence of a specific mandate, the very broad nature of the purposes of the UN, as expressed in Article 1 of the Charter, has allowed it to develop its environmental function within the context of its economic, social and humanitarian responsibilities.[1] This chapter discusses the role of two of the six principal organs of the UN – the General Assembly and the Security Council.[2]

While the General Assembly has a long history of involvement in environmental matters, the Security Council's only environmental intervention to date has been to address the pollution that occurred during the Gulf War. Because of this difference, the two parts of this chapter follow dissimilar styles. The General Assembly section is largely historical, analysing some of its more important environmental initiatives, whereas the discussion of the Security Council is exploratory, examining the issues raised by the prospect of an expanding environmental role for the Council.

GREENING THE GENERAL ASSEMBLY

Environmental Roles of the United Nations General Assembly

The General Assembly plays an important role in the international environmental sphere in a number of ways:

Policy/Consensus Building

The General Assembly serves as a universal forum for environmental policy-making, giving states an opportunity to exchange ideas and to build an international consensus on controversial issues. Its resolutions are expressions of world opinion and, as such, they can have a significant political and moral influence. This was illustrated by the 'consciousness raising' influence of the General Assembly prior to and during the two major global environmental initiatives, the 1972 UN Conference on the Human Environment and the 1992 UN Conference on the Environment and Development (UNCED).[3] Agenda 21,[4] the global 'action plan' adopted at UNCED, has identified the General Assembly as the 'principal policy-making and appraisal organ on UNCED follow-up'.

Development of International Law

In addition to its policy role, the General Assembly, through Resolutions adopted over the last 20 years, has made a contribution to the development of international law. While not themselves legally binding, General Assembly resolutions can influence the law-making process either through their being adopted into binding international treaties or through serving as a basis for the development of customary law, thereby contributing directly or indirectly to the development of substantive legal obligations.[5]

Creating Other UN Bodies

The power granted to the General Assembly to 'establish such subsidiary organs as it deems necessary for the performance of its functions'[6] has enabled it to create a range of UN specialized agencies, programmes and committees. Bodies with environmental functions that were created by the General Assembly include the United Nations Environment Programme (UNEP);[7] the United Nations Development Programme (UNDP);[8] and more recently the Commission on Sustainable Development (CSD).[9]

Convening Global Conferences

From as early as 1954, when it decided to convene the Conference on the Conservation of the Living Resources of the Sea, the General Assembly has been facilitating global conferences for the negotiation of binding conventions, hortatory ministerial declarations or illustrative programmes of action to protect different aspects of the global environment. Both the Stockholm Conference on the Human Environment and the United Nations Conference on Environment and Development (UNCED) were convened by the General Assembly. In the follow-up to UNCED, the General Assembly has a central role not only in policy appraisal, but also in managing the international negotiating process. Since UNCED, the arrangements for the UN Conferences on Climate Change, Desertification, Small Island Developing States, Straddling Fish Stocks and Highly Migratory Fish Stocks have all been facilitated by General Assembly resolutions. Post-UNCED, procedural General Assembly resolutions determining the arrangements for global environmental conferences under UN auspices have outnumbered the number of resolutions that are concerned with substantive aspects of environmental law and policy. [10]

Requesting Advisory Opinions

Article 96 of the UN Charter provides that the General Assembly may request the International Court of Justice to give an advisory opinion on any legal question. In 1994 the General Assembly requested an opinion on the following question: '[i]s the threat or use of nuclear weapons in any circumstance permitted under international law?'.[11]

Before discussing the General Assembly's influence upon environmental law and policy, this chapter will briefly outline the structure and general functions of the General Assembly, and the status of its resolutions.

General Assembly Structure

Each of the member states of the United Nations is represented in the General Assembly (UNGA) with equal voting power irrespective of their size, population or power.[12] This universal and democratic nature lends great weight to the General Assembly resolutions which can be seen as representative of world opinion. According to the Charter, decisions are to be taken on a simple majority basis, with important questions, such as the election of non-permanent members of the Security Council, requiring a two-thirds majority.[13] However, in practice most resolutions are now adopted without vote on a consensus basis.

The General Assembly meets in regular annual sessions which begin on the third Tuesday of September and run through to Christmas. Special sessions can be convened at the request of the Security Council or of a majority of the members of the United Nations. The General Assembly has been requested to convene a special session to review Agenda 21 and its implementation before the end of 1997.[14]

The bulk of the General Assembly's work on environmental matters is carried out in the Second (Economic and Financial) Committee, where draft resolutions are agreed upon before being put to the plenary session for adoption. The Second Committee also acts as the final reviewing body for the activities of several relevant UN bodies including UNEP, UNDP, CSD and UNCTAD (United Nations Commission on Trade and Development). The Sixth (Legal) Committee will occasionally look at issues of international environmental law – for example in recent sessions it has debated the legal protection of the environment in wartime.[15] Proposals have been made that a Committee could be created which would have environmental matters as its prime responsibility,[16] or that the now largely redundant Fourth Committee could be transformed into an Environment Committee. However, others question whether the environmental workload of the General Assembly is sufficiently large to warrant such a reform.

The Question of the Legal Effect of Resolutions of the General Assembly

One measure of the General Assembly's role in protecting the environment is the extent to which its edicts make law that compels changes in the way states behave.

The UN Charter granted a wide mandate to the General Assembly to initiate studies, discuss and make recommendations on matters within the scope of the Charter, or relating to the powers and functions of other UN organs.[17] Article 13(1) provides that the General Assembly shall make recommendations for the purpose of 'promoting international cooperation in the political field and encouraging the progressive development of international law'.

The law-making capabilities of General Assembly resolutions is a subject of perennial debate in international law and it is beyond the scope of this chapter to discuss this problem in any depth.[18] In contrast to the Security Council, resolutions of the General Assembly are not legally binding. While there are certain Charter provisions which expressly authorize the General Assembly to take decisions that have legal effects (these include establishing subsidiary organs;[19] determining the budget of the Organization and its apportionment among the Members;[20] admission of new members[21] and the election of non-permanent members of the Security Council),[22] in general the formal status of General Assembly resolutions is that they are recommendatory. However, the fact that resolutions are not legally binding does not prevent them from having an influence on the development of law and state practice. Resolutions of the General Assembly can have an effect on international law either by serving as the basis for the development of customary law (state practice accepted as law), or through the subsequent incorporation of the principles contained in the resolution into a legally binding instrument. The influence of General Assembly resolutions on the customary law-making process is particularly important. Resolutions have sought to codify, by declaration, existing customary law[23] to crystallize emerging law[24] or to develop international law.[25]

Examples of General Assembly Resolutions Influencing International Environmental Law and Policy

The Common Heritage of Mankind
There are numerous General Assembly resolutions that subsequently have been incorporated into international treaties. For example, the 1948 Universal Declaration of Human Rights led to the two international human rights covenants.[26] In relation to the environment, several General Assembly resolutions on legal principles have served as the catalyst for the development of international environmental law. One of the best known examples is the concept of the 'common heritage of mankind' which first appeared in 1967 in a draft resolution sponsored by Malta. The aim of the proposal was

> to provide a solid basis for future worldwide cooperation . . . through the acceptance by the international community of a new principle of international law . . . that the seabed and ocean floor and their subsoil have a special status as a common heritage of mankind and as such should be reserved exclusively for peaceful purposes and administered by an international authority for the benefit of all peoples.[27]

The principle was incorporated in Resolution 2749[28] which declared that 'The sea-bed and ocean floor, and the subsoil thereof, beyond the limits of national jurisdiction . . . are the common heritage of mankind'. Subsequently the common heritage principle was incorporated in the United Nations Convention on Law of the Sea 1982 and in the Moon Treaty of 1979.[29] Variations on this principle have helped to shape the international community's response to a range of environmental issues concerning areas beyond national jurisdiction, or of legitimate global concern. The principle has been re-expressed in the designation of climate change[30] and biodiversity[31] as the common concern of humankind.

While the Marxist character of the principle has mellowed, even in the context of the deep sea-bed,[32] without doubt it has laid the groundwork for the acceptance of a 'common but differentiated responsibility' shared by all states in responding to environmental threats of a global character.[33]

The Moratorium on Large-scale Pelagic Driftnet Fishing and Other Resolutions on Marine Living Resources

One area in which the General Assembly has been very active is in driftnet fishing regulation. This destructive fishing technique threatens not only to deplete the targeted species – ie tuna and swordfish – but also the by-catch – ie the other marine species such as dolphins, sharks and whales, which are caught incidentally in the 'walls of death' and subsequently discarded. In Resolution 44/225 on Large-Scale Pelagic Driftnet Fishing and its Impact on the Living Marine Resources of the World's Oceans and Seas, the General Assembly called for a global moratorium on driftnet fishing by 30 June 1992. The following year the General Assembly emphasized the importance of the international community's implementation of Resolution 44/225 and requested UN organizations as well as the various global, regional and sub-regional fishery organizations, to 'bear in mind' the goals of Resolution 44/225.[34]

In 1991 the General Assembly again called for full implementation of the moratorium by the end of 1992. Unusually, the Resolution went beyond merely calling for a ban and laid down interim measures to facilitate implementation. Under the Resolution there was to be no new driftnet fishing, and existing driftnet fishing was to be reduced by 50 per cent by 30 June 1992, and ultimately by 100 per cent by 31 December 1992.[35]

Even though the resolution is not legally binding, the three major driftnetting nations, Japan, Korea and Taiwan, all announced that they would respect the moratorium.[36] While this behaviour raises hopes that we are witnessing the emergence of a new norm of customary international law prohibiting large-scale pelagic driftnet fishing, other fishing nations continue to resist the moratorium.[37] Greenpeace has compiled evidence of continued high seas driftnet fishing by some 600 Italian vessels in the Mediterranean, and by 100 French and UK vessels in the Northeast Atlantic.[38]

In response to the reports of EU non-compliance, the General Assembly adopted another resolution in December 1994 in which it expressed 'further serious concern that . . . there are reports of continuing conduct and activities inconsistent with the terms of the moratorium' and urged 'authorities of members of the international community to take greater enforcement responsibility to ensure full compliance' and 'to impose appropriate sanctions consistent with international law against acts contrary to the terms' of the moratorium.[39] Despite the pressure exerted by the UN, Greenpeace and other organizations, the European Union fisheries ministers did not support a German proposal to ban driftnets.[40]

Climate Change

The objectives of the early General Assembly resolutions on climate change were a combination of consciousness raising and coordinating the activities of the various international organizations. Resolution 43/53, entitled 'Protection of the global climate for present and future generations of mankind' recognized that climate change 'is a common concern of mankind', a phrase of uncertain legal effect,[41] and urged governments and scientific institutions to treat climate change as a priority issue.[42] The following year the General Assembly emphasized the urgent need to address climate change and urged governments to make every possible effort to limit or prevent activities that could adversely affect the climate.[43]

At the same time as coordinating the activities of other institutions the General Assembly consolidated its central role by reaffirming 'that the United Nations system, through the General Assembly, owing to its universal character, is the appropriate forum for concerted political action on global environmental problems'.[44]

In 1990 the General Assembly established an intergovernmental negotiating process to prepare 'an effective framework convention on climate change, containing appropriate commitments' and stated that negotiations should be completed in time to have a convention ready for signature at UNCED.[45] The General Assembly provided institutional and financial support for the negotiations of the Climate Change Convention up to its entry into force in March 1994.

Antarctica

Developing states, seeking to designate Antarctic minerals as the common heritage of mankind, led to the 'Question of Antarctica' being placed on the General Assembly's agenda in 1983.[46] While the initiative to extend the common heritage principles to the 'last continental wilderness' failed, it helped to spur the negotiation of the 1991 Protocol on Environmental Protection (not yet in force) which will place a 50-year ban on mineral exploitation in the Antarctic. Where common economic aspirations failed, a common environmental concern may have succeeded.

Antarctica has continued to be an annual fixture on the Assembly's agenda and the ongoing concern of its members has been to try to persuade the Antarctic Treaty Parties that the universal nature of the General Assembly makes it the appropriate forum for the international community to determine Antarctic policy.[47] Currently, under the Antarctic Treaty of 1959, decision-making rights are restricted to the consultative parties – ie the 12 original signatories and those new countries that are conducting substantial scientific research in Antarctica. Therefore, in theory the fate of this precious environment could be determined by 26 nations rather than the more than 180 members of the United Nations. Despite the strengths of the General Assembly's position on this point, the Antarctic Treaty Parties have not capitulated. Lee Kimball states that the campaign to have Antarctic matters discussed within the United Nations irritated the Antarctic Treaty Parties and that the 'debate has deteriorated to a perfunctory exchange where the oversight role of the UN is asserted by one side and rejected by the other'.[48]

Where the General Assembly has had more modest ambitions, it has been more successful. Resolutions aimed at putting pressure on the Antarctic Treaty Parties to increase the access of the international community to the meetings of the parties and to Antarctic data have forced changes that increase the transparency of the Antarctic Treaty system. Non-party states, Inter-governmental Organizations (IGOs) and Non-Governmental Organizations

(NGOs) are now invited to attend the meetings as observers. The documents from the meetings are made publicly available, and annual reports are sent to the UN Secretary-General.

It is interesting to contrast the General Assembly's lack of influence over Antarctic policy with its relative success with climate change and driftnets. In these latter cases, the General Assembly established itself as the central body for coordinating international initiatives and developing policy at a very early stage whereas the Antarctic Treaty system had been in operation for 24 years before the General Assembly became involved.

World Charter for Nature

The World Charter for Nature (WCN), along with the Stockholm Declaration of 1972 and the Rio Declaration of 1992, is part of the quest to formulate general principles of international environmental law. Following a proposal of President Mobutu of Zaire, the International Union for the Conservation of Nature drafted the WCN which was then sponsored at the General Assembly by 34 developing nations and was finally adopted in 1982 by a vote of 111 to 1 against (the US) and 18 abstentions.[49]

The WCN is divided into four sections: the preamble; general principles; functions and implementation. The preamble proclaims that 'Mankind is a part of nature' and that 'Lasting benefits from nature depend upon the maintenance of essential ecological processes and life support systems, and upon the diversity of life forms, which are jeopardised through excessive exploitation and habitat destruction by man'.[50] Paragraph three, which states that 'Every form of life is unique, warranting respect regardless of its worth to man,' indicates a change from the prevailing anthropogenic approach to the environment towards a recognition of the intrinsic value of nature.

The principles include the requirement that 'Nature shall be respected';[51] that 'the genetic viability on earth shall not be compromised and the habitats necessary to maintain sufficient population levels for the survival of all life forms shall be safeguarded';[52] special protection shall be given to unique eco-systems and to the habitats of rare or endangered species.[53]

The 'Functions' section of the WCN aims to integrate the nature conservation principles into social and economic development planning. Persons involved in planning have to take account of the long-term capacity of natural systems to sustain human use.[54] Natural resources are not to be wasted but to be used with restraint.[55] Activities which are likely to cause irreversible damage to nature shall be avoided.[56] Activities which may disturb nature are to be preceded by an environmental impact assessment.[57] To implement the WCN's objectives, the last 11 principles contain several requirements for action by states, including a very progressive provision on access to justice that requires states to make available remedies for harm to a person's environment.[58]

That the WCN was intended to be a fundamental statement of principles for the conservation of nature is indicated by a number of factors. Firstly, it was solemnly proclaimed by the General Assembly. Secondly, Article 14 requires that the principles in the Charter 'be reflected in the law and practice of each state as well as at the international level'. Thirdly, the mandatory term 'shall', as opposed to 'should' or 'shall endeavour to', is used throughout the text. Yet in reality, despite this solemn intent, the WCN has achieved nowhere near the same status as the Stockholm Declaration, even though they were both concluded in non-legally binding soft law instruments.

From the New International Economic Order to Rio: Evolution of Policy Within the General Assembly

UNCED was formally convened by the General Assembly in Resolution 44/228, which directed the Conference to 'elaborate strategies and measures to halt and reverse the effects of environmental degradation'. Its importance was emphasized in subsequent resolutions which called for funding at generous amounts and urged nations to be represented at the Conference by their heads of state or government.[59]

It is interesting to note how some of the developments in international environmental law made at Rio were an evolution of policy on which consensus had been reached in the General Assembly. For example, consider the principle of common but differentiated responsibility which underlies the relationship between the commitments undertaken by the developed and developing countries in the Climate Change and Biodiversity Conventions. Two years prior to Rio, the General Assembly had adopted a resolution noting that 'the largest part of the current emissions of pollutants into the environment originates in developed countries, and recognizing therefore, that those countries have the main responsibility for combating such pollution' directed an Intergovernmental Negotiating Committee (INC) to prepare a climate change convention containing 'appropriate commitments'.[60]

On a broader level, some of what was agreed upon at Rio reflects parts of the New International Economic Order (NIEO). The NIEO included provisions for the increased flow of development assistance from the industrialized nations and reducing the cost and increasing the ease of technology transfer.[61] Attempts to implement the NIEO via General Assembly resolutions met with little success due to lack of support from the developed states which, throughout the 1970s and 1980s, remained fiercely opposed to the concept of a NIEO. In 1990 a special session of the General Assembly debated 'International Economic Cooperation, in Particular the Revitalization of Economic Growth and Development of the Developing Countries'. Although reference to the NIEO was avoided, the issues were much the same. The Declaration that resulted from the session is significant as it was the first time that a General Assembly resolution on the NIEO subject matter was adopted by consensus.[62] Various compromises were made in order to harmonize the North's position on the environment with the South's on development:

> The current threat to the environment is the common concern of all. All countries should take effective actions for the protection and enhancement of the environment in accordance with their respective capacities and responsibilities, and taking into account the specific needs of developing countries. As the major sources of pollution, the developed countries have the main responsibility for taking appropriate measures urgently. The economic growth and development of developing countries are essential in order to address problems of the degradation and protection of the environment. New and additional financial resources will have to be channelled to developing countries. Effective modalities for favourable access to, and transfer of, environmentally sound technologies, in particular to developing countries, including concessional and preferential terms should be examined.[63]

10

Conclusion

The General Assembly's treatment of environment and development issues in the past indicate a continuing potential to serve as forum for forging consensus and influencing state behaviour. Attempts, like those that characterized the NIEO movement, to create binding obligations through majority decisions, over-reached the powers vested in the Assembly by the UN Charter, and largely failed. These attempts did, however, leave behind a set of principles around which a new and more focused consensus could form. UNCED and the Rio Conventions demonstrate the important role the General Assembly can play in focusing government attention and public opinion on issues of global concern, and then launching the negotiation of legally binding agreements through other fora.

THE SECURITY COUNCIL

Introduction

The Rio Declaration, adopted at the 1992 United Nations Conference on Environment and Development, calls upon states to 'resolve all their environmental disputes peacefully, by appropriate means and in accordance with the United Nations Charter'.[64]

The Security Council is the organ of the United Nations with the primary responsibility for the maintenance of international peace and security.[65] Under Chapter VII of the UN Charter, the Council has the authority to carry out enforcement action against a state to restore peace if it determines that there is a 'threat to the peace, breach of the peace or act of aggression'.[66] Until recently it was considered that this mandate related only to military activity. However a new concept of environmental security has begun to emerge, with recommendations that the Security Council should have a role in environmental affairs. For example, Vinogradov has speculated that:

> With time, there could arise a need to endow the UN with functions similar to those given to it at present by the Charter only in cases of threats to international peace and security, in order to be able to cope with situations endangering environmental security. Such situations could be the consequence, for example, of the acts of ecocide, mass pollution of the atmosphere. There is a question whether certain activities of States with grave environmental consequences can be qualified as a threat to peace and security, thus giving the Security Council the right to intervene with measures provided for in Chapter VII of the Charter. This question should be the object of further study.[67]

This development was recognized at the highest level in January 1992, at a first-ever summit of the heads of state of the 15 members of the Security Council:

> The absence of war and military conflicts amongst States does not in itself ensure international peace and security. The *non-military sources of instability in the economic, social, humanitarian and ecological fields have become threats to peace and security.* The United Nations membership as a whole, needs to give the highest priority to the solution of these matters.[68]

Environmental problems could threaten peace and security in a number of ways. Firstly, disputes between states over shared natural resources or over transboundary pollution could escalate into military conflict, thus threatening international peace and security in its traditional sense. Secondly, environmental degradation, depletion of natural resources, the threats to the ozone layer and the climate system and unsustainable development may threaten human and economic health, and by implication, international peace and security. Thirdly, the environment can be used as a weapon in war. It is this final category that has seen the only instance of environmental intervention by the Security Council thus far, in relation to the Gulf War.

The development of an environmental role for the Security Council is an attractive proposition, in particular as the powers of the Security Council to take decisions binding on member states could fill what has been termed the 'institutional gap' in international environmental governance.[69] However, it is a development that will face many obstacles, both legal and political. This section will explore some of the issues raised by the proposition of an environmental role for the Security Council, but first it will look at the emergence of the concept of environmental security, the dispute settlement system, and will also study Security Council Resolution 687 on the pollution of the Gulf. Broadening the scope of the Council's mandate beyond military matters raises issues related to the broadening of its membership and its decision-making structure to redress the existing imbalances which favour the victors of World War II. The final part of this chapter will discuss the calls for reform to increase the democracy and transparency of the Security Council.

Environmental Security and International Peace and Security

The idea that the concept of security needed to be redefined so that it encompassed not only its traditional military aspects, but also to take into account environmental and economic aspects, has had a growing popularity in international relations literature.[70] The confluence of a number of factors in the late 1980s – primarily the end of the Cold War and the corresponding decline in military tension, coupled with the realization of the international and global nature of many environmental problems such as ozone depletion and climate change – resulted in environmental security coming on to the international agenda. For example, in the aftermath of Chernobyl, the Soviet proposal at the United Nations for a Universal System of International Security placed great emphasis on the environmental element of comprehensive security.[71] Recognizing the link between environmental security and the Security Council's mandate of maintaining international peace and security, numerous commentators have made proposals envisaging a role for the Security Council in environmental matters.[72]

Numerous forms of environmental disputes could escalate into threats to international peace and security. The two examples which will be discussed here are shared international rivers and environmental refugees.

International Rivers
Population growth, industrial expansion and the use of modern technologies for hydroelectric power and irrigation have resulted in much higher water consumption demands. In arid regions, competition for shared water resources

is increasing. Nowhere is this problem more acute than in the Middle East, leading the United Nations Secretary-General to warn that the next war in the area may well be over water.[73]

The Tigris–Euphrates system which flows through Turkey, Syria and Iraq is a source of dispute between the three nations. Turkey's 'Grand Anatolia Project' of harnessing the Euphrates with the construction of 20 dams would reduce the annual flow of the Euphrates within Syria from 32 billion m^3 to 20 billion m^3. The President of Turkey has expressed his belief in Turkey's absolute sovereignty over its water resources, denying any rights of the lower riparians to a share of the resource.[74] In January 1990 Turkey announced that for one month it would halt the flow of the Euphrates to fill the vast new Atatuk Dam. According to critics, the real reason behind this interruption was to demonstrate the possible consequences of continued Syrian support for Kurdish rebels in South Turkey. Faced with water shortages, Iraq and Syria united and plans were drawn up for armed retaliation.[75] Fortunately the river was allowed to flow as normal after three weeks and war was avoided; however it illustrates how disputes over shared natural resources can escalate into a threat to the peace. The Euphrates–Tigris system is not the only potential source of water conflict in the Middle East. Control over the Jordan river and the West Bank aquifer complicate efforts at a territorial settlement between Israel and Palestine. Egypt is concerned about actions of Sudan and Ethiopia affecting the flow of the Nile.

Environmental Refugees

The movement of large numbers of refugees across international frontiers has already been accepted by the Security Council, in a non-environmental context, as a threat to international peace and security.[76] Large-scale movements of people away from their traditional lands because of environmental disruption brought about by unsustainable agricultural practices, shortages of fertile land and growing population may lead to a major problem of environmental refugees. For example, in Haiti, an island which has become an ecological wasteground, severe erosion has left half the bedrock exposed and shrunk the area of arable land to 11 per cent. The exodus of refugees was as much due to environmental degradation as political circumstances. Environmental problems in Bangladesh have resulted in a large refugee movement to the Assam region of India, causing much ethnic strife.[77]

The changes that will be brought about by global warming, such as sea-level rise and changing rainfall patterns, may displace millions of people. Estimates of the number of environmental refugees that may be caused by climate change are as high as 150 million people.[78] Concern over the effects of climate change on international security has been expressed by the United Nations Environment Programme (UNEP):

> If climate change has its predicted impacts, conflicts could be sparked by competition over declining natural resources and by cross border movements of environmental refugees.

> If the economic and social costs of climate change prove severe, conflict between the industrialized nations of the North and the less-developed nations of the South would probably increase. Disputes over limited or diminishing resources such as water and arable land would proliferate, both between individual countries and within them.[79]

The Dispute Settlement System

The UN Charter establishes, in Chapter VI on the peaceful settlement of disputes and in Chapter VII on enforcement measures, a two-tiered system for Security Council action to fulfil the objective of maintaining international peace, with resort to the second tier only should the first tier fail.

Chapter VI sets out the various procedures available to the Council to assist in the peaceful settlement of disputes by making recommendations. Article 34 of the UN Charter states that the 'Security Council may investigate any dispute, or any situation which might lead to international friction or give rise to a dispute, in order to determine whether the continuance of the dispute or situation is likely to endanger the maintenance of international peace and security'. There are a number of courses of action open to the Security Council under Chapter VI. It may call upon the parties to settle their dispute by the conventional means of peaceful settlement;[80] recommend a particular means of settlement, taking into account that legal disputes, as a general rule, should be referred by the parties to the ICJ;[81] or if the Council deems that the continuance of the dispute may endanger international peace and security it may recommend the actual terms of a settlement.[82] There are two limitations on the Security Council when it is acting under Chapter VI. Firstly, recommendations of the Council under Chapter VI are not binding on states. Secondly, if the Council considers that a dispute is not 'international', then it is precluded from taking action by the prohibition on intervention in domestic matters in Article 2(7).

Where the Security Council has made a determination in accordance with Article 39 that a 'threat to the peace', 'breach of the peace' or 'act of aggression' exists, recourse may be had to the enforcement measures under Chapter VII. The drafters of the UN Charter did not attempt to define these three key phrases, preferring to leave a broad discretion to the Security Council. The two main types of enforcement action available to the Council to maintain or restore international peace are sanctions as described in Article 41, and where such sanctions have been or would be inadequate, then action involving the use of force may be authorized.

Resolution 687

The one occasion where Article 39 enforcement measures were applied to an environmental threat was in response to the setting on fire of the Kuwaiti oil wells by Iraq and the pollution of the Persian Gulf. Resolution 687, which officially ended the Gulf War, included environmental remedies against Iraq. It is an important resolution, in terms of the development of international environmental law, as it is the first determination under international law of a state's liability for harm to the environment itself, distinct from harm to persons or property. Resolution 687 stated that Iraq 'is liable under international law for any direct loss, damage, including environmental damage and the depletion of natural resources, or injury to foreign Governments, nationals and corporations, as a result of Iraq's unlawful invasion and occupation of Kuwait'.[83]

The Security Council envisaged the creation of a fund to pay compensation and the establishment of a body to administer the fund. The UN Compensation Commission was created as a subsidiary organ of the Security Council to carry out this task. In 1992 the Governing Council of the Compensation Commission defined the criteria for claims from governments and intergovernmental organizations (IGOs). Claims may cover, *inter alia*, depletion of natural resources, environmental damage, clean-up and rehabilitation. The Council intended that the compensation fund would be financed by Iraq contributing 30 per cent of the value of its oil exports. However Iraq has refused so far to resume exporting under these terms.[84]

Legal and Policy Aspects of Security Council Involvement in Environmental Affairs

The development of a role in environmental affairs for the Security Council faces many obstacles of both a legal and a political nature.

Legal Aspects
Right to Development
States have a sovereign right to pursue their own development policy as affirmed in Principle 21 of the Stockholm Declaration and more recently in the Rio Declaration adopted at UNCED. Principle 2 of the Rio Declaration provides that states have the sovereign right to exploit their own resources pursuant to their own environmental and development policies. This right is qualified by the obligation to ensure that activities within a state's jurisdiction and control do not cause damage to the environment of other states or to areas beyond national jurisdiction. Many states strongly assert this right to development and oppose international involvement in their domestic environmental policies, even when those policies may have international repercussions.

The involvement of the United Nations in domestic matters is governed by Article 2(7) of the UN Charter:

> Nothing contained in the present Charter shall authorise the United Nations to intervene in matters which are essentially within the domestic jurisdiction of any state or shall require the Members to submit such matters to settlement under the present Charter: but this principle shall not prejudice the application of enforcement measures under Chapter VII.

Therefore, in relation to the recommendatory peaceful settlement mechanisms of Chapter VI, which require the consent of the state concerned before intervention can take place, Security Council action may face objections on the grounds of domestic jurisdiction and the right to development. But these objections could not apply to enforcement action under Chapter VII.

Threats to the Peace
In recent years a variety of situations have been determined by the Security Council to constitute a threat to the peace, and the practical definition of this term has expanded far beyond its original scope – ie transboundary military invasions. Recent United Nations practice in Iraq, Somalia, Haiti and Rwanda indicates a trend to interpret threats to the peace in a broader fashion. Internal conflicts which do not threaten to destabilize or spread war to other countries, but which have international effects, such as refugee flows or humanitarian concern, have been identified as threats to the peace. Iraqi suppression of its Kurdish population after the Gulf War was an internal matter until the massive

flow of refugees into Iran and Turkey internationalized the affair. Resolution 688 determined that Iraqi actions in the Kurdish areas of Iraq were a threat to regional peace and security.[85] If the Security Council was to intervene in environmental matters in the absence of military conflict the question would surely be asked, just how far can the term 'threats to the peace' be expanded?

Limits to the Security Council Powers
When the Security Council is operating under Chapter VII, it has a very broad, if not unlimited discretion. This is true in relation not only to the Article 39 determination, but also it applies to the action that can be taken pursuant to that determination. Article 42 of the Charter permits the Security Council to 'take such action . . . as may be necessary to maintain or restore the peace'. Recent Resolutions of the Security Council contain determinations of a quasi-judicial nature and authorize actions that go further than may have been contemplated by the drafters of the Charter. For example, Resolution 678 determined that Iraq was liable for pollution damage and sequestrated the natural resource wealth of Iraq to pay compensation for that damage at an amount to be specified by a subsidiary organ of the Council. The same Resolution also ordered demarcation of an international boundary. In Haiti, the powers of the United Nations were used to restore one party to government.

These developments raise questions about what limits there may be to the permissibility of United Nations actions. The sole legal limitation imposed on the Council by the Charter is the requirement that it 'shall act in accordance with the Purposes and Principles of the United Nations'.[86] These fundamental Principles and Purposes are expressed in very general terms and may be difficult to apply in a given case.

The possibility remains that any environmental intervention undertaken by the Security Council may lead to the state concerned challenging the *vires* of the act before the International Court of Justice (ICJ). The ICJ has so far never reviewed the *vires* of a Security Council Resolution and the question of whether it has the power to do so remains unanswered. This issue was considered by the Court in the Lockerbie cases. The Court did not assert judicial competence to review whether resolutions of the Security Council comply with the UN Charter, or with international law in general. However, it was tacitly acknowledged that there are limits to Security Council powers and that the interpretation of these limits cannot be left exclusively to the Security Council.[87]

Policy Aspects
Characterizing environmental problems as security issues helps to alter the conceptual approach to environmental protection by placing the environment on the highest priority level, according it the same importance as other security issues. However the Security Council is used to dealing with questions of military security, whereas the issues involved in environmental security are fundamentally different as the following table indicates:

National Security	*Environmental Security*
Diffuse threats	*Specific threats*
Enemy as 'others'	Enemy as ourselves
Intended harm	Unintended harm
Short time-scales	Long time-scales
Mainly zero sum	Common benefits[88]

There is a risk that the involvement of the Security Council in environmental security could promote inappropriate responses to resolving environmental disputes. The Security Council's powers to maintain peace were designed to deal with transboundary military invasions. The use of Chapter VII enforcement action would be counter-productive to resolving the great majority of environmental disputes.

While the Security Council may have the capacity to respond to an event such as the diversion of an international river, what could it do where a State is losing its territory as a result of rising sea-levels caused by worldwide greenhouse gas emissions? The Council could be involved in alleviating the immediate crisis, such as humanitarian assistance to mitigate any refugee problem, but in relation to the causes of the problem very little could be done.

One of the main current problems in international environmental law is ensuring the widest possible participation in treaty regimes. If developing states, with rapidly growing populations and expanding industry, do not participate in the efforts to reduce pollution, then in the long term the efforts of the rest of the world will be severely undermined. Thus the current trend is to encourage broad participation in environmental treaties by the use of technology transfer provisions, financial incentives and the principle of common but differentiated responsibility. This facilitative approach is also apparent in relation to compliance with environmental law, where recent efforts have also sought to ensure that, where possible, enforcement and the settlement of disputes are addressed in a non-contentious and non-adversarial manner.[89] If the involvement of the Security Council in environmental affairs resulted in a shift in the approach from a facilitative to a coercive style this could be very harmful in the long term. It could cause friction between states, in particular by accentuating the existing North/South tensions, and could lead to states refusing to participate in environmental treaties.

Four years have elapsed since the Security Council summit meeting highlighted instability in the ecological field as a threat to peace and security, yet in this period no environmental security issues have been subject to the attention of the Security Council. The continued operation of the Chernobyl nuclear reactor, which is perceived by European states as the most serious current threat to their environmental security, was not placed on the agenda of the Security Council. In theory, a resolution could have been passed determining that the operation of Chernobyl constituted a threat to the peace and requiring that Ukraine close the reactor, yet the preferred course of action was to negotiate with Ukraine.

The legal obstacles and political risks entailed in environmental intervention will likely make it very difficult to muster the political support for Security Council action over environmental hazards such as Chernobyl. Any Security Council involvement in environmental matters may well be confined to environmental disputes that result from or threaten to escalate into military conflict.

Reform of the Security Council

For the first time since 1963, when the size of the Security Council was increased from 11 to the present 15, the Member States of the United Nations are seriously considering reforming the composition of the Security Council and its working methods.

In 1993 the General Assembly requested Member States to submit their opinions on the issue and established the Open-ended Working Group on Security Council Reform[90] to study increasing the size of the Council and other matters relating to decision-making by the Security Council. The Working Group reported back to the General Assembly and the issue was debated in the 49th session. The Working Group resumed its work in the fiftieth anniversary session but no conclusive outcome is expected for some time.

The granting of the extraordinary status of permanent membership to the five nations who, when the Charter was negotiated 50 years ago, were the great post-war powers, is now under challenge. Following on from the post-Cold War revitalization of the Security Council there have been doubts expressed about the legitimacy of the Council's use of the collective authority of the United Nations.[91] In particular, there is concern over the domination of the Council by the Western Permanent Members.[92] Moreover, with the increase in membership of the United Nations from the original 53 to over 185, there is now great pressure to enlarge Security Council membership.

Size and Composition

The consultation process among states that is taking place in the General Assembly reveals a very broad consensus among states that the Security Council needs to be enlarged to take account of the increase in the number of Member States of the United Nations. The balance that needs to be struck is between having a body that is large enough to be representative of the whole United Nations membership yet small enough to function efficiently and to fulfil the requirement of prompt and effective action under Article 24(1) of the Charter.

In the General Assembly debates there was overall agreement that expansion should not exceed 10 new members; the final total will likely be a Council of between 20 and 25 members. While there was consensus on the need for enlargement, there remains the major hurdle of agreeing what the criteria for new members should be.[93] Developing states argued that selection of new members should be based on principles of sovereign equality of states and equitable geographical distribution. Developed states argued that the ability to contribute to peacekeeping activities should be a major factor. The Permanent Members emphasized that reforms should not affect the effectiveness of the Council's work. There is broad support for Japan and Germany to have permanent seats. But if expansion of permanent membership was confined to Japan and Germany, this would exacerbate the existing regional imbalances with all seven Permanent Members coming from the northern hemisphere. The Non-Aligned Movement has stated that any expansion of permanent membership which excluded developing countries would be unacceptable.[94]

To enable Council membership to reflect better the current membership of the organization there is a need not only for a greater number of non-permanent seats for developing countries, but also for some permanent status for regional representatives from Africa, Asia and Latin America. Many of the state comments submitted to the General Assembly supported amending Article 23(2) of the Charter to remove the ban on immediate re-election of retiring non-permanent members. This would enable the creation of a new category of 'semi-permanent members'. A proposal by the Netherlands included permanent membership for Germany and Japan, and one extra seat of this semi-permanent category for each regional grouping. Under this proposal it would be up to each regional grouping to determine which of their non-permanent members should be granted the seat.[95]

The Veto

Concerns have also been expressed in relation to the veto. The Non-Aligned Movement of States see the veto as incompatible with the aim of democratizing the United Nations as it guarantees an exclusive and dominant role to the permanent members and marginalizes the role of non-permanent members.[96] The five holders of the veto and the states that they are willing to protect are potentially free from the governance of the Council. While the veto is now used only rarely, the indirect veto – that is, the threat to use the veto – still has a considerable influence.

While many states, especially those within the Non-Aligned Movement, would like to see the veto abolished, it is unlikely that the permanent members would be willing to relinquish their power of veto. Reform proposals will therefore focus on how to dilute or restrict the use of the veto to prevent states from obstructing the functioning of the Council. First of all, if the aim is to restrict the use of the veto, new permanent members should have no right of veto. Secondly, the veto could be diluted by requiring the support of two, or even three, of the permanent members as a condition of its use. This would prevent any single state from overruling the will of the majority.

Transparency

There is also the question of the lack of accountability and transparency in the decision-making process. The sole formal source of accountability of the Council to the rest of the UN member states is the annual report of the Secretary-General to the General Assembly. Important decisions are now taken secretively, prior to the Council meeting in public, in informal consultations with no written records.[97]

One method of increasing the transparency of the Council would be to improve its annual report to the General Assembly by making it into a more substantive document. Informal consultations held prior to Council meetings could be recorded and reported. Also there is a need to improve communication between the Security Council and the states affected by its decisions, both states involved in the dispute and the troop-contributing states.

Transparency is a two-way process, 'like light passing through glass, transparency suggests the free flow of information into and out from' the Council.[98] The Security Council could be better informed of the views of the wider UN membership and other international actors.

The fiftieth anniversary of the UN has served to focus the minds of member states upon reform. It would be appropriate if reforms could be adopted during the fiftieth anniversary. However, reform of the Council will require an amendment to the UN Charter. Amendment to the Charter will probably not be reconsidered for a long time. Thus it is important that a workable agreement is reached rather than a hurried reform package to coincide with the anniversary.

Conclusion

The power of the Security Council to adopt binding decisions gives it the potential to exercise an influential role in relation to environmental disputes or hazards that threaten international peace and security. Resolution 687 and the subsequent decisions which, by determining Iraq's liability for harm to the environment and allowing claims for necessary clean-up and restoration costs, are an important development of international environmental law, illustrate this potential. However due to the legal and political obstacles outlined above, states may not view the Security Council as the appropriate forum for environmental security. Thus the Security Council, even if reformed and enlarged, will probably be involved in environmental matters only in exceptional cases.

2 THE UNITED NATIONS COMMISSION ON SUSTAINABLE DEVELOPMENT

Chris Mensah

INTRODUCTION

The United Nations Commission on Sustainable Development (Commission or CSD), the institutional arrangement established as a follow-up to the United Nations Conference on Environment and Development (or UNCED) is perhaps one of the most important outcomes of the Earth Summit in Rio de Janeiro in 1992. The CSD promises to provide a forum for the continuing debate on the priorities for achieving sustainable development, for the negotiation of balanced solutions to the problems of the environment and development, and to assist in harmonizing and development of international and national environmental instruments.

This is not to say that existing institutions cannot provide the forum to achieve the above goals. The United Nations General Assembly (UNGA),[1] United Nations Environment Programme (UNEP)[2], United Nations Economic Commission of Europe (UN-ECE),[3] the United Nations Education, Scientific and Cultural Organization (UNESCO),[4] International Maritime Organization (IMO),[5] and other organizations of the United Nations system have played important roles in treaty making and policy development in the field of the environment.

Despite the tremendous contribution by existing institutions in the fields of environment and development, UNCED felt that there was still need to improve institutional arrangements at the international level to prepare the United Nations system for the challenges of sustainable development. Agenda 21, which seeks to integrate environmental and development goals would require coordination between the various United Nations agencies, and with other international bodies. Thus, it was felt that the focal point of coordination in the work on environment and development by all the relevant institutions, should come under the institutional arrangement for the follow-up of UNCED. This Chapter is mostly concerned with the background information which lead to the creation of the Commission on Sustainable Development.

THE CREATIVE STAGE

Principal Issues Under Consideration

Twenty years after the 1972 Stockholm Conference on Human Environment (Stockholm Conference),[6] the international community gathered once more. This time, the United Nations Conference on Environment and Development was convened to address and propose solutions to the problems of the environment and also of development.

At Stockholm, the international community was mostly concerned with what are known today as first-generation environmental problems relating to water, air and land degradation caused mostly by industrial activities and those activities exacerbated by poverty and underdevelopment.[7] The international community responded to these problems by concluding a framework of policies and institutional arrangements consisting of:

- The Stockholm Declaration.
- The Action Plan for Human Environment.
- The voluntary Environmental Fund.
- The United Nations Environment Programme (UNEP).

UNEP was the institutional mechanism established to act as a focal point for environmental action and coordination within the United Nations system, to promote international cooperation in the field of the environment and to provide general policy guidance for the direction and coordination of environmental programmes within the United Nations system.[8]

At UNCED in 1992, the international community was faced with addressing and finding solutions to what have become known as second-generation environmental problems – acid rain, depletion of the stratospheric ozone layer, climate change, deforestation and desertification, preservation of biodiversity, international traffic in toxic and dangerous products and waste, and the destruction of the environment in times of armed conflict.

At the centre stage of the discussion on the second-generation environmental problems, was the debate on the linkage between the environment and development and the need to find an acceptable point of equilibrium between the two. Specifically, on the one hand was the question of how much of the environment must be sacrificed in order for states to achieve their development objectives, and on the other hand was the question of how much and what kind of development states must forgo in order to protect the environment. Thus UNCED had to consider the extent to which a bias towards environmental protection of industrialized countries ('the North') would impact on the development of many developing countries ('the South'), and the extent to which an emphasis on development might lead to further degradation of the environment. What measures might be taken to offset any imbalance on either side?

The linkage between the environment and development, as reflected in the Report of the Founex preparatory meeting,[9] is not a new phenomenon; it had been recognized as far back as Stockholm. It was observed then, and observed again during UNCED discussions, that environmental dimensions must be integrated into developmental practices. After Stockholm, however, very little progress was made towards this integration for fear of the economic impact of environmental initiatives on the developmental objectives of these countries. At UNCED, the international community sought to strike a balance between preservation of the environment and the need for many countries in the developing world to continue exploiting their natural resources for their development.

Prevailing Views

The debate on the issue of linkage was very polarized throughout the negotiating process of the Conference. The North argued that environmental protection should be the principal focus of the domestic policies of every state, particularly policies for economic development. It went as far as insisting that the text of the various agreements reached at the Conference include language that emphasized the priority of environmental protection over economic development. In its view, such an emphasis would rehabilitate the current degraded state of the environment and further preserve the natural resources of the world for the present and for future generations.

The South, on the other hand, argued that it was unrealistic to expect that it would subject their development to environmental protection. To them, environmental protection could not take priority over the need to develop. It insisted that only when basic development had been achieved by the poorer countries would the environment be protected, only then would the world's poor, who form the majority of the world's population, no longer need consciously to over-exploit their environmental resources for their basic needs, such as food. The South characterized the North's position as an attempt by a group of rich countries, which had already achieved economic development at a great environmental cost, to stagnate the development of the South by introducing conditionalities to their development as a pretext to environmental protection. They wondered why the North did not address the issue of environmental degradation when they were engaged in their development. It was the North's development and current consumption patterns which had led to the current degraded state of the environment and was responsible for over 70 per cent of the world's pollution.[10] To the South, the North's proposal was a restriction on development, and it was deliberately being proposed at a time when the developing countries were overburdened with debt, poverty, malnutrition and lack of a viable health care for its citizens, all of which had brought on civil unrest in many parts of the developing world.

The South guarded its position by insisting that certain principles be emphasized in the agreements that emanated from the Conference. These principles were reflected in the 1992 Rio de Janeiro Declaration on Environment and Development and seek to make human development a priority and to reaffirm the right of states to exploit their natural resources.[11]

In Principle 1 of the Rio Declaration, for instance, the emphasis is on human beings, their entitlement to health and productive life. Principle 2 emphasizes the sovereign right of states to exploit their own resources pursuant to their environmental and developmental policies. This Principle is basically Principle 21 of the Stockholm Declaration, with the addition of the word 'development'. Principle 3 emphasizes the fulfilment of the right to development. Principle 4 emphasizes the South's view took that environmental protection is an integral part of the development process. In this way the concern for development was moved to the forefront.

It is important to point out that the disagreements between the North and the South were not over whether or not the environment should be protected – in fact, both sides were equally serious about environmental protection. Where the two sides diverged was in their perspectives as to the fundamental causes and solutions to environmental challenges. As indicated above, the North had argued all along that by protecting the environment, development would be enhanced because, in its view, environmental degradation was the major contributor to underdevelopment and poverty in many of the developing countries.

The South, on the other hand, had argued that development would enhance the protection of the environment. Development promises to alleviate poverty, one of the greatest causes of the depletion of the environment in the developing countries due to the need for food. Once poverty and underdevelopment are eliminated, there will be no need to overexploit the resources of the environment for food. Development would bring about alternative sources of food processing and energy, and would lead to a diminution in the exploitation of the environment.

This debate will go on for years to come. What is relevant is that both positions reflect practical and realistic concerns which neither side wants to give up. In this respect, it is important that the results of UNCED should not be seen as a win or a loss by either side, for certainly what emerged was a consensus document which neither side liked but which both sides agreed to live with.

SUSTAINABLE DEVELOPMENT

After a prolonged debate and various informal consultations, the international community reached a consensus whereby it agreed that environmental protection and economic development would have to live in a common jurisdiction that recognized that the developing world would need environmental space in order to achieve its economic development; in other words, development must go on, but in a sustainable way. That agreement was the international community's formal recognition and acceptance of the concept of sustainable development.

The concept of sustainable development has been defined by the World Commission on Environment and Development (WCED) established by the United Nations in 1983,[12] as '... development that meets the needs of the present generation without compromising the ability of the future generations to meet their own needs'.[13] The international community enshrined sustainable development in the following new cornerstones:

(1) The Rio Declaration on Environment and Development.
(2) Agenda 21, a plan of action for sustainable development for the twenty-first century and beyond.
(3) The Commission on Sustainable Development to oversee the coordination in the implementation of the cornerstones.[14]

Institutional Arrangements

At UNCED, the international community agreed that there was the need for an institutional arrangement to oversee and coordinate the implementation of the outcome of the Conference. Negotiating the institutional arrangements was very tedious because of disagreements on various issues, including disputes over whether to create a new institution or to use an appropriate existing institution. The disagreements on the institutional arrangement was exacerbated by the fact that public awareness of environmental issues had reached an all-time high during this decade. In addition, the Conference was perhaps the most popular issue on the United Nations agenda since its creation. Never had a United Nations activity received such attention from all sectors of the international community. There was participation, for instance, from public and private sectors, governmental and non-governmental organizations and the religious community. There was also a strong belief that any institution emanating from the Conference would be as significant and as popular as the Conference itself. After all, as expressed by one of the participants of the Conference, the institution would be the body with the responsibility to oversee some of the most important decisions that the international community had ever taken, and no state would want to be left out. Furthermore, the institution would be the forum where the continuing debate on balancing environmental protection and development, would be conducted.

Many states saw the institutional arrangement as a means to foster their positions on the environment. The North saw the institutional arrangement as a means through which it could stipulate that any financial aid contributed towards the implementation of the agreements reached at the Conference would be given on condition that the protection and preservation of the environment be given priority. Meanwhile, the South saw the institutional arrangement as a mechanism through which it could secure its development aspirations, which would include insisting that development should take priority over the protection of the environment, and to force or shame the North to contribute financially towards the implementation of what was agreed at the Conference. Those disputes and suspicions were carried over from the negotiations held during the Preparatory Committee meetings (PrepCom) of the Conference.

At this point, it may be relevant to provide a brief background to the substantive discussion on the institutional arrangements planned as a follow-up to the Conference which had begun during the fourth PrepCom.

PrepCom

The PrepCom was full of ideas, sometimes divergent, on the type of institutional arrangement that was needed as a follow-up to the Conference. There were debates on whether, given the proliferation of institutions in the United Nations system, a new institution was needed.

Some of the states, particularly those in the North, took the view that it was not rational to establish a new institution when the United Nations was going through a process of reform – restructuring, revitalizing and streamlining the system. They felt that it was better to bring follow-up arrangements under one of the existing United Nations institutions in order to enhance the reform process of the United Nations.

The South took the position that because there were still unresolved issues regarding the concept of sustainable development, there was the need for equal participation by all members of the international community, including non-state actors, in resolving those issues. Furthermore, many of the existing institutions within the United Nations system were not equitably and geographically representative enough of the Member States of the United Nations for that purpose. In addition, because of the financial implications of implementing the agreements reached at the Conference, these countries felt that there was the need for an institutional arrangement to counterbalance what they felt was the power of multilateral financial institutions to impose arbitrary conditionalities on financial assistance.

The PrepCom finally compromised and agreed on the need for a new institution in lieu of an existing one, but one which would be in conformity with the United Nations system and which would support the restructuring and revitalization of the United Nations in the economic, social and related fields.[15] It was also agreed that the arrangement would be based on agreements reached on financial resources, transfer of technology, the Rio Declaration and Agenda 21. It was envisaged that within the institutional arrangement, there would be a close and effective cooperation and exchange of information between the United Nations system and the multilateral financial institutions. This way, financial support would be ensured for substantive actions taken towards the implementation of Agenda 21.

The main objectives of the institution, the states agreed, would be post-Conference follow-up which would ensure that environmental and developmental issues were integrated at all levels – namely, at the regional, national and international levels, including within the United Nations system of institutional arrangements. Specifically, states wanted an institution which would:

- ensure the review and the implementation of Agenda 21 for the purposes of achieving sustainable development in all countries;
- enhance the functioning of the United Nations system in the field of the environment and development;
- improve upon the interaction and cooperation within the United Nations system and between it and other intergovernmental, non-governmental, subregional, regional and global institutions and organizations in the field of the environment and development;
- assist in the strengthening and coordination of national subregional, regional and national capacities and actions in the areas of the environment and development;
- remain seized of continuing and emerging issues relating to the environment and development.

Furthermore, the institutional arrangement was expected to support the revitalization, with clear division of responsibilities, to avoid duplication in the United Nations system through the cooperation and exchange of information between the United Nations organs, organizations, programmes and multilateral financial bodies, and to endeavour to achieve this mandate within the existing resources. However, while the PrepCom agreed on what the institution should do, it was unable to resolve the issues that related to the structure of the institution.

Institutional Structure

As is normal in the functioning of the United Nations and as provided for in its Charter, bodies established by the Organization report either to one of the organs or to the United Nations General Assembly through one of its organs. Bitter debates often ensue on which method should be used. The main debate on this issue during the PrepCom was whether the new institution should be placed under the General Assembly or under the Economic and Social Council (ECOSOC or Council).

The North and a few countries from the South argued that the type of structure envisioned for the institution, ie a 'functional commission', was already provided under Article 68 of the Charter, which allows the establishment of such commissions under ECOSOC auspices.[16] In addition, those countries felt that this approach would enhance the on-going restructuring and revitalization of the United Nations system. The South and, interestingly enough, a few countries of the North, felt that ECOSOC's smaller membership could not represent fully the universal membership of the General Assembly to the extent necessary to oversee such an important new institution.[17] They argued further that the provision in Article 68 did not preclude the establishment of other institutions under the auspices of any of the other organs of the United Nations. They proposed instead that the institution should be established as a 'subsidiary organ' under Article 22 of the Charter which would bring it under the auspices of the General Assembly. This way, all the members of the United Nations would be fully represented in the work of the institution.[18]

The PrepCom was unable to resolve the matter, at least not formally, but it agreed and forwarded to the Conference two proposals:

- either a high-level Commission on Sustainable Development should be established that would report to the General Assembly on matters of substance and to ECOSOC on matters of coordination;
- or a revitalized ECOSOC with a subsidiary mechanism, such as a third sessional committee or ECOSOC's high-level coordination segment, should be the institutional arrangement.

COMMISSION ON SUSTAINABLE DEVELOPMENT

Under the skilful chairmanship of Ambassador Razali Ismail, Permanent Representative of Malaysia to the United Nations, a compromise was struck at UNCED which provided for the establishment of a high-level Commission on Sustainable Development (Commission) which would be a functional commission of ECOSOC, with a high-level Advisory Board and a Secretariat support arrangement.[19] It is significant that in deciding on the institutional arrangements, the Conference considered and acknowledged the extensive experience of the UN agencies in the field of the environment and development. It also recognized, however, the need for an improved institutional arrangement at the international level to strengthen the United Nations system, and its coordination with other international bodies and relevant international agreements. It was felt that the Conference's formal recognition that the environmental and developmental issues were intricately linked, warranted a fundamental change in the way the United Nations and the international community as a whole, approached these issues. The Conference reaffirmed the General Assembly's role as the principal policy-making and appraisal body on matters relating to the follow-up of the Conference, and it recommended that the General Assembly should organize a regular review of the implementation of Agenda 21, with an overall review to occur no later than 1997.[20] In addition, it was also decided that the General Assembly would be assisted in that task by ECOSOC whose role would be to oversee system-wide coordination in the implementation of Agenda 21 and to make recommendations to the General Assembly, UN agencies and other bodies in the UN system, and Member States. UNCED decided that the Commission, a new body, should be created to undertake a third essential task, to spearhead new thinking and to coordinate the United Nations activities with respect to the environment and development.

The Conference then recommended that the 47th session of the General Assembly take decisions on the specific organizational modalities of the Commission and also on the number of members, and matters related to the frequency, venue and duration of the meetings.

After very intense negotiations, the General Assembly adopted Resolution A/Res/47/191 of 22 December 1992, requesting ECOSOC to establish a high-level Commission on Sustainable Development as a Functional Commission of the Economic and Social Council in accordance with Article 68 of the Charter of the United Nations.[21] The Commission is to ensure effective follow-up of the Conference, as well as to enhance international cooperation and to rationalize the intergovernmental decision-making capacity for the integration of environmental and developmental issues and to examine the progress in the implementation of Agenda 21 at the regional, national and international levels. Its work is to be guided fully by the principles of the Rio Declaration on Environment and Development and all aspects of the Conference, in order to achieve sustainable development in all countries.[22]

Functions

Specifically, the General Assembly recommended that the functions of the Commission should be:

> To monitor progress in the implementation of Agenda 21 and activities related to the integration of environmental and developmental goals throughout the United Nations system through analysis and evaluation of reports from all relevant organs, organizations, programmes and institutions of the United Nations System dealing with various issues of environment and development, including those related to finance;

> To consider information provided by government, including in the form of periodic reports regarding the activities they undertook to implement Agenda 21, problems they faced, such as those related to financial resources and technology transfer, and other environmental and development issues they found relevant;

> To review progress in the implementation of the commitments contained in Agenda 21, including those related to provision of financial resources technology;

> To review and regularly monitor progress towards UN target of 0.7 per cent of gross national product of developed countries for official development assistance;

That review process should systematically combine the monitoring of the implementation of Agenda 21 with review of financial resources available;

To review the adequacy of funding and mechanisms, including efforts to reach the objectives agreed in chapter 33 of Agenda 21, including targets applicable;

To receive and analyze relevant input from competent NGOs, including the scientific and private sector, in the context of the overall implementation of Agenda 21; to enhance the dialogue, within the framework of the United Nations with NGOs and the independent sector;

To consider, where appropriate, information regarding progress made in the implementation of environmental conventions;

To provide appropriate recommendations to the General Assembly, through ECOSOC, on the basis of an integrated consideration of the reports and issues related to the implementation of Agenda 21;

To consider the results of the Secretary General's review of all of the Conference recommendations for capacity building programs, information networks, task force and other mechanism to integrate environment and development at regional and sub-regional level, and

To promote the incorporation of the principles contained in the Rio Declaration on Environment and Development and the Non-Legally Binding Authoritative Statement of Principles for Global Consensus on Management, Conservation and Sustainable Development of Types of Forest in the implementation of Agenda 21.[23]

The General Assembly also resolved that the Commission should:

Monitor progress in promoting, facilitating and financing access to the transfer of environmentally sound technologies and corresponding know-how, in particular to developing countries, on favourable terms, including on concessional and preferential terms, as mutually agreed, taking into account, the need to protect intellectual property rights as well as the special needs of the developing countries for the implementation of Agenda 21;

Consider issues related to the provision of financial resources.[24]

Finally, the General Assembly recommended that the Commission should:

Keep the implementation of Agenda 21 under review with the recognition that it was a dynamic programme that could evolve over time, taking into account the agreement to review Agenda 21 in 1997, and make recommendations, as appropriate, on the need for new cooperative arrangements related to sustainable development to ECOSOC, and through it, to the General Assembly.[25]

Venue

The decision on the venue for the meetings of the Commission was negotiated throughout the 47th session of the General Assembly because of disagreement within the United Nations on which country should host the seat of the Commission. This time, however, polarization was not along the lines of developed and developing countries; instead it was a strange mix of countries. Member countries of the Alliance of Small Island States (AOSIS), under the chairmanship of Ambassador Robert Van Lierop then the Permanent Representative of the Republic of Vanuatu to the United Nations, took a common position and played a very prominent role.

One group wanted the venue to be in Geneva, Switzerland, to prevent the Commission from being turned into a politicized institution by what they called the 'New York Mafia', a term usually associated with a group of politically influential diplomats representing their countries in the Second Committee of the General Assembly. The other group, spearheaded by AOSIS and others, wanted the venue to be New York. Unlike Geneva, New York was seen as a place where every member state of the United Nations was represented. Poorer countries without missions in Geneva would have to spend a fortune to attend such meetings and would be at a negotiating disadvantage vis-à-vis those who had a Swiss base. Furthermore, they saw the effort to establish the seat of the Commission in Geneva as a European attempt to bring under its domination what it perceives to be perhaps one of the most important institutions of the international community.

Compromise on the venue issue appeared impossible for some time; suddenly rumours began to circulate around the corridors of the United Nations that the Secretary-General of the United Nations, Mr Boutros Boutros-Ghali favoured New York as the venue because it would enable him to attend the meetings of the Commission without being absent from his office. In addition, a significant number of countries began to realize that in order to give the Commission the attention and importance it deserved, it would have to be based in New York, the headquarters of the United Nations. After all, they argued, all the resources needed for the preparation of the meetings of the Commission were located in New York. Eventually the debate and negotiations on the venue broke down.

Under the skilful chairmanship of Ambassador Razali Ismail, it was agreed finally that the venue would be New York, with the understanding that the Commission itself could decide in the future to hold some meetings in Geneva if its members so wished. It was also understood that should the Commission decide to hold future meetings in Geneva, it did not mean that New York would cease to be its host. That understanding was the Member States' deliberate and convoluted way of saying that New York is the venue but the Commission could hold its meetings anywhere, including Geneva, should the Commission so choose. To have said otherwise would have meant that Geneva had lost the debate on the issue.

The final version of the General Assembly resolution recommended that the initial organizational session and the first substantive session of the Commission should take place in New York, but without prejudice to future venues.[26] Meetings following the organizational and substantive sessions of the Commission may take place in other venues, including Geneva.[27] The Secretariat, which would be funded from the regular budget of the United Nations and depend to the maximum extent possible on existing budgetary resources, would be located also in New York, with a liaison office in Nairobi.[28]

Membership and Participation of States

In the light of the fact that the General Assembly decided that the Commission should be a functional commission of ECOSOC, it was logically assumed that membership of the Commission would be governed by the Rules of Procedure of the Functional Commissions of the Economic and Social Council (Rules of Procedure of the Functional Commissions).[29]

There were, however, issues regarding the numerical composition, membership and participation of non-state entities in the Commission which needed to be clarified.

At the PrepCom and later at the Conference, the North proposed that the composition should be limited to a small number so that the work of the Commission would be more efficient. Actually, the North was concerned that they would be out-voted by the more numerous countries of the South. The South wanted a larger membership so that most Member States of the United Nations would be represented, to ensure equitable geographical representation.

It was agreed finally that the Commission should be composed of 53 members, one member less than the composition of ECOSOC.[30] It is rumoured that the number 53 was arrived at in order to keep in conformity with the practice in the United Nations that functional commissions of ECOSOC should not be larger, numerically, than the parent body.

Thus, at its 47th session, the General Assembly decided and recommended to ECOSOC that 53 members be elected to the Commission.

Participation of Specialised Agencies, Intergovernmental and Non-governmental Organizations

UNCED also recommended the participation of specialized agencies, intergovernmental and non-governmental organizations in the work of the Commission because the states considered that it was very important and necessary for the Commission to seek contributions and expertise from various sources, including those referred to above, on the subject of the environment and development.

Pursuant to that recommendation, the 47th session of the General Assembly recommended further that the Commission should provide for representatives of various parts of the United Nations system and other intergovernmental organizations to assist and advise the Commission in the performance of its functions within their respective areas of expertise and mandates, and to participate actively in its deliberations.[31] In that respect, bodies such as the General Agreement on Tariffs and Trade (now the WTO), regional development banks, subregional financial institutions, relevant regional and subregional technical cooperation organizations, and regional economic integration organizations were expected to assist and advise the Commission within its Rules of Procedure.[32] The General Assembly requested that the Secretary-General prepare for ECOSOC approval rules of procedure that would allow the full participation of the European Community, within its areas of competence, but without the right to vote. In addition, the General Assembly also recommended to the Commission to provide for non-governmental organizations (NGOs), major groups, industry and scientific and business communities to participate effectively in its work and to contribute within their areas of competence.[33]

The European Community

The request by the European Community (EC) that it should be allowed to 'participate fully' on the Commission as it had during UNCED raised a controversy that was not resolved until 1995. What the EC meant by 'participate fully' went beyond the provisions of the Rules of Procedure governing participation of intergovernmental organizations in the work of the Functional

Commissions of ECOSOC. Although it did not seek voting rights, the EC wanted to participate in the CSD's discussion to the same extent as a state member, and to secure access to informal meetings that are normally refused to intergovernmental organizations.

The EC request sought to rely on an earlier decision taken by the General Assembly pursuant to a recommendation by the PrepCom that the draft Provisional Rules of the Conference (draft Provisional Rules) should be amended to allow the EC to participate fully in the Conference.[34] That recommendation was adopted in resolution A/46/470 of 13 April 1992, but with the understanding that the amendment applied only to the EC's participation in the Conference and not beyond.[35] The draft Provisional Rules for the Conference were indeed amended, and were very clear with respect to their application.[36]

Pursuant to the amendment, the EC participated fully in the PrepCom and in the Conference as a distinct entity, in addition to its then 12 member states. However, it is important to clarify that the decision by the General Assembly on EC participation in the Conference could not be interpreted to grant to the EC a right to participate fully in all other gatherings of the United Nations, or indeed of the Commission itself. Whereas it was true that the General Assembly decided to include the EC among the full participants at the Conference, it was the same General Assembly that decided that the members of the Commission would be states;[37] thus excluding the EC from membership.

To 'participate fully' in the way that the EC had requested would have meant according it rights that would be equivalent to state membership of the Commission, even though it is an intergovernmental organization.[38] It would have meant also that in addition to the then 12 Member States of the EC who were eligible to compete for membership of the Commission, the EC itself would also become a *de facto* member. Many of the Member States of the United Nations were opposed to the EC request which they believed lacked a legal basis and because the EC was requesting a status that went beyond its own competence. They argued that the Member States could express their common views through their individual memberships of the Commission.

The Secretary–General recommended to ECOSOC that the EC be given rights of full participation as a non-member of the Commission equivalent to those provided in Rules 69 and 71 of the Rules of Procedure of the Functional Commissions applicable to non-members.[39] He observed, however, that the participation in informal meetings, consultations or negotiations would fall outside the formal Rules of Procedure of the Commission, and it was a matter in the first instance for the convener of such meetings to determine whether the EC could participate.[40] Thus, in the Secretary-General's view, participation of the EC in such meetings was a policy matter to be determined by the Commission. He recommended, for ECOSOC's consideration, that:

> The Commission shall invite the EC, within its areas of competence, to participate fully in its deliberations on any matter of particular concern to the EC. The EC shall not have a right to vote, but may submit proposals which may be put to vote at the at the request of any member of the Commission.[41]

The status of the EC in the Commission was not settled until 1995, after the Commission had already met twice. On 8 February 1995, ECOSOC decided that 'full participation' for the EC in the work of the Commission would consist of:

the right to speak and the right of reply, as well as the right to introduce proposals and amendments . . . The Community shall not have the right to vote but may submit proposals which shall be put to vote if any member of the Commission so requests. The participation of the representatives in the Commission shall in no case entail an increase in the representation to which Member States of the Community would otherwise be entitled. Subject to Council`s approval, similar arrangements shall apply to any other regional or subregional economic integration organization to which its Member States have transferred competence over a range of matters within the purview of the Commission on Sustainable Development, including the authority to make decisions binding on its Member States in respect of those matters.[42]

Non-governmental Organizations

One of the most unprecedented events at UNCED was the extent of NGO participation. Earlier on during the organizational session and the PrepCom, Member States acknowledged that it was essential for the Conference to enjoy the input of the NGO community. This is not to say that every Member State was in favour of extensive NGO participation. Some felt that NGOs were already represented by government delegates who spoke for the people of their country. Other countries worried that the NGOs would use the Conference as a forum for criticism of many countries for abuses or inaction. It was felt that there was a need to clarify on whose behalf the NGOs would be speaking. There were also concerns that NGOs from the North outnumbered Southern NGOs and were being used by the North to propagate the agenda of the developed countries.

Despite the various feelings about the attitudes of the NGOs, which one delegate characterized as 'loose cannon', all the states acknowledged that they had made a very significant contribution, both towards the preparations for and the results of the Conference. This is what led the General Assembly, in its Resolutions A/45/211 of 21 December 1990 and A/46/168 of 19 December 1991, to endorse the decision by the PrepCom, recognizing the significant contribution by the NGOs towards the Conference and its preparation. The General Assembly also emphasized the need to ensure equitable representation and participation as observers in the Conference and its preparatory process, of NGOs from the North and South and from all regions, as well as to ensure a fair balance between NGOs with environmental focus and those with developmental focus.[43]

The 47th session of the General Assembly agreed that it was important that the Commission continue to benefit from the expertise and competence of NGOs, and it resolved that it was necessary to ensure the continuity and further to enhance the dialogue between representatives of governments and NGOs as important partners of sustainable development.[44] The General Assembly further called upon the Commission to encourage the participation of NGOs, including industry and the business and scientific communities, and for procedures to be established for an expanded role of NGOs as regards the follow-up process of the Conference.

The balance that was struck provides that:

The NGOs may, at their own expense make written submissions, which will not be issued as official documents, to the Commission or its subsidiary organs through the Secretariats in the official languages of the United Nations.

The NGOs may be given an opportunity to address the meetings of the Commission and its subsidiary organ, and depending on the number that may wish to be accorded such opportunity, the Chairman of the meetings may request that they do so through one or more spokesperson. Any oral intervention by a representative of an NGO would be at the discretion of the Chairman of the Commission and with the consent of the members of the Commission.

NGOs shall not have any negotiating role in the work of the Commission, and with respect to consultations, it may be arranged at the request of the NGO, at the invitation of the Commission or on recommendation of the Secretary-General.[45]

THE COMMISSION MEETS

The Commission held its organizational session in New York from 24–26 February 1993. It elected Ambassador Razali Ismail as its Chairman and adopted its substantive work schedule for 1993–97.

The Commission recommended various clusters of chapters in Agenda 21 as the basis for the programme of work of the Commission; these are:

- Critical elements of sustainability.
- Financial resources mechanism.
- Education, science, transfer of environmentally sound technologies, co-operation and capacity building.
- Decision-making structures.
- Roles of major groups.

The Commission further decided that it would consider:

- Health, human settlements and fresh-water.
- Toxic chemicals and hazardous wastes.
- Land, desertification, forest and biodiversity.
- Atmosphere, oceans and all kinds of seas.

The first substantive session of the Commission was held on 14–25 June 1993 with a high-level segment of over 50 ministers participating. The Commission decided to establish two intersessional working groups to assist the Commission in the implementation of the recommendations from the Conference regarding the adequacy of financial resources and transfer of technology respectively. With respect to the multi-year thematic programme of work, the Commission adopted a programme which provides a framework for reviewing Agenda 21, consisting of nine clusters of chapters. Five of the clusters, which are also the cross-sectorial issues, would be considered annually; these are: critical elements of sustainability, including the chapters on poverty and changing consumption pattern; financial resources mechanisms; education, science, transfer of environmentally sound technologies, cooperation and capacity-building; decision-making structures; and roles of major groups. Clusters of sectorial issues to be taken up once during a three-year period are: health, human settlements and fresh water, which were taken up in 1994; toxic chemicals and hazardous waste were also taken up in 1994; land, desertification, forest and biodiversity were taken up in 1995; and the atmosphere, oceans and all kinds of seas were to be discussed in 1996. The 1997 session would be devoted to an overall review and appraisal of Agenda 21 for presentation to that year's special session of the General Assembly as provided for in Resolution A/47/190 of the General Assembly.[46] The Commission also decided to request governments and international organizations to provide information on their activities as a follow-up to the Conference.

Prior to the 1994 session of the Commission, several intersessional meetings were held on various clusters of Agenda 21. The government of Norway and the United Nations Commission on Trade and Development (UNCTAD) co-sponsored a workshop in Oslo on 13–15 October 1993 on the transfer and development of environmentally sound technology; Colombia and the United States of America co-hosted a meeting in Cartagena, Colombia, from 17–19 November 1993 on technology transfer, cooperation and local capacities; a symposium on sustainable consumption was held in Oslo, Norway, on 19–20 January 1994; the governments of Japan and Malaysia co-sponsored a preparatory meeting on finance in Kuala Lumpur, Malaysia, on 2–4 February 1994; France hosted a round table on water and health in underprivileged urban areas, in Sophia Antipolis, France, on 21–23 February 1994; an international workshop on health, the environment and sustainable development was held in Copenhagen, Denmark, on 23–25 February 1994; a ministerial conference on drinking water and environmental sanitation was held in Noordwijk, the Netherlands, on 22–23 March 1994; a symposium on sustainable development and international law in Baden bei Wein, Austria, took place on 14–16 April 1994, and an international conference on chemical safety was convened by UNEP, the International Labour Organization (ILO) and the World Health Organization (WHO) in Stockholm, Sweden, on 25–29 April 1994. The objective of those gatherings was to identify and seek ways to solve the problems that may impede the implementation of Agenda 21. The gatherings also facilitated the discussions on some of the issues during the meeting of the Commission.

The second substantive session of the Commission was held in New York on 16–27 May 1994 under the chairmanship of Klaus Topfer, German Foreign Minister. Various delegations expressed concern about the lack of adequate funding for the implementation of Agenda 21 and about the fact that the spirit of Rio seemed to be fading. The Commission first had a general discussion on the results of the various intersessional meetings and then moved on to address the contents of Agenda 21.

Working Group I of the Commission addressed the cross-sectorial clusters of the multi-year thematic programme of work. These include, progress in the implementation of Agenda 21; trade, environment and sustainable development; consumption; patterns; financial resources and mechanism; institutions; legal instruments; education; science; transfer of environmentally sound technologies; cooperation; capacity building, and major groups.

Working Group II addressed the sectorial clusters involving health, human settlements, fresh-water resources, toxic chemicals, hazardous waste, solid waste and radioactive waste. The high-level segment of the Commission was held on 26 May 1994 with about 40 ministers and officials in attendance.

At the end of the session, the Commission decided to establish a new ad hoc open-ended intersessional working group to examine issues on land, management, agriculture, desertification, mountains, forests and biodiversity. The Commission concluded the second session by determining that there was some progress had been made but noted that there was a serious lack of flow of the financial resources agreed to at the Conference.

OBSERVATIONS

The Commission has thus far had substantive sessions and various intersessional meetings. A proper evaluation of the Commission at this point, however, would still be premature, particularly in the light of the fact that the Commission's work has been scheduled in a manner that would allow for thorough evaluation in 1997. Moreover, it is also important to take into account the fact that at this early stage of the Commission's life, it is still trying find its own identity.

This is not to say that preliminary observations could not be made of the Commission's work thus far. Before making any observations, it is important to emphasize that too much should not be expected of the Commission. This is because right from its creation it was evident that the Commission would not be a body with legal competence beyond the collective will of its member states. It is a body whose success depends upon the willingness of the Member States of the United Nations, and is sharply curtailed by the economic and social realities in these countries. The Commission would be what the Member States of the United Nations want it to be because these are the countries that must implement Agenda 21, taking into account other competing sectors of their economies. Implementation of Agenda 21 is a very expensive venture for many countries, despite its overwhelming long-term benefits. It is the bitter-sweet pill that many nations have been asked to take, and have yet to swallow. In many countries of the developing world, the choice of poor people will always be between the struggle to gather that only meal of the day and destroy the environment or to watch a family starve so that the environment can be protected, even though they are aware that in the long run, sustaining the environment means more food in the future. The difficulty for many countries is to sustain the human self now. These are the countries whose activities towards the implementation of Agenda 21 the Commission is supposed to follow and make recommendations.

Thus far, the Commission has distinguished itself as the primary forum for review of the implementation of Agenda 21. The Commission has made it possible for the discussions to take place at the highest level, on issues involving the environment and development. In addition, the Commission has brought together different sectors concerned with the environment and development – namely NGOs, the other major groups, politicians, diplomats and experts. What is important is the fact that discussions are still being undertaken on the environment and development, and many countries are trying to implement certain aspects of Agenda 21 as best they can.

This is not say that the Commission does not need to be improved; in fact, the Commission has not been able to achieve the frank discussions among delegates that were envisioned. Delegates tend to speak more for the record and from prepared statements. This practice would be difficult to overcome because delegates simply do not speak candidly on a topic if they are present as representatives of their countries, except to state the positions of their governments, particularly when they know they are being watched by groups outside the diplomatic community. There may be a few countries who would venture to be candid but even those countries seldom criticize each other or other countries; instead, they simply agree to disagree. One just has look at how long it has taken Member States to criticize the United States government for non-payment of its contribution to the United Nations budget. The fact of the matter is that when one is living in a glasshouse one does not throw stones.

The Commission currently provides a good forum to discuss issues relating to the environment and development, a place where member states of the United Nations can report on measures they have taken to implement Agenda 21, a place which can serve as a focal point for the various organizations engaged in the work on the environment and development. Unfortunately, this may be all that the Commission can and is expected to do, as long as the financial and technological resources are not available in the form of aid or on concessional terms for the many countries of the South in their efforts to implement Agenda 21. There is nothing that the Commission can do beyond that, and that may be the reality of the situation; if the Commission becomes too critical of Member States for inaction, the sessions will simply end up being attended by ambassadors or lower level officials and not ministers.

The relevant question to ask is whether a government policy-maker can really be expected to tell its people to stop cutting down the vegetation for energy, food and survival so that the environment may be protected, which would enhance development so that food may be abundant tomorrow. Even the rich countries know that people cannot put their hunger on hold; miracles should not be expected of the Commission.

3 THE UNITED NATIONS ENVIRONMENT PROGRAMME AND THE UNITED NATIONS DEVELOPMENT PROGRAMME

Alexander Timoshenko and Mark Berman

The United Nations Conference on Environment and Development (UNCED) brought the concept of sustainable development into the focus of the international community. The comprehensive and holistic nature of this concept implies close involvement in its practical implementation of relevant international agencies, specifically those with clear environmental and developmental mandates: the United Nations Environment Programme (UNEP) and the United Nations Development Programme (UNDP). UNCED had been mandated to elaborate strategies and measures to halt and reverse the effects of environmental degradation in the context of increased national and international efforts to promote sustainable and environmentally sound development in all countries.[1] However, the above strategies and measures integrated in Agenda 21 have had a different impact on the respective activities of UNEP and UNDP.

Agenda 21 is to be implemented through an effective division of labour between various parts of the United Nations system, based on their respective competence and comparative strengths.[2] Its Chapter 38 clearly reaffirmed UNEP's role as the principal body within the United Nations system in the field of environment, while taking into account the developmental aspects of environmental questions.[3] UNEP's comparative strength lies in its unique experience and expertise in dealing with a wide range of environmental issues, including developmental perspectives.

With regard to the role of UNDP, Agenda 21 emphasized that, like UNEP, it also has a crucial role in the follow-up to UNCED. The comparative advantage of UNDP was specifically indicated: through its network of field offices it would foster the United Nations system's collective thrust in support of the implementation of Agenda 21, at the country, regional, interregional and global levels.[4]

The process of 'greening international institutions' as applied to UNEP and UNDP translates differently into their mandates. For UNEP it is to focus more precisely on the goals of sustainable development. For UNDP is to integrate the environmental component into its operational activities. These processes are expected to be complementary and coherent within the framework of the overall objective 'to strengthen cooperation and coordination on environment and development in the United Nations System'.[5] The recent and on-going cooperation between the two agencies provides excellent examples of how they can engage effectively in coordinated common action[6] or function jointly within a common structure.[7] The need and ability to cooperate closely in order to respond to sustainable development goals has been pointed out explicitly in the joint statement issued by J G Speth, Administrator, UNDP, and E Dowdeswell, Executive Director, UNEP, to the Commission on Sustainable Development in May 1994: 'We hereby propose that our two organizations work even more closely together by combining our relative strengths in support of Agenda 21'.

UNITED NATIONS ENVIRONMENT PROGRAMME (UNEP)

Integrating the Environment and Development

The 'new face' of UNEP in the post-UNCED era reflects not only innovative approaches to challenges of sustainable development but also a continuity of policy aimed at integrating environmental and developmental concerns.

The concept integrating the environment and development had been put at the very basis of UNEP by its constituent act – UN General Assembly resolution 2997 (XXVII) – which stressed the need 'to assist developing countries to implement environmental policies and programmes that are compatible with their development plans'.[8]

Right from the beginning, the UNEP Governing Council kept the relationship between the environment and development among its priority areas. This issue had been considered through a number of consecutive sessions of the Governing Council. At its first session (1973) the concept of 'eco-development' was launched.[9] The fourth session of the Governing Council (1976) adopted a detailed decision on the 'Environment and Development'.[10] The decision had clear connotations for the concept of sustainable development emerging as 'recognizing further the relevance of eco-development in planning for better development and long-term sustainable use of the environment' and requested the UNEP Executive Director to devote increased attention to the relationship between the environment and development. Another conceptual evolution drawn from this decision was the introduction of the concept of 'environmental costs and benefits of development, including social costs'.

UNEP's evolving role in pursuing sustainable development goals was consequently recognized by the World Commission on Environment and Development (Brundtland Commission). While recommending reorientation of major international bodies and agencies towards sustainable development through improved coordination and cooperation, the Commission viewed the UNEP as playing a central role in this process.[11]

The policy integrating environment and development has been pursued by the UNEP not only through its own activities but also in collaboration with other agencies. In 1980, UNEP, together with the World Bank, UNDP and six other development assistance agencies, signed the Declaration of Environmental Policies and Procedures Related to Economic Development. The Declaration called for the creation of systematic environmental assessment and evaluation procedures for all developmental activities and to support projects that enhanced the environment and natural resource base of the developing nations. The agencies then established the Committee of International Development Institutions on the Environment (CIDIE) to review regularly the implementation of the Declaration.[12]

Even during the pre-UNCED period, UNEP envisaged that its catalytic functions should encompass fully the problems of sustainable development. As early as 1987, UNEP's Report entitled 'Sustainable Perspective to the Year 2000 and Beyond'[13] stated that one of UNEP's major priorities and functions should be to provide leadership, advice and guidance to the United Nations System on restoring, protecting and improving the environmental basis for, and in general be a catalyst, in the promotion of sustainable development.

Throughout the UNCED process, UNEP stimulated and coordinated the UN System-Wide Medium-Term Environment Programme 1990–1995[14] which stressed that the relationship between people and the environment is the substance of, and the justification for, sustainable development.

Within its own, on-going programmes, the concept of sustainable development has been introduced in the long-term planning of UNEP's activities in the field of environmental law. The first long-term Programme for the Development and Periodic Review of Environmental Law (Montevideo Programme) was prepared by the Meeting of Senior Government Officials Expert in Environmental Law in 1981. The governmental experts in their conclusions stressed that the Programme should be directed at harmonizing developmental and environmental concerns by the adoption of an integrated and coordinated approach in all aspects of environmental legislation and its application.[15]

The growing legal response to the need for the integration of the environment and development is reflected increasingly in various international treaties that have been elaborated and adopted under UNEP auspices. A group of regional seas conventions which address sectoral issues of marine pollution have consistently included provisions supporting the integration of environmental and developmental concerns. In earlier conventions, the need for cooperation was established 'in order to ensure sustainable environmentally-sound development'[16] with the obligation 'to ensure appropriate environmental management of natural resources'.[17]

In later agreements, the requirements for the integration of the environment and development are stated in more detailed terms such as 'the need ... to ensure co-operation and comprehensive development without environmental damage'.[18] The agreements also recognized that a threat to the marine environment was posed 'by the absence of sufficient integration of an environmental dimension into the development process'.[19] They expanded the obligations of states to ensuring 'sound environmental management and development of natural resources'.[20]

Yet another regional instrument developed with UNEP assistance – the 1987 Agreement on the Action Plan for the Environmentally Sound Management of the Common Zambezi River Systems – expressly formulated its sustainable development goal: 'to develop regional cooperation ... on environmentally sound water resources management of the common Zambezi River System and to strengthen their regional cooperation for sustainable development'.[21] The Zambezi Action Plan that was elaborated as an integral part of the Agreement also had as its objective 'incorporation of environmental considerations in water resource management while increasing long-term sustainable development in the river basin'.[22]

Besides the international legal regimes referred to above, UNEP significantly contributed to the elaboration of a number of environmental agreements which by the nature of the subject of regulation cannot be considered other than as substantively focused on the integration of the environment and development. The 1985 Vienna Convention for the Protection of the Ozone Layer and its 1987 Montreal Protocol provided an effective legal framework to safeguard global ecological values in the course of developmental activities. The 1989 Basel Convention on the Control of Transboundary Movements of Hazardous Wastes and Their Disposal further contributed to making the economic activities environmentally sound and sustainable. The Basel Convention states in particular 'that enhanced control of transboundary movement of hazardous wastes and other wastes will act as an incentive for their environmentally sound management'.[23]

Two global environmental treaties had been negotiated by the time of UNCED and were brought to Rio for signature by the Member States. The Convention on Biological Diversity was prepared under UNEP auspices. The UN Framework Convention on Climate Change was elaborated by an independent negotiating forum established by the UN General Assembly.[24] UNEP, however, played a distinct role in climate negotiations, both at the early stage of the preparatory process by providing assistance in identifying elements for the future convention, and also by providing continuous support to the Secretariat of the Intergovernmental Negotiating Committee for a Framework Convention on Climate Change.

Both the Biological Diversity and Climate Change Conventions can be seen as incorporating into positive law the concept of sustainable development and being in line with UNCED recommendations. Of the first and foremost significance is the conventions' role in integrating environmental and developmental concerns into the web of the sustainable development concept. The Convention on Biological Diversity has been recognized as 'bridging the gap between conservation and development'.[25] Indeed, both the 'conservation of biological diversity' and 'the sustainable use of its components' are the parts of the objectives of the Convention on Biological Diversity.[26]

The Climate Change Convention aims at stabilization of greenhouse gas concentrations in the atmosphere to pursue environmental as well as developmental goals: '... to allow ecosystems to adapt naturally to climate change, to ensure that food production is not threatened and to enable economic development to proceed in a sustainable manner'.[27] Moreover, the Convention expressly stresses as one of its principles the right to sustainable development in conjunction with the protection of the global climate system.[28]

UNCED Results

The history of UNEP demonstrates that the institution had confronted the challenge of pursuing the integration of the environment and development well before UNCED. However, UNCED brought a new and more precise dimension in UNEP's activities. The outcome of UNCED has had both conceptual and practical, operational and institutional, implications.

Firstly, UNCED resulted in the political legitimization of the concept of sustainable development which, in turn, constitutes the new context for all major UNEP functions – monitoring the environment, environmental management and catalysing action.

Secondly, UNCED requested that implementation of Agenda 21 and of its other conclusions be based on an action- and result-oriented approach and that it should be consistent with the principles of universality, democracy, transparency, cost-effectiveness and accountability.[29] The above requirements, although they were not novel to UNEP, needed to be pursued in their aggregate.

Thirdly, UNCED created a 'new infrastructural environment' within the UN system by establishing the Commission on Sustainable Development and introducing related changes in the UN Secretariat. The role and functioning of UNEP as defined by Agenda 21 needs to be implemented along with such changes.

Finally, UNCED ignited the speedy process of 'greening international institutions' within and outside the UN system which requires UNEP to strengthen existing and to establish new collaboration and coordinating ties with other partner-agencies.

Post-UNCED Mandate

UNCED, while reaffirming UNEP's role as the principal body within the United Nations system in the field of the environment, also requires that UNEP takes into account the development aspects of environmental questions, leading to a new, expanded and strengthened mandate for UNEP.

Agenda 21 provided for a wide array of priority areas on which UNEP should concentrate, including catalysing action, promoting international cooperation, monitoring and assessment, further developing international environmental law, research, dissemination of information and raising awareness, dealing with environmental emergencies and generally providing technical, legal and institutional advice and assistance to governments.[30]

The new expanded mandate should be mentioned specifically with regard to international environmental law. Chapter 38, 22 (h) identified it as follows:

> further development of international environmental law, in particular conventions and guidelines, promotion of its implementation, and coordinating functions arising from an increasing number of international legal agreements, *inter alia*, the functioning of the secretariats of the Conventions, taking into account the need for the most efficient use of resources, including possible co-location of secretariats established in the future.

Apparently the above mandate contains two major elements: further development of international environmental law and coordinating functions arising from an increasing number of international environmental agreements

When read in conjunction with other parts of Agenda 21 and with the relevant principles of the Rio Declaration, the first element could be viewed as the progressive development of international environmental law towards the goals of sustainable development.[31] The 'international law for sustainable development' and other similar formulas[32] could be understood subsequently as a process rather than as a new body or branch of international law. Furthermore, the relevant discussions at the Second Session of the Commission on Sustainable Development (CSD-2, May 1994) have evolved in a similar direction. In this regard it is to be mentioned that CSD-2 requested UNEP 'to study further the concept, requirements and implications of sustainable development and international law', including major environmental conventions 'related to sustainable development'.

The new mandate has already activated a prompt response by UNEP. In particular, the requirements of Agenda 21 have been reflected in UNEP's law-related activities. This impact is apparent in UNEP's process of long-term planning of the progressive development of environmental law. Indeed, shortly after UNCED, the elaboration of the long-term Programme for the Development and Periodic Review of Environmental Law for the 1990s (Montevideo II) was finalized and subsequently adopted by the 17th Session (1993) of UNEP Governing Council.

Montevideo II calls for legal action in 18 programme areas, including consideration of 'concepts and principles which may be applicable to the formation and development of international law in the field of environment and sustainable development'.[33] The Programme is, to a large extent a response to new environmental challenges and specific recommendations and decisions by UNCED. Most of its programme areas can be cross-referenced easily to relevant chapters of Agenda 21.

The second element of the mandate relates to the coordinating functions which can be traced to the constituent act of UNEP. However, in the context of Agenda 21, a new dimension of the coordinating functions, made necessary by the quantitative growth of the body of international environmental law, has been provided. Apparently, this mandate is wider than just the coordination of the environmental conventions secretariats, and includes the coordination of the whole process of international law-making in the field of sustainable development.

When adopting Montevideo II, UNEP Governing Council underlined UNEP's role in the continued progressive development of international environmental law and its relevance to Agenda 21, specifically its Chapters 38 and 39.[34] In the same decision, the Governing Council also referred to the other new element of UNEP mandate (coordinating functions) by requesting the Executive Director 'to continue to promote the coherent coordination of the functioning of environmental conventions, including their secretariats, with a view to improving the effectiveness of the implementation of the conventions'.[35]

A thorough reading of the relevant provisions of Agenda 21 – relating to 'coordinating functions arising from an increasing number of international legal agreements' - leads to an assumption that the UNEP coordinating functions are not limited only to existing conventions. In the light of a more general mandate – 'further development of international environmental law' – these functions should also relate to the development of new environmental regimes to achieve coherence and compatibility, and to avoid overlapping or conflicting regulation.

UNEP has already begun to execute its new coordination mandate. During 1994–96, coordination meetings of the environmental conventions' Secretariats were held. Targeting primarily the secretariats of the UNEP-administered conventions, the meetings led to the identification of the areas which would benefit specifically from the coordinated action and to an institutionalized coordination mechanism. The experience of the first coordination meetings, suggests that UNEP proceed by gradually expanding the scope and magnitude of its coordinating functions.

The meetings of the Conference of the Parties to the Convention on Biological Diversity have provided another example of practical recognition of the new post-UNCED role of the UNEP. In particular, the Conference of the Parties selected UNEP as a competent international organization to carry out the functions of the Secretariat of the Convention,[36] and has requested the Secretariat to coordinate its activities with relevant biodiversity-related conventions.[37]

In the light of Agenda 21 (Chapter 39) and in response to the request by the second session of the Commission on Sustainable Development 'to study further the concept, requirements and implications of sustainable development and international law' UNEP has undertaken a number of related empirical studies. Using its comparative strength which stems from the long-term practice of administering the Secretariats of major conventions related to sustainable development, UNEP has a unique opportunity to assess the practice of the legal enforcement of sustainable development regimes, in particular, the practical results and needs in such areas as implementation and compliance, efficacy of trade-related provisions, liability and compensation mechanisms, avoidance and the resolution of disputes.

The issue of the further development of international environmental law aiming at sustainable development was also considered by the 18th session of the UNEP Governing Council (1995). Recalling Chapter 38 of Agenda 21 and believing that innovative approaches are required in the field of the progressive development and codification of international environmental law in order to achieve sustainable development, the Governing Council, by its decision 18/9 requested the UNEP Executive Director, in preparing the periodic review for the Montevideo-II Programme, to develop a position paper for international environmental law and new instruments aiming at sustainable development.

In response to the above requests, UNEP Secretariat, in consultation with governments and relevant international organizations, is conducting a number of expert meetings and studies in order to provide a new insight into the complex process of the continuous evolution of international environmental law towards the goals of sustainable development, based on scientific soundness and political realism.

Institutional Developments

Even before UNCED, it was expected that the Conference would adopt measures to strengthen and supplement existing international institutions and the institutional processes of environmental governance.[38] Institutions were expected to play a paramount role in responding to the imperatives of sustainable development. New institutional arrangements were needed to meet the general requirements of participation, equity, transparency, accountability and subsidiarity, as well as the challenges of integrating the environment and development.

Some recommendations of UNCED related to institutional arrangements for sustainable development. As translated into relevant resolutions and decisions by the UN General Assembly and the ECOSOC, the recommendations were twofold, providing for both the creation of new UN mechanisms and the strengthening of the existing institutions. The major new institutional development was the establishment of the Commission on Sustainable Development (CSD) (see Chapter 2). Being formally a subsidiary body of ECOSOC, the CSD was charged with an impressive list of functions. These functions, as provided by the UN General Assembly[39], can be summarized as those of monitoring the progress of the implementation of Agenda 21 by bodies and organizations of the UN system as well as by national governments. Competent non-governmental organizations, including the scientific and the private sector, as well as other entities outside the UN system, were also invited to report to the CSD on the implementation of Agenda 21.

Among the existing institutions affected by UNCED, UNEP should be singled out as assigned with a new and additional mandate for sustainable development. According to commentators, UNEP was called to be strengthened in its mandate to promote international cooperation in environmental policy, environmental monitoring and assessment and early warning, and general information dissemination and awareness-raising.[40] UNCED culminated in reaffirming and strengthening UNEP as the principal organization in the environmental field.

Thus, the new infrastructure created by UNCED consists not only of new bodies, but also of the existing agencies which have undergone appropriate reshaping. The process of the 'greening of international institutions' is not limited to the strengthening and consolidation of the environmental components of the various agencies. It also requires a general reorientation towards sustainable development.

The efficiency of the new system will depend, to a large extent, upon its ability to ensure a smooth and complementary interaction of its constituents. The goals of sustainable development are to be achieved within the same limited resources. This is why the synergy to be generated by the new system is of the utmost importance.

The UNCED decisions formulated the sustainable development mandates of CSD, UNEP, UNDP and other agencies with sufficient clarity to avoid duplication and overlapping. The new institutional paradigm raised by UNCED needs to be implemented through the practical and harmonious application of the relevant mandates. The formation of new bodies and the reshaping of the existing ones can be seen as an on-going process, continuously adapting to the evolving requirements of sustainable development. This demands the maintenance of an inherent balance and coherence of the system of international institutions as provided by UNCED.

In the light of UNCED decisions, UNEP is consistently rethinking both the planning process and the concrete actions to further its results and client needs-oriented nature. From its very inception, UNEP activities have been developing at three functional levels:

- environmental assessment;
- environmental policy development and coordination;
- environmental management.

This 'three-layer approach' remains valid in the post-UNCED era. However, the new international environmental agenda, oriented at sustainable development, requires an innovative translation of this 'three-layer approach' in changed circumstances. In the light of the new requirements, the 18th session of the UNEP Governing Council specifically addressed the following issues: major directions of UNEP action in 1996–97 and the relationship between the UNEP and the CSD. The Council endorsed the strengthening of UNEP as the authoritative voice and catalyst of environmental action within the UN system. It underlined that priority must be given to monitoring the state of the environment, assessing and addressing emerging critical environmental issues, and promoting international cooperation. The Council further approved an integrated approach to programme formulation and implementation in UNEP which would focus on four major themes: sustainable management and the use of natural resources; sustainable production and consumption; a better environment for human health and well-being; and globalization of the environment.

The Governing Council also clarified the relationship between UNEP, CSD, UNDP, other UN agencies and bodies, the private sector and NGOs. The CSD acts as the high-level policy forum for the discussions in order to follow up the decisions and recommendations of UNCED. UNEP brings the environmental dimension to that debate through the provision of scientific, technical and policy information and advice. Another instrument to ensure enhanced coordination in the field of the environment is the Inter-Agency Environment Coordination Group (IAEG). Established in 1994 the IAEG is expected to facilitate UNEP's catalytic and coordination role.

UNEP continues to reach out further in order to involve other actors besides the Member States. It consolidates its strategic thinking while strengthening the regional delivery. UNEP acts as coordinator and catalyst both within and outside the UN system. A successful fulfilment of its catalytic function must be based on a comprehensive approach, dealing with a combination of global, regional and local problems.

UNITED NATIONS DEVELOPMENT PROGRAMME (UNDP)

Pre-UNCED Period

The UNDP was established in November 1965, through the merger of the United Nations Programme of Technical Assistance (EPTA) and the United Nations Special Fund, pursuant to Resolution 1020 (XXXVII) of the Economic and Social Council, approved by the General Assembly in Resolution 2029 (XX). Originally consisting of 37 Member States, the aim of the Programme has been to assist developing countries in building self-reliance through technical assistance. The Programme was created to help develop the human and natural resources required to meet basic needs: economic growth and human development. Specifically, UNDP, at the request of governments, supports projects which are designed to help them to attract development capital, to train personnel and to apply modern technologies that are needed for their economic and social advancement.

By promoting human development in more than 150 developing countries and territories in Africa, Asia and the Pacific, Latin America and the Caribbean, the Arab States, the Commonwealth of Independent States (CIS) and parts of Europe, UNDP has created opportunities through which people's abilities, talents and creativity can find full expression. With varying success, the Programme has helped countries to develop the capacity to manage their economies, to fight poverty, ignorance and disease, to conserve the environment, to control their natural resources, to stimulate technological innovation, and to enhance the contribution of women to society.[41]

Since the 1950s, the UNDP and its predecessor agencies have promoted a number of environmental initiatives, such as organizing programmes to eradicate malaria, restoring soil fertility, managing farming systems without poisoning ecosystems, restoring water quality and helping to prevent sand encroachment of roads and farmland.[42] Such projects have helped developing countries to meet their current needs without jeopardizing the ability of future generations to meet their requirements.[43]

In its decision 90/34 of 23 June 1990, the Governing Council of the UNDP recognized the importance of such activities by selecting the environment and natural resource management as one of six areas of focus in the Organization's fifth programming cycle. The UNDP responded by:

- Developing environmental management guidelines.
- Ensuring that all UNDP programmes support sustainable human development.
- Assessing and strengthening its internal capacity to integrate environmental concerns into the mainstream of its work.
- Assessing the capacity of developing countries to develop and redirect their policies and strategies in order to enable them to become more sustainable.
- Developing information systems and networks in support of capacity-building for sustainable development.[44]

Subsequently, UNDP launched the Sustainable Development Network (SDN) to make relevant information on sustainable development readily available to decision-makers who are responsible for planning sustainable development strategies. The SDN was developed to foster interlinkages and informed dialogue between governmental, non-governmental, grass-roots and entrepreneurial organizations and institutions which could benefit and/or contribute to economic development that is sustainable and environmentally sound.[45]

Prior to the Earth Summit, the UNDP also published a *Handbook for Environmental Management and Sustainable Development* to help development practitioners to incorporate environmental concerns into the developmental process, and to encourage people's participation in formulating programmes and projects.[46] This initiative is intended to dovetail with the SDN and other UNDP environmental activities to strengthen the governmental and independent-sector institutional, professional, scientific and human resource capacities of developing countries, allowing them to manage more effectively their own needs for environmentally sound and sustainable development.[47]

The Earth Summit

The 1992 United Nations Conference on Environment and Development, building on the foundations laid in 1972 at Stockholm, committed governments to the eradication of the socio-economic causes of environmental degradation. To achieve this important milestone, nations have had to accept, at least in principle, that it is not possible to maintain a healthy economy without action to arrest environmental degradation.

Agenda 21, the programme of action agreed to by governments at Rio, serves as a blueprint for reconciling a healthy environment with a sound economy. Chapter 38.3 of Agenda 21 recognized that:

> The United Nations system, with its multisectoral capacity and the extensive experience of a number of specialized agencies in various spheres of international cooperation in the field of environment and development, is uniquely positioned to assist Governments to establish more effective patterns of economic and social development with a view to achieving the objectives of Agenda 21 and sustainable development.

Paragraph 38.4 continues by stating that all agencies of the United Nations system have a key role to play in the implementation of Agenda 21 within their respective competence.[48]

Both UNEP and UNDP are given significant roles in the implementation of Agenda 21: for UNEP with regard to policy guidance and coordination in the field of the environment, taking into account the development perspective, and for the UNDP as the lead agency in mobilizing donor assistance and organizing efforts by the United Nations system to build expertise for sustainable development.

It is significant that in the aftermath of UNCED, both UNEP and the UNDP underwent changes in their top echelons. In 1993 Elizabeth Dowdeswell, formerly an Assistant Deputy Minister at Environment, Canada, was elected by the United Nations General Assembly as UNEP's Executive Director. James Gustave Speth, founder and former president of the World Resource Institute and senior adviser on natural resources, energy and the environment to US President Clinton's transition team, was similarly appointed as Administrator of UNDP. Both individuals bring to their respective organizations the kind of experience which will be required to meet the challenges set by Agenda 21 to achieve the overall goal of sustainable development.

UNDP's role in implementing Agenda 21 is defined principally in chapters 12, 33, 37 and 38, which call on the Programme to:

(1) play a leading role in coordinating the United Nations system efforts in capacity-building, in mobilizing donor resources for capacity-building and in assisting recipient countries on request;
(2) to strengthen coordination mechanisms;
(3) to undertake programmes that address the problems of desertification and drought;
(4) to promote the role and involvement of women, youth, NGOs and other major groups in the implementation of Agenda 21.[49]

Response to UNCED and Agenda 21

The UNDP, in response to UNCED and Agenda 21, initiated a process in 1993 of extensive consultation as well as internal and external assessment of the Programme. Prior to UNCED, the Programme had focused its activity on the human aspects of development. While in the past this had been narrowly viewed as investment in human skills, in recent years human development had taken on a wider meaning by recognizing that development is sustainable only if human beings are increasingly capable of taking charge of their own destiny.[50]

Although UNDP had promoted the concept of sustainable development prior to UNCED, it became more of a systematic concern for the Programme following the Earth Summit.[51] The challenge for the Organization was to integrate sustainable and human development into an operational reality. The process of consultation and assessment resulted in a vision of 'sustainable human development' which 'not only generates economic growth but distributes its benefits equitably; that regenerates the environment rather than destroying it; that empowers people rather than marginalizing them'.[52]

Assessment of UNDP also pointed to the need for change within the Programme, the need for better support by the UN and the lack of a clear mission and focus, particularly with regard to sustainable development.[53] The following improvements were also recommended:

(1) Streamlining activities at headquarters to improve efficiency and co-ordination, to strengthen substantive thematic support to the field and to ensure the full integration of actions to promote human development with actions relating to environment and natural resource management.

(2) Adopting personnel and training policies that will strengthen UNDP internal capacity to support sustainable human development and the implementation of Agenda 21.

(3) Strengthening UNDP field officers so that they are better able to deliver integrated solutions in support of sustainable development.[54]

UNDP's core mission in the aftermath of UNCED has been expressed in the following terms: 'To assist programme countries in their endeavour to achieve sustainable human development'.[55] To meet the need for change and to pursue this mission statement, three priority areas have been identified:

(1) To strengthen international cooperation for sustainable human development and to serve as a major substantive resource on how to achieve it.

(2) To help the United Nations family become a unified and powerful force for sustainable human development.

(3) To focus UNDP's strengths and assets to make the maximum contribution to sustainable human development in the countries served by the Programme.[56]

In achieving the goals in these three priority areas, the UNDP must utilize its comparative strengths, its broad mandate in the social and economic areas, its coordination responsibilities for humanitarian and development operations and, most importantly, its unique network of 132 country offices. With regard to strengthening international cooperation for sustainable human development, UNDP's field offices allow the Programme to offer development alternatives which are responsive to local needs and priorities. This network also provides UNDP with the capacity to deliver solid analysis and understanding of what sustainable human development entails at the local level to other agencies and organizations at the international level. This intersectoral expertise complements the activities of other specialized agencies, strengthening international cooperation by building consensus, coalition and partnership at the national, regional and local level.

Building developing countries capacities' for sustainable human development requires the Programme to identify countries' priority needs, the most effective action to achieve those priorities, and identification of partners and other resources to help countries to pursue their development objectives in a sustainable manner. UNDP has focused on four objectives which are seen as priority goals of each of its programme countries: giving priority to the poor, creating employment, advancing the status of women and regenerating the environment.[57] The most effective action to achieve those goals has been identified as capacity-building, development management, grass-roots development, promoting access to technology, and finance and technical cooperation among developing countries.[58]

Making the United Nations an integrated, effective force for sustainable human development recognizes the United Nations' indispensable role in the promotion and realization of sustainable development. It also highlights UNDP's role in fostering the United Nations system's collective thrust in support of the implementation of Agenda 21, at the country, regional, inter-regional and global levels, drawing on the expertise of the specialized agencies and other United Nations organizations and bodies involved in operational activities.[59]

Capacity 21

Chapter 37 of Agenda 21 states that the ability of a country to follow sustainable development paths is determined to a large extent by the capacity of its people and its institutions. Building endogenous capacity to implement Agenda 21 will require the efforts of the countries themselves in partnership with relevant United Nations organizations, as well as with developed countries. As indicated above, UNDP has been given a special role in Chapter 38 of Agenda 21, acting as the lead agency in organizing United Nations system efforts towards capacity-building at the local, national and regional levels.

As a major vehicle by which to achieve the goal of sustainable development in the developing world, UNDP has launched Capacity 21, an initiative to assist countries in developing sustainable development strategies and to enhance national and local capacities to implement related programmes. Capacity 21 is not a separate facility but rather it builds on UNDP's strengths, including its long-term experience in technical cooperation and capacity-building, its multisectoral approach to development, and its strong in-country presence. The initiative complements existing programmes and the capacity-building initiatives of such facilities as the Global Environment Facility (GEF) (see Chapter 9) and the Montreal Protocol's Multilateral Fund (MFMP).

Capacity 21, which became fully operational in July 1993, is a catalytic fund which facilitates the integration of environmental considerations in all programmes and strengthens the sustainable development aspects of these programmes. The objectives are to assist developing countries to integrate environmental issues into development policies, to facilitate the involvement of all stakeholders into development planning and environmental management and to create a national body of expertise in sustainable development and capacity-building.

Translating Agenda 21 into action, Capacity 21 assists countries by providing capacity at the national level to design strategies that promote sustainable development, drawing on appropriate policy, legal, regulatory and enforcement frameworks and on local information sources. Capacity is also strengthened to develop and adapt the appropriate technology to promote sustainable development, and to develop mechanisms for popular participation in deciding and implementing sustainable human development issues.[60]

In its first 18 months, Capacity 21 has operated in a limited number of countries. The experience gained will serve as the basis for full programmes in 1995–96. For UNDP to initiate a programme, certain minimum conditions must be met. Governments must demonstrate a strong commitment to Agenda 21 and to capacity-building, as well as a clear perception of how Capacity 21 will be linked to relevant activities funded by such other means as the IPF, the International Development Association, the GEF and the MFMP. A national policy framework must exist or at least there must be a commitment on the part of the government that one will be created. There must be assurances that programme beneficiaries and stakeholders will be involved at the appropriate stages of the programme development and implementation. UNDP must also be assured that an enabling environment exists which ensures that the desired impacts can be achieved and sustained, and which allows UNDP to play a coordinating and catalytic role.[61]

UNDP is not the executing agent for Capacity 21, but rather a facilitator, coordinator and mobilizer of activities. While the Programme is strengthening its own substantive capacity to allow it to make informed decisions with the governments it serves, as with most of its activities, the UNDP relies on the experience and expertise of others, including the United Nations system agencies, bilateral agencies, NGOs, private sector institutions, and research and academic institutions.

Accordingly, the Programme taps the skills of existing and future partners, utilizing its well-established mechanisms to facilitate on-going dialogue, information sharing and collaboration among both public and private agencies on the subject of capacity-building.

UNDP/UNEP COLLABORATION

Until but a few generations ago, the natural environment was thought of as relatively independent from human activity, with an almost limitless capacity. Today, the human impact on the physical environment has radically changed the condition of both the natural and the human environment. The actual state of the environment is the result of a complex of interactions in which human beings interfere in their natural surroundings, the degradation of which impacts on human development. Although environmental resources are the life-blood of socio-economic development, many of the environmental problems faced today are rooted in inappropriate development patterns.

With an overall objective of integrating environmental and developmental issues at national, subregional, regional and international levels, Chapter 38 of Agenda 21 specifically requires strengthened cooperation and coordination on environmental and developmental issues in the United Nations system.[62] Agenda 21 recognized the vital roles that both the UNDP and the UNEP have to play in realizing those objectives.

There are a number of examples of successful collaborative partnerships between UNDP and UNEP in which their complementary strengths facilitate the goals of sustainable development. UNDP and UNEP cooperate closely with their partner agencies – the United Nations Industrial Development Organization (UNIDO) and the World Bank – in programme implementation under the Multilateral Fund of the Montreal Protocol. The Fund, a financial mechanism to assist countries to comply with the measure of the Montreal Protocol, offers assistance to developing countries to acquire technologies to substitute substances that deplete the ozone layer by those which do not.

Within this cooperative effort, UNEP provides the organizational umbrella for the Fund's Secretariat, serves as the Fund's Treasurer and through the Secretariat of the Vienna Convention for the Protection of the Ozone Layer (1985) which is administered by UNEP, provides technical and institutional advice to governments, upon request, in establishing and enhancing their national ozone policy frameworks. UNDP, following a sector-based approach, assists eligible parties in the planning, preparation and implementation of country programmes, projects, institutional strengthening, as well as with training and demonstration programmes. Although this process is still experiencing some difficulty because of the lack of awareness and technical knowledge in developing countries, the efforts of UNEP, UNDP and their partners continue to enhance national frameworks and to improve the overall effectiveness of the ozone instruments.

Collaboration is also highly visible within the context of the Global Environment Facility. Responsibility for managing and implementing the GEF is shared by UNDP, UNEP and the World Bank. UNDP is responsible for technical assistance activities, capacity-building and, through its worldwide network of country offices, ensuring that GEF programmes complement other development activities. UNDP is also responsible for running the Small Grants Programme which awards grants of up to $50,000 to local NGO activities that contribute to one or more of the four GEF themes. Grants of up to $250,000 are awarded to NGOs carrying out regional projects.

UNEP is charged with integrating environmental concerns in GEF operations, in particular, by catalysing the development of scientific and technical analysis in GEF-financed activities and by managing the Scientific and Technical Advisory Panel (STAP), an independent advisory body providing scientific and technical guidance to the GEF. The World Bank, the actual repository of the Trust Fund, is responsible for investment projects and mobilizing resources from the private sector.[63]

A third example of collaborative effort between UNEP and UNDP has been the development of a joint project funded by the government of the Netherlands for the development of environmental legislation and institutions in Africa. This project reflects the reorientation of both organizations' activity programming in the post-UNCED era and aims at improving the legislative and institutional capacity of selected African countries to meet the challenges of sustainable development.

The project employs a holistic approach by linking its activities to on-going bilateral and multilateral assistance programmes and seeks to develop integrated legal and regulatory regimes. The activities contemplated, therefore, range from the development of cross-sectoral and sectoral laws, through the preparation of appropriate regulations, to training of manpower and institutional support. The project proposes new criteria for the selection of project countries, proper assessment of the needs of project countries and a systematic and integrated response to those needs. This project is being implemented by UNEP and UNDP in close collaboration with such bodies as the Food and Agriculture Organization (FAO), the World Bank and the IUCN, again giving effect to the spirit of partnership which is central to Agenda 21.

In response to the challenges posed by the UNCED process, UNEP and UNDP are proposing to work more closely together by combining their relative strengths in support of Agenda 21. This collaborative effort recognizes that environmental issues cannot be framed in isolation from the development and policy sectors in which they emanate and implies the integration of environmental concerns into all aspects of economic and social-decision-making. It also recognizes that achieving sustainable development requires a combination of the organizations' skills, experience and expertise.

Three areas of cooperation are envisaged:

(1) The development of national frameworks for sustainable development.
(2) Assistance to governments in the servicing and implementation of the Rio and post-Rio conventions.
(3) Mobilizing UNDP's country-based strengths for the dissemination of environmental information.[64]

In the context of this collaborative relationship, several specific agreements have been concluded, including the Memoranda of Understanding on information exchange, desertification control and capacity building.

Requirements set by donors and international agreements for National Conservation Strategies, Agenda 21 implementation plans, biodiversity, desertification and forestry action plans, and National Environmental Action Plans are stretching the human resources of many countries. These strategies should also be harmonized with national economic plans and structural adjustments to ensure the integration of environmental and socio-economic development. UNEP and UNDP have invited the World Bank and IUCN to cooperate in helping countries to develop their plans within a coherent national framework.

Assistance to governments in the servicing and implementation of the Rio and post-Rio conventions is particularly needed in the light of what Agenda 21 referred to as 'an increasing number of international legal agreements'.[65] The two organizations have agreed to cooperate in providing support to the Climate Change, Biological Diversity and Desertification Conventions, in furtherance of the special mandates assigned to UNEP and UNDP by Chapter 38 of Agenda 21.

Making environmental information more accessible is a role which has been carried out successfully by both organizations over the years. Since its creation, UNEP has devoted considerable resources and developed considerable expertise in monitoring and data collection through its Global Resource Information Data Base (GRID), the Global Environmental Monitoring System (GEMS) and the system-wide Earthwatch, and other specific programme areas. UNDP, as mentioned previously, is developing its Sustainable Development Network and deploying resources for capacity-building to facilitate the effective dissemination of information on sustainable development. The complementary roles of the organizations provide an opportunity for collaboration and increased effectiveness of such activities.

Cooperation between UNEP, UNDP and other agencies is being promoted not only from within those agencies. At the Second Session of the Commission on Sustainable Development, the CSD underlined efforts to make trade and environment mutually supportive through strengthening technical assistance in the capacity-building undertaken by UNCTAD, UNDP and UNEP.[66] The Commission also encouraged UNEP, UNDP, UNIDO and UNCTAD to conduct, in collaboration with other international organizations, a survey on the assessment of the available sources of information, as well as supporting systems and inventories, and their effective use, focusing on selected environmentally sound technologies.[67] These agencies and other appropriate organizations were further invited to assist countries, in particular developing countries, in applying conditions and modalities for the involvement of small and medium-sized enterprises in long-term international technology partnership arrangements, including assistance in the preparation, execution and post-servicing of sustainable development projects at the local level.[68]

In the context of freshwater resources, the Commission urged UNEP and other agencies, in collaboration with UNDP, the World Bank and other organizations to strengthen their efforts towards a comprehensive assessment of freshwater resources with the aim of identifying the availability of such resources, making projections of future needs and identifying problems to be considered by a special session of the United Nations General Assembly in 1997.[69]

Agenda 21 clearly underlined the need for strengthened cooperation and coordination on the environment and development in the United Nations System. This objective is being highlighted further in such international forums as the meetings of the Commission on Sustainable Development. In the light of the urging of the international community for inter-agency cooperation, the inter-agency collaboration in the past should be thoroughly analysed, and the pressing needs and limited resources of today fully taken into account. There is obviously a myriad of opportunity for cooperation between UNEP, UNDP and other agencies in such areas as the environment and trade, environmental economics, energy and forestry, to name but a few. The collaboration between organizations must ensure common understanding and objectives and avoid duplicative effort or activity which is at cross-purposes. Through the sharing of information, frequent dialogue and common goals, the ambitious agenda set at Rio can be met successfully.

4 THE CONFERENCE OF PARTIES TO ENVIRONMENTAL TREATIES

*Jacob Werksman**

INTRODUCTION

'What is missing from the present institutional arrangements is the equivalent of a legislature.'[1]

Despite growing concerns about the planet's fate, proposals to empower a new or an existing international institution with the authority to make and enforce global environmental regulation remain Utopian.[2] While many UN institutions have been encouraged to search for greener agendas, their member states have denied any of them the authority to legislate with binding force or to adjudicate disputes compulsorily.[3] The fear of global environmental catastrophe has not yet proved sufficient to create an ambitious new world order in which the nation state willingly yields up its sovereignty for the greater collective good.

Instead, the bulk of international environmental issues are being addressed one at a time, by a series of negotiations that lead to self-contained, legally binding treaties, or Multilateral Environmental Agreements (MEAs). By addressing global environmental governance one issue at a time, states appear to make minor, piecemeal concessions of sovereignty. However, while dispersed, ad hoc and relatively low-profile, these MEAs establish independent intergovernmental bodies[4] (Conferences of Parties, or 'COP') with the potential to develop powers over states that may far exceed those of more formally established international institutions. This chapter will explore, not the greening of a particular institution, but rather the extent to which global environmental imperatives, as reflected in Multilateral Environmental Agreements, have sought to change the way in which states make law.

In the traditional process of law-making, states protect their individual

* The author is grateful for the extremely helpful comments of Hermann Ott, Wuppertal Institute, Gilbert Bankobeza, UNEP Nairobi. The views expressed the author's.

interests by exercising their sovereign right to withhold their consent to be bound and their prerogative to demand reciprocal concessions of their bargaining partners. Negotiation by consensus has been criticized, however, as being slow, cumbersome and as generating weak, least common denominator agreements.[5] Furthermore, strict reciprocity may prove inequitable or unfeasible in the global environmental context, where states at vastly different stages of economic development bear different levels of responsibility for environmental damage and cannot shoulder similar burdens in responding to that damage. The urgent and universal character of many global environmental threats is such that regulation cannot await the moment that all states unanimously agree the rate at which steps must be taken. Many now feel that if MEAs are to provide the rules necessary for sustainable development, they must create institutions with law-making authority capable of taking decisions that may override traditional conceptions of consent and reciprocity.[6]

This chapter will deal generally with MEAs that address transboundary environmental issues of a global character. Typically, these agreements are ambitious in their objectives, seeking profound changes in the *status quo*; are universal in membership, requiring the full participation of the international community; and implicate a wide range of conflicting interests. Specific reference will be made to two MEAs that, in many ways, display a pattern of law-making and institution-building that is illustrative of regimes designed to protect the global environment: the 1987 Montreal Protocol on Ozone Depleting Substances,[7] and the 1992 United Nations Framework Convention on Climate Change.[8]

The success, or effectiveness, of MEAs and the institutions they create can be assessed on a number of levels. A final judgement, reserved for future generations, must be based on whether the parties have been able the achieve the MEA's objectives.[9] Rather than speculate whether the treaties themselves are likely to achieve change, this chapter will focus instead on an interim assessment of whether MEAs have succeeded in creating legislative institutions capable of generating rules that are adequate to their ambitious objectives.

NEGOTIATING A MULTILATERAL ENVIRONMENTAL AGREEMENT

In the absence of a powerful and unitary international legislature, MEAs have sprung up when a convergence of scientific evidence, public concern and political momentum leads the international community to coalesce around a particular issue area. An MEA typically begins its life as a general set of principles and objectives, basic procedural obligations, and a framework of institutions designed to carry them out. Having reached a consensus that there is a problem of common concern to all parties, and having established conduits for scientific and technical advice to identify the means for resolving the problem, the parties are to follow a rhythm of procedures, intended to lead incrementally and ineluctably towards the adoption of rules in support of an ultimate objective.[10]

There can be said to be two stages in the life of an MEA, each of which creates its own set of institutional demands. The first stage is the process of treaty-making, the negotiation and adoption of the text of an international agreement.

The second stage is the more open-ended process of implementing the agreement's provisions. Most commonly, the formal process of treaty-making begins with the establishment of a diplomatic conference or Intergovernmental Negotiating Committee (INC) to which states are invited to send representatives.

Because of their essentially global character, the MEAs considered here were initiated by the United Nations system, and were open to the virtually universal participation of countries.[11] The scope of the negotiations, both in terms of their length and their subject matter, is determined by the mandate adopted by the parent institution that convenes the negotiating committee. The negotiating mandate is typically general in nature, allowing the countries to determine, as they negotiate, the extent of their mutual obligations.

Once the text enters into force, the negotiating committee dissolves and the MEA is carried forward by the institutional structure established by the agreement's own terms, the Conference of the Parties. While the participants and the *modus operandi* of the states involved in an INC and a COP is outwardly similar – the same people may meet in the same rooms discussing the same issues – with the entry into force of the treaty, the legal relationship between the states changes profoundly, from participants in a negotiating process, to parties to a legally binding agreement. In addition to undertaking the substantive commitments contained in the treaties, states' parties become members of the COP, and entitled and subject to its unique procedural rights and obligations.

Sir Geoffrey Palmer and others have proposed that the modular and organic development of the law through distinct MEAs might be replaced by a single institution, a 'super-treaty' system equivalent to an international legislature. Such proposals are attractive for a range of reasons, including promises of improved efficiency and the avoidance of overlapping or contradictory law-making.[12] Other observers of MEAs, however, attribute certain agreements' success to the specialized, modular approach to law-making that develops within each MEA. The principles, functions and structures agreed in each MEA provide the framework for a distinct institutional culture which can allow parties to develop common expertise and expectations around a specific issue, and that enables them to move away from self-interested political posturing to coordinated and targeted action.[13]

In any event, the process of law-making does not end with the adoption of the MEA. The general 'framework' character of many MEAs leaves much of the more difficult and detailed rule-making to the COPs and the specialized institutions they establish as the treaty enters into force.

PRINCIPLE, FUNCTION AND STRUCTURE

MEAs that address issues of global concern can be seen to share a set of principles which in turn, demand a similar set of functions and institutions:

- MEAs often depend upon science to inform their policy-making and have built scientific and technical advice, and precautionary approaches to decision-making, into their institutions and procedures that, combined, place pressure on sovereign states to strengthen their commitments.
- MEAs incorporate the general principle of international law that seeks a balance between sovereign rights and sovereign duties to the shared

environment. This balance between individual national priorities and collective responsibility is reflected in the universal membership and decision-making structures of the MEAs' governing bodies, which encourage the adoption of rules based on inclusiveness, rather than reciprocity.

- The obligations contained in each agreement are often differentiated on the basis of the stage of economic development of the parties, and consequently contain varying levels of substantive commitments. These multi-track concentric regimes can allow states with insignificant legal obligations to participate on equal terms with those undertaking more substantive commitments.

As these regimes have begun to operate, they have challenged traditional concepts of sovereign consent and reciprocity. The outcome of these challenges will determine the effectiveness with which MEAs are able to adopt new and stronger rules.

Scientific Imperative and Sovereign Consent

Despite the ground swell of concern that led to their adoption, many MEAs suffer from continuing scientific and political uncertainty as to the environmental, social and economic costs of responding, or failing to respond effectively. MEAs adopted as empty frameworks are intended to be filled by substantive obligations as the scientific evidence of potential impacts and responses matures. Thus, many MEAs recognize the link between environmental risks and scientific evidence and anticipate that:

(1) Parties' substantive commitments will change over time in response to scientific advice.
(2) Parties will adopt measures in a precautionary manner, not allowing a lack of full scientific certainty to be used as a reason for postponing such measures.

This built-in momentum for ratcheting up Parties' obligations collides with an equally inherent deference for the sovereignty of states and the principle of consent. While all may agree on the general desirability of closing the hole in the ozone layer or stabilizing the global climate system, when general principles are distilled into specific and individual commitments, states begin to balk. The collision places the institutions created by the MEAs – required to fulfil the regime's objective and yet designed to operate by consensus – under stress. The success of a Multilateral Environmental Agreement as a means of protecting the global environment will be determined by the ability of its institutions, through political and legal means, to resolve points of difference and to induce consent.

In order to assist parties to make complex trade-offs between scientific uncertainties and political judgments, many MEAs have established a subsidiary body on scientific, technological and technical advice. The institutional structure and mandate of each of these bodies reflect the degree to which Parties have decided to allow the discipline of scientific or other expertise to direct political action. Under the Montreal Protocol and its 'mother', the Vienna Convention on the Protection of the Ozone Layer,[14] the international community has reached a considerable level of agreement on the political and economic costs of reducing production and consumption of ozone-depleting substances. As a result, the Protocol's Parties have allowed its scientific advisory panels to consist of members who are selected on the basis of internationally recognized expertise. This criterion is qualified only by assurances that selection will strive for the widest possible geographical balance of representation.[15] Panellists are not selected as representatives of their governments, and, indeed, may even be drawn from non-parties, ie representatives of the relevant inter-governmental organizations.[16]

The Climate Change Convention takes an approach very different from that of the Montreal Protocol. The institutional structure and mandate of the Climate Change Subsidiary Body for Scientific and Technological Advice (SBSTA) is designed to retain the political character and influence of the COP. Neither the size nor the qualifications for membership of the SBSTA is selective, as it is 'open to participation by all Parties and shall be multidisciplinary'.[17] In practice, SBSTA of the Climate Change Convention has proved, as of this writing, a highly politicized forum which is virtually indistinguishable in its membership or its negotiating dynamic from the Convention's policy bodies. More objective, authoritative and influential scientific advice is being provided by the Intergovernmental Panel on Climate Change (IPCC), a body of experts who are supported by the World Meteorological Organization (WMO) and UNEP, and who are wholly independent from the Convention.

Scientific advice in both the ozone and the climate regimes is clearly designed to spur policy-makers to adjust their substantive commitments in the light of maturing scientific evidence. Parties to both agreements are required to confront the latest relevant scientific findings, to assess the adequacy of their commitments and to take decisions accordingly. For both the ozone and the climate parties, such decisions are to be taken in a precautionary manner, giving the environment the benefit of any remaining scientific doubt.[18] Assuming that the scientists have been able to reach a consensus on what new commitments are necessary, policy-makers find themselves under extreme pressure to legislate.[19] As of December 1995, these pressures have helped to lead the parties to the Montreal Protocol to strengthen their commitments three times since the protocol was adopted in 1987.[20]

The analogous regime that was established for climate change is also urging the commitments of parties onward. Since 1989, prior to the adoption of the Convention, climate change policy-makers have been informed by the scientific advice of the IPCC. The IPCC's First Assessment Report was sufficiently convincing to help lead to the adoption of the Convention in 1992 and to shape the Convention's central objective. While the treaty negotiators were unable to agree on specific, binding emissions reductions obligations, they committed the parties to taking as their objective the stabilization of concentrations of greenhouse gases in the atmosphere at a level that would prevent dangerous anthropogenic interference with the climate system.[21] In the context of this objective, and in the light of the best available scientific information and assessment on climate change, parties undertake to review their commitments at their first meeting and regularly thereafter. Having conducted this review, they are legally *bound* to 'take appropriate action, which may include the adoption of amendments' to these commitments.[22]

At its first meeting in Berlin in 1995, the Climate Change COP formally acknowledged that the Convention's commitments were not adequate and adopted a mandate to negotiate strengthened commitments. The Berlin Mandate negotiations, which should be completed as early as possible in 1997, must again be carried out 'in the light of the best available scientific information and assessment'.[23] Meanwhile, as average global temperatures continue to rise, scientific evidence confirming the causal link between climate change and human activity accumulates. The IPCC's Second Assessment Report, which provides the most authoritative evidence to date of the need for fundamental changes if catastrophic climate change is to be avoided, was adopted in late 1995.[24] It is difficult to see how the COP could act consistently with the Convention and the Mandate, and fail to strengthen Parties' commitments.

Yet bringing the Parties to face the scientific imperative is not enough to ensure that they will legislate. The failure thus far of the climate change negotiators, in contrast with the Montreal Protocol, to adopt meaningful commitments, can be attributed to a wide range of factors: the strength and breadth of vested interests implicated by greenhouse gas-emitting activities, the longer time-scale associated with the impacts of global warming, and greater scientific and economic uncertainties with regard to the risks associated with action and inaction. But in part failure can be attributed to the structure of the institutions and the decision-making rules that were adopted by the Convention's negotiators when they sought a balance between sovereign and global interests.

Balancing Sovereign and Global Interests[25]

The COPs' institutional structure and decision-making procedures are shaped by Principle 21 of the Stockholm Declaration, which recognizes that states have 'the sovereign right to exploit their own resources pursuant to their own environmental policies' and the responsibility 'to ensure that activities within their jurisdiction or control do not cause damage to other states or to areas beyond the limits of national jurisdiction'.[26] While each state party to an MEA has ceded some degree of sovereignty by consenting to the substantive and procedural obligations in the agreement, each also retains control over the agreement's ability to impose future restrictions on their use of resources through the COP's universal membership and its decision-making rules, which operate primarily by consensus.

Should the parties to an MEA fail to reach consensus, most COPs are designed to resort to majority voting procedures in which each party is entitled to an equal vote.[27] Thus, even within these universal and democratic bodies, the sovereignty of individual member states can be limited through decision-making rules that operate other than by consensus. The pressing nature of the threats to areas of common concern have begun a shift away from preferences for individual sovereignty towards multilateralism and majority voting. This move reflects a growing level of recognition by states of the need for 'such decision-making procedures as may be effective even if, on occasion, unanimous agreement has not been achieved'.[28]

However, the COP's universal membership makes decision-making inherently problematic. One hundred countries with a vast variety of interests are unlikely, despite the availability of scientific and technical advice, to reach the same conclusions as to what new rules should be created. Consensus decision-making is therefore likely to lead to least common denominator solutions. Majority decision-making, on the other hand, may lead a numerically larger group to overwhelm the interests of a more adversely affected minority.

The parties to the climate change and ozone agreements have each responded differently to the challenge of balancing sovereign and global interests, in ways which already have had important implications for the future direction of each regime. Perhaps to the same extent that the unique procedural provisions of the Montreal Protocol have allowed decision-making to be pushed forward by science, the provisions of the climate change convention have allowed it to be hobbled by deeply held parochial interests.

Under the ozone regime, the Parties have delegated the authority to the COP to negotiate the amendment of the Protocol to expand its scope to control additional ozone-depleting substances (ODS), and to adjust the targets and timetables associated with those substances for the reduction and elimination of their use.[29] Amendments to the Protocol become law through traditional procedures that protect each Party's sovereign right of consent. Adjustments to the regulatory schedules for controlled substances, however, have been subject to revolutionary procedures, which have enabled the COP to legislate effectively in response to scientific evidence as it emerges.

For example, in 1991, the Protocol's science panel reported that emissions of methyl bromide, a widely used pesticide, were having a significant ozone-depleting effect in the upper atmosphere. In 1992, at the Parties' fourth meeting, held in Copenhagen, it was proposed that the substance should be controlled through the amendment of the Protocol. The Protocol and its rules of procedures empower the Parties to adopt amendments by consensus, or, should Parties fail to agree, by a two-thirds majority of the Parties present and voting. At Copenhagen, the Protocol Parties reached consensus without having to vote. While the adoption of the amendment would not have required the affirmative vote of all the Parties, the Protocol's amendment procedures respect the sovereign right to consent to be bound by providing that amendments to the Protocol enter into force only for those Parties to the Protocol that take the additional step of ratifying the amendments through their domestic legal systems.

Procedures for the adoption and entry into force of amendments to the Protocol are set out in the Protocol's mother Convention,[30] and require that 'at least two-thirds of the parties to the protocol concerned' must ratify the amendment before it will enter into force. In order to expedite the development of the regime, the Parties to the Protocol have effectively overridden these provisions, adopting, on two occasions, amendments that have entered into force with the ratification of only twenty parties to the Protocol.[31]

But it is the Protocol's provisions on the adjustment of the 'scope, amount and timing' of the measures related to a controlled ODS that have made major inroads on traditional principles of sovereign consent. In text that represents a revolutionary departure from previous MEAs, the Protocol allows the Parties, should they fail to reach consensus, to adopt binding, substantive adjustments by a two-thirds majority of Parties.[32] Thus, a minority of parties, objecting to a strengthening of commitments, could be outvoted by a majority of Parties in favour of such an adjustment. The decision, according to the Protocol, 'shall be binding on all Parties'[33] and enters into force without ratification. At its second, fourth and seventh meetings, the Parties adopted, without resorting to a vote, adjustments affecting the amount and timing of control measures for various controlled substances.

While the Protocol parties have yet to resort to a formal vote, the majority voting provisions help to set the parameters of the Parties' expectations. When becoming Parties to the Protocol, states commit themselves not only to the existing obligations, but to procedures that would bind them to the outcome of future adjustment negotiations, agreed by a majority vote, should such a vote be necessary. The amendment and adjustment procedures are well-tailored to the scientific imperative of ozone depletion: once parties have agreed, through traditional forms of consent (amendment), that emissions of a particular ODS should be controlled, the eventual elimination of the ODS can be accelerated by the Protocol's revolutionary procedures provided for adjustment.

The procedures for strengthening commitments under the Climate Change Convention are considerably more constrained, and have been complicated by steps taken by negotiators prior to and after the adoption of the Convention. The universal character of the Climate Change Convention, which, perhaps more than any other MEA, seeks to include and respect the interests of all states, has among its parties countries who remain unconvinced of the urgency of the climate issue. Indeed, among the long catalogue of specific needs and concerns that the COP must take into account when implementing the Convention are those of Parties adversely affected by the Convention's own rules, including countries 'with economies that are highly dependent on income generated from the production, processing and export, and/or consumption of fossil fuels and associated energy-intensive products and/or the use of fossil fuels for which such Parties have serious difficulties in switching to alternatives.'[34] Relying in part on these provisions certain parties, primarily oil producers, have, with some efficacy, steered the Convention away from the path of progressive law-making.

Although the COP was and continues to be required to 'take appropriate action' in response to the inadequacy of current commitments, neither the Convention, nor the Berlin Mandate indicates the appropriate legal mechanism whereby strengthened commitments should be legislated. The Convention indicates that the 'adoption of amendments' *may* be the appropriate response,[35] while the Berlin Mandate seeks to strengthen commitments 'through the adoption of a protocol or another legal instrument'. The core objective of the Berlin Mandate process, however, is to strengthen industrialized Parties' commitments.[36] While negotiators could not reasonably have committed themselves to adopting an instrument of a particular form and character before they had agreed upon its content, the Mandate points to a strengthening of both the *qualitative* and the *quantitative* character of new commitments.

Industrialized Parties' commitments are currently embodied in the text of Article 4.2 (a) and (b) of the Convention, a legally binding agreement. However, the famously opaque drafting of this article has led a number of industrialized Parties to interpret the aim of returning emissions of CO_2 to their 1990 levels as not creating a legally binding target. In the light of the now universally acknowledged inadequacy of Article 4.2 (a) and (b), a qualitative strengthening of industrialized Parties' commitments would be consistent with the adoption of a *legally binding* instrument containing *legally binding* commitments.[37]

Like the ozone agreements, the text of the Convention sets out the various legislative mechanisms at present available to the parties. Legally binding changes to the Convention may be enacted through the adoption by the COP of amendments or protocols.[38] The process of amending the Convention, which might otherwise have offered the most straightforward means of fulfilling the Berlin Mandate, was made more difficult by procedural rules built into the text of the Convention. Should Parties fail to reach a consensus on the adoption of a proposed amendment, it can only be adopted if a three-quarters majority of the Parties agrees. Significantly, those who wished to protect individual interests ensured the inclusion of language that requires three-quarters of the Parties to 'accept' or ratify an amendment before it could enter into force. In effect this language allows a minority of Parties (one-quarter plus one), whose own commitments may be unaffected by a proposed amendment, to prevent its entry into force by withholding their ratifications, thereby blocking a significant majority from moving forward under a binding regime.[39]

For these reasons, many Parties have favoured the adoption of a protocol as the appropriate means for strengthening commitments. While the requirements for the entry into force of a protocol are to be determined by the text of the protocol itself, the Convention is largely silent as to what decision-making rules should govern how protocols are to be adopted by the COP in the first place.[40] Normally, specified voting majorities for decisions of substance would be provided for by the COP's rules of procedure, which the Convention provides will be adopted by the COP at its first session, and which it was anticipated 'may include specified majorities required for the adoption of particular decisions'.[41] Such rules themselves must, however, themselves be adopted by consensus.[42] Thus far, individual sovereign interests have been able to prevent the adoption of these rules.

Many COPs are empowered by the underlying treaty to take decisions or actions that may be required for the achievement of the agreement's objective or purposes.[43] Some parties have sought to use this generally expressed authority to achieve quickly substantive changes in the MEA's rules that might otherwise have been delayed or prevented by the process of ratification of an amendment or protocol. Such attempts have raised questions about the scope of COP's implied legislative powers and the legal character of its decisions: can a decision adopted by the COP by consensus be considered legally binding upon the parties if the COP is not explicitly empowered by the treaty to legislate?

The Parties to the Montreal Protocol have done so on a number of occasions in order to promote the development of the regime. The ozone parties have used the tool of a COP decision to make authoratative interpretations of a substantive nature, to establish and grant legal personality to its financial mechanism, and, as was described above, to override the entry into force of provisions for amendments as set out in its mother Convention.[44] Although they may share similar treaty language, other MEAs have not enjoyed the same flexible and dynamic operation as the Montreal Protocol.

The issue was raised most recently by the Parties to the Basel Convention on the Transboundary Shipment of Hazardous Wastes.[45] At its second COP, a coalition of developed and developing country Parties pushed through the adoption of a decision which sought to prohibit immediately all transboundary movements of hazardous wastes which are destined for final disposal from member states of the Organization for Economic Cooperation and Development (OECD) to non-OECD states, and to prohibit, as of 31 December 1997, all transboundary movements from OECD to non-OECD states of hazardous wastes which are destined for recycling or recovery operations.

Although COP-2's decision to impose the ban was taken by consensus (no Party present formally objected to its adoption), controversy has surrounded its operative and legal effect since its adoption. Disagreement, reminiscent of the political and academic debates that have followed controversial UN General Assembly resolutions,[46] centred on whether Parties to the Convention, by consenting to the adoption of the decision, were legally bound to comply. While the COP is empowered, under Article 15, to '[c]onsider and undertake any additional action that may be required for the achievement of the purposes of th[e] Convention', a number of Parties argued, after the decision had been passed, that such power did not extend to changing Parties' substantive legal obligations. Decision II/12 itself, nevertheless, speaks in absolute, mandatory terms and does not anticipate the need for any further action before it would take immediate effect.

Proponents of the ban have sought to overcome this dispute by tabling an amendment to the Convention in time for its adoption at COP-3. The amendment was also adopted by consensus and will contain substantively the same provisions as the COP-2 decision. It will formally enter into legal force and become part of the Convention when it is ratified by three-quarters of the Parties. Even then, however, it will only bind those parties that have chosen to ratify it. Once in force, the amendment will ban the shipment of hazardous wastes for disposal or recycling (after 31 December 1997) from states listed in a new Annex VII of the Convention (which will include the 27 OECD countries, the European Community and Liechtenstein), to states not so listed. In the interim period before the amendment enters into force, the ban imposed by the decision, and the legal controversy surrounding its status, remains.

As has been seen, while COPs are generally reluctant to exercise majority voting, the possibility of voting necessarily shapes Parties' expectations and the outcome of their negotiations.[47] The prescience of progressive forces behind the design of the Montreal Protocol was able to establish a regime that was flexible enough to respond, thus far, in some relationship to the demands of scientific advice. A similar foresight from those opposed to the rapid development of the Climate Change Convention was able to build in substantive and procedural obstacles to its ability to legislate effectively. Limited to taking all decisions by consensus and to contending with the Convention's own principles of inclusiveness, the climate change parties are at risk of responding ineffectually to the scientific imperative of global warming.

One characteristic that has been credited with enabling states with different agendas to move forward, in spite of these procedural obstacles, has been the use of common but differentiated responsibilities. As will be seen, this approach has its own institutional implications.

Common but Differentiated Responsibilities

The obligations under a number of newer MEAs, either explicitly or otherwise, are structured on the basis of Parties' relative level of economic development. As regimes designed to protect areas of common concern, these MEAs recognize that while the responsibility to contribute to a solution is a shared one, the burden of responding may be differentiated on the basis of a Party's economic ability to take action. Because many environmental threats stem from the cumulative effects of industrial development, the structure of these commitments also reflects a tacit acknowledgement that industrialized countries bear a greater historical and present responsibility. The inclusion of developing countries in these MEAs is, nevertheless, essential, as their accelerating economic development has the potential to wipe out any achievement by industrial countries acting alone.

Bargains are struck and regimes are designed, not on the principle of strict reciprocity but, rather, on the basis of equity and inclusiveness. This approach to the design of legal obligations, known as 'common but differentiated responsibility', allows Parties with profoundly different legal obligations to participate as equals in the same regime. Such MEAs challenge traditional notions of consent and reciprocity and this has led parties to design new structures and procedures for decision-making. In particular, two fundamental effects on the institutional development of MEAs can be noted:

- The development of 'concentric regimes' in which parties share a basic objective, but are bound by substantially different commitments.
- The establishment of financial mechanisms to support the implementation of the commitments of poorer parties.

Concentric Regimes

Concentric regimes develop out of two related phenomena: the differentiation of commitments between developed and developing countries, and the incremental growth of a treaty through a process of adoption and ratification of amendments and protocols. Both the Montreal Protocol and the Climate Change Convention were designed to distinguish between Parties on the basis of their stage of economic development. Developing countries are simply not required to do as much as quickly as their industrialized counterparts.

The Montreal Protocol provides those developing countries with a minimal annual calculated consumption level of the controlled substances, with a compliance grace period of ten years beyond the deadline for developed country Parties.[48] The Climate Change Convention separates its Parties into three general categories of countries:

(1) Annex I: developed country Parties.
(2) Annex II: countries selected from Annex I and comprising the wealthier OECD countries.
(3) Developing country Parties, which are those countries not listed in either Annex.

Under the Convention's present text, only Annex I parties are expected to demonstrate that they are reducing their net emissions of greenhouse gases.[49] In the medium term, this distinction is preserved by the Berlin Mandate which will result in new commitments for Annex I countries only.[50]

For both the Protocol and the Convention, the process of negotiating new commitments allows a further differentiation within each regime. While all Parties who sign up to new commitments must first be parties to the underlying legal agreement, all Parties to the underlying agreement need not become party to the new commitments. All Parties are bound by the treaty's core objective (eg the elimination of ODS or the protection of the climate system), but only those states that formally ratify the new amendments or protocols are bound to the increasing outer circles of strengthened commitments.[51]

Despite the legal distinctions built into these agreements, developing country Parties continue to participate in the full range of formal negotiations over the implementation and future development of commitments. The treaties' COPs and subsidiary bodies are open to all parties. Procedure and practice for formal meetings allow all parties to join the list of speakers and to shape the sense and the momentum of the debate. The traditional system of regional representation, borrowed from decades of UN practice, and the South's numerical strength, ensures that developing country Parties have a significant membership on the influential intergovernmental bureaux that help to set negotiating agendas and chair meetings.[52]

The institutional complexities arising from this situation have been thrown into the sharpest relief at the meetings of the Montreal Protocol at which all Parties to the Protocol have participated in the negotiation of the adjustments of commitments related to substances controlled through amendments that only some countries have ratified. India and China were credited with leading a coalition of developing countries, to require phase-outs of methyl bromide (an ODS first added to the Protocol's annexes through the Copenhagen amendments) in industrialized countries, while allowing developing countries virtually unrestricted production of the substance until 2016. Neither China nor India was a party to the methyl bromide amendment at the time the adjustments were adopted.

Legal purists might argue that each amendment or protocol creates its own, largely distinguishable treaty, which encompasses only those states that are parties to it. Each concentric ring of Parties, having reciprocally ratified the same new legal agreement, should be entitled to form their own COP and to legislate future commitments accordingly. Other Parties should be allowed to participate only with regard to decisions affecting whatever inner rings of obligation they have ratified. Pragmatists might respond that the current rings of differentiation are only temporary anomalies. While all countries may not at present be bound by the same obligations, all share a legitimate interest in the future development of the treaty as a whole. As developing countries grow, they will be expected to graduate to the outer ring. Allowing them to participate in the design of their future obligations may help to ensure their longer term involvement in the regime.

State practice thus far has sought to strike a balance between both approaches. As has been described, under the Montreal Protocol, non-Parties to later amendments and, indeed, non-Parties to the Protocol itself, have been allowed to participate fully in the development of consensus decisions through formal negotiations in the COP and its subsidiary bodies. However, if the COP were ever pressed to a vote, only those countries' Parties to an amendment would be entitled to vote on an adjustment to that amendment. The Climate Change Convention anticipates a similar procedure, providing explicitly that 'decisions under any protocol shall be taken only by parties to the protocol concerned'.[53]

However, these formal procedural rules rarely, if ever, invoked, may not be enough to placate the resentment felt by countries that have taken on greater burdens.

The Berlin Mandate[54] and developments under other MEAs[55] indicate that powerful coalitions of developing countries have been able, thus far, to use their participation within the COP to help perpetuate a continued strengthening and differentiation of industrialized countries' commitments, without taking on substantial commitments of their own. The tensions that arise from these processes may have a knock-on effect on the operation of other aspects of MEAs, such as the treaties' financial mechanisms, that are designed to take into account the special needs and circumstances of developing countries.

Financial Mechanisms

A further institutional manifestation of the concept of 'common but differentiated responsibilities' are the MEAs' financial mechanisms that are to provide the incremental costs of developing country Party compliance. Several MEAs, in an attempt to ensure the participation of as many developing countries as possible, provide that the richer parties will meet the agreed incremental costs incurred by developing countries in fulfilling their commitments under the agreements.[56] The need to include developing countries in the long-term development of the agreements so outweighed concerns about strict reciprocity that climate change parties, in language similar to the Montreal Protocol, openly acknowledged that the 'extent to which developing country Parties will effectively implement their commitments under the Convention will depend on the effective implementation by developed country Parties of their commitments under the Convention related to financial resources and transfer of technology'.[57]

To ease the administrative process of determining how funds contributed to the agreements' financial mechanism should be spent and on which individual projects, both the climate change and the ozone Parties decided to subcontract the detailed funding decisions to uniquely structured entities. The ozone COP established the Multilateral Fund for the Montreal Protocol (MFMP); the climate change parties designated the Global Environment Facility (GEF) (see Chapter 9) to operate its financial mechanism. Both the MFMP and the GEF have developed unique constituency and voting rules that are designed to allow a smaller body to take decisions representative of all the Parties. A balance in membership and power seeks to respect donor countries' interests in seeing their contributions spent in a cost-effective manner and recipient countries' interests in designing projects that are suitable to their national circumstances.

The MFMP operates under the direct authority of the Conference of the Parties represented by an Executive Committee composed of seven developed country and seven developing country Parties. If the Executive Committee should fail to reach consensus, decisions are to be taken by a 'double majority' system which requires a two-thirds majority of developing country parties and a two-thirds majority of developed country Parties to adopt a decision. The GEF is a legal entity separate from the COP, but is expected to operate under its guidance. Parties are represented through the near-universal overlap between GEF participants and COP member states. GEF operations are supervised by a Council, made up of 32 constituencies, 14 from developed countries, 14 from developing countries and 2 from countries with economies in transition. In the absence of a consensus, voting in the GEF Council is to be taken by a 'double weighted majority', which requires the concurrence of both a 60 per cent majority of the total participants and a 60 per cent majority of total contributions to the fund.

The authority to set overall policy decisions for the financial mechanisms was retained by the COP, backed up, in the case of the climate regime, by the discretion to terminate the relationship with the GEF, should the COP so decide. The creation of financial mechanisms has required the development of new mechanisms that balance the interests and the powers of developed and developing countries both within the mechanism itself and between the COP and the mechanism. Perhaps the most divisive issue that these new mechanisms will have to confront over the next few years, is not which individual projects should be funded, but how much funding overall developed countries should make available to support developing country implementation. Neither the ozone nor the climate regime is precise in indicating by what criteria that amount should be determined, but discussions will, no doubt, test the strength of each regime's ability to respond to scientific imperatives in a balanced and responsible manner.

CONCLUSION

The complexity and subtlety of the institutional dynamics developing under the COPs of MEAs reflects the tremendous challenges presented by the geophysics and geopolitics of sustainable development. Some progress has been made towards the design of international institutions capable of reconfiguring traditional notions of consent and reciprocity, but the day when nations regularly subject themselves to binding majority decision-making for the global environment, seems very far off. The Montreal Protocol and the Climate Change Convention may provide a first indication of the way forward. While concessions of sovereign interests appear at present to be asymmetrical rather than reciprocal, with industrialized countries offering more and asking less of developing countries, they in fact reflect a principled and necessary attempt to compensate for past damage done. But continued good faith efforts are required from both sides. Only a consistent pattern of equitable decisions, taken by consensus and promptly complied with, will build the confidence necessary to convince the individual sovereign to subject itself to the will of the majority.

PART II

Trade

5 THE UNITED NATIONS CONFERENCE ON TRADE AND DEVELOPMENT

*Mehmet Arda**

THE INSTITUTION

The United Nations Conference on Trade and Development (UNCTAD) is the principal organ of the General Assembly in the field of trade and development. It was established as a permanent intergovernmental body in 1964 in Geneva as a result of the first session of the Conference, with a view to accelerating economic growth and development, particularly that of the developing countries. UNCTAD discharges its mandate through policy analysis; intergovernmental deliberations, consensus-building and negotiation; monitoring, implementation and follow-up; and technical cooperation. These functions are interrelated and call for constant cross-fertilization between the relevant activities. In accordance with its mandate, UNCTAD deals in an integrated manner with development and interrelated issues in the areas of trade, finance, technology, investment and sustainable development.

UNCTAD is composed of 188 member states. Many intergovernmental and non-governmental organizations participate in its work as observers. The UNCTAD Secretariat forms part of the United Nations Secretariat. With staff of about 480 and located at Geneva, the Secretariat is headed by a Secretary-General. UNCTAD's annual operational budget is approximately $55 million, drawn from the United Nations regular budget. Technical cooperation activities, which have developed as a result of UNCTAD's sectoral expertise, financed from extrabudgetary resources, amounted to approximately $20 million in 1993.

The Conference is the organization's highest policy-making body. It normally meets every four years at ministerial level to formulate major policy guidelines

* The views expressed are those of the author and do not necessarily reflect the views of UNCTAD. The author would like to thank staff members of UNCTAD who have worked or are working on sustainable development and, particularly, Mr John Cuddy, Coordinator, Sustainable Development, for their assistance.

and to decide on the programmes of work. At the eighth session of the Conference (UNCTAD VIII), held in Cartagena de Indias, Colombia, in February 1992, Member States made the first major move in reforming the United Nations in the economic and social fields. Through this reform, the traditional North–South cleavages were replaced by a new Partnership of Development, embodied in what is known as the 'Spirit of Cartagena'. One of UNCTAD's main tasks is to study and build consensus on international measures in support of national development efforts. That role was enhanced by agreement in Cartagena that UNCTAD is the focal point within the United Nations for the integrated treatment of development and the interrelated key issues in its mandate.

The Conference also recognized the need for institutional adaptation and revitalization in order to enable UNCTAD to seize new opportunities to foster international cooperation. Guidelines were set for expanding work in UNCTAD on sustainable development, focusing on issues such as the interaction between trade matters and environmental policies, measures to foster the sound management of natural resources, the generation and dissemination of environmentally sound technologies and the impact of patterns of production and consumption on sustainable development.

UNCTAD VIII undertook far-reaching reforms of UNCTAD's intergovernmental machinery and methods of work. In addition to setting out the Trade and Development Board's programme of work, it established four Standing Committees and five *ad hoc* Working Groups. A more detailed description of UNCTAD's intergovernmental machinery is given on p 83 where the place of sustainable development in this machinery is discussed.

In the context of reforming the United Nations system, and following the establishment of the World Trade Organization (see Chapter 6), some views have been expressed which question the role of UNCTAD. One of these views is that of the Commission on Global Governance, a group of 28 eminent personalities. The Commission, in its report entitled 'Our Global Neighbourhood', proposed that a United Nations Economic Security Council be set up to improve global economic governance. In this connection, the Commission suggested that UNCTAD and the UN Industrial Development Organization (UNIDO) be shut down.[1] It added, however, that balanced governance arrangements will not result if policy leadership is preserved in the hands of a small directorate of countries while such institutions as UNCTAD, set up to correct imbalances, are dismantled.

While an Economic Security Council remains a proposal, the World Trade Organization has come into being and the question is being asked legitimately, what role, if any, the United Nations will now have in relation to international trade.[2]

The Agreement Establishing the World Trade Organization is an institutional and procedural instrument. It provides for a set of institutional arrangements by which specific aspects of international or national policy can be made the subject of contractual obligations which could be enforced eventually through recourse to trade sanctions. Other than general references in its preambular paragraphs, the Agreement does not contain any substantive rules, disciplines or principles on the relation between trade and other aspects of the world economy or of national economic policy, such as those relating to employment or commodities.

A majority of governments seem to subscribe to the view that intergovernmental debate in the WTO should focus on the implementation of existing multilateral agreements or negotiation of new ones. Broad debate of policy issues is not encouraged, as it might prejudice subsequent negotiating positions. Furthermore, according to this view, the contractual nature of the WTO requires that the Secretariat should be responsive essentially to the requirements and demands of the contracting parties, rather than have a pro-active role of initiating independent analysis and proposing policy approaches.

International governance in the field of trade requires an additional set of arrangements. It is there that United Nations institutions have a role to play. UNCTAD, in the context of its mandate, can provide constructive approaches, as well as viewpoints, and can generate political impulses to be considered by the WTO and other relevant institutions with decision-making powers.

The complementarities between the United Nations and the WTO cover three principal areas. A first important expression of that complementarity arises in connection with the need to define the areas that can be brought under the scope of trade disciplines – the 'frontiers' of the WTO regime. The general question has come up of what are the limits to the inclusion in international trade disciplines of policy areas other than trade itself, and conversely, what issues are best dealt with through instruments other than international trade disciplines. The United Nations can offer a universal forum in which the question can be debated and consensus built both on general principles and on specific cases.

A second area in which the United Nations can be complementary to the WTO relates to the groundwork needed to prepare the negotiation of further international trade agreements. While the WTO will clearly be the forum where most of such negotiations will take place, the UN institutions can help to identify and explore the issues and policy options, as well as build consensus on the basic parameters for new international agreements.

This leads us to a third element of complementarity of the roles of the WTO and the UN in the emerging system of international governance in trade. The United Nations has a specific role to play in providing a development perspective to international trade debate. The Uruguay Round represented something of a reversal of a trend in the General Agreement on Tariffs and Trade (GATT) to introduce a development orientation. This trend had begun in the 1960s with the adoption of Part IV of the Agreement, which deals with trade and development, and had progressed through the creation of the Committee on Trade and Development, and the acceptance in the Tokyo Round of the principle of differential and more favourable treatment for developing countries. The WTO has removed a great deal of the flexibility previously enjoyed by developing countries, and reduced differential treatment essentially to longer time spans for the full implementation of the obligations agreed in the Uruguay Round. There is a need, therefore, for a forum for the identification of the development aspects of major trade issues with a view to improving the understanding of member countries, particularly developing countries, and for the promotion of development objectives in current and future negotiations. The United Nations can provide such a forum.

THE EARLY DAYS

In order to discuss UNCTAD's involvement in environment-related issues, a distinction needs to be made between intergovernmental activities in the

UNCTAD forum and those of the secretariat. Although the latter are normally determined by the former, the secretariat has a duty to undertake research and to bring emerging issues to the attention of the governments. Therefore, work initiated by the secretariat within its broad mandate on trade and development issues may precede governmental deliberations in UNCTAD on a given subject.

The involvement in environmental issues by the UNCTAD Secretariat goes back to the preparations for the 1972 Stockholm Conference on the Human Environment. Several staff members participated, in their personal capacity, at a meeting held in Founex, near Geneva, where substantive preparations were undertaken for the Stockholm Conference. In spite of its informal character, this meeting had a significant influence on the Conference itself and on a major part of the subsequent activities on sustainable development.

The first really visible and official emergence of UNCTAD on the 'environment' front was at a meeting which it organized, jointly with UNEP, on 8–12 October 1974, in Cocoyoc, Mexico. This symposium on 'Patterns of Resource Use, Environment and Development Strategies' was a direct consequence of the Founex meeting. It gathered 25 eminent personalities and resulted in the 'Cocoyoc Declaration'.[3] Coming shortly after the adoption by the UN General Assembly, on 1 May 1974, of the 'Declaration on the Establishment of a New International Economic Order' (NIEO) (Decision 3201, S-IV) and the 'Programme of Action on the Establishment of a New International Economic Order' (Decision 3201, S-IV), the Cocoyoc Declaration focused on poverty, population and environmental issues and their interrelationship, which had not been emphasized by the General Assembly in these two decisions.

The NIEO 'Declaration' and 'Programme of Action' refer to the environment only indirectly by calling for the improvement of the competitiveness of natural materials facing competition from synthetic substitutes, and putting an end to the waste of natural resources. The Cocoyoc Declaration, on the other hand, 'fully endorses' these decisions but stresses at the very beginning the importance of environmental problems by stating that 'environmental degradation and the rising pressure on resources raise the question of whether the "outer limits" of the planet's integrity may not be at risk'.

The analytical reasoning behind this observation also establishes a strong link with development.

> Unequal economic relationships contribute directly to environmental pressures. The cheapness of materials has been one factor in increasing pollution and encouraging waste and the throw-away economy among the rich. And continued poverty in many developing lands has often compelled the people to cultivate marginal lands at great risk of soil erosion or to migrate to the physically degraded and overcrowded cities.

In a long section, the declaration supports 'strong international regimes for the exploitation of common property resources' and the taxation of the use of international commons 'for the benefit of the poorest strata of the poor countries'. It calls for 'imaginative research into alternative consumption patterns, technological styles, land use strategies as well as the institutional framework and the educational requirements to sustain them', and for 'low waste and clean technologies [to] replace the environmentally disruptive ones'. The declaration also foreshadows an underlying element of UNCTAD's subsequent approach to environmental issues by saying that environmental considerations add 'new strength to the legitimate aspirations of the poor countries'. Finally, the participants 'affirm their belief that since the issues of development, environment and resource use are essentially global and concern the wellbeing of all mankind, governments should fully use the mechanisms of the United Nations for their resolution and that the United Nations System should be renewed and strengthened to be capable of its new responsibilities'.

1974–1988 PERIOD

UNCTAD's activities in this period were dominated by the decisions taken in the fourth United Nations Conference on Trade and Development (UNCTAD IV) held in 1974, in Nairobi, and in particular, on Resolution 93(IV) which set out the Integrated Programme for Commodities (IPC). Efforts were focused on the establishment of International Commodity Agreements and the Common Fund which aimed at stabilizing world prices of commodities. Certain commodity negotiations recognized, however, that the production and pricing of natural resources were having a critical impact on the environment.

While intergovernmental negotiations on international cooperation between producers and consumers of most commodities mentioned in Resolution 93(IV) focused on price stabilization, the tropical timber discussions followed a different path. Since it had become obvious that the rapid destruction of tropical forests would soon endanger the supply of tropical timber itself and inflict heavy damage on the ecological systems of producer countries, the main issue for negotiations was not price stabilization but conservation and development. Thus, the preamble to the International Tropical Timber Agreement (ITTA), 1983, negotiated under UNCTAD auspices, refers to 'the importance of, and the need for, proper and effective conservation and development of tropical forests with a view to ensuring their optimum utilization while maintaining the ecological balance of the regions concerned and of the biosphere'.[4] The agreement even defines 'producing member' in such a novel way that equal treatment is given to forest countries if they choose not to export timber in order to preserve their forests. It is an intergovernmental instrument reflecting the consensus reached among states. The World Commission on Environment and Development which formulated many UNCED recommendations recognized the ITTA as a notable exception to international commodity agreements which, at that time, included no environmental resource considerations. The UNCTAD secretariat played a key intermediary role in the negotiations leading to the final result. Similar environmental principles were later introduced in other international commodity Agreements.

During this period the text of the International Agreement on Jute and Jute Products, 1989,[5] was renegotiated to give 'environmental aspects due consideration in activities of the Organization, particularly by creating awareness of the beneficial effects of the use of Jute as a natural product'.

Although environmental issues, as a specific topic, were absent from the agenda of the intergovernmental machinery of UNCTAD, during the late 1970s the Research Division of the secretariat carried out a joint project with UNEP on environmental issues. This led to the publication of a series of research reports,[6] and, in 1982, *The Control of Resources*.[7] This publication, the first draft of which was discussed at a meeting in Paris in February 1980, includes discussions on conceptual problems such as common property resources, externalities, the distribution of income and environmental control under uncertainty, as well as applied theoretical analyses of fisheries, forestry and pollution control.

1988–92 PERIOD, UP TO AND INCLUDING UNCTAD VIII AND UNCED

It was in 1988 that work on environmental issues and sustainable development appeared as an explicit duty of an organizational unit of UNCTAD. In a reorganization of the secretariat in 1988, an Inter-sectoral Issues Unit was established. It was to be the 'focal point for promoting work, relevant to UNCTAD's mandate, on disarmament and development, ecologically sustainable development and the role of women in development'. The unit was to be kept small to the extent possible, so that work on these topics could be integrated with related activities within programmes in different areas of the secretariat. Initially, these different areas of the secretariat comprised the Commodities Division and International Trade Programmes, in addition to the Resources for Development Programmes in which the Intersectoral Issues Unit was located.

Research Activities

During the period up to early 1992, there was no significant activity on environmental issues in the intergovernmental machinery of UNCTAD. The secretariat, however, was involved in a series of studies which, at the conceptual level, introduced and elaborated some of the modern thinking on environmental issues and, at the empirical level, provided evidence of the linkage between the environmental and developmental policies. At the same time there was active collaboration with the UNCED secretariat on substantive preparations for the Rio Conference.

Thanks to extrabudgetary support, a series of studies on environmental principles and developing countries was prepared and published as a book.[8] The essays provide a critical review of the polluter–pays, user–pays, precautionary and subsidiarity principles from the point of view of developing countries. The purpose of the volume was 'to explore what the implications would be for developing countries if the four principles . . . were more widely applied, in particular in international trade and global agreements'.[9]

Extrabudgetary support was also instrumental in launching a series of studies on the links between market conditions, the intensity of resource use, and particular environmental effects. Four studies analysed the issue in agriculture, fisheries, mining and forestry.[10] Together with two other studies contributed by experts, these were discussed at a round table meeting held in Geneva in January 1992. The meeting identified a number of major themes and guidelines for UNCTAD's work at the interface between commodities and environment. These ideas, later elaborated by governments in the context of the Committee (later Standing Committee) on Commodities, led to empirical work linking policies which affect the commodity sector with environmental impacts of commodity production and processing. In 1993, several country/commodity case studies were undertaken in this area, in particular on cocoa, coffee and rice

(UNCTAD/COM/17–24). Some conceptual work on the internalization of environmental externalities was also carried out during this period.[11]

In May 1990, at a high-level meeting in Bergen, Norway, the Secretary-General of UNCTAD invited the international community to give serious consideration to controlling carbon dioxide (CO_2) through a system of tradable permits. This was a bold and challenging idea. In 1991, with extrabudgetary financial support, the secretariat launched a programme of research into the technical and institutional aspects of a global system of tradable CO_2 emission entitlements, both as a cost-effective and technically efficient means of controlling CO_2 emissions, and as an innovative financial mechanism which is capable of transferring substantial amounts of finance, environmentally sound technologies and technical assistance to developing countries. In this period a series of research reports were prepared and discussed at a round table meeting in Rio just before UNCED.[12]

Second UN Conference on LDCs

The relationship between the environment and development was among the issues that were considered by the Second UNCTAD United Nations Conference on least developed countries (LDCs) held in Paris in 1990. The Programme of Action for the LDCs for the 1990s[13] adopted by the Conference recommends policies and measures in this area. UNCTAD acts as the focal point for the follow-up and review of progress in the implementation of the Programme of Action. In particular, the Programme stresses the need for an integrated and multidisciplinary approach to confront the twin problems of poverty and environmental degradation in the countries, covering the following broad elements:

(1) Incentives to motivate better environmental management and to ensure high efficiency of energy use, as well as to discourage environmental degradation.
(2) Education of the local communities in both urban and rural areas, aimed at enhancing awareness of the economic and social benefits of environmental protection.
(3) Developing human resources to deal with environmental problems, as an important component of capacity-building in the LDCs.
(4) Addressing the intertwined problems of poverty eradication and improvement and management of the environment in an integrated way.
(5) Facilitating the access to and the transfer of environmentally sound technologies to the least developed countries.
(6) Developing new techniques to rationalize the use of traditional energy resources, and developing low-cost alternative fuel sources, in particular new and renewable sources, which could provide an alternative to the use of fuelwood, thus alleviating pressure on the environment.

The Programme of Action also underscores the importance of strengthening human, institutional and technological capacities of LDCs to identify environmental problems, to assess the relationship between developmental and environmental trends, and to prepare national environmental management plans for conservation and protection strategies. It calls for involving women in these plans, especially in forest- and land-management programmes. They should also be involved in the choice and dissemination of appropriate technologies which would facilitate their household and productive activities while respecting the rhythm of renewal of the natural resource base.

The Programme of Action for LDCs highlights the particular needs of LDCs which are prone to drought and desertification, and recommends improved natural resources management and increases in productivity in agriculture and livestock on a sustainable ecologically sound basis as measures to protect their productive base.

The Programme of Action also recognizes that implementing these policies would be beyond the capacity and resources of LDCs and emphasizes the importance of external financial and technical support. A key provision of the Programme in this regard is that the 'assistance provided to the least developed countries for programmes for environmental protection should, as much as possible, be additional to regular flows of assistance'.[14]

UNCTAD VIII and UNCED

This period also covered the preparatory process for both UNCTAD VIII and the Rio Conference as well as for the conferences themselves. These two conferences gave UNCTAD its specific mandate on sustainable development and environment, and laid the ground for its work programme in these areas which is described below.

UNCTAD VIII

Secretariat's Report
The report by the UNCTAD secretariat to UNCTAD VIII[15] contains special sections on issues related to sustainable development and the environment in each of its five chapters which corresponded, respectively, to the five areas of interest mentioned in the agenda of the Conference.[16] These areas were resources for development, international trade, technology, services and commodities.

In terms of the environment and sustainable development, Chapter I, 'Resources for development', focused on the need for 'adequate financial and technological assistance to increase [developing countries'] contribution to the protection of the global and domestic environment, including through the enhancement of their development efforts' (p 35). It emphasized the need for ensuring 'that new resource flows for global environmental protection are put on a more automatic and stable footing, and . . . be clearly additional to current ODA flows and development commitments' (p 35). It mentioned 'the possibilities for the imposition of taxes and user fees on environmentally damaging activities and products' (p 36). On the subject of a system of tradable permits for controlling carbon dioxide emissions, it was reported that 'some initial investigations have shown that tradable permits are among the most cost-effective means of limiting emissions of greenhouse gases that cause global warming' (p 36).

The section on sustainable development in chapter II, 'The changing international trading environment', was based on the observation that there appears to be a broad consensus that ultimately there should be no conflict between trade and sustainable development. However, there has been an increasing concern that in the short and medium run, measures adopted for environmental considerations may have adverse impacts on trade and impede economic growth, particularly in developing countries' (*Analytical Report*, p 87).

These impacts could be the result of 'environmental protection measures introduced by Governments [and] could reduce the competitiveness of a specific industry with lower environmental requirements' (pp 87, 88).

After a brief discussion from the point of view of developing countries of the GATT provisions with implications on such competitiveness, the report pointed out that 'the ability and capacity of developing countries to respond to the concerns for the environment were impeded by a number of external constraints' (p 89). It identified 'four areas in the Uruguay Round context where the outcome could have an impact on the ability of governments, particularly those of developing countries, to implement policies consistent with sustainable development' (p 90). These were anti-dumping and countervailing duties, agriculture, natural resource-based products and trade-related investment measures (TRIMs). Harmonization of standards was another area which was of particular importance to developing countries. Concerning UNCTAD's role in the area of trade and development policies and the environment, emphasis was placed upon identifying measures taken on environmental grounds that might have a bearing on international trade and on maintaining a database on such measures; undertaking research on the linkages between environmental policies and international trades, particularly through case studies, with a view to proposing policy recommendations; working towards a general consensus in this area which would be useful for governments, international organizations and the private sector in adopting a common approach to environmental problems, and making policy recommendations with a view to enabling the developing countries to improve their market access for resource-based products, to increase their export earnings, to reduce over-exploitation and the export of their natural resources and raw materials, to overcome obstacles to sustainable development, and to cope with environmental degradation' (p 91).

In Chapter III on 'Technology', the section on 'technology and sustainable development' stresses that technology is both the source of assaults on the eco-system and the potential solution to the apparent conflict between increased material prosperity of all and improvement in environmental quality (*Analytical Report*, p 156). After identifying several problems raised by the promotion of environmentally sound technologies in developing countries it concludes that 'although the main responsibility for developing and promoting environmentally sounder technologies rests with the developed countries, the increasingly global character of contemporary environmental problems means that both developed and developing country governments have an interest in ensuring the promotion of such technologies' (p 161). Among policy proposals, concessional financial support for developing countries 'not only for attacking the more universal environmental problems, but also for reducing the dependence of their economies on resource exploitation and special attention to financing schemes and incentives (tax-credits, tax-exemptions, etc) for users in developing countries adopting environmentally sound technologies' (p 161) are emphasized. To determine 'principles which would ensure that the price of environmentally sound technologies provides an incentive to producers of such technologies and is equitable to users' (p 161) is also among the recommendations.

Chapter IV on 'Services' identifies several environmental measures, such as noise regulations concerning aircraft, with potentially large effects on the service sectors of developing countries, and draws attention to the impact on the environment of expanding tourism sectors.

Chapter V on 'Commodities' points out that

> an important factor behind environmental degradation is that costs and prices of commodities often do not fully reflect their social cost (including that of environmental degradation). In certain cases, natural resources such as water and air are treated as being virtually costless. As a result, incorrect price signals are given to producers and consumers. This leads to significant cost distortions, over-exploitation and mismanagement of resources. It also recalls that such distortions and, therefore, sustainability of development is crucially affected, in all its facets, by governmental policies. Government decisions affect the rate and extent of utilization of all non-renewable and renewable resources, whether it be through the issuance of mining permits, fishing and logging concessions, or the provision of subsidies to stimulate agricultural production' (*Analytical Report*, pp 269–270).

In terms of proposals, it calls for principles and guidelines to be established by the international community to ensure that costs incurred for the protection of the environment and the management of natural resources are properly reflected in the prices of final products, whether they are natural or synthetic. It also suggests that 'in the negotiation and renegotiation of commodity agreements specific attention must be paid to the impact of the commodity in question on the environment and its contribution to sustainable development'. 'Promoting the sustainable production and usage of natural products with environmental advantages as well as the commercial exploitation and usage of waste, particularly when these are found to be environmentally advantageous' is also emphasized. In this context, international cooperation is called for to 'identify such products and their environmental advantages, and to propose policies and measures for promoting their utilization and trade' (pp 277–278).

Thus, the *Analytical Report* to the eighth Conference contains the Secretariat's views on the basic approach to work on the environment, sustainable development and related issues in UNCTAD. The main focus is on making environmental protection and development mutually supportive. The work on the environment was to be integrated into the traditional sectoral issues being followed by the Secretariat rather than creating an organizational unit working exclusively on the environment. It was a decentralized approach which called for considerable coordination and cooperation.

The Outcome of UNCTAD VIII

The 'Cartagena Commitment'[17] which is the final agreement reached by governments at UNCTAD VIII, contains explicit references to the environment and sustainable development issues in many places. In fact, it is the first internationally agreed text which affirms the principle that all countries have a common but differentiated responsibility for the main environmental problems. It further states that international cooperation is essential not only for the adoption of a concerted global strategy on the environment, but also to assist developing countries in implementing plans and policies aimed at achieving sustainable development.

The Cartagena Commitment is also an elaboration, by governments, of the conceptual framework for the UNCTAD Secretariat's work on sustainable development and environmental issues. The focus is on sustainable development which 'places environmental concerns firmly within the context of growth ... and implies changes in the economies of all countries, as well as enhanced international economic cooperation, so as to make economic growth [and] environmental protection mutually supportive' (paragraph 39). Further discussion of the issue emphasizes 'a common but differentiated responsibility for the main environmental problems', and discusses the fundamental principles of this responsibility.

Governments spelled out the general mandate of UNCTAD in the area of sustainable development in the following terms:

> The Conference reaffirms the need for UNCTAD's intergovernmental machinery and the secretariat to continue to integrate the concept of sustainable development and its environmental dimension into their respective programmes of work. The orientations ... relating to the environment and sustainable development should be guided by the following objectives, taking into account the work in other forums:
>
> - To contribute within its mandate to innovative thinking on the establishment of a framework for coexistence between environmental measures and international trade rules, and thus aiming at preventing the use of environmental measures for protectionist purposes.
> - To contribute to the exploration of all possibilities of providing developing countries with additional resources for environmental protection and development, notably through the improvement of existing financial mechanisms such as the Global Environment Fund (GEF).
> - To explore and promote policies aimed at generating, adapting and disseminating environmentally sound technologies.
> - To foster the sound management of natural resources, taking into account the special conditions and development requirements of developing countries, through enhanced international cooperation, and to complement and support their national policies and efforts, respectively. (paragraph 42)

The Conference also stated that UNCTAD should provide technical cooperation to developing countries

> for the design and implementation of national policies in the fields presented above, including the preparation of national sustainable action plans, and in their preparations for ongoing or future international environmental deliberations, including those concerning flows of finance and technology, the management of natural resources related to exports, and issues having implications for international competition and trade. For that purpose, UNCTAD should assess and monitor the impact of the results of these deliberations on the growth and development prospects of developing countries. (paragraph 43)

The Conference, having agreed that sustainable development will be one of the main orientations of the organization's activities, also adopted a message for sending to the Rio Conference.

United Nations Conference on Environment and Development

UNCTAD staff members participated in substantive preparations on several specific topics in preparation for UNCED and the drafting of Agenda 21, in particular Chapter 2 (International cooperation to accelerate sustainable development in developing countries and related domestic policies) and Chapter 11 (Combating deforestation), as well as on 'forest principles'. Regarding Chapter 2, UNCTAD's contribution was mostly based on its work on general principles for sustainable development, international trade and commodity problems. UNCTAD's experience in the negotiation and renegotiation of the International Tropical Timber Agreement made it a natural participant in discussions on issues related to deforestation and related policies.

The fact that UNCTAD VIII preceded the last stages of the preparatory process for the Rio Conference allowed another important, although indirect, contribution from UNCTAD. Being an intergovernmentally negotiated text, the language of the Cartagena Commitment was used to resolve several contentious points during the drafting of Agenda 21, particularly in Chapter 2. In several places, the exact wording of the Cartagena Commitment was used to resolve deadlocks over language.

The Rio Conference also provided an important mandate for UNCTAD's activities in the area of the environment and sustainable development. Agenda 21, Section IV, Chapter 38, on the international institutional arrangements, singles out UNCTAD, together with UNEP and UNDP, as having an important role to play in the follow-up to the Rio Conference. It states that:

> The United Nations Conference on Trade and Development should play an important role in the implementation of Agenda 21 as extended at the eighth session of the Conference, taking into account the importance of the interrelationships between development, international trade and the environment and in accordance with its mandate in the area of sustainable development (paragraph 38.26).[18]

1992–95 PERIOD

Since late 1992, UNCTAD's mandate on the environment and sustainable development stems from both the Cartagena Commitment and the results of the Rio Conference.

After the Cartagena and Rio meetings, sustainable development and environmental issues appeared explicitly and prominently both on the agendas of various intergovernmental meetings held under UNCTAD's auspices and in the work programme of the secretariat. The secretariat, which provides substantive support to the intergovernmental machinery, has organized its work on these issues by integrating analysis and (to the extent that it was feasible and as supplemented by extrabudgetary resources) technical assistance activities into the regular work programmes of the substantive divisions of the institution. No overheads or central 'core' staff are allocated to this work. Rather, the officer-in-charge of one of the substantive divisions serves also as a secretariat-wide coordinator of work on sustainable development within the substantive divisions.

Sustainable Development and the Environment in the Post-Cartagena Intergovernmental Machinery of UNCTAD

The Terms of Reference of UNCTAD's Intergovernmental Bodies

One of the decisions of the Cartagena Conference changed the intergovernmental machinery of UNCTAD which had been in operation since the early days of the Organization. The intergovernmental structure consists of the Trade and Development Board, which is the highest organ of the Conference, and the subsidiary bodies of the Board. The Cartagena Conference established 'Standing Committees' on Commodities, Economic Cooperation among Developing Countries (both of which also existed under the old structure), Poverty Alleviation, and Developing Services Sectors. Apart from these Standing Committees, upon the request of the Conference, the Trade and Development Board created five 'ad hoc working groups'.

The terms of reference of these newly created subsidiary bodies were agreed upon by the Trade and Development Board during its meeting in May–June 1992.[19] The terms of reference of all the Standing Committees included issues related to sustainable development and the environment. In this regard, the Standing Committee on Commodities would explore the links between commodity policies, sound management of natural resources and achievement of sustainable development. The Standing Committee on Poverty Alleviation would identify the linkages between the alleviation of poverty and the achievement of sustainable development. The Standing Committee on Economic Cooperation among Developing Countries was to consider studies and proposals on economic cooperation and integration, on operational activities and policies in sectors such as trade, money, finance, investment, technology, environment, transport and communication, information, education and training.

Among the *ad hoc* working groups, it was only the terms of reference of the *ad hoc* Working Group on Interrelationship between Investment and Technology Transfer that included an explicit reference to the environment.[20]

One recent development with regard to the intergovernmental machinery of UNCTAD is the establishment, in May 1994, of the *ad hoc* Working Group on Trade, Environment and Development, which will focus, in particular, on the effects of environmental policies, standards and regulations on market access and competitiveness, and emerging environmental policy instruments with a trade impact. It will also explore the market opportunities and implications for exporters which may flow from the demand for 'environmentally friendly' products and study eco-labelling and eco-certification schemes, and possibilities for international co-operation.

Intergovernmental Work Programme on the Environment and Sustainable Development in UNCTAD

In 1993, the General Assembly endorsed the Trade and Development Board's specific plans to implement Agenda 21 within its mandate[21] These plans present the work programme of UNCTAD as a whole on the issue of the environment and sustainable development, and most of it is reproduced below as an annex to this chapter.

In accordance with this mandate the Trade and Development Board as well as the Standing Committees, have regularly included topics on sustainable development.[22] Thus, for example, one specific issue taken up by the Trade and Development Board, was 'the effects of internalization of external costs on sustainable development'.[23] The Board agreed that the internalization of external environmental costs was of general importance in the follow-up to UNCED, particularly in the light of the Rio Principles, especially Principle 16, and noted that it requires a careful balancing of equity and efficiency and, within the former, of intra- and intergenerational considerations of a domestic and international nature. Indeed, internalization was agreed to be a means towards the ultimate goal of the efficient avoidance of environmental costs, not a goal in itself.

The Board considered the impact of environment-related policies on export competitiveness and market access. The analysis and debate on this issue, undertaken in UNCTAD's intergovernmental bodies, so far has shown that the complexity of the linkages between trade and environment pose significant challenges to the pursuit of sustainable development. Two categories of issues dominate the debate. The first set of issues relate to the trade and competitiveness impacts of changes in environmental regulations in a formal sense, as well as to the growing public concern for a better environment. The second set of issues has focused on the environmental impacts of the various attempts at trade liberalization. The discussions in UNCTAD have shown that environmental problems should, be resolved, as far as possible, through environmental policies rather than trade restrictions. Moreover, improved market access for developing countries' exports, in conjunction with sound macroeconomic and environmental policies, are more likely to make an important contribution to sustainable development. On issues related to market access, discussions in UNCTAD's intergovernmental bodies have shown that, with regard to product-related environmental policies and standards, measures which address consumption and disposal externalities should be regarded as any other quality standard, provided they are adopted in an open, equitable and non-discriminatory manner. With regard to process measures, UNCTAD's intergovernmental discussions have shown that more stringent requirements generally result in environmental benefits, provided that the specific environmental situation of each country is taken into account.

The Standing Committee on Commodities has discussed 'analysis of national experiences in the management of natural resources with regard to commodity production' at its second session in February 1994. It observed that, while commodity production and processing could cause local or global environmental damage in some cases, it could also provide significant environmental services when carried out sustainably. The Committee included the following topics as requiring special attention: the examination of national experiences in terms of environmental impacts of commodity production, in particular the determinants of these impacts and their relationship with economic policies and market conditions, and the facilitation of the exchange of experiences in this regard; and policies for the sustainable development of mineral-dependent economies, including policies for the sound macroeconomic management of these economies, and for the establishment in all countries concerned of an adequate legal, fiscal and regulatory framework for the management of mineral resources. In October 1994, at the third session of the

Committee, the 'identification of means by which the competitiveness of natural products with environmental advantages could be improved' was considered. It was concluded that emphasis should be placed on theoretical and practical work regarding the internalization of environmental externalities, with particular focus on the impact on the environment of the main distortions in price formation mechanisms, in particular the impact of subsidies, and on experimental studies for some specific products where internalization would appear to be most readily addressed. In this connection, it was recognized that internalization had to be universal and undertaken collectively. The UNCTAD Secretariat was also urged to undertake work to improve the applicability of life-cycle analysis to commodity issues. The Committee has included 'examination of the manner in which prices of natural commodities and their synthetic competitors could reflect environmental costs, taking into account policies relating to the use and management of natural resources and sustainable development' in the agenda of its fourth session to be held in the autumn of 1995.

The *ad hoc* working group on the Interrelationship Between Investment and Technology Transfer considered the issue of the transfer of environmentally sound technologies (ESTs) at its second session in December 1993. This discussion was based on the outcome of a workshop organized in Oslo (in October 1993) by the UNCTAD Secretariat, jointly with the government of Norway.[24] Some of the issues addressed were:

- The relative nature of 'environmental soundness' of technologies.
- The fundamental role of the private sector in the transfer of ESTs and the need to build a dialogue between host countries and transnational corporations.
- The role of governments in providing the necessary framework for creating demand for ESTs.
- The special problems and the creative potential of small and medium enterprises.
- The importance of creating domestic capacities in developing countries.
- The need for financial resources.

The group recommended that further consideration be given by UNCTAD to the examination of measures, in particular in the field of training and education, aimed at engaging more fully the creative potential of small- and medium-sized enterprises in the generation and dissemination of ESTs. In this context, a study has been undertaken on the determinants of the demand for ESTs by small- and medium-sized enterprises (SMEs) and their policy implications. The study covers factors both internal to the firm and those relating to its environment including market conditions and policy stances towards small- and medium-sized enterprises.

At its fourth session in April 1994, the ad hoc working group on Comparative Experiences with Privatization deliberated on the links between privatization and the environment. Discussions included the need to address, prior to privatization, the environmental liabilities of public enterprises selected for privatization, the reasons why privatization may be beneficial to the environment (public enterprises tend to use older and more polluting technologies and can more easily evade enforcement), as well as why it may be harmful to the environment (private enterprises tend to give higher priority to profit and growth, they may hide incriminating information from the government, they may prefer fines, particularly during high inflation, rather than redress an environmentally undesirable situation).

At its first session, in November 1994, the newly established *ad hoc* Working Group on Trade, Environment and Development considered the issue of eco-labelling. In this connection, the report of a workshop organized by UNCTAD on 'Eco-labelling and Trade', was made available to the group (TD/B/WG 6/ Misc 2). The work programme of this group includes the impact of environmental standards on trade and competitiveness, starting from the premise that the potential adverse effects of environmental product standards and regulations can be mitigated or avoided by adequate transparency and notification procedures, and that ways will be sought to ensure that the impact of environmental policies on trading partners, in particular developing country exporters and countries in transition, are considered as early as possible.

In 1993, The Commission on Transnational Corporations and The Commission on Science and Technology for Development were integrated into the intergovernmental machinery of UNCTAD. As the work of these two Commissions includes sustainable development and environmental issues, the coverage by the intergovernmental machinery of UNCTAD of these topics will expand considerably.

The terms of reference of the Commission on International Investment and Transnational Corporations (formerly the Commission on Transnational Corporations) does not include a specific reference to the environment and sustainable development. However, the Intergovernmental Working Group of Experts on International Standards of Accounting and Reporting, whose work is kept under review by this Commission, acts as a unique forum for discussions on an equal footing among experts from all continents with a view to developing tools for transparent and reliable information. This group held discussions, at its thirteenth session in March 1995, on a 'Survey of environmental performance indicators: indicators currently in use; evaluation of the usefulness of these indicators; other indicators that might be useful' and a 'Review of national environmental accounting laws and regulations'.

The reports prepared for the meeting investigate:

- The awareness of transnational corporations of the concept of sustainability, the factors behind changes in corporate behaviour, and the causes of the failure to take account of sustainability.[25]
- The integration by transnational corporations of environmental performance indicators with financial information.[26]
- National environmental accounting laws and regulations.[27]
- Transnational corporations in the food and chemical industries in India, Malaysia and the Philippines.[28]

The last report confirms that discrepancies exist between voluntary environmental accounting disclosure standards adopted by some transnational corporations in their home (developed) country and those implemented in host (developing) countries.

The Commission on Science and Technology for Development (CSTD) set up a panel to examine the science and technology aspects of integrated land management and to report its findings to both the CSD and the CSTD in 1995. The report of the panel identifies the ways that science and technology contribute to improving land management, the barriers to the effective application of integrated land management methods and useful approaches for their implementation.

The Non-sessional Research Work of the Secretariat

Many reports by the secretariat are presented to the sessions of UNCTAD's intergovernmental bodies, but research also provides the background for these reports or helps to develop new thinking. This section discusses this aspect of the secretariat's work.

Trade

Policy-oriented research covers country case studies on the interrelationship between trade and the environment and also thematic studies carried out by national experts. UNCTAD's work also aims at building an empirical base for the debate on trade, the environment and development. In-house research has concentrated on the issue of eco-labelling and trade. In this area, particular attention is paid to examining how the special conditions and development needs of the developing countries could be considered, for example, in the selection of products and in the determination of the criteria a product must meet to qualify for the label. The secretariat also undertakes capacity-building activities whose main purpose is to help increase awareness and understanding of the complex linkages between trade, the environment and development, and to contribute to building institutional capacity to deal with the interface of environmental and trade policies. Such training also helps negotiators in international deliberations on trade and environment by providing them with the necessary information on emerging issues.

Commodities

In the area of commodities and natural resources, the secretariat's work centres on three issues:

- Improved natural resources management and environmental protection in the commodities sector.
- Expanding the utilization, production and trade of environmentally friendly products.
- Internalization of environmental costs and resource values.

In the context of improved natural resources management and environmental protection in the commodities sector, the objective has been to assist in the design and implementation of national and international policies which would ensure that the development of the commodity sector and commodity trade are consistent and mutually supportive, with a better management of natural resources and protection of the environment.

Several case studies covering selected commodities in specific countries were undertaken to establish a solid factual basis aimed at assisting developing countries in designing and implementing policies which promote environmentally desirable production and processing of commodities, and increasing the awareness in developed countries of the difficulties faced by governments and producers in developing countries in terms of environmental protection in the commodities sector. Environmental legislation and practices in the mining and metals industries are also analysed with an aim to assist developing countries in institution and capacity-building activities. The secretariat's work on expanding the utilization, production and trade of environmentally friendly products aims to assist developing countries in increasing export earnings through expanding sustainable production and exports of products which are environmentally preferable from the point of view of producing and consuming countries, and benefiting from enhanced recycling programmes. One of the goals of this work is to contribute to a shift of consumption towards more sustainable patterns. Work on the internalization of environmental costs and resource values is also carried out in the context of the environment and commodities. This issue has been regarded as being of overriding importance in changing consumption, production and trade patterns. The programme activities aim at developing the conceptual, institutional and practical aspects of internalization.

UNCTAD's work on biodiversity is coordinated by the Commodities Division. The main objective is to contribute to the design and implementation of economic policies and measures, ensuring that developing countries attain economic benefits from the full use of the Convention on Biological Diversity. In this context, activities focus on:

- The use of specific economic instruments for the internalization of costs and values related to biodiversity, ie tradable development rights for conservation and sustainable use of biological diversity.
- Property rights issues and the development and transfer of technology aiming at an equitable sharing of benefits from biodiversity.
- Local control of biodiversity for the needs of local communities and indigenous people.
- The interrelationship between trade and the conservation and sustainable use of biological diversity.
- The promotion of sustainably produced products from biodiversity.

Environmental Finance
Research in this area has focused on:

- The design and implementation of a global system of tradable carbon dioxide (CO_2) emission entitlements as a cost-effective means of controlling global warming.
- A 'joint implementation' demonstration initiative as a contribution to the development of appropriate guidelines under the United Nations Framework Convention on Climate Change.
- The revenue potential, equity and efficiency implications of and administrative arrangements for an internationally agreed tax on air transport.
- The use of fiscal mechanisms for environmental protection at the national level, focusing on carbon taxes and energy subsidies, and their implications for the development of internationally agreed fiscal mechanisms for financing sustainable development.
- The use of debt for environmental swaps.

In the case of the global system of tradable permits, a number of policy concerns for developing countries as well as industrial countries have been addressed:

- The case for greater reliance on the use of market-based economic instruments in dealing with environmental problems and their financing.
- The policy conflicts between the imperative of development based on rapid industrialization (and therefore rising levels of CO_2 emissions well into the future for most developing countries) and the commitments to protect the planet's environment.
- Permits allocation, equity and resource transfers.
- Feasibility and implementation strategies.

The main recommendation to date calls for the launching of an experimental pilot scheme for trading CO_2 emission permits. Such a scheme could be established among the major emitters that have undertaken to stabilize their emissions of CO_2 at 1990 levels by the year 2000, with suitable opt-in provisions for the participation of developing countries. The main purpose of the pilot scheme would be to collect information, to carry out studies and to gain experience in this area.

Transnational Corporations

In addition to studies which are prepared for the Working Group of Experts on International Standards of Accounting and Reporting, a case study on Accounting for Sustainable Forestry Management[29] has been undertaken. It investigates a hypothetical enterprise that produces its own definition of 'sustainability' and then describes the changes in operations that would be necessary to comply with the definition. In doing so, accountancy is used to measure the monetary implications and to assist management throughout the decision-making process.

CONCLUSION

UNCTAD members have declared as their ultimate goal 'to achieve steady rates of sustained growth in all countries and accelerate the development of developing countries, so that all peoples can enjoy economic and social well-being'. In the pursuit of this goal 'the functions of UNCTAD comprise policy analysis, intergovernmental deliberation, consensus building and negotiation; monitoring, implementation and follow-up; and technical cooperation. These functions are interrelated and call for constant cross-fertilization between the relevant activities.[30]

The issues of the environment and sustainable development have been integrated into the work programmes of the intergovernmental machinery and the secretariat with an eye to fulfilling all of the functions mentioned above. Parallel to the relative emphasis currently attached to these functions in most areas of UNCTAD's mandate, however, the 'policy analysis' function appears to be at the forefront in the area of the environment and sustainable development as well. This analysis is used for 'intergovernmental deliberations' (without necessarily leading to a 'negotiation' stage). The monitoring, implementation and follow-up function is associated with the policy proposals emanating from the analysis and results of deliberations. As the organization has no power to enforce implementation, however, persuasion through sound analysis remains the only avenue for ensuring that a positive impact is generated on sustained growth by UNCTAD's work.

Technical cooperation activities in the area of the environment and sustainable development depend on the availability of extrabudgetary resources, as UNCTAD itself has no budget for this purpose. The resources generated provide a substantial contribution to the substantive work of the organization, in particular with regard to specific developing countries, and allow the results of this work to be disseminated to much wider audiences than would be possible through the meetings in Geneva.

ANNEX

The Work Programme of UNCTAD as a Whole on the Issue of the Environment and Sustainable Development

(a) *Taking into account the importance of the theme 'Trade and environment', the Board will consider a topic under this theme at the first part of each of its annual sessions; and*

(b) *It will consider another theme or themes on sustainable development at the second part of its annual sessions.*

. . .

– *The Board will have the overall responsibility of submitting to the Commission on Sustainable Development the results of its own deliberations, as well as those of its subsidiary bodies.*

. . .

– *The Trade and Development Board and its subsidiary bodies have adopted the practice of organizing input to their discussions from three actors singled out in Agenda 21 as playing an important role in the implementation of Agenda 21, namely the private, academic and NGO sectors.*

A. *Agenda 21 and trade*

– *The Board will give consideration to the following areas as elements of its substantive intergovernmental work programme on trade-related aspects of sustainable development. Paragraphs of Agenda 21 to which the work programme elements are relevant are indicated in parentheses for ease of reference.*

   – *Trends in the field of trade and environment within the framework of international cooperation; (para. 2.22 (b))*
   – *The reconciliation of environmental and trade policies, including the necessity to ensure that environmental measures do not become an instrument of protection; (paras. 2.21 and 2.22 (c,d,e,f,i))*
   – *Analysis of the impact of environment-related regulations and standards on export competitiveness, particularly of developing countries; (para. 2.22 (f, g)*
   – *Building of increased awareness and understanding of the interlinkages between trade, development and environment; (para. 2.22 (g,h,i))*
   – *Collection, analysis and dissemination of information on environmental regulations and measures which may have an impact on trade, especially that of developing countries; (paras 2.15, 2.22 (c))*

- *Comparative analysis of country experiences with ways and means of promoting trade expansion and diversification without deteriorating or depleting the natural resource base (with specific focus on export competitiveness). (paras 2.11, 2.14, 2.24, 3.5, 4.17, 4.18)*
- *In addition, the Board's Ad Hoc Working Group on Expansion of Trading Opportunities for Developing Countries has adopted a work programme which contains the element 'Environmental measures', under the terms of which the Working Group would consider the impact of environmental policies and measures on trading opportunities of developing countries with a view to making recommendations for enhancing those opportunities (paras 2.10 (a,c,d), 2.12 and 2.22 (a)).*

B.   *Agenda 21 and commodities*

- *The Board's Standing Committee on Commodities has agreed on a work programme which singled out sustainable development as one of its four priority areas. This work programme contains the following elements relevant to the implementation of Agenda 21:*

  - *Analysis of national experience in the management of natural resources with regard to commodity production; (para 3.8 (m))*
  - *Exploration of the links between commodity policies, use and management of natural resources and sustainable development; (paras 2.11, 2.13, 2.16 (a), 4.10 (b))*
  - *Identification of environmental problems that are specific to commodity production and processing and examination of ways of improving developing countries' access to international financial and technical support including environmentally sound technologies to cope with such problems; (paras 4.17(c), 4.18)*
  - *Identification of means by which the competitiveness of natural products with environmental advantages could be improved; (paras 4.19 (c), 4.20, 4.22 (a, b))*
  - *Examination of the manner in which prices of natural commodities and their synthetic competitors could reflects environmental costs. (paras 2.14 (c), 4.24, 8.31 (a, b), 8.37)*

C.   *Agenda 21 and technology*

- *The Board's Ad Hoc Working Group on the Interrelationship between Investment and Technology Transfer has agreed on a work programme composed of three priority areas, of which one is entitled 'Transfer and development of environmentally sound technologies'. This latter contains the following elements relevant to the implementation of Agenda 21:*

  - *Issues involved in the generation, transfer and diffusion of environmentally sound technologies which have an impact on competitiveness and development: (paras 34.14 (b), 34.26).*
  - *Policies and measures for the promotion, development, dissemination and financing of environmentally sound technologies, particularly in developing countries, taking into account the need to provide incentives to innovators that promote research and development of these technologies. (paras 34.11, 34.14, 34.18, 34.27, 34.28).*

D. *Agenda 21 and services*

The Board's Standing Committee on Developing Services Sectors, which deals with services in general, shipping and insurance, has adopted work programmes containing the following elements relevant to the implementation of Agenda 21:

– The role played by the services sectors in contributing to growth and sustainable development; (paras 2.16 (a), 4.18, 4.26, 8.14, 8.19, 8.33, 8 (a) and 40.22)
– Comparative analysis of the factors which can contribute to sustainable development of ports and related port services; (paras 17.6 (b,i), 17.30 (d) and 17.38 (d))
– Alternative mechanisms to meet the insurance and reinsurance needs in respect of environmental impairments. (Although insurance does not appear as such as an issue in Agenda 21, this work element is relevant to chapters 4, 14 and 17 to 22 of Agenda 21)

E. *Agenda 21 and poverty*

The Board's Standing Committee on Poverty Alleviation has agreed on a work programme of six priority areas which contains the following elements relevant to the implementation of Agenda 21:

– Analysis of the linkages between poverty and sustainable development; (para 3.10 (a))
– Examination of the implications for the poor of national and international policies relating to environment (eg applications of the polluter-pays principle; environmental standards that might adversely affect the poor). (para 3.8 (d,f,h,o))

F. *Agenda 21 and privatization*

The Board's Ad Hoc Working Group on Comparative Experiences with privatization has adopted a work programme which includes an element on environmental aspects of privatization (paras 2.13 (a), 2.31, 2.37 (c), 2.38, 30.3, 30.4, 30.19 and 30.28).

Studies and projects related to sustainable development funded by extrabudgetary resources

The UNCTAD secretariat is pursuing and completing studies, funded by extrabudgetary resources, on market-based instruments for financing environmental protection; this work is focused primarily on the costs and benefits of CO_2 abatement, including tradeable entitlements, joint implementation of commitments, and tax-based instruments. The UNCTAD secretariat has also designed studies and projects related to sustainable development funded by extrabudgetary resources, and the work carried out by the secretariat is indicated in the appendix.

<u>*Technical cooperation*</u>

> *In the field of technical cooperation, the overall objective of UNCTAD is to strengthen the capacity of the developing countries to implement Agenda 21 effectively. This is being carried out in accordance with paragraph 43 of the Cartagena Commitment and chapter 37 of Agenda 21.*

POSTSCRIPT

Since this review was written, the ninth session of the Conference on Trade and Development (UNCTAD IX) took place in Midrand, South Africa, from 27 April to 11 May 1996. The Conference took steps to provide a sharper focus to UNCTAD's work. The final document, entitled 'Midrand Declaration and a Partnership for Growth and Development' (TD/377) includes (i) an analysis of the challenges associated with the promotion of 'growth and sustainable development in a globalizing and liberalizing world economy', (ii) a series of recommendations that member states agree to apply in order to 'maximize the development impact of liberalization and globalization and minimize the risks or marginalization and instability' and (iii) the contribution expected of UNCTAD to sustainable development. Sections of the final document dealing with UNCTAD's work enumerate the areas where activities should be concentrated.

Sustainable development has been identified as a cross cutting issue in UNCTAD's work. However, references have also been made to specific areas of activity. These include 'promoting the integration of trade, environment and development and continuing UNCTAD's special role in this field, in accordance with General Assembly resolution 50/95, paragraph 27, by examining trade and environment issues, from a development perspective, in close cooperation with UNEP and WTO and as task manager for the Commission on Sustainable Development by: undertaking work that the fourth session of the Commission on Sustainable Development proposed for UNCTAD, including in the field of competitiveness, market access, ecolabelling, multilateral environmental agreements, positive measures and trade liberalization and sustainable development' (paragraph 91 (iv)). A second specific reference to the issue is work on 'promoting the sustainable management of commodity resources, in the context of sustainable development' (paragraph 91 (v)).

6 THE WORLD TRADE ORGANIZATION AND THE GENERAL AGREEMENT ON TARIFFS AND TRADE

Zen Makuch[*]

INTRODUCTION

Since its inception in 1947, the General Agreement on Tariffs and Trade (GATT), its processes and institutions have operated within a closed system. The emergence of transparent participatory models in other international institutions and processes and the further consolidation of this trend through the United Nations Conference on Environment and Development (UNCED) signals an important change in international policy-making. When coupled with the increased influence of environmental non-governmental organizations (NGOs) on domestic policy-making in the 1980s and 1990s, these developments may constitute a potent force for institutional and procedural change towards a more open and greener trading system in GATT's successor, the World Trade Organization (WTO).

Trade law experts have expressed concern that, like labour and social standards, trade-related environmental measures (TREMs)[1] are merely a new form of protectionism designed to repel foreign firms that are seeking a larger share of domestic markets, particularly for primary and manufactured goods. In the words of WTO Director-General, Renato Ruggiero, '(t)he risk now is of an insidious neo-protectionism which could try to use trade restrictions as a response to widespread concerns over labour, social or environmental standards'.[2] He is critical of efforts by Canada, the United States and Mexico to link labour and environmental standards to the North American Free Trade Agreement (see Chapter 7). In his view, environmental, social and labour

---

[*] This work is influenced by the synergy of ideas produced in association with my colleague and friend James Cameron (Director, Foundation for International Environmental Law and Development (FIELD)), since October 1993.

concerns, though legitimate, call for international cooperation not trade barriers. Indeed, coping with the direct and indirect protectionist effects of environmental measures, especially those implemented unilaterally, is the single largest challenge for the WTO Committee on Trade and Environment (CTE).

Still, environmentalists have legitimate concerns. Some oppose trade liberalization for causing unchecked growth and pollution. A recent econometric analysis of this phenomenon in the context of the North American Free Trade (NAFTA) Agreement sponsored trade liberalization proved this point.[3] Such groups opposed the Uruguay Round Agreement and trade liberalization, as a matter of principle, on environmental and social grounds. Others seek the interpretation and amendment of the Uruguay Round Multilateral Trade Agreements to make them consistent with principles of environmental protection[4] law and policy, including international, national and sub-national environmental law. Both positions reflect a concern for the effect of WTO disciplines on environmental regulation.

Although no comprehensive environmental assessment of a trade deal has yet taken place, liberalized trade has led to export-driven destruction of tropical forests for timber exports, the depletion of fish stocks and the development of energy megaprojects that have damaged the environment. Such illustrations and the widely publicized GATT Tuna/Dolphin No 1 decision[5] have generated the trade and environment debate. Consequently, groups such as the World Wide Fund for Nature (WWF), Greenpeace and Friends of the Earth have called for such measures as the internalization of environmental costs in all WTO-related activities and decisions, the inclusion of environmental factors in evaluations of process and production methods related to the trade in goods, and an environmental assessment of the Uruguay Round Multilateral Trade Agreements.[6]

In the international arena, UN agencies such as the United Nations Environment Programme (UNEP) (see Chapter 3), the Commission on Sustainable Development (CSD) (see Chapter 2) and international environmental convention secretariats are hopeful of protecting the right to employ TREMs. Pressure by states will increase for the use of TREMs to counteract low or poor environmental standards for goods production. This is why the integration of the WTO into the UN system or, at least, greater interaction among these institutions, is a necessary development. Tentative steps in this regard are already being made by some institutions. The Organization for Economic Co-operation and Development (OECD) (see Chapter 11) Trade and Environment Programme brings together its trade and environment branches to encourage OECD member states to coordinate their policy-making. The CSD, UNEP and the UN Conference on Trade and Development (UNCTAD) (see Chapter 5) have conducted similar integration ventures.[7]

The international trade community is concerned instead with the trade effects of environmental policies. Trade policy analysts are without the tools to identify empirically the protectionist effects which, they suspect, are at the heart of most TREMs. They can only point to trade distortions that are related to isolated instances like the tuna–dolphin debate or the GATT Superfund case;[8] or they argue that trade actually pays environmental dividends. As countries gain more revenues from trading activities, they are able to devote more finances to the design and enforcement of environmental measures.

In view of the above, the legal disciplines created by the Uruguay Round Agreements are in need of clarification and improvement in a manner which will permit the perpetuation and further adoption of needed national and international environmental protection and sustainable development goals. In particular, new trade rules which are codified pursuant to the Uruguay Round Agreement on Technical Barriers to Trade and the Agreement on the Application of Sanitary and Phytosanitary Measures could impede these goals. WTO members have a unique opportunity to use the CTE as a springboard for interpreting and modifying the Uruguay Round Agreements in a manner which will create greater balance between trade and environmental protection. After a brief description of the WTO's institutional structure and its stated environmentally related agenda, this chapter:

(1) Explores the GATT/WTO disciplines related to TREMs particularly in the international environmental law context.
(2) Describes the challenges associated with the integration of Multilateral Environmental Agreements (MEAs) and GATT/WTO disciplines.
(3) Suggests a series of institutional reforms that WTO Members should undertake to ensure the effective balancing of the trade and environment agendas.

THE WORLD TRADE ORGANIZATION

Structure and Goals

It is anticipated that the inauguration of the World Trade Organization and the entry into force of the Uruguay Round of Multilateral Trade Agreements signals the dawn of a larger and more effective global trading system. More than anything else, this depends on the political will of the 120 (and growing) members of the WTO. There are high expectations for the WTO and members have set themselves a very daunting task – the creation of a stronger, more comprehensive and more efficient framework for the accelerated liberalization of economies worldwide. This task features the coordination of policy responses and related trading activities in a highly integrated fashion.

Optimism should be cautious because, unlike the International Monetary Fund (IMF) and the World Bank, the WTO must rely on the force of policy rather than the influence of funds. The WTO's ability to make policy depends upon harmony among the world's trading powers. As the length of the Uruguay Round negotiation indicates, the achievement of international consensus on trade matters is a precarious exercise. This exercise will be made all the more difficult as international trade law penetrates deeper levels of national policy-making such as environmental protection, labour standards, social programmes, intellectual property systems and foreign investment. One means of traversing these potential pitfalls is through the introduction of greater openness, public participation and transparency into a system which, for the most part, has remained hermetically sealed.

The WTO faces a far more demanding workload than GATT, with more than 30 committees and councils, more than twice as many as its predecessor. Many of these bodies will be dealing with issues which are new to the GATT system. In some areas, particularly services, further negotiations will be required if goals set in the Uruguay Round Agreements are to be met. Briefly, the immediate challenges facing the new WTO are:

(1) Fostering and ensuring harmony among the world's trading powers.
(2) Overseeing the completion of the remaining negotiations concerning Uruguay Round objectives, particularly financial services.
(3) Providing that dispute settlement procedures produce predictable results, particularly as regards their enforcement.
(4) Ensuring that trading activities are consistent with or do not undermine the delivery of social goods (ie environmental protection, labour standards, public programmes).

Longer-term goals would include the following:

(1) Developing disciplines aimed at controlling the activities of transnational corporations.
(2) Creating rules concerning competition law, including mergers and acquisitions, restrictive business practices and cartels (perhaps along the lines of the European Union's community-wide competition law).

The central purpose of the WTO is to provide a 'common institutional framework' for trade relations among the members.[9] It will act as a vehicle for future multilateral trade negotiations among the Member States and will co-ordinate international policy with the World Bank and the International Monetary Fund.

The *loci* of decision-making power pursuant to the WTO Agreement consists of the Ministerial Council and the General Council. They have exclusive authority to interpret both the WTO Agreement and the Multilateral Trade Agreements.[10] The Ministerial Conference, in which all WTO members are to be present, will take place at least every two years.[11] The Ministerial Conference has powers of decision-making concerning all of the Uruguay Round Multilateral Agreements.[12] Between ministerial conferences, the General Council, composed of all WTO members, carries out the duties of the Ministerial Council.[13] Beneath these bodies are the WTO Secretariat, Councils and Committees, all of whom are answerable to the Ministerial Council and the General Council.

The WTO has a broader mandate than its GATT predecessor and, at least theoretically, possesses greater procedural powers. For instance, the WTO is to preside over the Uruguay Round Agreements, which themselves include areas heretofore untouched or only indirectly addressed by GATT 1947 (ie services, intellectual property, agriculture, government procurement and investment measures). Secondly, according to the Agreement Establishing the World Trade Organization, the WTO will be the institutional base for ensuring the conformity of Member State laws with the Uruguay Round Agreements.[14] This will take place under a new requirement in which all members must comply with each of the Multilateral Trade Agreements comprising the Uruguay Round.[15]

Dispute Settlement

The WTO's enhanced procedural powers are also illustrated in the new Dispute Settlement Understanding. Whereas previously it was not uncommon that GATT dispute settlement panel decisions were not adopted, the new 'automatic adoption' and 'unanimous consent to reject' provisions make it much more likely that dispute settlement panel decisions will be accepted and observed.

Both unappealed dispute panel and appellate body decisions are to be adopted automatically unless the Dispute Settlement Body decides by consensus not to adopt a decision.[16] This approach should provide a dose of badly needed legitimacy to a system in which parties have regularly disregarded or prevented the adoption of dispute settlement panel rulings that were adverse to national interests.

The WTO Committee on Trade and Environment[17]

The April GATT ministerial meeting in Marrakesh marked the beginning of serious, transparent discussions concerning environmental reform of GATT. As the Uruguay Round talks neared completion in December 1994, the GATT Trade Negotiations Committee issued a decision on Trade and Environment (Trade and Environment Decision). The Decision requires that GATT Contracting Parties (now WTO Members) draw up a programme of work 'to identify the relationship between trade measures and environmental measures, in order to promote sustainable development . . . [and] to make appropriate recommendations' on changes to the world trading system. The decision was approved at the April ministerial meeting. The Trade and Environment Decision accepts the following premises:

(1) The continued liberalization of international trade.
(2) The objective of sustainable development, consistent with the commitments made by the international community at UNCED in Rio.
(3) The need for special consideration of the requirements of developing countries.
(4) The need for transparency.

From this starting point the Committee initially is discussing a number of issues, some of which are also being addressed in various other international institutions. The issues include the relationship between the GATT multilateral trading system and the following:

- Trade measures taken for environmental purposes, including those taken pursuant to multilateral environmental agreements.
- Environmental policies relevant to trade and environmental measures with significant trade effects.
- Transparency of trade measures used for environmental purposes and environmental measures which have significant trade effects.
- Requirements for environmental purposes relating to products, including charges and taxes, standards and technical regulations, packaging, labelling and recycling.
- The relationship between the dispute settlement mechanisms in the multilateral trading system and those in multilateral environment agreements.
- The effect of environmental measures on market access, especially in relation to developing and least developed countries, and the environmental benefits of removing trade restrictions and distortions.
- The export of domestically prohibited goods.

Prior to the entry into force of the Uruguay Round Agreements on 1 January 1995, the GATT Sub-Committee on Trade and Environment held meetings that were designed to establish an agenda for the immediate work of the new WTO/

CTE. It was decided that at the first meeting of the Committee on Trade and Environment (CTE), the Committee would consider exports of domestically prohibited goods. Prior to the completion of the Uruguay Round Agreements, GATT Contracting Parties came close to finalizing a draft decision on domestically prohibited goods (1991), but the urgency of the Uruguay Round took their attention away from this matter.

On 26–27 October 1994, members began preliminary deliberations over the issue of TREMs that had been taken pursuant to MEAs. Several countries made statements against the use of unilateral measures, but there appeared to be general support for the use of TREMs as a last resort in multilateral environmental agreements. Consistent with suggestions made later in this paper, the parties turned their attention to a definition for a 'legitimate' MEA. Then, various states made submissions concerning the best means of making TREMs and WTO disciplines compatible. Central to this discussion was the notion of an agreed interpretation of Article XX. Two other important issues that were raised included the treatment of non-parties to MEAs and the problems of the participation of developing countries in MEAs. The discussion was very preliminary in that members are only just now beginning to assemble positions on these issues.

Meetings of the Committee on 23–24 November 1994 examined the effects of environmental measures on market access for developing countries. A key issue concerned the need to eliminate trade-distorting subsidies that pay for unsustainable, environmentally damaging agricultural practices. Concerns were expressed about the potentially protectionist effects of environmental measures.

The Committee has also served as a forum for the discussion of environmental taxes and charges. Central matters that have been addressed include voluntary standards, production and process methods, life-cycle analyses and the compatibility of eco-labelling schemes with the TBT Agreement.

Ten intergovernmental bodies (the UN CSD, EFTA, FAO, IMF, OECD, UN, UNCTAD, UNEP, UNDP and the World Bank) were invited as observers to the first meeting of the WTO/CTE. There was general agreement that the 1991 draft decision on domestically prohibited goods would serve as the basis for further work in this area. Members were in general agreement about the need to ensure full transparency with respect to domestically prohibited goods regimes. The United States and the European Commission took the view that the WTO should leave it to other fora, such as those under MEAs, to handle the regulation of domestically prohibited goods. The WTO would act merely to reinforce these regimes by adopting an approach that was consistent with MEA provisions on products regulated under multilateral domestically prohibited goods regimes.

In April 1995, the CTE commenced discussions concerning: TREM transparency requirements under the WTO, TREMs and the dispute settlement system, and the role of NGOs in the CTE. It was generally felt that WTO transparency disciplines were comprehensive in scope, although there were still potential gaps from WTO notification, such as with labelling, packaging and waste-handling requirements. On dispute settlement issues, there was a central concern that the CTE should address potential conflicts between WTO dispute settlement processes and MEAs. The general preference was for using MEA dispute settlement processes first, leaving recourse to WTO dispute settlement on environmental matters as a last resort.

In June 1995, members met to discuss the effect of the WTO Agreement on Trade-related Aspects of Intellectual Property Rights, including Trade in Counterfeit Goods (TRIPs or TRIPs Agreement), on environmental protection and sustainable development. At the time of publication of this book, a report has not yet been released on the results of this meeting. Thereafter, the CTE will issue a report covering TREMs and market access for developing countries, MEAs, economic instruments and eco-labelling and packaging requirements to the first WTO Ministerial Conference in Singapore (December 1996), when its work and terms of reference will be reviewed.

GATT/WTO TRADE AND ENVIRONMENT DISCIPLINES

Introduction

It is well established that the market economics upon which WTO disciplines are based can lead to failures in the delivery of social goods. In this regard, environmental protection is no exception.[18] The regulation of trade, however, can be used to achieve specific environmental objectives. Trade measures featured in some of the Multilateral Environmental Agreements that have come into force in the past 15 years discourage free riders (eg the 1987 Montreal Protocol on Substances that Deplete the Ozone Layer penalizes non-parties by placing restrictions on their access to foreign markets) and act as enforcement mechanisms (eg under the 1989 Basel Convention on the Transboundary Movement of Hazardous Wastes, non-compliance with prior informed consent requirements can result in bans on the importation of hazardous wastes). These trade-related environmental measures are known in GATT parlance as 'TREMs'.

While some have suggested that GATT rules operate in an environmental vacuum, this is false. Even prior to the Uruguay Round, the GATT Article XX(b) and (g) exceptions concerning, respectively, the 'protect[ion] of human, animal or plant life or health' and the 'conservation of exhaustible natural resources' would have permitted some unilateral and multilateral environmental protection regulations.

Article XX provides exceptions from the application of GATT provisions for acts designed to protect human, animal or plant life or health (Article XX(b)), as well as for acts relating to the conservation of exhaustible natural resources (Article XX(g)). Exemption for TREMs under Article XX is possible in some cases, but several obstacles may arise. First, there may be difficulty in showing that discrimination against non-signatories is neither arbitrary nor unjustifiable. Secondly, the exemption may fail if a regulation applies extraterritorially. Finally, it may be difficult to show that a measure was 'necessary' to protect life or health under Article XX(b) or 'relating to' the conservation of exhaustible natural resources under Article XX(g) and that no less trade restrictive alternative was available.

The Uruguay Round has taken further tentative steps towards the inclusion of environmental protection and sustainable development considerations within the WTO context. The Preamble to the Agreement Establishing the World Trade Organization (WTO Agreement) has introduced language showing both a commitment to environmental protection and sustainable development and recognition that economic and trade relations must allow for the optimal use of the world's resources. The Dispute Settlement Understanding (DSU) also calls for the interpretation of WTO annexed agreements 'in accordance with customary rules of interpretation of public international law' including international environmental law.

TBT and SPS Agreements[19]

The GATT has never ruled that a TREM contained in an international environmental agreement is prima facie GATT-inconsistent. In part, this is because such a decision, if taken amid the present conflict-oriented trade and environment climate, might cause a political backlash far outstripping any trade benefits accruing to a victorious complaining party. Some of the key environmental treaties that contain or could promote TREMs are the Montreal Protocol, the Basel Convention, the 1973 Convention on the International Trade in Endangered Species (CITES), the 1992 Convention on Biological Diversity, and the Framework Convention on Climate Change. A large majority of WTO members are Parties to these environmental conventions. Therefore, a dispute challenging the GATT consistency of an international environmental treaty would place many WTO members in the uncomfortable position of either ignoring their WTO obligations or reversing an international environmental treaty commitment with the accompanying losses of political capital in their national jurisdictions. Hence, parties to both trade and environment regimes have a vested interest in integration rather than conflict.

To date, however, neither GATT nor WTO authorities have been able to convince citizens or environmental policy-makers that such a clash will not occur. This has arguably had a 'chilling effect' on environmental law-making nationally and internationally,[20] discouraging environmental law-makers from using command and control models and economic instruments which may have a WTO dimension. The absence of clear authoritative WTO disciplines for TREMs constrains lawmakers' ability to develop the best possible environmental protection regimes. For these reasons, the CTE has identified international environmental agreements as a top priority for its deliberations.[21]

To encourage progress in this area, it is useful to note that the Charter of the International Trade Organization (ITO), which was to provide the institutional home for the GATT but never entered into force, specifically allowed countries to take measures pursuant to any intergovernmental agreement relating to the conservation of fisheries resources, migratory birds or wild animals.[22] The ITO approach, not yet followed by the WTO, could have enabled a harmonization of trade rules with MEAs in a manner far less threatening to trade interests. TREMs authorized multilaterally through MEAs (as opposed to those taken unilaterally) are more likely to be specific in scope, and have limited trade-distorting effects. In contrast, unilateral trade measures often seek to impose trade-distorting charges to counteract environmentally harmful (foreign) production and process methods.

The Role of TREMs in MEAs

Many commentators regret the absence of strong enforcement provisions in MEAs.[23] In this regard, trade remedies such as sanctions are a welcome addition to MEA enforcement paradigms. The threat of trade measures carries positive compliance effects. In addition, the adverse publicity that often accompanies the threat of trade actions can impose strong political and even economic pressure upon MEA transgressors. Equally, TREMs utilizing economic instruments (ie Climate Change Convention-based energy taxes), although potentially WTO violative, can serve as effective tools in the form of graduated penalties that are designed to deter production of a given greenhouse gas by increasing the costs of producing emissions. As further evidence supporting the international effectiveness of TREMs, there are at least 19 treaties which authorize some form of trade measure in pursuance of their objectives.[24]

Without the threatened use of trade sanctions by the United States to enforce compliance with the United Nations resolutions on high-seas driftnet fishing, it is doubtful whether Japan, South Korea or Taiwan would have ceased these destructive activities. This circumstance highlights both the effectiveness and the necessity of utilizing trade measures to ensure compliance with an international environmental objective. The CITES and Montreal Protocol regimes stand as leading examples of effective MEA compliance and enforcement through the threat or use of trade sanctions. For example, the Montreal Protocol now has over 136 parties representing 99 per cent of the world's population. All major producers of ozone-depleting substances are parties to the treaty, and it is the view of the Ozone Secretariat that the Protocol's trade measures have played a significant part in encouraging such wide participation.

The most effective TREMs are those which directly affect violating companies. Trade bans represent a prime example since they seriously compromise the ability of a company to carry on business in foreign markets. Limitation of access to major markets poses a severe operational threat for firms which are bound to communicate their consternation to their national governmental representatives. Such was the case for oil tanker owners facing detention in ports in order to satisfy segregated ballast tank and other equipment requirements.[25] Some countries have shown a strong willingness to use sanctions against nations that threaten the effectiveness of an MEA. The United States' threatened sanctions against non-member whaling states and states impeding progress through CITES provide examples of compliance successes.[26] A recent ban by many states of wildlife purchases from Thailand because of its violations of the CITES Treaty provides another example.[27]

Furthermore, there is already a precedent for a trade regime that permits the use of trade sanctions as remedies for the non-enforcement of environmental laws – the NAFTA Environmental Side Agreement, also known as the North American Agreement on Environmental Cooperation.[28] In the absence of a multilateral enforcement body, trade sanctions were viewed as an effective remedy for coping with domestic regulatory intransigence. In view of these findings, the use of TREMs in MEAs will continue to be seen by states as effective implementation, compliance and enforcement mechanisms.

Potential Inconsistencies Between GATT/WTO Disciplines and MEAs

The following examples serve as indicators of the types of conflicts which may arise between GATT/WTO disciplines and TREMs contained in international environmental agreements. While MEAs tend to enjoy a large membership of parties, TREMs adopted under these treaties can effect trade impacts not only between fellow parties, but between parties and WTO members that have not joined the environmental agreements. Both CITES and the Basel Convention feature import restrictions which may constitute violations of GATT Article XI, which prohibits the use of quantitative restrictions. CITES bans would probably not be exempted under Article XX(b) or (g) because their purpose is to conserve endangered species (extraterritorially) in exporting states. Recent bans imposed on the shipment of hazardous wastes, including wastes with recyclable value, from certain industrialized to developing countries under the Basel Convention, may also fall foul of Article XI.[29]

The disciplines of the Basel Convention can, furthermore, be used to justify discrimination, in potential violation of the GATT's most favoured nation provisions, between exporters and importers of wastes on the basis of the technical capacity of exporters to dispose of such wastes themselves, or on the basis of the requirements of the importers for raw material contained in the wastes.[30] Furthermore, the Basel Convention may violate the GATT by prohibiting the export or import of wastes to or from non-parties to the Convention.[31] Such bans on trade run counter to GATT disciplines as they make distinctions based on the characteristics of the countries involved in the trade, rather than on the character of the product being traded.

The Montreal Protocol phases out controlled-substance trade between parties at the same time as it bans the import of like products from non-parties. As a result, non-parties will be prohibited from exporting controlled products to parties that continue to have the capacity to trade in these products. WTO members that impose these import restrictions may violate GATT's non-discrimination principles.

In addition, restrictions applying to products manufactured with (rather than containing) controlled substances would be characterized as restrictions on production and process methods. This could result in violations of Article III, concerning national treatment, and Article XI, which prohibits quantitative restrictions on trade.

Fiscal measures passed to meet Climate Change Convention targets for reductions of dangerous anthropogenic emissions may also be interpreted as running foul of GATT disciplines. A prime example has been the European Community's proposed tax on both carbon dioxide emissions and non-carbon dioxide emitting sources of energy.[32] For example, if an EC state imposed the tax on imports from a state which already taxed energy production in a manner similar to that of the EC state, a clear case for discrimination under Article III(1) could be made on the basis that the imported product is being taxed twice while the domestic product is being taxed only once.

Such proposals often involve the granting of exemptions from payment of the CO_2/energy tax to domestic industries which may be viewed as a subsidy, especially when the exemption only operates on export. This is likely to make the price of the product more expensive in the domestic market than it is on export, action expressly prohibited under GATT Article XVI(4). Such subsidies may be the subject of countervailing duties according to GATT Article VI(2).[33]

The WTO Agreement on Trade-Related Aspects of Intellectual Property Rights (TRIPs Agreement) may also present obstacles to environmental protection and sustainable development. It could permit the further implementation and enforcement of intellectual property protection regimes in a manner which is inconsistent with the objectives of the Biodiversity Convention. Southern governments, non-government organizations, farmers and other private individuals have reason to believe that the enhanced intellectual property rights protection which is related to goods and processes approved under TRIPs could remove some of the advantages to be gained by the South from their ownership and conservation efforts regarding the major proportion of the world's biodiversity resources resting within their borders. As well, TRIPs-endorsed patenting of genetic materials could turn more and more life forms into patentable commodities, thus imposing long-term environmental, economic, cultural and ethical impacts. In the absence of concerted efforts by Biodiversity Convention Parties to interpret authoritatively and implement equitable benefit-sharing arrangements concerning access to genetic resources and appropriate technologies, biodiversity prospecting and product development may take place under contractual arrangements and intellectual property rights protection devices that are not consistent with the objectives of the Biodiversity Convention.

Finally, it is anticipated that TRIPs Article 27 exceptions related to the patenting of plant and animal life and the protection of public order and morality will be narrowly construed. This will place an onerous burden upon members to demonstrate unequivocally the link between patent protection and its detriment to human, animal or plant life, its detriment to health protection or its prejudice to the environment.

What Constitutes an MEA?

If WTO members are to move forward in the debate and provide a form of exceptions for MEAs, there must be an agreed upon definition within the WTO context of what constitutes an MEA. To constitute a genuine multilateral agreement, an MEA should:

(1) Be open to all relevant least-developed, developing and developed countries on equitable terms.
(2) Include nations involved in production or consumption activities related to the MEA.
(3) Be negotiated under the aegis of the United Nations or a duly authorized body with an explicit environmental goal.
(4) Contain clear and enforceable obligations.
(5) Feature an environmental problem that has transboundary trade-related environmental, conservational or human health impacts.
(6) Be international or regional in scope.

WTO Corrective Measures Concerning MEAs

What follows in this section is a range of options for the integration of international environmental law and WTO disciplines.

Article XX(k)
Potential conflicts between the WTO and MEAs could be avoided by clarifying that TREMs undertaken pursuant to an MEA qualify for a general exception under GATT Article XX. The chapeau paragraph could be amended, and an

additional paragraph XX(k), based on existing paragraph XX(h) could be included as follows (new text is marked in brackets).

A WTO MEAs exception clause could simply replicate the language of Article XX(h) within a new Article XX(k) with the following revision (see parentheses):

> Subject to the requirement that such measures are not applied in a manner which would constitute either a means of arbitrary or unjustifiable discrimination between countries where the same conditions prevail or a disguised restriction on international trade, nothing in this Agreement shall be construed to prevent the adoption or enforcement by any [Member] of measures:

> (k)   undertaken in pursuance of obligations under any [multilateral environmental agreement] which conforms to criteria submitted to the Members and not disapproved by them or which is itself so submitted and not so disapproved:

This proposal mirrors the provisions of the founding charter of the International Trade Organization (mentioned previously) which would have exempted measures 'taken in pursuance of an intergovernmental agreement which relates solely to the conservation of fisheries resources, migratory birds or wild animals'.

An annex on the definition and scope of MEAs together with a proposed test for evaluating the WTO compatibility of TREMs contained in MEAs would be included as part of this option.[34]

Perhaps discrimination against imported products should be 'justified' if they are being exported in violation of a legitimate MEA. In effect, this approach suggests that where Article XX(k) listed MEAs that conflict with the Uruguay Round agreements, the MEA provisions will prevail. This clear, unambiguous position is preferred and should be endorsed by the General Council of the WTO. It will ensure that Article XX(k) listed MEAs will not be subject to WTO challenges.

Stand-Alone Environmental Protection Provisions

A more ambitious alternative would be to introduce new stand-alone environmental protection provisions or environmental override sections in the WTO. The Maastricht Treaty on European Union provides the best precedent in this regard. For instance, Article 130(r)(2) requires that 'environmental protection requirements . . .be integrated into the definition and implementation of other Community policies'. This approach recognizes that from time to time environmental protection and free trade policy goals may conflict, and that environmental protection and conservation goals must not be undermined.

Article 130(r)(2) further provides that, 'in this context, harmonisation measures ensuring these requirements shall include, where appropriate, a safeguard clause allowing Member States to take provisional measures for non-economic environmental reasons, subject to a Community inspection procedure'. A new provision of the WTO Agreement, based on Article 130r(2), would state that, 'Members shall not undermine international environmental protection, natural resource conservation and sustainable development policies in applying the provisions of GATT 1994 and the WTO Agreements'.

Following the EC example, the WTO/CTE should also consider how to incorporate the widely held 'polluter pays', 'user pays', 'subsidiarity' and 'precautionary' principles into the GATT/WTO Agreements. These principles would include a commitment to protecting the 'common heritage of mankind' (eg the global commons, including shared environmental resources). Trade restrictions aiming to protect such resources would then be judged as within the jurisdiction or control of a member. The codification of these principles in Article 3.2 of the Understanding will require that they be considered in any dispute settlement process that contains an aspect of environmental protection or sustainable development.

Article XXV: Waiver

Article XXV(5) permits the use of a waiver in exceptional circumstances, not provided for elsewhere in the GATT/WTO Agreements. The waiver would be applied in circumstances where international agreement exists among signatories on the need to use TREMs in an existing or future MEA. Of course, the waiver technique is rarely used for this purpose and offers a somewhat temporary solution. Its main limitation is that it considers environmental protection measures as something to be used only in 'exceptional circumstances'. In these respects it is less favourable than the more permanent amendment strategy. Nevertheless, it may provide a useful transition mechanism pending the negotiation of GATT/WTO amendments or a new multilateral agreement on TREMS.

NAFTA Type List

NAFTA Article 104 allows for the creation of a list of environmental protection or conservation treaties which would be immune from NAFTA challenges. It states that: 'In the event of any inconsistency between this Agreement and the specific trade obligations set out in ... [CITES, The Montreal Protocol on Substances that Deplete the Ozone Layer, the Basel Convention and other agreements set out in an Annex, which may be expanded], such obligations prevail to the extent of the inconsistency,' provided that 'the party chooses the alternative that is the least inconsistent with the other provisions of this Agreement'. This hierarchical approach is promising, but it suffers from the limitations of the ambiguous 'least inconsistent' test introduced in 1989 by the GATT Salmon and Herring panel. This test, which has been used to strike down environmental and health measures, is too broad and unwieldy to be of assistance to regulators. Therefore, it should be removed from any similarly worded GATT/WTO clause.

A GATT waiver or amendment would identify the list as being within the GATT exceptions. Consistent with the NAFTA approach, a procedure for adding conventions to the list should also be adopted. At present, the most obvious candidates for the list are the Montreal Protocol, CITES and the Basel Convention. However, there are as many as 19 other MEAs which contain TREMS that will also have to be considered in any discussion of a list of existing treaties.

The EC Proposal

Another option would include the preparation and endorsement of an 'agreed interpretation' of Article XX(b) or (g) as it applies to environmental protection exceptions from GATT/WTO disciplines. The purpose of such an agreed-upon interpretation would be to clarify and broaden the 'environmental circumstances' for the application of these provisions.

In GATT Doc TRE/W/5, the European Community supports the idea of a collective interpretation of Article XX by WTO members. On the one hand, it suggests certain substantive criteria to ensure that such trade measures:

(1) Are not discriminatory merely because a country is not a party to an MEA, but instead only reflect actual differences between the environmental protection commitments applied by parties and non-parties.

(2) Are not a disguised restriction to international trade (ie are not taken, in fact, for protectionist purposes.

(3) Are necessary to achieve the environmental goal set by the MEA (ie they represent the least trade-restrictive option and apply to products which are themselves environmentally damaging or which, on the basis of their production, are directly and specifically linked to the environmental damage).

On the other hand, the Community proposes certain formal criteria to ensure that exemptions from GATT obligations are limited to cases in which environmental protection commitments have been established through a genuine multilateral process (ie one that is open to all WTO members or, in cases of regional agreements, to all countries within the region in which the trade measures may apply).

While this position improves upon existing GATT/WTO disciplines as they apply to TREMs, the third part of the proposal is unacceptable. This is because the 'necessity' test contained therein (as presently defined by GATT panel decisions) greatly restricts the use of the Article XX exception to protect TREMS.

Supersession[35]

The relationship between international environmental agreements and the GATT/WTO agreements may be characterized as one of 'peaceful co-existence'. GATT/WTO dispute settlement processes have never been invoked to challenge the GATT/WTO compatibility of an international environmental agreement. However, for the reasons stated above, a conflict is possible. The general rules of international law which would apply in the event of a conflict between the provisions of an MEA and GATT/WTO provisions are as follows:[36]

- Later treaties take priority over earlier ones.
- More specific treaties take priority over the general.
- Where a treaty says that it is subject to or incompatible with another treaty, that other treaty will prevail.
- As between parties to a treaty who become parties to a later inconsistent treaty, the earlier will apply where provisions are not incompatible with the later.
- As between a party to both treaties and a party to only one of them, the treaty to which both are parties will govern the mutual rights and obligations of the states concerned.
- In determining which treaty is the earlier and which the later, the relevant date is the date of adoption, not the date of entry into force.

The most relevant dates for determining which treaty is later in time, and therefore supersedes the other, are the dates on which negotiators agreed to a final text of each treaty, assuming that both treaties have entered into force for both parties. It is important to note that the Uruguay Round Agreements are more recent than virtually all MEAs, giving them precedence, all other matters being equal.

There is also the central concern that if a dispute were heard pursuant to WTO dispute settlement procedures, there might be little sympathy for policy goals other than free trade, leaving the decision-maker with a ruling that insufficiently considers an MEA and all of its important nuances. There are at least two policy reasons why WTO dispute settlement should not be the appropriate process for interpreting the relationship between an MEA and the GATT/WTO Agreements. First, it has been widely stated by WTO members and the WTO Secretariat that the WTO has no role in environmental standard setting. Yet the WTO Council or dispute settlement-based interpretation of the Convention is a form of *de facto* environmental standard setting and, thus, should not be countenanced by WTO members or the MEA parties. Secondly, the WTO is neither well equipped with experts on environmental law or policy, nor is its mandate concerned with general applications of international law or the resolution of conflicts of international law. Hence, the interpretation of the relevant MEA should be left to its Conference of the Parties on the basis of cooperation.

As Sands has observed, there is a crucial provision of the Vienna Convention on the Law of Treaties under Article 31(3)(c) which directs the adjudication to take into account, 'any relevant rules of international law applicable in the relations between the parties'. Even within the limited jurisdictional confines of WTO dispute settlement, it is totally appropriate for a panel to look outside the GATT/WTO system to other rules. The provision does not limit those rules to treaty provisions. Therefore, one could go beyond GATT/WTO disciplines to consider rules of customary law and international treaty law relating to environmental protection and conservation regulations.[37] But should these sorts of evaluations be left to a dispute settlement process where the sole emphasis and expertise is traditionally placed upon the interpretation of trade law disciplines to the virtual exclusion of international law in general?[38]

It has been suggested consistently by GATT decision-makers that GATT is ill-equipped to consider environmental policy matters.[39] This prompts the suggestion that, where there are conflicts in international law between WTO and MEA regimes, there should at least be a right of appeal against a dispute resolution panel decision to the International Court of Justice (ICJ). Perhaps these conflicts should be decided in their entirety by the ICJ which has now established a chamber on environmental matters. In addition, the WTO Dispute Settlement Body should have the power to seek advisory opinions from the ICJ on these conflicts and other matters of international law as was envisioned in the original Charter of the International Trade Organization. In this regard, WTO members should be encouraged to endorse the appropriate jurisdiction clauses.

RECOMMENDATIONS FOR WTO INSTITUTIONAL REFORM[40]

Institutional Mechanisms – Introduction

The creation of an environmental protection and sustainable development programme for the GATT system is overdue. WTO members should undertake a concerted effort to adapt the rules and institutions that govern international trade to contemporary understanding of the threats to natural resources, environmental quality, human health and sustainable development. More environmental safeguards are needed in Uruguay Round trade disciplines. It is important that the WTO/CTE (Committee on Trade and the Environment) promote comprehensive reforms on environmental issues. However, it would repeat past GATT mistakes to emphasize the trade impacts of environmental measures rather than giving equal consideration to the environmental effects of international trade. The following discussion is designed to assist decision-makers in the development and implementation of WTO institutional reforms as part of the effort to integrate international trade, environmental protection and sustainable development goals.

Successful environmental reform of the WTO will not be achieved without new institutional mechanisms. It is a welcome development that the Trade and Environment Work Programme has been conducted by an interim Preparatory Committee and succeeded by a permanent CTE.

As soon as possible, WTO members should be asked to endorse the creation of an advisory panel or process for the Trade and Environment Committee. This panel should be designed to inform and assist, but function independently of, the WTO Trade and Environment Committee. The panel should have a broad mandate to conduct research and develop policy options on trade and environmental issues that involve the complex issues of science, economics, institution-building and development.

WTO Committee on Trade and Environment

It is critical that the WTO/CTE feature expertise in environmental law and policy, ample opportunities for public participation and transparent procedures. The work of the Committee should be coordinated with other relevant bodies such as the OECD Joint Session of Trade and Environment Experts, UNEP, UNDP, UNCTAD, MEA Secretariats and the UN Commission on Sustainable Development. Each of these bodies should be granted *ex officio* participant status at WTO Committee meetings, not just the muted observer status which they now possess. In addition, the CTE should coordinate its activities with other relevant WTO committees and working groups such as the Committee on Trade and Development and the Council for Trade in Services, which are authorized by the Uruguay Round Agreement.

The CTE should continue to meet on a regular basis, with short time-lines for the completion of recommendations in preparation for the next ministerial meeting. This is necessary to assure prompt multilateral attention to reform measures on issues where a high level of international consensus already exists and to enable individual countries to integrate environmental concerns fully into their implementing legislation. Quick time-lines are also important to ensure that implementation of WTO provisions governing technical standards, sanitary and phytosanitary standards, dispute settlements, subsidies, agriculture, services, intellectual property and investment do not proceed with insufficient environmental safeguards or accompanying negative environmental impacts in either developing or developed countries.

Thus far, the meetings have produced some well-informed comments about the trade and environment interface. However, they have been rather unfocused. In this regard, it is hoped that this necessary discursive step is a prelude to the future identification of a hierarchy of issues which will be tackled quickly and efficiently. For strategic reasons it is submitted that the CTE should take on the least contentious issues first, those concerning the work on domestically prohibited goods and the integration of MEAs into the WTO system. Draft decisions on these topics should be completed by a small representative drafting group for consideration by the wider membership of the CTE. Thereafter, a one year time-line should be imposed for the finalization of these decisions. The completion of these tasks should give the CTE the necessary momentum and credibility to attack some of the more intractable issues with which it is faced, such as the regulation of process and production methods and the grant of concessions to developing countries seeking to improve both their environmental protection/sustainable development programmes and their trade balances.

Intergovernmental Panel on Trade and Environment

Outside the WTO, a new Intergovernmental Panel on Trade and Environment (IPTE) should be established to provide the CTE and other institutions with the background information and analysis which is needed to formulate effective trade, environmental protection and sustainable development linkages. While many issues remain to be discussed, not the least of which are those affecting developing countries, the IPTE should be comprised of: representatives of national governments (including external affairs departments and the departments with responsibility for environmental protection and sustainable development), with special emphasis on Southern country participation (not less than 50 per cent); the relevant international organizations mentioned above; and internationally recognized experts from a wide range of disciplines – eg international law and policy, environmental law and policy, sustainable development policy, economics and natural sciences – which are related to trade and the environment. The IPTE should exist for as long as the CTE exists.

The IPTE's agenda should be open enough in the future to address, but not be limited to, issues surrounding:

- Environmental cost internalization.
- Eco-labelling (geographic: 'tropical' timber; process: 'hormone-treated' agricultural products).
- Eco-dumping and competitiveness.
- Production and process methods.
- Upgrading of environmental standards.
- Economic instruments.
- Environmental subsidies.
- Recycling content laws.

- PPMs.
- 'Like' products.
- Waste trade.
- Elimination of environmentally damaging subsidies.
- Domestically prohibited goods.
- Greening the WTO Trade Policy Review Mechanism.

Consideration should also be given to working with the Committee on Trade and Development so that the environmental protection and sustainable development implications of structural adjustment, foreign debt, commodity and transnational corporation regulation policies may be reviewed.

Of significance to the trade and environment context, a multidisciplinary approach was applied successfully by the Intergovernmental Panel on Climate Change (IPCC), which provided the essential scientific data, policy options and international consensus behind the 1992 Climate Change Convention. The IPTE's work should build upon other relevant efforts, in particular the trade and environment analyses prepared under the auspices of the OECD, UNEP and UNCTAD. Both the IPTE and the CTE should make an annual report publicly available on their preliminary work and findings, beginning in 1995 and annually thereafter.

CSD Committee on Trade and Sustainable Development

If the United Nations Commission on Sustainable Development (CSD) were to convene a CSD Committee on Trade and Sustainable Development, as was proposed at its meeting on 27 May 1994 in New York, and it were along the lines proposed above, this would also provide a comparable institutional solution for addressing trade, environment and sustainable development linkages outside the WTO in support of the CTE.

In addition to having the mandate and organizational structure of the IPTE, the CSD Committee, if backed by genuine political will, should have the task of coordinating UN agency trade, environment and sustainable development activities for reasons of efficiency and for ensuring the cross-fertilization of ideas among the various agencies. The Uruguay Round Trade and Environment Decision requires the work of the CTE to be consistent with the Rio Declaration on Environment and Development and Agenda 21. The integration of environment and development objectives served as the *raison d'être* for UNCED and is a central theme of its related documents and conventions. In particular, Agenda 21 (Chapter 2, paragraph 2.3) recognizes the following as objectives of the international community:

(1) Making trade and environment mutually supportive.
(2) Encouraging macroeconomic policies conducive to the environment and development.
(3) Providing adequate financial resources to developing countries dealing with international debt.

Furthermore, Agenda 21 calls upon the international community (including NGOs) to engage in a dialogue on trade, the environment and development policy-making, with specific reference to such issues as the promotion of environmentally sound investment measures, the elimination of tariff escalation policies, the role of TREMs, the elimination of tariff escalation practices and the implementation of environmental and social cost accounting.

Trade, environmental and developmental issues were formally addressed in the First Session of the Commission on Sustainable Development in June 1993 and were addressed again in the Report of the Secretary-General in the Second Session (E/CN 17/1994/2). To date, GATT has been consistent in its position that it is not an environmental policy-maker and that it is exclusively concerned with trade measures. However, the very existence of the WTO Trade and Environment Committee suggests that WTO multilateral trade agreements and decisions do have effects on the environment, sustainable development and related policy-making in national and international jurisdictions.

Given the CSD's institutional mandate of advancing the Rio Declaration, Agenda 21, and related environmental conventions, several of which contain or permit TREMs (ie Biodiversity Convention, Climate Change Convention, Basel Convention, Montreal Protocol, CITES), juxtaposed with its environmental expertise, it is recommended that the CSD should act as the main agency for the coordination and streamlining of trade, environment and sustainable development efforts that are presently being undertaken by UNDP, UNEP, UNCTAD, OECD and the WTO, noting their relevant contributions to date. The CSD should also seek the establishment of the CSD Committee as an advisory body to the WTO Committee on Trade and Environment. The CTE Work Programme should seek, without delay, to build international consensus, consistent with the activities of the CSD Committee or the IPTE, on the adoption and implementation of environmental reforms of the Uruguay Round Agreements.

Sustainable Development and Developing Countries

No WTO environmental reform initiative will be successful in the absence of a broad international consensus that reflects the concerns of developing countries. It is regrettable that, at present, the CTE has no working relationship with the Trade and Development Committee whose work on UNCED follow-up issues is highly relevant. This situation should be remedied.

The CTE should address how WTO institutions and rules need to be interpreted or reformed and what terms of market access need to be negotiated in order to promote sustainable development in developing countries. Priorities for consideration in this regard include trade policies affecting subsidies, food security, market access, intellectual property rights, domestically prohibited goods, investment, tariff escalation, and commodity production and pricing. An additional priority will be to conduct research and implement measures which ensure that a portion of revenues associated with expanded trade are dedicated to providing developing countries with the appropriate technology and financial resources to meet environmental objectives. As well as on those occasions in which environmental regulations decrease equity, special precautions will be necessary to redress the imbalance in the priority areas stated above.

Ultimately, consideration must be given to granting further trade concessions to developing countries as part of the package of negotiable elements if developed countries are to advance green reform measures through the WTO. Discussions on this point thus far have had little to do with such an approach. Yet trade concessions are likely to pay the economic and environmental dividends that developing countries need to achieve sustainable development through international trade. More favourable market access terms will provide developing countries with greater opportunities to internalize environmental costs as they are absorbed into production costs and consumer prices through the implementation of the polluter pays principle. For the time being, revenues collected as a result of border taxes having an environmental policy basis should be channelled back to developing country exporters to assist in refining their pollution control or sustainable resource management efforts. This should be done under the supervision and guidance of the WTO.

In addition, further efforts should be made using WTO good offices to develop and extend international commodity agreements to stabilize and raise developing countries' financial returns from commodity exports. Environmental resource management factors must be added to these agreements, especially where the limits of environmental sustainability are felt during periods of low market supply. In these situations, funding should be made available from the IMF Compensatory Financing Facility. Ultimately, these measures should be designed to encourage greater market penetration for developing country goods in general. In particular, they should allow for an expanded range of market access and production opportunities for green products which are made in developing countries using sustainable processes and environmentally sound production methods.

Public Participation and Transparency in WTO Dispute Settlement Processes and Bodies

Like its GATT predecessor, the WTO limits opportunities for public participation and generally requires that proceedings and documents be kept secret. Regarding public participation and transparency, the WTO is considerably less progressive than other international institutions dealing with environmental matters. The insularity of the WTO system is inappropriate. Other equally important international legal processes, ie the UNCED negotiations, the Global Environmental Facility and the Multilateral Environmental Agreements, have managed to combine closed session negotiations with a degree of public access. The effective integration of public input will improve the quality and representativeness of WTO decisions.

Priorities for the CTE should include the access of NGOs to meetings, expanded public access to all documents produced in connection with WTO dispute resolution panel cases, and the production of panel decisions, official reports, negotiating texts, documents related to WTO institutional proceedings and notices of pending disputes in a timely manner. Access to all documents should be unrestricted unless there is a clear and convincing reason why they should be so restricted.

The dispute settlement system would benefit from procedural changes, allowing for amicus interventions in dispute settlement cases, including appeals, by NGOs with a sufficient interest. There should be greater opportunities for NGO representation as delegates or observers to negotiating sessions. These requirements build upon a standard to which members of the public and NGOs have become accustomed in most legal systems. They will add public legitimacy and democracy to WTO processes.

The Work Programme should also examine the possible creation of an autonomous office within the WTO dispute settlement body modelled along the lines of the Advocate General in the European Court of Justice. Such an office could help to synthesize, evaluate and report on arguments made by disputing WTO members, as well as on information and requests for standing brought forward by interested persons and NGOs. It would also ensure that timely submissions made by NGOs are inserted in the record of trade dispute panel and appellate proceedings.

Article 13.2 of the Dispute Settlement Understanding is the only provision to relate to participation by individuals and NGOs in the WTO dispute resolution process. It does not give them a right to be consulted or to participate in the process. Article 13.2 allows panels to obtain written analysis from technical or scientific expert review groups. In disputes concerning sustainable development matters or TREMs, the report of a group of experts in these matters could represent an important advance. Disputing Parties should be granted the right to comment on the report. As well, they should have the right to adduce environmental policy evidence independently. However, this is all subject to the concern that unless appropriate amendments are made to the TBT and SPS Agreements, technical and scientific expert reports may be used solely to undermine environmental and sustainable development policies. Expert reports should not be used for this purpose.

A more direct way of ensuring a higher standard of dispute panel decisions concerning environmental protection and sustainable development decisions, is to develop a pool of WTO panellists with expertise in environmental protection and sustainable development policy areas. This could be supported by granting any member a right to require that at least one panellist hearing the dispute has such expertise.

CONCLUSION

It is no longer possible to suggest that the WTO is confined to the regulation of trade restrictions. The very existence of TREMs, and indeed the CTE, serve as evidence that the WTO is in the business of regulating environmental law. The same can be said when it presides, as GATT has in the past, over dispute settlement processes which determine the fate of environmental measures, and when it encourages the harmonization of environmental regulation methodologies and standards.[41]

The WTO should not be viewed as the source which solves trade and environmental problems. Its expertise is in advancing liberalized trade. But, the WTO must be seen as addressing environmental protection problems, lest it be seen as the cause of them. In resolving trade and environmental protection conflicts, the hermetic seal placed around the evolution of GATT/WTO trade disciplines must be broken. The self-recognition that the WTO is without environmental expertise compels greater transparency and openness, coupled with a new ethic of cooperation with environmental experts in member environment ministries, intergovernmental organizations and NGOs.

This effort within the WTO should have the CTE as its focus. It is submitted that there should be a moratorium on any future WTO panel judgments concerning MEAs or harmonization processes concerning environmental protection standards under the TBT and SPS Agreements in order not to prejudge the results of the Committee's work. What remains to be seen is whether WTO members will accept the growing international recognition that environmental protection considerations must be infused into economic policy decisions.

7 THE NORTH AMERICAN FREE TRADE ASSOCIATION

Aradhana Kumar, Jean Milner and Annie Petsonk

INTRODUCTION

The North American Free Trade Agreement,[1] adopted by the governments of Canada, the United Mexican States and the United States of America in September 1993, was, together with its associated North American Agreement on Environmental Cooperation[2] (NAAEC), heralded by many as the 'greenest' trade agreement ever concluded, and an embodiment of the integration of trade and the environment called for by the Earth Summit.[3] Have the NAFTA and the associated environmental side agreement lived up to these lofty goals? The evidence is mixed. While the text of the NAFTA goes a long way towards the aims for trade and environmental integration laid down at Rio, the institutions established by the NAAEC are without precedent and their effectiveness remains to be proved. This chapter identifies Agenda 21 principles aimed at integrating trade and environmental goals; examines the text of key environmental components of the NAFTA, the NAAEC and the institutions they established in the light of the specific trade and environmental objectives laid down at the Earth Summit; and highlights developments in the evolution and implementation of the institutions and agreements that will merit scrutiny in the years to come.

THE TRADE AND ENVIRONMENT PRINCIPLES OF AGENDA 21

The Rio Declaration and Agenda 21, adopted by governments at the Earth Summit, contain a number of important principles on the integration of trade and the environment. The Rio Declaration and related provisions of Agenda 21 emphasize the importance of open trading systems to economic growth and sustainable development;[4] national sovereignty and the need for flexibility in the establishment of environmental standards;[5] and mechanisms for discouraging polluting industries from relocating to other countries.[6] They also specifically address trade measures used for environmental purposes, urging governments to ensure transparency and compatibility with international obligations; to avoid the use of trade restrictions as a means of offsetting differences in cost due to differences in environmental standards; to ensure that environmental regulations do not operate as a means of arbitrary or unjustifiable discrimination or a disguised restriction on trade; and to avoid unilateral actions to deal with environmental issues outside national jurisdiction.[7]

The Rio trade and environmental objectives themselves fall far short of what many environmentalists would have preferred. Many, particularly in the North, would have preferred broader latitude for unilateral trade measures in the service of environmental goals. The Rio objectives, however, represent a balancing of these concerns with the development, environment and sovereignty priorities of the South. How do the NAFTA and the NAAEC stack up against the Rio objectives?

THE ENVIRONMENTAL COMPONENTS OF THE NAFTA AND THE NAAEC

The NAFTA

The NAFTA has been described as the first multilateral trade agreement ever to incorporate sustainable development principles and objectives formally into both its preamble and its articles. The Preamble of the NAFTA announces the resolve of the three governments to 'promote sustainable development' and to 'strengthen the development and enforcement of environmental laws and regulations'; it also asserts the governments' resolve to undertake specific trade-related objectives 'in a manner consistent with environmental protection and conservation'.[8] These assertions, though hardly enforceable solely by virtue of their inclusion in the preamble, nevertheless provide a framework for interpreting the entire remainder of the text of the NAFTA. Because they can serve as important legal tools for resolving tensions that may arise from any substantive articles of the NAFTA, whether in dispute settlement or in other contexts, they make a substantial contribution to giving legal vitality to the Rio goals.

But these statements are preambular only. The more complex test of the relationship between the NAFTA and the Rio principles rests on an analysis of the specific operative language of the NAFTA articles. This discussion will explore how the NAFTA has sought to deal with potential conflicts between trade liberalization and trade restrictive environmental measures taken pursuant to international environmental agreements; national environmental standards; and restrictions on the movement of polluting industries.

The NAFTA Consistency of International Environmental Agreements

The first environmentally specific operative article in the NAFTA deals with the relationship between the NAFTA and other international environmental agreements. Chapter One of the NAFTA establishes the Agreement's specific objectives. In this Chapter, Article 104 describes the relationship between the NAFTA and other environmental and conservation agreements. In the event of any inconsistency between the NAFTA and the specific trade obligations set out in the Convention on International Trade in Endangered Species of Wild Fauna and Flora (CITES),[9] the Montreal Protocol on Substances that Deplete the Ozone Layer,[10] and the Basel Convention on the Control of Transboundary Movements of Hazardous Wastes and Their Disposal,[11] the obligations of the environmental agreements shall prevail to the extent of the inconsistency, provided that when complying with such NAFTA-inconsistent obligations, Parties shall utilize the least inconsistent option reasonably available.[12] Article 104 further provides that Parties may add to an Annex additional environmental agreements to which the consistency provisions of Article 104 will apply. Currently, that Annex contains references to two agreements, both of which are bilateral agreements concerning principally the movement of hazardous waste across national borders.[13]

By giving these environmental agreements, all of which can authorize the use of trade-restrictive measures, priority over its own trade liberalization provisions, Article 104 effectively 'grandfathers' the environmental agreements into the NAFTA. This savings clause for the environmental agreements is particularly important, not only because it responds specifically to the Rio call for the integration of trade measures in a manner that 'ensure[s] transparency and compatibility with international obligations',[14] but also because it insulates those agreements against challenges similar to those argued by Mexico in its tuna–dolphin case – under the General Agreement on Tariffs and Trade (GATT)[15] (see Chapter 6). Mexico had argued that it was GATT inconsistent for the US to impose unilateral trade embargoes against high-seas origin tuna caught by foreign vessels whose incidental dolphin mortality exceeded comparable dolphin mortality of the US tuna fleet. This challenge arose at the same time as the negotiation of the NAFTA. A GATT panel report issued in Mexico's favour in 1991 found that the US embargoes were inconsistent with the GATT, and in dicta further speculated that the trade provisions of the Montreal Protocol, the Basel Convention and CITES might also be GATT-inconsistent. That panel report, although never formally adopted, sparked fears among environmentalists that the issue of NAFTA consistency with these agreements should be addressed head on. Article 104 thus achieves a significant gain for environmentalists, furthering the Rio objective of ensuring that trade-related environmental measures are compatible with international obligations.

Standards

A significant portion of the Rio trade and environment texts deals with standards. The Rio texts seek to strike a balance among a number of competing standards-related concerns. The first of these is the concern of each state to retain sovereign capacity to establish environmental standards at levels that it deems appropriate, taking into account its environmental and developmental priorities and its relative environmental fragility or resiliency. Conflicts often arise between countries or groups of countries at different stages of economic development, and there is a tendency to view high environmental standards as placing restrictions on economic development. A competing concern, from the free trade perspective, seeks to harmonize international standards to ensure that they do not operate as non-tariff trade barriers in an arbitrary or unjustifiably discriminatory manner. Finally, also from a trade perspective, states have an interest in maintaining transparency in the setting and application of national standards.

Each of these concerns is reflected in Principle 11 of the Rio Declaration, with its special emphasis on ensuring that standards 'reflect the environmental and development context to which they apply'. These themes are echoed in Agenda 21 para 2.22(e) and (f), which speak of the importance of avoiding environmental standards that 'could lead to trade distortions and increase protectionist tendencies', or which otherwise constitute arbitrary or unjustified discrimination or a disguised restriction on trade.

Both NAFTA's Sanitary and Phytosanitary (SPS) Measures chapter and its chapter on Standards-Related Measures (SRMs) are quite responsive to these concerns. While a detailed analysis of SPS and SRMs is beyond the scope of this discussion, it is worth noting that each chapter specifically affords significant environmental protection in the context of trade concerns. For example, in the SPS, Article 712 establishes the right of each Party to adopt, maintain or apply any sanitary or phytosanitary measure considered necessary for the protection of human, animal or plant life or health, including a measure more stringent than an international standard, guideline or recommendation. The Article further establishes the right of each party, notwithstanding any other provision of the SPS, to establish 'its appropriate levels of protection', in accordance with transparency-oriented risk assessment provisions laid down in Article 715.

These SPS provisions represent potentially significant gains for environmentalists, since they clearly announce the right of each NAFTA party to maintain SPS standards at whatever level of protection a Party deems appropriate. The provisions make clear that international standards shall not operate as a 'ceiling' for national SPS measures. Similarly, Article 904.2 of the SRMs text provides that, notwithstanding any other provision of that chapter, each Party may establish the levels of protection that it considers appropriate in pursuit of its legitimate environmental objectives. Article 907 of the SRMs text provides that legitimacy is to be determined, as in the SPS chapter, on the basis of assessment of risk.

The SPS text specifically limits the right to establish SPS standards to measures taken to address human, animal or plant life or health in the territory of the Party taking the measure.[16] The SRMs text is less clear on this point.

Discouraging Relocation of Polluting Industries
The NAFTA takes a very interesting approach to the Rio objective of discouraging the relocation of polluting industries.[17] On the one hand, by allowing countries to establish their own environmental standards at levels more stringent than those internationally agreed, it provides a basis for countries to prevent the involuntary in-migration of polluting industries. On the other hand, the NAFTA's Investment chapter contains a particular provision prohibiting countries from voluntarily lowering their national environmental standards for the purposes of encouraging in-migration of polluting industries. The NAFTA Investment chapter contains two paragraphs responsive to both the involuntary and voluntary in-migration concerns. It provides, at Article 1114:

(1) Nothing in this Chapter shall be construed to prevent a Party from adopting, maintaining or enforcing any measure otherwise consistent with this Chapter that it considers appropriate to ensure that investment activity

in its territory is undertaken in a manner sensitive to environmental concerns.

(2) That parties recognize that it is inappropriate to encourage investment by relaxing domestic health, safety or environmental measures. Accordingly, a Party should not waive or otherwise derogate from, or offer to waive or otherwise derogate from, such measures as an encouragement for the establishment, acquisition, expansion or retention in its territory of an investment of an investor. If a Party considers that another Party has offered such an encouragement, it may request consultations with the other Party and the two Parties shall consult with a view to avoiding any such encouragement.

These provisions, while a significant step forward in addressing the environmental concerns embodied in the Rio Declaration, are not subject to dispute resolution under the NAFTA. As described more fully below, a new request to the NAFTA environmental bodies will test the vitality of this provision.

The NAAEC

The objectives of the NAAEC include promoting sustainable development through cooperative economic and environmental policies; cooperation on development and improvement of environmental laws, procedures and practices; enhanced enforcement of environmental laws; promotion of transparency and public participation; and the promotion of economically efficient and effective environmental measures.[18]

The NAAEC establishes the Commission for Environmental Cooperation ('the Commission').[19] The Commission is comprised of three separate bodies: the Council, the Secretariat and the Joint Public Advisory Committee.[20] While the NAAEC embraces some institutional features that are typical of international institutions, others are novel. These ground-breaking provisions relate specifically to the inclusion of the public in various aspects of the Commission's activities and to enforcement.

Structure of the Commission

The Council
The governing body of the Commission is the Council comprising 'cabinet-level or equivalent representatives of the Parties, or their designees'.[21] The Council shall meet at least once a year in regular session and in special session at the request of any party.[22] The Council may delegate responsibilities to *ad hoc* or standing committees, working groups or expert groups[23] and may also seek the advice of NGOs[24] or individuals, including independent experts.[25]

The Secretariat
The Secretariat directs the day-to-day affairs of the Commission. It is located in Montreal and is headed by an Executive Director chosen by the Council.[26] The position of Executive Director rotates consecutively between nationals of each Party.[27] Staffing of the Secretariat is the responsibility of the Executive Director and will be effected according to general guidelines.[28] The intention is that the

staff and the Executive Director will be politically independent in the performance of their duties.[29]

The Secretariat has three major functions: to prepare the Commission's annual report;[30] to prepare reports on other matters;[31] and to evaluate complaints brought by individuals and NGOs about a Party's failure to enforce its environmental laws effectively.[32]

The annual report covers the activities and expenses of the Commission during the previous year[33] and the approved programme and budget of the Commission for the subsequent year.[34] More interestingly, it includes 'relevant views and information submitted by NGOs and persons, including summary data regarding submissions'.[35] The report must also periodically address the state of the environment in the territories of the Parties.[36] The report is reviewed by the Council, and the final report is to be released to the public.[37]

The Secretariat is also empowered to draw up other reports on any matter falling within the ambit of the annual work programme.[38] The programme proposed for 1995 covered an ambitiously broad range of topics. Should the Secretariat wish to draw up a report on a matter not provided for by the work programme, it must notify the Council and may proceed only if, within 30 days, the Council does not object by a two-thirds majority.[39] This requirement of positive action by the Council does seem to favour preparation of the reports. The Secretariat is prohibited, however, from reporting on whether a party has failed to enforce its environmental laws.[40] These reports will also be made public, unless the Council decides otherwise.[41]

In the preparation of its reports the Secretariat can draw upon a diversity of sources, including NGOs, independent experts, public consultations and the Parties themselves.[42] These reports, although subject to some constraints, can function to raise the political visibility of environmental issues. The role these reports come to play will undoubtedly depend upon the vigour and independence of the Secretariat and the Executive Director.

Advisory Committees

The Joint Public Advisory Committee   The Secretariat and the Council are advised by the Joint Public Advisory Committee (JPAC), which is made up of five individuals from each of the Signatory Parties.[43] The JPAC members serve in their individual capacity. However, the NAAEC does not clearly define the role of the JPAC. Instead it states:

> The [JPAC] may provide advice to the Council on any matter within the scope of this Agreement [including on the proposed annual program and the budget of the Commission, the draft annual report and any report the Secretariat prepares], and on the implementation and further elaboration of this Agreement and may perform such other functions as the Council may direct.[44]

(It may also provide technical, scientific or other information to the Secretariat. This could be for the purpose of compiling the factual record.)[45]

The JPAC intends initially to meet quarterly and to conduct its work through working groups when necessary.[46] The JPAC has stated that it will seek to achieve public participation and transparency in the activities of the full Commission.[47]

The lack of specificity in the NAAEC can be viewed as the freedom for the JPAC to define its own role. JPAC members, representatives from industry, academia, government and NGOs, have the skills to make this body more proactive and less simply reactive to the needs of the Secretariat and the Council.[48] Again, this will depend on the role the JPAC and other Commission staff envision that the Commission will fulfil. Budget constraints will obviously also be determinative.

The National Advisory Committee (NAC) Each Party may also choose to have a National Advisory Committee (NAC) to guide its government representative to the Council[49] on the 'implementation and further elaboration' of the NAAEC.[50] NACs are to be composed of representatives of environmental groups, business and industry, government agencies and educational institutions.[51] The diversity of the groups, as with the JPAC, is intended to provide governmental representatives with the range of perspectives considered necessary to evaluate effectively the various issues that will be addressed in the implementation of the NAAEC.[52]

Enforcement Procedures

The central aim of the enforcement procedures is to ensure that each Party effectively enforces its own domestic environmental laws. The NAAEC establishes two procedures with different remedies, depending on the status of the disputants and the nature of the claim. Thus, claims can be brought by the NAFTA Parties themselves or by concerned individuals or NGOs.

Actions brought by NAFTA/NAAEC parties Where a Party believes that another Party has exhibited a persistent pattern of failure to enforce its environmental laws effectively,[53] it can request consultations with that party.[54] If the consultations fail to achieve a 'mutually satisfactory resolution of the matter', either Party may request a special session of the Council.[55] The Council may seek the advice of expert groups, have recourse to good offices, conciliation, mediation or other dispute resolution procedures, or may make recommendations in an effort to resolve the matter at issue. Any recommendations may be made public, where two-thirds of the Council agrees.[56]

If still unsuccessful, the Council (on a written request and by a two-thirds vote) shall convene an arbitral panel of five members.[57] In order for such a Panel to be convened, the dispute has to relate to goods or services involved in NAFTA trade.[58]

The panel shall prepare an initial report, determining whether or not the party has failed to enforce its environmental laws effectively.[59] If the panel makes an affirmative determination, the initial report will likely provide that the Party complained against must adopt and implement an action plan sufficient to remedy the pattern of non-enforcement.[60]

A Party to the dispute may comment in writing on this initial report within 30 days.[61] The Panel will present a final report, including any separate opinions on matters that are not unanimously agreed upon, within two months. The final report will then be given to the Council and must be published five days after it is transmitted to the Council.[62]

In implementing the recommendations resulting from an affirmative finding by the panel, the disputing Parties may agree on a satisfactory action plan to remedy the persistent pattern of non-enforcement.[63] Alternatively, if there is a failure to agree on an action plan or on whether a Party is implementing an action plan fully, the Council shall reconvene the panel upon the request of a disputing party.[64] This reconvened panel may determine that the Party, in fact, is implementing the action plan fully. If, however, it decides that this is not the case, it 'shall' impose a monetary enforcement assessment.[65] The Party complained against will also have to implement an action plan fully – either the one previously decided on or a new one.[66]

Where a Party fails to pay a monetary enforcement assessment within 180 days after its imposition, any complaining Party/Parties may suspend trade benefits as against that Party in an amount no greater than that sufficient to collect the monetary enforcement assessment.[67]

Complaints brought by individuals or NGOs   Private citizens or NGOs who believe that a Party is failing to enforce effectively its environmental laws can submit a complaint ('submission') to the Secretariat.[68] Such a submission need not relate to goods or services involved in NAFTA trade, but can pertain to a general lack of environmental enforcement. If the submission meets several threshold requirements,[69] the Secretariat will determine whether, in fact, it merits a request for a response from the Party complained against.[70] In making this decision, the Secretariat will take into account factors such as whether the submission raises issues whose consideration 'would advance the goals of [the NAAEC]'; whether private remedies under the Party's law have been pursued; whether the submission is drawn exclusively from media reports; or whether it alleges harm to the person or organization making the complaint.[71]

If a Party from whom a response has been requested states that the matter is the subject of a pending judicial or administrative proceeding, the Secretariat cannot proceed further.[72] This could complete the submissions process. The Party can also offer other information; it might, for example, show that appropriate private remedies are available and that they have not been pursued.[73] Should the Secretariat determine that the submission warrants further examination and if two-thirds of the Council agrees, it can compile a factual record.[74] The Secretariat does not have many investigative powers available to it in drawing up this record.[75] It can consider information that any Party has provided, is publicly available, has been submitted by interested NGOs or individuals, or the JPAC, or has been developed by the Secretariat or by independent experts.[76]

After a draft of the factual record has been given to the Council, further comments on its accuracy are restricted to the Parties.[77] The Secretariat shall include any such comments it deems appropriate. This will constitute the final factual record which is then submitted to the Council.[78] It can be made public by a two-thirds vote of the Council.[79] Expectations of release of a final document will have been raised by input by the public in earlier stages of the process, so it seems unlikely that the Council would readily deny publication. Unfortunately the factual record does not trigger any further action by any Party or by the Secretariat – a significant shortcoming.

The positive aspects of this process should, nevertheless, be recognized. Should a two-thirds Council vote be achieved, the behaviour of the Parties will be placed in the public eye. Negative publicity can be an effective catalyst for improvement of environmental enforcement and might serve further to inhibit environmentally irresponsible behaviour by a Party or its domestic industry. The factual records, combined with media pressure, can also be used to identify patterns of non-enforcement that could lead to a Party bringing an action against another non-enforcing Party.

Neither the Council, the Secretariat nor the JPAC has the authority to initiate investigations or to bring proceedings against a Party on their own behalf. Thus, the Commission has to rely completely upon complaints brought by individuals, NGOs and the Parties.

Criticisms

The NAAEC does not comprehensively address environmental concerns in the North American free trade area, nor does it attempt to. It does seek to address some of the environmental consequences of burgeoning trade arising out of the NAFTA accord. It does this firstly by supplying a forum in which these issues will be addressed, discussed and made known to the public. The enforcement procedure, reinforced by penalties, gives the Commission teeth and, perhaps more importantly at this point, hopes of credibility.

First, criticism levelled against the Commission's enforcement procedure is that, by sanctioning a Party's 'failure to effectively enforce its environmental laws', it holds a Party accountable for the conduct of an industry within its territory rather than holding the offending entity itself accountable for that conduct. It would be more time-efficient and would produce speedier results if the Commission could proceed against a polluting company, rather than involve itself in lengthy diplomatic negotiations (which necessarily incorporate a host of political considerations) to reach a solution ('action plan') that is amenable to all.

Second, while the distinction made between whether an action is brought by a state or by an individual or NGO broadens the range of complaints that can be brought ('submissions' need not relate only to goods or services involved in NAFTA trade), it seems unnecessarily limiting in other ways. There is no rationale to explain why a citizen's complaint should only be capable of triggering an investigative procedure, resulting at best in the publication of a factual report, while a Party's complaint, on the other hand, will result in a procedure which seeks to achieve a solution. The value of the Secretariat's factual report, arising out of the citizen's complaint, is limited by restrictions on the Secretariat's investigative powers in drawing it up. Another drawback is that comments on the draft factual report are limited to Parties and that the citizen or citizens' group that originally brought the complaint are denied the same procedural rights. In fact, after making the initial submission, the participation of the complaining citizen/NGO is limited to providing information for the draft factual record. It would be more effective if the complainant citizen/NGO was permitted to participate actively throughout the process.

Thirdly, the independence of the Secretariat is limited by the requirement that two-thirds of the Council must provide approval to draw up even a *draft* factual record and to publicize the final factual record.

Fourthly, the fact that the Secretariat is prohibited from reporting on whether a Party has failed to enforce its environmental laws and regulations[80] substantially restricts its ability to act as an independent body and renders it less effective as a monitor of the environmental consequences of expanded trade in the NAFTA region.

Fifthly, lack of information available to the public on the existence, purpose and functioning of the Commission for Environmental Cooperation constitutes a serious impediment to its success. Education of the public is essential: citizens need to be taught how they can involve themselves in protecting their environment by participating in Commission processes and the Commission itself needs to learn from interaction with NGOs and individuals.

Activities of the Commission – 1995

The Commission held six meetings in 1994 to invite proposals for its work plan. These were open to the public and were attended by representatives of NGOs, academia and governmental agencies of the three countries. The Commission has been receptive to the ideas and suggestions of these groups. From the outset, the Commission for Environmental Cooperation, unlike many existing international organizations, has placed substantial emphasis on public participation. The Commission is supposed to promote environmental protection, review environmental enforcement and recommend policy changes to the three Parties.

Among the mandatory activities that the Council will undertake 'is the creation of a database of relevant environmental laws, regulations, norms and technical standards of the Parties'.[81] It will also 'prepare a comparative study on criteria and methodologies used by the three Parties in establishing domestic environmental standards, including the work done by industry and trade associations'.[82] Janine Ferretti, Director of the Secretariat, informed us that preparation of the databank of comparative environmental laws in the three countries, which would be available to any interested person, is on the list of priority activities for 1995. Also high on the agenda is a comparative study of current environmental impact statement legislation and practice in the Parties, including the assessment process. Also included in the proposed activities is a trinational study of public access to information concerning the environment that is held by the public authorities of each Party.[83] A status report and recommendations to the Council will ultimately be drawn up by the Secretariat. In conjunction with this, a comparative study will be done to identify and analyse existing domestic mechanisms for public participation in the environmental decision-making process under the laws of each Party. Case studies will be done of particular problems and the final report will include recommendations for follow-up action nationally.

There will be special emphasis on the enforcement of laws and regulations relating to transboundary environmental effects. The latter half of the 1994 work plan focuses on the complementary and supporting activities to be undertaken; some of these include Secretariat reports, NGO meetings and State of the Environment Assessment methodologies.

The Commission will begin a NAFTA environment effects programme which the Executive Director described as a 'study of the most important sectors we should be focusing on' in terms of their environmental effects in the party countries.[84]

The 1995 work plan covers a wide range of issues ranging from Conservation and the Ecosystem Protection, Pollution Prevention, Environmental Policy Instruments, including Economic Instruments, Technology Cooperation and Capacity Building, Transboundary Environmental Issues to Enforcement Issues, and Environmental Laws and Regulation. The Commission intends to identify areas of common concern for the parties.

The real question, however, is the implementation of the Agreement – ie will the Parties be in a position to incorporate the standards set? The comparative study of current environmental legislation and practices in the three countries will focus on the 'special circumstances posed by projects which may generate transboundary environmental consequences'.[85] Despite the common objective of protecting the environment, the three countries have different priorities. Transboundary conflicts arise from the problem of difference in environmental standards. The challenge of proving that an activity is actually harming the environment is the key to the whole issue: 'Mexicans enjoy clean air and vistas as much as anyone else, but their lower incomes and need for economic development may make them unable or unwilling to spend as much on the environment as the Americans would like.'[86] The Commission has undertaken to determine the 'cleanest technologies' or the 'best available technology (BAT)' for all sectors and is trying to develop 'appropriate limits for specific pollutants, taking into account the differences in ecosystems'.[87] The Commission thus intends to play a major role in encouraging the enforcement of national laws. The three parties have comparable environmental regulations, but substantial differences in levels of enforcement of these laws.

The work plan of the Commission is comprehensive in that it addresses the issues it was instructed to under the NAAEC. Furthermore, it includes several recommendations made by the NGOs. Unfortunately the first stages of the Secretariat's functioning have been extremely slow. Until the end of 1994 the Secretariat had a staff of only ten people. Given this level of staff, the Commission may have difficulty achieving the exhaustive agenda it has created for itself.

Recent Issues

Environmentalists in all three countries are beginning to use the mechanisms and the institutions established by the NAFTA and the NAAEC, particularly their public/governmental attention aspects, to illuminate policies and issues of environmental concern in the three countries, and to press for action to address those concerns. A recent petition filed by the Sierra Club Legal Defense Fund on behalf of 20 environmental organizations in the United States, Canada and Mexico asked the Commission to investigate the newly enacted 'salvage logging' law that allows significantly increased logging in US national forests. The logging law exempts significant cutting of trees in national forests from regulations protecting fish and wildlife, and suspends the Endangered Species Act and other laws in order to expedite salvage timber harvests. It directs the Forest Service to allow logging without environmental constraints in some of the Pacific Northwest forests that are home to the embattled spotted owl and marbled murrelet. Most troubling, provisions of the logging law appear to preclude citizen enforcements, as they bar administrative appeals or court challenges in US domestic fora. Therefore, environmentalists sought recourse to the NAFTA/NAAEC.

Under the NAAEC, the groups alleged that the law violates the NAFTA investment provision that requires countries to avoid waiving or derogating from environmental measures to attract or retain investment. The argument was a clever one, since it skirts two problems: first, that the NAFTA investment provisions are not themselves subject to dispute settlement under the NAFTA; and second, that even if those provisions were subject to the NAFTA dispute settlement procedures, only a NAFTA party, not an environmental group, could initiate a dispute under NAFTA itself. Instead, the groups argued that the apparent violation of the NAFTA investment provisions constituted an actionable event, ie one that is subject to trade sanctions, under the NAAEC. The Commission is currently considering its response.[88]

The Commission has also responded to a request for an investigation into the deaths of 40,000 native and migratory waterfowl at the Silva Reservoir in Mexico's Turbio River Basin. A petition submitted by US and Mexican groups asserted that the waterfowl disaster is one of the worst bird kills ever reported. The groups sought to determine as whether the cause of the kill was one-time dumping of pesticides, or, more ominously, chronic pollution upstream of the reservoir. Attention focused on tanneries that discharge waste-water directly into the San German Reservoir, upstream from the Silva. The Commission was also asked to investigate the possibility that whatever triggered the bird kills would also adversely affect thousands more birds and, if chemical contamination were the cause, it might also be harmful to people who harvest the birds during the hunting season.

In late September 1995, a nine-member panel of scientists from each of the three NAFTA countries concluded that although heavy metals pollution from the 1000 upstream leather tanneries may have been a factor, the main killer was botulism. The botulism occurred because rivers of raw human sewage flowing into the reservoir turned the water into an incubator in which botulism-producing bacteria flourished. The finding underscores what Mexico's environment minister, Julia Carabias Lillo, has repeatedly identified as one of her country's health problems: lack of sewage treatment facilities.[89] Moreover, while the resources of two other NAFTA-related institutions, the North American Developments Bank (NAD Bank) and the binational (US–Mexico) Border Environmental Cooperation Commission (BECC), are available to support sewage treatment in the border region, more resources clearly are needed to address the vast public health and environmental concerns raised by the need to provide adequate water treatment facilities throughout Mexico.[90]

A third request for an environmental investigation has been filed and a fourth case is brewing. Groups focusing on pollution along the US–Canada border are considering filing a petition urging the Commission to investigate the alleged failure of the US Environmental Protection Agency to regulate the disposal of toxic waste at a General Motors plant along the St Lawrence River.

As this Chapter goes to press, the Commission is slated to decide soon whether to launch a full-scale inquiry into allegations that Mexico failed to enforce its environmental impact assessment laws when it decided to allow the construction of a US$230 million resort complex along a fragile coral reef on Cozumes Island on the Caribbean coast.

CONCLUSION

These matters and others that are likely to arise in the near future will test the vitality of the NAFTA/NAAEC environmental provisions, and the technical and legal capability of the Commission to deal effectively with highly complex pollution and natural resource-related controversies. They will also test the effectiveness of the Commission's procedures, adopted after public comment and input, for receiving, hearing, investigating and acting upon such claims. On the one hand, the Commission will be beset by calls for speedy action to address pressing environmental concerns; and, on the other hand, it will be beset also by demands that the mechanisms the Commission utilizes to address these claims be absolutely credible. The Commission will do well to proceed carefully and firmly. It remains to be seen whether the Commission will be able to muster the resources, the technical and legal capabilities, and the political resolve to discharge its responsibilities effectively.

PART III

Finance

8 THE WORLD BANK AND THE INTERNATIONAL MONETARY FUND

Korinna Horta

'If I knew for a certainty that a man was coming to my house with the conscious design of doing me good, I should run for my life ... for fear that I should get some of his good done to me' Henry David Thoreau, *Walden, or Life in the Woods and On the Duty of Civil Disobedience*.[1]

In a recent internal document prepared by the World Bank's External Affairs Department, the Bank quantifies the benefits that its largest shareholders receive from contributing to the Bank: 'Over the years, for every dollar in paid-in capital and IDA contributions [the Bank's soft loan window intended for the world's poorest countries] that the US Government has invested in the World Bank, US companies have received back about $1.10.' The other major shareholders are not faring badly either. Income accruing from procurement contracts when compared to every dollar contributed to the Bank leads to benefits amounting to $1.90 for the United Kingdom, $1.78 for France, $1.47 for Germany. Only Japan with $0.97 appears to receive a little less than its contribution.[2]

These profits to the planet's wealthiest countries from the World Bank, the world's pre-eminent agency for international development, are remarkable in the light of the overarching goal of the organization which is to alleviate poverty in poor developing countries. Theoretically, both lending and borrowing countries could profit from Bank loans. But these successful rates of return to the world's richer countries become difficult to reconcile with the Bank's poverty reduction goals when contrasted with the increasing failure rate of World Bank projects, documented in the 1992 World Bank 'Wapenhans Report'.[3] The Wapenhans Report concluded that over one-third of all World Bank projects recently evaluated did not meet basic economic goals. The loans contracted for these expensive project failures must still be repaid, a cost that is being borne entirely by people in developing countries.

How do these different issues of profits, mission to help the poor and project failure rate relate to the question of the greening of the Bretton Woods institutions? It is in the fundamental issue of accountability where the various threads come together. To whom is the institution accountable and for what? The question of accountability is at the very centre of the battle for ecological and social reform at the Bretton Woods institutions.

When world leaders met in the small New Hampshire town of Bretton Woods in 1944 to put in place the pillars of a post-World War II international economic order, they envisioned the creation of three institutions: the World Bank, the International Monetary Fund (IMF) and the International Trade Organization.[4] This chapter deals primarily with the World Bank and will focus only briefly on its sister organization, the International Monetary Fund. It will examine the extent to which environmental reforms are taking hold at the World Bank by reviewing the issues of transparency and participation, including the Bank's new information disclosure policy, the question of vastly increased lending for environmental projects, the Bank's record with regards to forests, structural adjustment and the environment and last, but not least, the promising new development of the Bank's recently established inspection panel. Environmental policy changes have come about as a result of a decade of environmental activism marked by close cooperation between grass-roots movements for social and ecological change in the South and non-governmental organizations in the North. These groups have become increasingly successful at bringing their case to the public and to law-makers in their countries. The United States Congress played a special role in giving the impetus for policy reforms by conditioning part of the direct US contribution to the World Bank on the implementation of new policies, such as the policy on information disclosure.[5]

One cannot look, however, at these new policies without taking into account both the institutional culture of the organization and the reality of project implementation in developing countries. The overall conclusion which emerges is that policies and research, in both of which the Bank is far ahead by comparison with other multi- and bilateral development agencies, remain largely divorced from day-to-day Bank operations which continue to be driven by the imperative of meeting lending targets. In other words, true to the nature of a bank (albeit a bank whose loans are government subsidized and guaranteed and entail no financial risks), the World Bank focuses on approving loans. The environmental and social sustainability of what these loans are financing remains a largely rhetorical preoccupation.

ACCOUNTABILITY

With a portfolio of $148 billion dollars financing about 1900 projects throughout the developing world,[6] the World Bank remains by far the single most influential development agency in the world and it is leaving its imprint on the environment and the fate of poor people in a large number of countries.

Critics who claim that World Bank-funded projects have needlessly contributed to environmental destruction and social problems, received unexpected support through the conclusions of the already mentioned Wapenhans Report. This 1992 internal World Bank study, named after the then World Bank Vice-President, Willi A Wapenhans, who led the task force which wrote the report, revealed a systemic failure within the Bank to monitor the implementation of its own projects. The study found that 37.5 per cent of all recently evaluated World Bank projects were rated as unsatisfactory on Bank assessment criteria.[7] The report also observed a clear and growing tendency towards further degradation in the Bank's portfolio, noting that in 1981 only 15 per cent of Bank projects received the same negative rating.[8]

Wapenhans attributed responsibility for this state of affairs to the Bank's 'approval culture', a term which describes the institution's emphasis on rapid loan approval and lack of attention to the actual implementation of the projects it approves. There are no financial consequences to the Bank or to its rich country shareholders from the badly performing loans because, given the Bank's status as a 'preferred creditor', developing country governments repay their World Bank debts out of general revenue or new loans. Interrupting this cycle of approval will require Bank operations to become more transparent and participatory, so that those affected by projects can have a decisive voice in decisions affecting their lives.

Transparency and Participation

Improving the quality of projects by making them environmentally sustainable and socially beneficial requires the active participation of local communities and their local or regional governmental and administrative structures. Information is power and makes meaningful participation possible. Grass-roots movements and environmental organizations have been able to exert considerable pressure to erode the World Bank's tradition of withholding information about its projects from the public. In the United States, numerous Congressional hearings which documented environmental and social negligence in World Bank projects led to a series of legislative efforts to increase transparency in the Bank's operations, such as the 1992 law which required the timely availability of draft and final environmental assessments to the public in both recipient and donor countries.[9]

As a result of the mounting pressure, World Bank statements reiterating Bank support for accountability and transparency in the development process and as a tool in increasing local participation in decision-making have become commonplace.[10] A new Information Disclosure Policy became effective in January 1994. A public information centre was established at World Bank headquarters in Washington and the commitment has been made to provide information at World Bank offices in Tokyo, Paris and London, as well as at field offices.

The approval of the Bank's new Information Disclosure Policy was preceded by an internal debate about how open the Bank should become. When drafts of the new policy were circulated first within the Bank, staff in the Bank's Environment Department responded with an internal document that was highly critical of the 'overriding presumption of confidentiality' which characterizes the new policy and proposed an alternative. The alternative which, in the view of the Bank's outside critics represented real positive change, ensured the confidentiality of certain documents during critical stages of negotiations with governments, but in general guaranteed public access to all relevant documentation, especially the environment and social reports.[11]

In the end the alternative point of view lost out and despite some critical voices on the World Bank's Board, a new policy was approved which continues to emphasize confidentiality.[12] Despite assurances of a 'presumption in favour of disclosure', the new policy adopts a case-by-case approach in which the prior authorization of borrowing governments is a precondition for the release to the public of most essential documents, including the environmental assessments.[13] Even more important, the Staff Appraisal Reports, which are the most important documents defining a project, can only be made available once a project has already been approved and even then only after the government in the project country has had a chance to delete all the information from it that it considers to be sensitive. Delaying access until after a project has been approved and all important decisions have been taken, offers little possibility of meaningful input from affected parties, academic experts or non-governmental organizations.

Finally, the new Information Disclosure Policy makes no provisions for ensuring that project information at the early stages of project preparation is made available at the local level in languages that local communities can understand. The opportunity for constructive suggestions regarding project design or possible alternatives from local communities is made very difficult, if not impossible. The serious limitations of the new Information Disclosure Policy are not conducive to promoting much needed improvements in project quality and sustainability.

Social Assessment and Participation

'Participation of stakeholders' has become one of the most frequent expressions pervading literature, including that of the World Bank, on the environment and sustainable development. What indicators are there to demonstrate that this shift in the development paradigm, giving a decisive voice to intended project beneficiaries, is actually taking place? First, stakeholders must be identified. For this purpose, the World Bank developed draft social assessment guidelines in 1994 which, if applied, could lay a solid basis for a participatory process from the design through to the implementation and evaluation stages of a project.[14] At present, however, these guidelines remain in draft form, and it is unclear when and if they will be approved. Approval of these guidelines will be an important step towards making participation more real. As with all Bank policy, successful and consistent implementation will depend, in part, on the status the policy is assigned within the Bank's institutional culture. The social assessment guidelines will be part of the Bank's 'best practice' guidelines and, therefore, will not be considered mandatory. Implementing these guidelines will be left to the discretion of individual World Bank task managers, who often will not only be overburdened with the new task, but will also have had little social science training to prepare them for it.

In addition to social assessment guidelines, the World Bank approved a 'Participation Action Plan' in September 1994 and is now in the process of identifying key flagship countries and projects where the action plan could be put to work.[15] Some development and environmental organizations, which have prodded the Bank in the direction of participatory approaches for many years, are now expressing some concern that the Participation Action Plan may turn out to be a social marketing exercise, and promise to monitor closely how it will be implemented.[16]

In conclusion, it is hardly surprising that Willi A Wapenhans, the now retired World Bank Vice-President, after reviewing the steps announced by the World Bank in response to his 1992 report, concludes that: 'It is perhaps noteworthy that the Bank's management response to the Wapenhans report does not yet address recommendations concerning accountability. The "cultural change" required is, however, unlikely to occur unless the recognized performance criteria change.'[17]

Vastly Increased Lending for the Environment – a Benefit?

In addition to 'greening' its regular investment portfolio, the World Bank is seeking to direct more funds towards projects with specific environmental objectives. The Bank recently announced that there are now more than 100 Bank-supported environmental projects representing a commitment of $5 billion and total investments of more than $13 billion.[18] Closer evaluation of these claims yields mixed results. While part of the environmental funding is for what is called the 'brown agenda', ie projects that are designed to address pollution in urban areas, most of the 'environmental projects' deal with the 'green agenda', ie projects concerned with natural resource management in mostly rural areas, such as forestry, fisheries and agriculture. As of 1994, the Bank had committed nearly $3.2 billion for 'green agenda' projects.[19] Many of the projects have been characterized as green because they involve natural resource management; whether they are actually environmentally beneficial is open to question.

Anecdotal information about some of the individual projects listed suggests that claims about environmental benefits can be misleading. For example, a 1991 fisheries project for the central African nation of Malawi is on the Bank's list of environmental projects. This particular project supports the increase of industrial fisheries in Lake Malawi without even the benefit of an environmental assessment.[20] Yet the aquatic biodiversity of Lake Malawi is at high risk, a problem that the Bank's environmental experts have recognized and seek to address through a separate project funded by the Global Environment Facility (GEF).[21] One may ask why the problem of biodiversity loss was not taken into account in the fisheries development project, which is described as an environmental project. This particular case also raises the disturbing question of the potentially perverse effects of GEF funding, when GEF funds are used to pay for the externalities of regular Bank operations. The availability of funds for this purpose, even if they are very limited as in the case of the GEF, undermines much-needed efforts to ensure that development projects internalize their social and environmental costs, a pre-condition for sustainability.

As the section on forestry later in this chapter will describe in more detail, claims of the environmental benefits of forestry projects continue to be especially questionable. The $80 million forestry loan for Côte d'Ivoire, listed as an environmental project in the Bank's last annual environment report,[22] is a historical case in point. The vote on the project at the Bank's Board represented the first time that the United States Executive Director to the World Bank did not support a project for environmental reasons. His concerns related to commercial forest exploitation and the project's large forced resettlement component.[23]

The Bank's record on forced resettlement and questions about the effectiveness of its environment impact assessments are indicative of the caution that must be exercised concerning the Bank's environmental claims.

FORCED RESETTLEMENT

The problem of forced resettlement is a sad example of the Bank's lack of adherence to its own policies. The Bank's Policy on Involuntary Resettlement,[24] which is accepted as a valuable policy by people both inside and outside the Bank, states that the Bank must ensure that people forcibly displaced under Bank projects will not be made worse off as a result of resettlement. Most often the populations to be resettled are among a country's poorest and most marginalized. At present there are 2.5 million people displaced as a result of Bank-financed projects and another 2 million will be added over the next few years. Yet an internal Bank review published in 1994, assessing resettlement operations under Bank-assisted development projects between 1986 and 1993, concluded that despite some improvements over the seven-year period, '[u]nsatisfactory performance in reestablishing settlers at an equal or better level of living still persists on a wide and unacceptable scale'.[25] The explanation for resettlement failures was, once again, that unambiguous Bank requirements were not being followed by the Bank or the borrower, and that 'in most projects restoring incomes is not a project objective from the outset'.[26]

Environmental Assessments

Environmental Assessments (EAs) can be an invaluable tool for understanding the environmental consequences of proposed development projects and for ensuring the consideration of alternatives with less damaging impacts. Since 1989 EAs have become a formal requirement for all Bank operations that are expected to have significant adverse environmental impacts.[27] It is encouraging that an increasing percentage of World Bank projects in more sectors and subsectors is scrutinized through EAs. But there is evidence – anecdotal but worrying – that the effectiveness of EAs, especially in the natural resources management sector, is undermined by a range of factors.

A study by then Stanford University researchers Rafik Hirji and Leonard Ortolano examines the effectiveness of EAs with regard to World Bank-funded hydroelectric projects in Kenya. They found that the EA process was simply being used to legitimize previously established project concepts. EAs were carried out to comply with World Bank conditions, but the lack of follow-through and the absence of controls created little incentive to take the EA seriously. In the opinion of the authors, this raises important questions about the Bank's commitment to the process in the first place.[28]

An example from the forestry perspective is the EA carried out for the 1992 'Forestry and Environment Project' for Gabon in West Africa. The EA recognizes that increased pressure on the land and increased poaching are the main environmental risks of the project and recognizes also the central role of landownership for forest conservation.[29] But the $30 million project addresses only marginally – if at all – the question of land tenure, strengthened rural economies and improved basic village infrastructure as recommended by the EA.[30]

Another crucial element in EA effectiveness is the abundant use of foreign consultants in carrying out the EAs, often with minimal input of national experts or affected communities. Edward V K Jaycox, the World Bank's former Vice-President for the Africa Region, delivered a brave and impassioned speech in 1993 in which he described how the Bank's excessive use of foreign consultants has effectively contributed to undermining local capacity in African countries. While Jaycox's remarks refer to the overall development process, they apply in particular to the EA process. He states that the annual $4 billion international technical assistance to Africa is being used up to pay for the salaries of the expatriate advisers and that the prevalence of foreign experts has been a 'systematic destructive force which is undermining the development of indigenous capacity in Africa'.[31] While foreign consultants can play a very useful role in the EA process, there needs to be a systematic participation of national experts and local communities. Otherwise, the EA will often remain a merely formal exercise with little follow-up on its recommendations and lacking in relevance to on-the-ground project reality.

The Problem of Hard Currency Loans for the Environment

The arguments made here to caution against an optimistic view of the Bank's new environmental portfolio have to be placed in a larger context. The function of the Bank is to make hard currency loans for projects that can generate foreign exchange for repayment. A study by Francis F Korten on Asian Development Bank environmental loans to the Philippines demonstrates that 'environmental loans' generate pressures for exports that often involve unsustainable practices or outright destruction of the natural resources the 'environmental project' intended to protect.[32] For example, the already mentioned forestry/environment loans for Côte d'Ivoire and Gabon were made on non-concessional terms, which means that the interest rates on the loans are almost as high as those of the international financial markets. Given the extreme volatility of most traditional primary export commodities, such as coffee and cocoa, the most likely alternative for these countries is to increase vastly their exports of raw logs and to do irreversible damage to their tropical rainforest, its people and biodiversity in the process.

Instead of promoting 'environmental projects', the World Bank would do a greater service to the environment if it would ensure that its regular lending activities internalize their environmental and social costs. Environmental problems are often caused by social and institutional conditions, which are not susceptible of being solved with large hard currency loans. Just providing more loans seems to be more advantageous to the lender than to the borrowing nation, which is driven ever deeper into debt and outside dependence.

Forests: From Financing Geopolitical Forest Colonization to Financing Environmentally Sustainable Forest Management?

The World Bank is the largest financier of forestry projects in the world and its lending for the forestry sector has increased recently at an unparalleled rate. Forestry loans more than doubled in the three years between 1992–1994 as compared to the previous seven years (1984–1991). Over this period, the Bank has approved about $1.65 billion for forestry projects, whose total project costs are close to $3 billion.[33] But forestry projects are only a small slice of a whole range of World Bank-financed activities that have direct and indirect impacts on forests. Infrastructure projects, such as dam and road construction, have immediately visible effects on forests. World Bank-promoted policy reforms through structural adjustment programmes (about 20 per cent of the World Bank's annual loans commitments of *circa* $23 billion) have more indirect effects. In some cases, for example in Cameroon, the promotion of forest policy legislation is part of a World Bank-structural adjustment programme.[34]

In addition to providing livelihoods for an estimated 500 million people worldwide who live in and near forests, and playing a critical role in maintaining local and regional ecological balance, forests are essential to the health of the global environment. They shelter most of the planet's terrestrial biodiversity and absorb and store carbon dioxide, protecting the world's climate system. For these reasons, forests are central to the two international agreements emerging from the 1992 United Nations Conference on Environment and Development – the biodiversity and climate conventions. Funding for projects to help countries to meet the goals of the conventions will be provided through the Global Environment Facility (GEF), a funding mechanism that was established in 1991 and of which the World Bank is both the trustee and the main project implementing agency.

Given the Bank's role in the GEF and its vast influence over both the world's tropical rainforests and now, increasingly, the boreal and temperate forests of Eastern Europe and Russia, a brief sketch of some of the Bank's past lending which has affected forests helps to put the greening of the Bank in perspective.

Settling Indonesia's Outer Islands

In the early 1980s, the military governments ruling the two single countries with the world's most extensive areas of tropical rainforest, Indonesia and Brazil, were successful in obtaining large World Bank loans to open up and colonize the outer edges of their respective empires. The World Bank contributed about $500 million directly to Indonesia's transmigration programme, a contribution that helped to mobilize hundreds of millions of additional dollars from other bilateral and multilateral sources. The goal of the transmigration programme was to move millions of Indonesian peasants from Java and some of the smaller central islands to Indonesia's outer islands of Sumatra, Kalimantan, Sulawesi and West Irian. Between 1979 and 1984 alone, an estimated 1.8 million people were resettled by the Indonesian government under this programme.

Indonesia's outer islands, which contain an estimated 10 per cent of the world's remaining tropical rainforest and half of that remaining in Asia, are home to indigenous peoples whose traditional claims on the land are often in conflict with the claims of the transmigrants. While traditional shifting cultivation and forest gathering activities have provided livelihoods for indigenous peoples, the agricultural practices of the transmigrants are mostly unsuitable for food-crop production on the poor soil. Severe social hardship for both local people and transmigrants and the relentless ecological destruction of forest lands as a result of the transmigration programme have been widely documented.[35]

Estimates put the rate of deforestation in Indonesia at up to 4600 square miles a year,[36] placing Indonesia among the world's tropical countries with the highest rate of deforestation.[37] While logging contributes significantly to this high deforestation rate, experts estimate that the transmigration programme has, and will continue to be, responsible for four to five times as much annual deforestation as that directly attributable to logging.[38]

Colonizing Brazil's Amazon Frontier

In Brazil, the military governments perceived the wilderness of the Amazon frontier as a threat to national security and embarked on massive programmes of highway construction, agricultural colonization and mineral exploitation that have entailed the systematic destruction of the Amerindian cultures of Brazil.[39] Critical funding for the mammoth enterprise was either directly provided by the World Bank or through World Bank-sponsored negotiations with other international and national agencies and private banks. The 1982 World Bank loan of $304.5 million to finance the infrastructure for an iron-ore mine, a railway and a deep-water port, is a case in point, as the World Bank project became the centre-piece of the much larger Greater Carajas development scheme totalling $4 billion in investments and catalysing a much broader destruction that was not considered in the environmental assessment. The loan agreement contained provisions to protect the environment in the heavily forested project area, as well as a Special Project to assist the 40 Indian communities who lived near the iron-ore mine and the railroad.[40] The environmental and indigenous people's protection provisions, however, were inadequately implemented, leading to a resolution by the European Parliament in May 1992 which denounced the iron-ore mine as an ecological disaster.[41]

Another well-known example is the Bank's support for Brazil's Northwest Region Development Programme, known by its Portuguese acronym Polonoroeste. Between 1981 and 1983 the World Bank provided $440 million in loans for Polonoroeste, a substantial part of which was used to build the 1500-kilometre Amazon highway which links south-central Brazil with the northwestern Amazon state of Rondônia. Tens of thousands of settlers, many of them made landless by the ever-increasing concentration of land in the hands of large landowners in southern Brazil, were lured to the area with promises of land. Analogous to the situation in Indonesia's outer islands, the Amazon soils are largely unsuitable for permanent agricultural settlement and a year or two after cultivating a plot of land, the settlers would see the land become barren and be forced to move on and clear a new patch of forest. In addition, government subsidies for equally unsustainable cattle ranching attracted investments by wealthy Brazilians who sought to hedge their money against inflation by acquiring land in the proximity of the World Bank-financed infrastructure development in the Amazon frontier. Provisions made for protecting the region's approximately 10,000 Amerindians were mostly flouted and the needs of other forest-dwelling communities, such as the *seringueiros*, or rubber-tappers, whose livelihoods depend directly on a variety of products that the intact forest provides, did not receive attention. Polonoroeste transformed the state of Rondônia, which is about the size of the United Kingdom, into the burning inferno that, documented by NASA satellite photographs, began to make international headlines.

GROWING ENVIRONMENTAL PRESSURE

Environmental organizations in the United States, which had been spearheading a growing international movement to make the environment an integral part of World Bank policy, were successful in obtaining support from leaders of both political parties in the US Congress. About two dozen congressional hearings about the Bank's environmental negligence helped to bring forward legislation requiring that the US Executive Director to the Bank should promote environmental reform and report back on the progress being made by the Bank on a regular basis.

Reflecting the growing pressure on the Bank was the admission in 1987 by the then World Bank President, Barber Conable, that the World Bank shared the responsibility for the ecological problems of its loans and his announcement of sweeping environmental reforms.[42] Barber Conable announced a 16-fold increase in staff in a newly created Central Environment Department as well as the creation of regional environmental units for each of the Bank's four operational regions (Africa, Asia, Latin America and the Caribbean, and Europe and the Middle East), which would closely monitor the environmental impact of Bank projects. In addition he announced increased World Bank efforts to alleviate tropical deforestation by vastly increasing Bank lending in the forestry sector and promised greater cooperation with non-governmental organizations.[43]

Nine weeks before his assassination in December 1988, Francisco Alves (Chico) Mendes Filho, the leader of the struggle of rubber-tappers and other forest peoples in Northwest Brazil to protect the Amazon rainforest, followed up Barber Conable's promise of greater cooperation with the non-governmental sector. He wrote a letter to the World Bank President in which he expressed the opposition of the rubber-tappers to one of the World Bank's new generation of so-called environmental projects. In his letter, Mendes warned that the $317 million Rondônia and Mato Grosso Natural Resource Management project, which had been prepared without proper consultation with the people who were directly affected by it, would be a sad replay of the earlier forest colonization schemes that had been funded under the Polonoroeste loans: '. . . a lot of money will be spent on infrastructures which do not mean anything to the peoples of the forest and the maintenance of which will not be sustainable'.[44] Chico Mendes' letter never received a response from the World Bank. But the world-wide publicity surrounding his brutal murder captivated world public opinion and created awareness about the tragic destruction of the world's rainforest as no previous event ever had.

Increased Lending for Forestry as an Environmental Solution

The Bank did follow up Barber Conable's other promise. Its response to the crisis was to increase loans for forestry projects, including its participation in the Tropical Forestry Action Plan (TFAP), an $8 billion plan which was coordinated by the UN Food and Agriculture Organization to spur forest investments. Non-governmental organizations began to analyse TFAPs for individual countries and concluded that the TFAP was largely focused on industrial forest exploitation, with only lip-service being paid to the ecological functions of forests and the value of non-timber forest products which provide for the livelihoods of hundreds of millions of forest-dwelling people worldwide.[45] After the World Resources Institute, a Washington think-tank which helped to develop the TFAP concept, published its own devastating TFAP critique,[46] the World Bank increasingly distanced itself from the TFAP.

But TFAP-style projects were what was coming out of the newly enlarged forestry project pipeline. In 1989 the World Wide Fund for Nature (WWF) prepared a critique of a forestry sector loan to the West African nation of Guinea, which official Bank statements had been promoting as a model project for the management and protection of Guinea's forests. Quoting the Bank's Staff Appraisal Report, the WWF found that the economic feasibility of the $8 million project was entirely based on increased government revenues from stumpage fees collected on logging operations, which would be facilitated further by building 75km of roads around the Ziama and Diecke forest areas, Guinea's last two areas of still largely intact rainforest.[47] Guinean environmentalists were very critical of how the project was being entirely prepared and run by foreign experts, who were paying no attention to the needs and priorities of local people and even excluded the local forest administration from participation in the project.[48]

It took the next West African forestry loan, an $80 million loan for Côte d'Ivoire lent on non-concessional terms, to raise questions in the minds of some members of the World Bank's Board as to the veracity of the environmental claims made by Bank management when presenting forestry projects to the Board for approval. World Bank documents state that the project was '... designed to substantially check forest destruction and to protect wildlife through demarcating 1.5 million hectares of rain forests'.[49] But environmental groups were able to raise questions about the increased logging the project was promoting in Côte d'Ivoire, a country which is suffering from one of the highest rates of deforestation in the world. They also showed that the project would entail the forced resettlement of up to 200,000 people without adequate planning.[50] *The New York Times* reported that the Côte d'Ivoire forestry project was set to include the largest forced resettlement under a World Bank-financed project in Africa.[51]

E Patrick Coady, then the Executive Director to the World Bank representing the United States, the Bank's largest shareholder, took the unprecedented decision to abstain from voting for the project on environmental grounds. He was concerned that neither the 'sustainable forest management' nor the resettlement component of the project were satisfactorily addressed during the project's preparation.[52]

The New Forest Policy and its Aftermath

The environmental storm surrounding the Côte d'Ivoire project led to a significant development. The Bank's Board of Directors requested that World Bank management prepare a new Forest Policy to guide lending operations in the future and to avoid new ecological disasters and, one may add, public relations débâcles.

During preparation of this new policy, non-governmental organizations were consulted by the World Bank team in charge and had several opportunities to comment on draft policy documents. Although the final result, the 1991 World Bank Forest Policy, was a compromise, it was largely welcomed by the environmental community as an important step towards an ecologically and socially responsible approach to forests by the world's leading lender to the forest sector. At the centre of the new policy are the principles of a precautionary approach toward forest utilization and the ban on all Bank financing of commercial logging operations in primary moist tropical forest. The policy establishes a clear mandate for Bank operations in the forest sector: to empower local people, to help governments to reform their policies and to develop their institutions.[53]

But what has actually happened as a result of the new Forest Policy? After adoption of the new Policy, the Bank's annual lending for forestry doubled in comparison to the previous seven years, amounting to over $500 million per year supporting projects with a total cost of about $1 billion. Has the increase in quantity been accompanied by an increase in quality? A recent Bank review of the forest sector policy gives reason to doubt that on-the-ground Bank operations have actually improved as a result of the policy. The Bank maintains its ban on financing logging in moist tropical rainforest (although, as logging in these forests is so profitable, direct financial support is hardly needed). Although carefully phrased, the review makes it clear that the Bank continues to finance forest production in, for example, the African countries of Cameroon, Côte d'Ivoire and Gabon, where primary moist tropical forests are definitely at stake.[54] Although public participation in forest projects by affected communities has been recognized by the Forest Policy to be an essential element in making projects sustainable, the review notes that social issues remain essentially neglected. Addressing social questions and the needs of indigenous peoples has once again been postponed to the future, while lending for forest protection has been modest.[55] In her statement about the review, the US Executive Director to the World Bank regrets that 'coverage of social issues is inadequate, as is participation by stakeholders in decision-making'.[56]

The Bank's struggle with the development and implementation of its Forest Policy illustrates that, despite policy reforms, key aspects that are necessary for the long-term survival of forests and their biodiversity remain marginal in Bank operations. The loan portfolio has instead revealed an unprecedented increase in forestry lending to support large-scale commercial forestry (including indirect support for logging in primary tropical rainforest), while the ecological and social aspects of forests are neglected. The new Forest Policy is adequate and plenty of useful studies have been conducted by World Bank staff, but a significant overhaul of the Bank's on-the-ground operations remains an urgent task to be carried out.

Adjustment Lending and the Environment

The International Monetary Fund has traditionally been charged with lending to countries with balance-of-payments problems. In exchange for the loans, countries commit themselves to adjusting macroeconomic policies, such as opening up their economies to international trade and practising fiscal austerity to reduce domestic deficits. Since the onslaught of the international debt crisis in the early 1980s, the World Bank has also begun to lend for policy reforms, dedicating about one-fifth of its lending resources to it. Often, the two sister organizations work in tandem, and a country will only be eligible for a World Bank loan if it has adopted an IMF-sponsored adjustment programme.

The monetary and fiscal policies promoted through structural adjustment loans create an economic framework that can determine land-use patterns, which in turn have decisive influence on the way water, soil and other natural resources are used. For example, a currency devaluation, which is routinely prescribed by structural adjustment programmes to address balance-of-payments problems, may increase the export profitability of a natural resource and set the incentives for unsustainable exploitation. The threat that IMF programmes place on the environment is exacerbated by even greater difficulties with accountability, transparency and participation than those that plague the Bank's projects.

Harvard economist Jeffrey Sachs, himself an active supporter of structural adjustment in the formerly Communist countries of Eastern Europe, has criticized the extreme secrecy with which IMF operations are negotiated and implemented.[57] The general outline of IMF-promoted policy reforms are known all too well to the point where former Russian Finance Minister Boris Fedorov jokes 'they are citing the IMF, the way they used to cite Karl Marx'.[58] But the details of agreed structural adjustment programmes are kept tightly confidential and rarely reach the public domain. Pressure for environmental and social reform in IMF operations has barely made a dent in the armour of this powerful institution. The prevailing orthodoxy is that IMF-supported adjustment programmes lead to macroeconomic stability, which is a motor of economic growth. Economic growth is what will solve both social and environmental problems. In other words, orthodox economic policies promoted through structural adjustment are also good environmental policies. While this may hold true in some cases, such as the removal of subsidies that encourage the overuse of energy, for example, the simple aphorism that growth is good is unlikely to bring about the much-needed coordination of developmental and environmental policy that is required for sustainable development.

Several US legislative efforts starting in 1989 called for environmental reforms at the IMF and IMF Managing Director Michel Camdessus has spoken of the need for 'high quality growth', rhetorically acknowledging the importance of considering the link between macroeconomic measures, poverty and the environment. The result has been a few token gestures, such as instructing IMF staff to be 'mindful of the interplay between economic policies, economic activity and environmental change'.[59]

The World Bank, like the IMF, largely ignores the disproportionate penalties that structural adjustment imposes on the socially disadvantaged classes and environmental protection. Unlike lending for projects, structural adjustment lending is exempt from environmental assessments. Increasing research efforts in the Bank's Environment Department, however, recognize that the sectoral and macrolevel economic policies promoted through structural adjustment are of 'great importance in determining environmentally related behaviour'.[60] The Environment Department's most recent research paper notes that the sectoral and macroeconomic policies promoted by the Bank continue to be divorced from the Bank's work in the areas of National Environmental Action Plans (NEAPs) and Country Environment Strategy Papers (CESPs). The paper proposes that economic documents should systematically discuss environmental issues, while environmental documents should strengthen their analyses of economic linkages. This proposal is very useful and will lay the groundwork for the much needed integration of the Bank's economic and environmental work.

Balance-of-payments sustainability, an expression used by the IMF to indicate that a country is in a position to pay for its imports and to service its foreign debt, is not the same as environmental sustainability. Reduction of developing countries' foreign debts, however, is one measure which is likely to benefit both areas. Unfortunately, the Bretton Woods institutions have made little progress towards reducing multilateral debt.[61]

INSPECTION PANEL

In the light of the general slowness of environmental reforms, the establishment of an independent inspection panel at the World Bank represents a promising and potentially path-breaking new development, because it introduces an element of Bank accountability to the people who are the intended beneficiaries of Bank-funded projects. For the first time in the Bank's 50-year history, community organizations or non-governmental organizations representing citizens harmed by Bank projects can request a full-scale investigation of the situation if there are indications that the Bank is ignoring or violating its own policies and procedures.

A string of well-publicized World Bank-funded development débâcles over the past decade have created the public pressure and support from law-makers for the establishment of such an inspection unit. The final impetus, though, came through legislation in the US Congress which instructed the US Treasury Department to urge the establishment of an inspection panel.[62]

An important precedent had already been established when the controversy over the Sardar Sarovar Dam on India's Narmada River led to an independent review of the project by a high-level commission known as the Morse Commission. In its well-documented investigation, the Morse Commission concluded that the Bank was failing to implement its policies on involuntary resettlement and on energy.[63] On the occasion of the release of the independent review, Bradford Morse, a former member of the US Congress and head of the United Nations Development Programme, summarized the Commission's findings: 'We think the Sardar Sarovar Projects are flawed, that resettlement and rehabilitation of all those displaced by the projects is not possible under prevailing circumstances, and that the environmental impacts of the projects have not been properly considered or adequately addressed'.[64] The combined effects of the Morse Commission Report and the above-mentioned Wapenhans Report generated the adverse publicity and pressure that caused the Bank to take action.

The World Bank Inspection Panel was created by a resolution of the World Bank's Board of Directors[65] and officially opened its office one year later in September 1994. The Panel consists of one full-time chairman and two part-time panel members, who were nominated by the Bank's President and appointed by its Board of Directors. The current structure will be in place until April 1996, at which time the Bank's Board will review the experience of the inspection function and decide if and how it will continue in the future.

The nomination process and the intricate operating procedures of the Inspection Panel have led some organizations to question the independence and accountability of the Panel.[66] For example, while the Inspection Panel will receive complaints from citizens' groups that feel adversely affected by Bank projects, the Inspection Panel's initial role is limited to requesting Bank management to provide the Panel with evidence on how Bank policies and procedures have been or are intended to be implemented. Based on the Bank's management response, the Inspection Panel will make a recommendation to the Executive Directors as to whether the matter should be investigated. It is the Executive Directors who will then decide if an investigation is warranted or not, and it is only at this point that the documentation on the complaint and the recommendations made will be available to the public.[67] Even if an investigation has been commissioned, there is no obligation for the Executive Directors to act on its findings. Despite these possible constraints, the work of the Inspection Panel could be ground-breaking and it will be the first cases to be brought to the Panel that will ultimately reveal the Panel's real independence from the institution that created it.

NEPAL'S ARUN III HYDROELECTRIC DAM – A PRECEDENT-SETTING CASE

The first such request for the investigation of a particular project was received by the Panel in November 1994 and concerned the proposed Arun III hydroelectric dam project in Nepal. The request was made by Nepalese citizens who stated that they had been adversely affected during the design and appraisal of the project by violations of several Bank policies and procedures, especially the policy relating to involuntary resettlement and the operational directive on environmental assessment.[68]

Although confidential, copies of the Inspection Panel's recommendation to the Executive Directors reached the public through unofficial channels. The Panel's memorandum states that, in the light of the cost of the project, which is larger than the entire annual budget for the kingdom of Nepal, and the extensive impact that this concentration of investment will have on living conditions throughout Nepal, the Panel found that alternatives to this mega-project had not been sufficiently studied. In conclusion, the Panel's memorandum to the Executive Directors states '... the Panel has reached a unanimous recommendation: that apparent violations of policy do exist that require further investigation'.[69]

Apparent efforts of the Bank staff to derail a full investigation of the project,[70] were overtaken when the Bank's new President, James D Wolfensohn, decided to withdraw support for the Arun III project proposal. Although the project was stopped, no full investigation was ever authorized, allowing Wolfensohn to maintain that the Inspection Panel's initial findings had confirmed that the environmental and social mitigation actions 'currently stipulated for the proposed project were satisfactory'. Wolfensohn acknowledged, however, that the public debate on the project, amplified by the Inspection Panel complaint, had helped to identify environmental and social risks associated with the project that Nepal could not realistically have managed at present.[71]

While they are pleased that the dam project was halted, NGO observers of the Panel process remain concerned that the Inspection Panel is being side-lined, and its limited independence compromised by an increasingly defensive Bank management and Bank staff.[72] More recent claims to the Inspection Panel have been frustrated. Two additional claims were registered by the Panel in 1995, one challenging the environmental impacts of a power project in Tanzania, the second a natural resources management project in Rondônia, Brazil.[73] The Panel did not recommend an inspection for the Tanzanian project, but it did find that the Rondonian claim justified further investigation.

The Board was unconvinced, however, and has asked the Panel to justify further its recommendation before the Board would determine whether investigation should take place. The growing level of tension between the Board, Bank management and the Panel is not leaving much room for the Panel to take effective action. A review of the resolution which established the Panel is scheduled to take place during 1996. NGOs will call for fundamental changes in the resolution with the goal of enabling the Panel to decide, independently, whether to pursue investigations into a project in the initial phase of a request, without interference from the Board or Bank management.

An additional, longer-term threat to the Inspection Panel's effectiveness is the fact that the World Bank is in the process of simplifying and shortening its existing policies and procedures, including those related to environmental and social impact. The reason for the new system, which will be put in place gradually, is to avoid overwhelming task managers with the complexity of the existing policies and to introduce more flexibility into the process.[74] An inherent risk in this shift is that at least some of the new policies might be sufficiently open-ended to make it difficult to claim that violations of Bank policies and procedures have occurred, leaving the Inspection Panel with a significantly diminished mandate.

However, the Inspection Panel promises to be a path-breaking innovation which is likely to have an impact on the evolution of international policy. The World Bank's General Counsel, Ibrahim Shihata, describes the new situation as part of a 'phenomenal expansion of rights of individuals and private groups derived directly from international law'.[75]

A GREEN LIGHT AT THE END OF THE TUNNEL?

In an interview which was granted on the occasion of the 50th anniversary of the Bretton Woods institutions, former World Bank President, Lewis Preston, stated, 'I think that the mistake the Bank has paid the highest price for was not recognizing the importance of the environment'.[76] But he went on to argue that environmental criticism was now 'very much out of date', because, among other developments, in the 1980s the Bank employed three environmental specialists on a staff of 11,000, while today there are 200.[77] This is important progress and much of the research and policy work being done in the Environment Department, as well as in some other departments, is pioneering and is making an important contribution to the international debate on the environment and development. Other multilateral and bilateral aid agencies would clearly benefit from emulating some of the Bank's work. For example, important work has been done recently by Robert Picciotto, the Director-General of the Bank's Operations Evaluation Department, on the Bank's project cycle. In view of the fact that about one-third of all Bank-supported operations completed recently do not reach their major relevant goals, Picciotto proposes a new project cycle for Bank operations, which would replace the existing one, which, grounded in engineering tradition, is excessively rigid and non-participatory, and suited only to a very narrow set of infrastructure development projects.[78] The new project cycle, described as a 'learning cycle', would place emphasis on 'listening' and would actively involve project beneficiaries in decision-making and thereby eliminate costly project failures.[79]

At present, however, as Willi Wapenhans notes, the 'cultural change' within the institution has not taken place, because the 'recognized performance criteria' have not changed.[80] As long as 'meeting lending targets', ie approving large amounts of money speedily, is the yardstick for advancing careers at the Bank, the well-intentioned, competent and sometimes brave World Bank staff who work hard to implement the Bank's stated goals of poverty reduction and environmental protection, will remain at a definite disadvantage. As critically important as the work of these staff members is, it remains marginal in an institution that continues to be geared towards loan approval at the expense of other considerations. There appears to be a dim green light at the end of the tunnel. How brightly it burns will depend on growing commitment within the institution, and the continued scrutiny of the outside world.

9 THE GLOBAL ENVIRONMENT FACILITY

Helen Sjöberg

We see the weakness of the exposed foundations – perhaps we can learn how, and where, to rebuild the institutional fabric so it can better withstand the shocks of change. (*R M MacIver, 1944*)[1]

INTRODUCTION

The inability of the international system to go beyond problem identification to effective common action is frequently blamed on the inertia of international institutions. Hardly a day goes by when frustrations are not vented on the main international organizations in the UN and Bretton Woods systems. These systems are now 50 years old, and although the problems we encounter have changed dramatically, adaptation to a new reality has been difficult to institute. Theories of international relations have no problem in showing why this is the case; now, as before, the underlying reason for inaction rests with the structure of the international system which, far from inducing governments to expand their vision beyond the national horizon, encourages states to act in accordance with narrowly defined self-interests. As a result, the international arena is characterized by pervasive collective action problems, in which both good intentions and urgent problems become trapped.[2]

The environmental regimes that are currently being developed are not exempt from these larger constraints.[3] But as relative newcomers to the international arena they differ from older forms of international organization, and display some more modern characteristics that are of interest if we want to understand the potential for qualitative change in international arrangements.[4]

Rather than creating comprehensive formal organizations, recent efforts at regime building have focused on the creation of a number of separate legal agreements which are implemented nationally. In addition to reducing the collective action problems that commonly stand in the way for agreement, one additional advantage of this procedure is its flexibility: it becomes worthwhile to agree to weak agreements since they can be strengthened incrementally in successive rounds of negotiations.[5] Initial investigations into these agreements have suggested that they have been effective in terms of raising political concern, improving domestic capacity for environmental management, and overcoming uncertainty and mistrust that prevent cooperation.[6]

The very success of this method, however, gives rise to problems. The sheer number of new environmental agreements causes concerns about implementation – so called treaty congestion – in particular in developing countries where both capacity and resources are limited. This worry is compounded when we consider the difficulties of mobilizing significant multilateral financial resources to assist developing countries with the process of implementing the agreements.

The most successful attempt to add funding to an agreement is the Multilateral Fund for the Montreal Protocol. In this case, countries managed to agree on a moderately sized fund for the purpose of assisting developing countries with the incremental cost of complying with the Protocol's provisions to phase out ozone-depleting substances.[7] As a rule, however, funding has not been forthcoming, and the multiple conventions have been accompanied by a fragmented system of small trust funds that primarily cover administrative expenses.[8] In essence, the result is that effective international action on the environment via treaty is limited to areas where national resources are available. It has made cooperation between developed countries relatively successful, while seriously hampering the participation of developing countries.

These concerns about the treaty method brings us to the subject of this chapter: the Global Environment Facility (GEF). This facility was created to assist developing countries in their efforts to address global environmental problems. It is a specialized mechanism that provides financial resources only to developing countries and only in four global problem areas: climate change, biodiversity, ozone depletion and international waters.

The institutional form of the GEF is unusual in its reliance on existing international instruments. Where the above focal areas are covered by a treaty, as in the climate change and biodiversity areas, the GEF is designed to serve the Conventions by translating their input into financed work programmes. In addition, the GEF is connected on the more practical level to three established formal organizations, UNDP, UNEP and the World Bank, which are referred to as implementing agencies. These agencies collaboratively manage the work programmes. It follows that the GEF holds a key position if action on global environmental problems is to be integrated. The GEF function is to incorporate input from more than one Convention, transforming it into programmes for action, and employing the three implementing agencies for delivery. In other words, integration does not take place through coordination from above, but rather at the level where decisions on action are made.

This novel type of arrangement has been controversial from the beginning. Although created as recently as 1990, the GEF is already a facility with a past. After a contentious pilot phase, it was restructured and replenished in a highly political process to become a permanent mechanism in 1994. Despite the changes made in this process, the debate continues as to the role the GEF should play in the larger regime for global environmental action. This chapter seeks to increase the understanding of what the GEF is, how it emerged as a pilot facility, the context in which it was restructured, and why it came to be surrounded by controversy. Following the account of the evolution of the GEF, a brief assessment of the restructured facility is provided. Finally, the argument is developed that the GEF 'model' holds considerable merit when viewed in relation to the overall institutional arrangements that are emerging to address global environmental problems.

Bringing About the Pilot Phase

The creation of the Global Environment Facility was a break with the cumulative step-by-step process that characterizes regime-building in the environmental area. It was swiftly launched into action as a $1 billion dollar experiment. The boldness of the initiative betrays that it was not created via the regular diplomatic process. It did not follow a pattern whereby all concerned countries craft a legally binding agreement and to which funding is added in accordance with an agreed burden-sharing formula. In the case of the GEF, many aspects happened in reverse order. Funding was offered before a clear purpose was articulated, operations began before funding criteria were established, and the Facility was up and running with essential components of its governance system deliberately left to be worked out in practice. If we consider that the mobilization of multilateral resources is an area where international cooperation regularly fails, the magnitude and the speed stand out as highly unusual. It calls for a closer investigation into how the GEF was made possible.

Riding on the wave of concern for international environmental problems in the late 1980s, France had taken the initiative in September 1989.[9] The French Finance Minister proposed to the Development Committee that the World Bank should investigate the possibility of establishing a programme for environmental funding in developing countries.[10] The Minister declared France's willingness to sponsor the programme with FFr 900 million over three years, an offer that was quickly seconded by Germany.[11] The idea to provide additional finance for environmental purposes was not new. Following the publication of the Brundtland Report in 1987, a number of proposals had been forwarded.[12] Concern for the lack of funding for international environmental problems was widespread by 1989, and the time for proposals opportune. September alone brought two notable proposals in addition to that of the French: one by the World Resources Institute for an International Environmental Facility,[13] and another by Indian Prime Minister Rajiv Gandhi who suggested a Planet Protection Fund for the transfer of environmentally benign technologies to developing countries.[14] These and many other proposals remained on the level of general discussion.

The viability of the French initiative was enhanced by a number of distinctive features. Without a doubt, the audacious move of putting money on the table before the purpose was specified had a decisive effect. The decision to hand the proposal to the World Bank also had a significant influence on the outcome. Settled with the task of developing the proposal and mobilizing resources, the World Bank turned to potential contributors first. Within governments, the World Bank finds its constituency among ministries dealing with development finance. The ability to mobilize support via this group was effective since their institutional connection to finance made it possible to mobilize funds on a large scale, and agreement was made easier by the relative coherence of views and values that exist within the professional coalition.[15] Following bilateral consultations, the World Bank gathered 17 developed countries for a first meeting in March 1990. By November, 24 participants, including seven developing countries,[16] managed to complete the negotiations. They had created a Facility that reflected the priorities from a financial perspective.

The result was innovative by any standards. More than a trust fund, but less than a new institution, the GEF was a new breed on the international arena. The mandate of providing funds for the global, as distinct from the national, benefit was a novel feature. The consequence was that, although funding in practice would be provided to developing countries, everyone would stand to benefit – this was not a case of charity or development assistance.[17] The attempt to combine existing management capabilities of the UNDP, the UNEP and the World Bank was an unusual approach. Establishing a bridge between the Bretton Woods and the UN systems through a substantial venture was seen to have value beyond the GEF. Finally, entrusting $1 billion for exploring how the mandate was best fulfilled was nothing less than daring. Since the design was novel – and soon to be controversial – a brief explication of the reasoning behind the purpose, the pilot strategy and the management arrangement is provided.

The GEF's purpose was to make it financially possible for developing countries to participate in efforts to combat global environmental problems in four areas: climate change, biodiversity, ozone depletion and international waters. The choice of global problems as well as the selection of the four areas was made on political grounds. These were problems that had received considerable attention from scientists, environmental activists and the media; as a result, they had passed through the informal test of reaching general public acceptance as issues of global concern.[18] An additional factor was the concern in developing countries that environmental issues would be used to impose so called 'green conditionalities' on the development process. This spoke in favour of an approach whereby funds allocated for the environment could be 'additional' to, or separated from, development assistance.

From a financial perspective, the concept of additionality was important. First, contributions for global purposes had to be additional to regular development assistance in order not to divert funding from national development priorities. This requirement was particularly important to representatives from developing countries. Secondly, it had to be additional to efforts by development agencies to incorporate environmental considerations into the regular development programmes; the GEF could not be allowed to serve as an excuse for not improving environmental practices generally. Finally, it had to be additional, or incremental, to the measures undertaken by developing countries to deal with their national environmental priorities. These requirements pointed to a conceptual division of labour whereby national environmental concerns were handled via regular development channels, leaving the GEF to finance projects or that part of a project which had environmental benefits of global relevance. In more technical terms, the GEF would finance the incremental cost of making a project yield global environmental benefits.[19]

The problem was that no agency had experience in putting together work programmes for the funding of global environmental issues. It was well known that conventional methods for calculating costs and benefits were not well suited for environmental resources where benefits may be uncertain, diffuse and/or far into the future. In this case the benefits were global by definition and it was not known how such projects would best be approached. The strategy was to start the facility off on an exploratory basis to learn in practice how these problems could be addressed in a cost-effective manner.[20] To establish the facility as a three-year pilot phase made sense from this perspective.

Another reason that made the pilot concept attractive was that participants had different visions for the future. Some European countries took note of the Conventions on Climate Change and Biodiversity (see Chapter 4) for which negotiations had just begun. While it was too soon to guess the outcome of the negotiations, these countries envisioned a set of environmental conventions for which the GEF could serve as the financial mechanism. Other countries, eg the United States, focused on the need to integrate global environmental problems into mainstream environmental and developmental activities. In this view, the GEF was a temporary arrangement that should be wound down once methods for integration were better developed. Both perspectives could support a pilot programme with the aim of exploring how global problems in the four areas could be tackled effectively.

The tripartite management arrangement by the GEF's three Implementing Agencies, the UNDP, the UNEP and the World Bank (see Chapter 8), fitted well into the exploratory rationale. It grew out of the resistance against the creation of a new international institution, which would add to a growing international bureaucracy. The notion of building on existing capabilities found unanimous support from the governments involved. Since the GEF was to be an operationally oriented financial mechanism, France's decision to put the proposal to the World Bank was not controversial within financial circles; they supported a design that made the World Bank central. A number of countries with close ties to the UN system, however, pushed for including the UNDP and the UNEP. Since these agencies find their constituencies within other ministries, their inclusion broadened the appeal of the GEF both among and within governments.

The GEF's Implementing Agencies had both common and differentiated tasks. The UNEP was to contribute scientific and technical expertise, and ensure that the GEF was in coherence with other international environmental agreements. The UNDP was given key responsibility for technical assistance and was expected to draw on its broad-based network of representatives within recipient countries. Investment projects, which were expected to be the dominant project type, remained the domain of the World Bank. Beyond this general division of labour, the interrelations were based on informal arrangements which the agencies were expected to work out among themselves. The founders had ensured that the World Bank would have the upper hand in this situation. The World Bank was assigned two formal roles in addition to being one of three Implementing Agencies: it was the administrator of the facility on a day-to-day basis, and it was the trustee for trust fund which was the financial and legal centre-piece of the GEF. The dominant role of the World Bank was to become a continuous source of criticism.

In this account, then, the main factors that allowed the GEF to pass through the hurdles which tripped up other proposals were:

(1) The initial bait of the French proposal.
(2) A coalition made up by governmental branches connected to finance and led by the World Bank.

(3) The global environmental purpose as distinct from development-related environmental problems.
(4) An agreement on an exploratory pilot phase over three years, which allowed potential conflicts to be deferred.[21]

The idea had been to test the GEF model operationally during the three pilot years. Before the experiment could find and mend its ways, however, the GEF was put through a political test. The same factors that gave the facility a thrust into action became political liabilities when the GEF was related to the broader international arena where its legitimacy was seriously questioned.

Controversy and Decisions in the Context of Rio

External developments generated pressure to revise the GEF arrangements already during the first months of its operational phase. The momentum for change derived from the preparatory processes for the Conventions on Climate Change and Biodiversity, and the United Nations Conference on Environment and Development (UNCED). A main outcome of UNCED was to be Agenda 21, a blueprint for action towards a sustainable future.[22] All three processes – the two Conventions and Agenda 21 – were to be completed by the Rio Conference in June 1992, and although they were negotiated separately, there were strong political linkages between them. These processes mobilized a broad set of actors around issues of the environment and development. The Conventions were negotiated primarily by people from environmental ministries and the UNCED brought in people from the areas of foreign affairs and development planning. In addition, the UNCED process strengthened the network of non-governmental organizations. Most importantly, the broader participation in these fora was accompanied by a shift towards the perspective and priorities of developing countries. When environmental issues first emerged, the developing countries had remained sceptical. Over time, however, they came to see sustainable development as an opportunity, not only to improve the environment, but also to establish a more equal relationship between the North and the South. Issues of governance and finance were both essential in this vision.

It was therefore not surprising that financial arrangements became the most controversial issue in the negotiations of the Conventions as well as Agenda 21. In early 1992, estimates for the cost of funding Agenda 21 were published, pointing to amounts more than double the total levels of existing development assistance.[23] It was followed by a complete deadlock between the North and the South on financial issues in all negotiating fora in the spring. The South put forward a demand for a large generic Green Fund to finance the activities of Agenda 21.[24] For the global environmental problems under negotiation, they envisaged separate windows as part of each Convention. (This preference was shared by most of the NGOs, as well as by some environmental ministries in developed countries.)

Most OECD countries – the United States being a notable exception – did accept that some new and additional funding was needed for Agenda 21, although they rejected any notion of a new generic environmental fund. They were unified by a common aversion for funding mechanisms where allocations would be 'politically' determined. Instead, they argued that efficiency was better served by mechanisms where technical and financial criteria were decisive. Both developing and developed countries consistently pushed for financial arrangements where they would have a controlling interest: the former preferred UN-style arrangements where one-country-one-vote favours their advantage in numbers; the latter connected financial arrangements to the Bretton Woods system, which rewards contributions. This perspective informed the developed countries when they offered the GEF as their preferred vehicle for additional funding of the global environmental problems that were soon to be covered by conventions.[25]

The GEF was irrevocably drawn into the larger political debate that surrounded the UNCED and the Conventions, where it did not receive a warm welcome. From the very beginning, the GEF had been criticized for its connection to the World Bank. The NGO network, which was concerned with environmental issues, had for a long time targeted the World Bank for promoting environmentally destructive projects and development approaches. The critique intensified as the implementing agencies of the GEF rapidly developed two large tranches of projects before scientific and technical criteria were in place, and in a manner that followed the regular procedures of the agencies. A number of NGOs had hoped that the GEF would have an impact on World Bank conduct; they were concerned by the 'business as usual' approach. The NGOs found the GEF projects wanting in terms of transparency, accountability, consultation with local communities and project quality. They were joined in their dislike for the World Bank by the Group of 77, which spoke for the South. The UNCED agenda also reintroduced the national and local perspectives, which for a time had been overshadowed by global problems. The argument that global problems are inextricably linked to local and national problems gained general acceptance in the UNCED context. From this perspective, the GEF scope of four global problems was seen as narrow and unresponsive to the environmental concerns of developing countries.

It was apparent that, as currently structured, the GEF would not be approved as the financial mechanism of the Conventions. Clearly, the Conventions could not entrust the funding arrangement to a pilot programme; the GEF would have to be a permanent structure. In addition, the narrow scope, inattention to national priorities, the informal and donor-dominated governance system, and the dominant role of the World Bank caused concern among many negotiators. The GEF participants therefore discussed future options for the Facility. On 30 April 1992 they agreed on the principles that should guide the restructuring process. They were developed with more than an eye towards the financial arrangements of the Conventions. (Timing was crucial: the International Negotiating Committees for the Conventions had to break the stalemate on finance at their May meetings in order to meet the deadline in Rio in early June.)

The agreed principles reaffirmed that the purpose of the GEF was 'to provide funding of the agreed incremental cost for achieving agreed global environmental benefits'.[26] On the sensitive issue of scope, a compromise was reached whereby the GEF would remain limited to the four original focal areas, but issues of land degradation, such as desertification and deforestation, would be eligible for funding 'as they relate to the focal areas . . .'[27] The principles also reflected a move away from the top-down, experimental approach that had characterized the pilot agreement; in the restructured facility, programmes and projects would be 'country driven and consistent with national priorities designed to support sustainable development'.[28]

The governance system in the permanent facility would strive towards universal membership and be 'transparent and accountable to contributors and recipients alike'. A Participants' Assembly was envisaged that would normally decide by consensus. For occasions when consensus could not be attained, a voting system would be developed that 'would guarantee both a balanced and equitable representation of the interests of the developing countries, as well as give due weight to the funding efforts of the donors'.[29]

The general sense conveyed by the April agreement was more open to the interests of the developing countries, and answered to a number of frequently voiced concerns. It proved sufficient to break the stalemate on financial arrangements, and persuaded the Conventions to give an appropriately restructured GEF permission to operate the financial mechanisms on an interim basis, ie until the Conventions were signed, ratified and the Conferences of the Parties could decide on permanent arrangements.[30] While 'if' and 'but' characterized the endorsement of the GEF, it none the less facilitated and motivated the restructuring process by not ruling out the possibility of an integrated and unified financial mechanism to support Conventions on global environmental issues. The discussion on the appropriateness of such a construction would continue.

Financial Offers at Rio

As thousands of people gathered for the Rio meeting in June 1992, the text on Financial Resources and Mechanisms in Agenda 21 was still in brackets. It would prove the most contentious issue at Rio, and negotiations continued throughout the Conference. Officially, the South held on to their demand for a Green Fund; in practice, they used this notion as a bargaining chip in order for the North to mobilize an alternative financial package. To provide a credible alternative, a number of OECD leaders announced their intentions to provide additional funding for environmental purposes, including the GEF. The single most encouraging statement came from the President of the World Bank, Lewis Preston, who announced that he would seek an 'Earth Increment' as part of the tenth replenishment of the International Development Association (IDA–10).[31] These declarations of prospective funding, combined with a vaguely worded section in Agenda 21 that developed countries should use 'their best efforts' to raise the level of assistance to the UN target of 0.7 per cent of GDP 'as soon as possible', persuaded the developing countries to drop the notion of a Green Fund and agree to include the GEF in Agenda 21.[32] This agreement was based on the understanding that the GEF should not only be restructured, but also that it should be replenished to ensure 'new and additional' financial resources.

A series of financial disappointments followed Rio; it began with the G-7 meeting in July and was followed by an IDA–10 replenishment which did not muster sufficient resources for an additional 'Earth Increment'.[33] It became clear that additional funding for Agenda 21 would not be forthcoming via the UN or Bretton Woods. When participants of the GEF met in late 1992, it was apparent that when it came to new and additional resources, the GEF was, as one representative put it, 'the only game in town'.

Restructuring the GEF

The negotiations to restructure and replenish the GEF began in December 1992. The task, in essence, was to give practical effect to the principles of Rio without sacrificing the operational focus of the pilot phase. The parties involved in the negotiations had grown to represent a wide spectrum. At the first meeting after Rio, the participants decided to abandon the 'entrance fee'[34] in accordance with the agreement to make membership universal.[35] It proved an effective policy: 32 governments had attended the April 1992 meeting; a year later, the number had grown to 61. (By July 1994, the GEF had 115 participating countries.) In terms of the outcome of the negotiations, however, the crucial difference was that the developing countries began to articulate a unified position in the name of the Group of 77. This was a shift away from finance and development ministries which had close ties with the World Bank; instead, the developing countries harmonized their views by way of their representatives to the UN in New York. These were people from the foreign ministries who had also been involved with the UNCED; they brought with them the Southern perspective from that process. Over time, the unified negotiating stance of the Group of 77 contributed to a correspondingly close coordination between the OECD countries. While there were differences also within the groups, the polarization into two camps divided along North–South lines became a reality.

A similar division can be detected with regard to the principles the groups were defending. Put simply, the struggle was argued in terms of legitimacy versus efficiency. The Southern countries invoked the 'spirit of Rio' and put forward their positions in terms of universality, democratic decision-making and transparency. The Northern countries claimed not to be against any of those principles; their concerns, however, centred around cost-effectiveness, efficient management and operational criteria. These two sets of principles corresponded to different governance models: the Southern countries favoured a UN-style system on the basis that it was more democratic and, presumably, because it rewards the many; the North wanted to keep a connection to the Bretton Woods system which they associated with competent management and where votes are weighted according to contribution. In the dynamic of the negotiations, these broad preferences were progressively condensed into specific positions on various governance issues.

The restructuring and replenishment were conducted in separate but parallel negotiations. The linkage between the two was crucial. While replenishment by definition is a situation where the donor countries hold the ultimate vote, the Group of 77 credibly made the case that the level of funding was symbolic of the commitment of the developed countries to the Rio process. In May 1993, the first formal replenishment meeting indicated support for a target of SDR 2–3 billion (which corresponded to US $2.8–4.2 billion).[36] This target was in line with the informal pledges made at Rio. Funding levels, however, are assessed based on an agreed burden-sharing system and therefore vulnerable to domino effects. The European countries had contributed disproportionately large voluntary shares to the pilot phase; in a permanent facility they insisted on a fair burden-sharing system. This led to a complication in the autumn when it became apparent that the United States – which neither promised additional funding at Rio nor indicated their intended funding level in May – was unable to contribute their share of the envisaged total. As a result, the target that had seemed possible just a few months earlier could no longer be attained. A new, reduced goal was set at US $2 billion. While this amount was double that of the pilot phase, it was clearly lower than many had hoped for. The developing countries showed considerable understanding for the distributional problems among the developed countries; they declared that the new target would not get in the way for an agreement, on condition that it was an irreducible final offer. From then on, the amount of US $2 billion became inviolable.

The last meeting was scheduled for December 1993. Since the principles were agreed in April of 1992, they had been manifested in a number of concrete issues. Now they were reduced to a few highly charged issues of governance, which were linked to a delicate balance of burden-sharing. The December meeting showed just how narrow the range of possible agreement was, and how easily a wobble in one area could spread to bring the process down. The meeting ended in failure. In the months that followed, the GEF was left hanging as both the G–77 and the OECD countries withdrew to redefine their bottom lines. Having re-established a certain measure of confidence, the Chairman set the date for a new meeting to take place in Geneva on 14–16 March 1994.

In the meantime, a number of developed country delegations and the Resource Mobilization Department of the World Bank worked hard to convince budget authorities to make funds available. Everybody knew the US $2 billion target was non-negotiable, but a new budget year, linkages to the shares of other countries, doubts about the agreement going too far in the direction of developing countries, and the overall change in priorities on the international agenda – towards, for example, peace-keeping and emergency relief – made money for the environment difficult to mobilize. The efforts were successful; when the final meeting opened with an initial pledging session, the US $2 billion seemed assured. The restructuring negotiations could proceed on firmer ground.

Cautious optimism characterized the mood in Geneva. Preparations were thorough and expectations more realistic. Despite the favourable conditions, agreement did not come easily. A day and a half into the meeting, little progress had been made by the two representatives who negotiated on behalf of the groups. They asked the GEF Chairman to prepare a proposal which could function as the basis for a settlement. The Chairman's mediation succeeded and an agreement to establish a restructured GEF was finally reached.

Agreement on GEF I was a classic compromise solution, oriented towards a careful balance of gains and concessions. An overview of the complex anatomy of the governance system gives an indication of the multiple bargains that were struck. The main components are an Assembly, a Governing Council and a Secretariat. The Assembly is constituted by all participating countries; it will meet every three years to review the general policies of the GEF. The Council is the main governing body with responsibility for operational policies and programmes. It meets every 6 months and is made up of 32 constituencies, distributed as 16 seats for developing countries, 2 for the so-called transitional economies and 14 from developed countries. The decisions are made by consensus. However, should there be a dispute, a voting system is in place where decisions are made on a double-majority basis. (Approval requires 60 per cent of the votes of all countries, as well as votes representing 60 per cent of the contributions.) The voting system hence has characteristics from both the UN and the Bretton Woods systems. Another hybrid solution can be found in the chairmanship of the meetings. It is divided, depending on the subject matter, between a chairperson, a government representative elected from the participants for the duration of the meeting (UN system), and the CEO of the GEF, an international civil servant (Bretton Woods). The CEO also heads the Secretariat and reports to the Council and the Assembly. The Secretariat, although administratively supported by the World Bank, is 'functionally independent' and is responsible for implementing the Council's decisions. The Implementing Agencies remain the same as in the pilot phase.

The Restructured GEF in Perspective

Compromise between the institutional models of the UN and Bretton Woods also represents a compromise in terms of the other dichotomies involved in the process, ie Northern versus Southern power, financial versus broader perspectives on global environmental issues, and efficiency versus legitimacy claims.[37] It remains to be seen how the system will perform in practice. It is possible, however, to point to aspects of the agreement on the GEF that may be of wider significance, and to identify decisive tests in terms of its future role in an emerging framework for handling global environmental problems. The following assessment does not pretend to be a comprehensive evaluation of the facility; instead, it attempts to generate some tentative conclusions through viewing the facility from a number of different analytic viewpoints.

NORTH–SOUTH POWER STRUGGLE

It is tempting to cast an evaluation of the outcome in terms of power and to interpret the GEF as yet another expression of an endemic North–South struggle. To be sure, environmental negotiations on global issues have developed into vivid illustrations of North–South divisions, and the GEF was no exception. The compromise struck on the GEF lends itself to investigation into how the power balance is evolving. The negotiations on the decision-making system, for example, sought to resolve which group would have the primary influence over decisions, and the compromise confirms that the bargaining position of the South is relatively strong when it comes to global environmental issues. Compared with traditional financial mechanisms, the GEF system clearly gives more 'voice' to the South.

One test of this balance will come in the successive replenishments of the GEF. Empirically, the North has been unwilling to entrust large sums of money to UN-style mechanisms where allocations of money are based on what is euphemistically called 'political' criteria. The hybrid system of the GEF may point to a middle road whereby the demands of the South for participation in decision-making are adequately fulfilled, while providing sufficient reassurance to the North that management of the funds is efficient. If the present level of US $2 billion is indicative, it suggests that the level of funding will be significantly higher than in a UN style system, although lower than the amounts entrusted to the Bretton Woods system. Any such assessment should be treated with caution, however, as many other factors influence levels of funding.

A power perspective is oriented towards identifying shifting balances within a given set-up. A North–South focus forcefully illustrates how this was played out in the GEF, but it also covers up more complex and informal actor alliances underneath these obvious divisions, and contributes little to understanding the evolving institutional framework.

Informal Actor Alliances

International environmental agreements usually involve, in one capacity or another, scientists, environmental activists,[38] international lawyers and officials from governmental branches. Since different perspectives are cultivated in different settings, opinions on the appropriateness of an institutional arrangement are likely to vary with institutional membership and loyalty. Informal alliances are found both between different levels in the international governmental hierarchy, and with scientific and other non-governmental networks. For example, a symbiotic relationship often exists between ministries and international agencies. The international agency that sponsors the negotiations commonly relies on its 'constituency' for support. The UNEP calls on environmental ministries, for example, while the UNDP draws on ministries of development planning and foreign affairs. Environmental issues are therefore susceptible to the so called 'where you stand depends on where you sit' syndrome.

The multiconstituency character of the GEF makes it vulnerable in this situation. The restructured GEF reflects the ambition to contain and balance both the financial perspective that dominated the pilot phase, and the perspective that was articulated and legitimized at Rio. And as we have seen, the resulting facility can be viewed as in institutionalized hybrid of these two perspectives. The problem is that there is no corresponding 'hybrid' ministry at the national level.[39] The GEF therefore risks being the victim of a bureaucratic situation where each ministry promotes the interest of that international agency which most closely corresponds to its perspective. A similar situation can be detected in the environmental community at large. The GEF remains a funding mechanism, and financial criteria will continue to play an important part in its decision-making. But the singlemindedness and moral conviction which are the greatest assets of environmental groups – and which were essential in putting the environment on the political agenda – fit uneasily with practical matters of finance. It is therefore not unlikely that many environmental groups will continue to have an ambivalent relationship to financial criteria, and by extension also to the GEF.

Applying an actor perspective to the GEF reinforces the trend observed in other international environmental processes: alliances are formed which are based on institutional perspectives that transcend hierarchical levels in the intergovernmental system, and are significantly influenced by international networks outside the governmental system. In the case of the GEF, these alliances did not prove sufficient to override the North–South divisions – government preferences were determined by group-belonging based on income levels – but it informed and played into the positions that were put forward, and significantly influenced the issues on the agenda.[40]

Institutional Learning

Broadly speaking, the entire restructuring process can be viewed as a learning process. But not all changes in the GEF derived from bargaining in the negotiations. Some components resulted from an internal process of institutional learning in the pilot phase. This period was characterized by exploration both in terms of the governance system and on an operational level.[41] The functionally independent secretariat, for example, is a lesson learned from the weaknesses of the governance system in the pilot phase.[42] The restructured GEF also incorporates some positive institutional innovations that were generated as part of experiments on an operational level – eg a Small Grants Programme which provides funding for small projects to be implemented by NGOs, and regional and national trust funds for biodiversity. It goes without saying that the permanent facility has a more formal governance system; a decisive test of the GEF will be whether this system has sufficient flexibility to continue to spawn innovative institutional mechanisms on an operational level. This relates to the overwhelmingly important issue of how well the permanent facility will be able to connect its global mandate to local projects generated in coherence with national development plans.

The issue of how agendas developed on an international level can be harmonized with action organized from below goes far beyond the GEF. It is at the core of debates in various disciplines that involve development assistance, environment and multilateral action. Some partial answers have emerged with regard to how implementation can be improved. Generally, they emphasize capacity and institution-building, recipient commitment and the need to involve actors with detailed local knowledge.[43] Creative financial arrangements are a much needed complement to these efforts. Whether or not the GEF will be able to build on the trust-fund experiments and extend the small grants programme will depend on decisions in the Council; a recent proposal for a regional fund in Central America indicates that novel arrangements will continue to emerge. Its size, institutional form and specialization in finance suggest that the GEF holds a comparative advantage relative to convention bound funding when it comes to assisting in creating a diversity of novel funding arrangements to complement the regular project development process by the three Implementing Agencies.

Before the verdict is delivered on how well the GEF can develop operational tentacles towards lower institutional levels, however, it will be tested, again, in the context of the Conventions. The issue is whether the Conventions on Biodiversity and Climate Change will accept the GEF as the entity to operate their financial mechanisms on a permanent basis. The implications for the future landscape of regimes for global environmental issues are considerable.

THE CONTOURS OF A BROAD REGIME FOR THE GLOBAL ENVIRONMENT

The choice presented to the Conference of the Parties (COP) for each Convention is whether they will make use of the GEF as a permanent financial mechanism, or follow, instead, the model of the Montreal Protocol Multilateral Fund. In this Fund, which was established under the auspices of the Parties to the Protocol, an Executive Committee elected by the Parties themselves directs the allocation of resources.[44] The choice of institutional model for the financial mechanism will be determined on political grounds within each Convention. The argument presented here attempts to stand back from the specific political considerations of the Conventions to show the consequences of these choices in terms of the larger regime of global environmental problems. The choice can then be viewed as a classic problem of organization: integration or differentiation.[45]

So far, international agreements on environmental issues have followed a pattern of differentiation. Once an issue is defined as suitable for international action, separate and incremental negotiations follow. As mentioned above, this approach has effectively circumvented collective action problems. Compared to the integrated negotiations of, for example, UNCLOS,[46] the differentiated pattern has proved to be fast, flexible and efficient. Theories predict that the downside of organizational differentiation will reveal itself in the form of coordination problems; the worry about treaty congestion seems to confirm the prognosis.[47] As long as cooperation involves mainly the developed world, national capacity for implementation has been sufficient. As the number of agreements grow, coordinating national implementation will become more difficult. When it comes to global problems, however, effective action must involve developing countries with limited capacity and resources. Unless multilateral resources are made available to implement the agreements on a national level in developing countries, this may well become the limiting factor for global environmental action.

In this context, it is disturbing to note that the pattern of differentiation has not been successful in terms of mobilizing resources. Historically, developed countries have not made significant resources available unless they have confidence that the resources will be used in accordance with criteria of efficiency. This is an issue area where international collective action problems have been severe, regardless of the seriousness of the problem. Arguments based on what urgently 'should' or 'must' be done have not managed to change this situation. Available finance tends to depend more on issues such as the design of a decision-making system and the basis for allocating resources than the demonstrated need for funding. The problem of mobilizing resources is also likely to become exacerbated with a growing number of funding arrangements. Peter Sand has warned 'the growing number of special funds raises problems of transaction costs and operational inefficiency... The real risk here is that acute "trust fund congestion" could lead to chronic funding fatigue'.[48]

An additional problem that will grow with the number of agreements is a diminishing ability to draw on cross-functional synergies. The strong linkages that exist between different environmental problems offer ample opportunities for programmes and projects that address more than one problem. Separate agreements make such operational linkages more problematic. In sum, a systemic vantage point suggests that the marginal benefits of a differentiated approach will decrease as the number of agreements increase.

The GEF offers a way out of this dilemma. Should the Conventions decide to use the GEF as an integrated financial mechanism for global environmental problems, the contours of an entirely new type of regime emerges. In this model, the different Conventions have primacy and provide guidance to the GEF which receives and integrates the information and translates it into operational work programmes. The projects are then transferred to the GEF Implementing Agencies in accordance with their specialization. No other regime on the international arena has a similar design. It institutes a division of labour between the realm where rules are made and the realm where they are translated into practice. It thereby introduces a differentiation according to function rather than issue, and integration at the level of operations – as opposed to the traditional, in international affairs generally unsuccessful, attempt to coordinate from above. Given what we know of the weaknesses of international cooperation, much speaks in favour of this model.

In contrast to attempts to build large and comprehensive regimes, this approach does not prevent a continued step-by-step process for building and strengthening legal agreements. Instead, this regime would be founded on the proven capability of the international community to negotiate international agreements for defined environmental problems, while compensating for the correspondingly poor record of raising the funds needed to enable the participation of developing countries. The negotiators and the Conventions can focus on what they do well: identifying problems, setting priorities within the area of concern, and deciding on policy guidance and rules. The GEF mechanism has different strengths: its comparative advantage lies with developing operational programmes and mobilizing resources. The division also makes it possible to draw on different networks for different purposes – eg environmental ministries are most appropriate when it comes to developing environmental conventions, but their expertise does not necessarily extend to management of large-scale financial resources.

A regime established along these lines preserves the flexibility that has been the hallmark both of the process whereby legal agreements have been created and the evolution of the GEF. Rather than create a formal organization, this regime is more decentralized and builds on linkages between units with different purposes. Its design is in line with findings in organizational theory, which suggests that while a hierarchical model works well in a stable environment, an organic and decentralized form is most appropriate in areas and times of change.

That these are times of change is beyond question. John Gerard Ruggie proposes that we find ourselves in a situation similar to that expressed by Theodore H White 50 years ago – yet again, 'the world is fluid and about to be remade'.[49] The remaking, Ruggie suggests, 'involves a shift not in the play of power politics but of the stage on which that play is performed'. This chapter has presented the argument that the GEF is central in building a stage for global environmental problems that is sufficiently flexible to be adjusted in accordance with changing circumstances. The process of building the GEF reflected the power play that we see in many other areas; it is only when we look beyond the political interests of the day and focus on the institutional result that we see the potential for a unique regime for global environmental issues.

10   NATIONAL ENVIRONMENTAL FUNDS

*Kyle Danish**

Growing international concern for sustainable development is evident in the increasing number and scope of declarations, conventions and plans of action that address international environmental issues. The success of most of these initiatives, however, depends on actions in countries with the least capacity to undertake them. Biologists estimate that anywhere from 50–90 per cent of the earth's remaining species are concentrated in the tropical forests of developing countries in South America and Asia.[1] If current trends of industrialization and deforestation in developing countries continue, greenhouse gas emissions from those countries will exceed emissions from the OECD countries in a few decades.[2] The future of desertification, ozone depletion and deforestation depends largely on the course of development in the world's poorest nations.

For those developing countries, environmental protection is a new priority, if it is a priority at all. Government agencies are small, expertise is lacking, and funding is sparse and unpredictable. The emergence of scores of grass-roots non-governmental organizations (NGOs) in these countries is encouraging. Often, these NGOs are undertaking projects and programmes that governments will not or cannot undertake. However, their high levels of concern and expertise notwithstanding, NGOs in developing countries also lack resources. In the Southern Hemisphere particularly, governments and NGOs both need long-term funding for hiring and training personnel; for purchasing and maintaining equipment; and for undertaking research and monitoring resources.[3]

If the international community is to achieve the myriad goals of sustainable development, external aid must be channelled towards building the capacity of developing countries for environmental protection. The quantity of official aid seems unlikely to grow significantly in the near future. The question, therefore, is how policy-makers can ensure that existing levels of financial transfers are directed to the greatest needs.

* I would like to acknowledge Marc Levy and Jeffrey Dunoff for their helpful comments on earlier drafts.

One element of this question is the extent to which the international community can and should rely on traditional approaches to development aid to also finance *sustainable* development. Since the end of World War II, donor countries have routed development aid largely through bilateral official development agencies and through international financial institutions such as the World Bank. Certain recurring institutional shortcomings have marked these bilateral and multilateral aid channels. One is the persistent neglect of the long-term needs of capacity-building. Another has been a failure to engage the meaningful participation of recipient country stakeholders. The Global Environment Facility, the donor countries' chosen mechanism for financing responses to global environmental problems, will be largely dependent on those same channels.

Since the early 1990s, an innovative alternative to traditional aid mechanisms has been diffusing rapidly throughout the developing world – the National Environmental Fund (NEF).[4] NEFs are national-level financial mechanisms that can collect, manage and disburse money for environmental protection over long periods of time. NEFs are administered by boards consisting of representatives of both donors and stakeholders. Nearly all national environmental funds are essentially independent of the national governments.

Although none of the NEFs have been operating long enough to allow a comprehensive evaluation, it is possible to outline their significant potential. NEFs are demonstrating a special ability to support capacity-building. They can reinforce local participation not only in implementation but also in planning. NEFs can be highly responsive to local needs and conditions. They can coordinate and rationalize external aid and domestic initiatives.

This chapter reviews the defects in traditional aid that inspired NEFs; evaluates the potential effectiveness of NEFs; and looks ahead to issues affecting the development and success of NEFs.

FAILURES OF DEVELOPMENT AID

Capacity-building would seem to be a natural objective for development aid in all sectors. By most accounts, however, donor efforts to develop human and institutional resources in poor countries have not been particularly successful. At the World Bank, projects can be divided into a 'hard investment' component – which is directed at developing physical infrastructure – and an 'institutional development' component – which is directed at the promotion of planning, training, maintenance and other technical support. Internal assessments at the Bank have determined that the institutional development component of projects fails approximately twice as often as the hard investment component. The United States Agency for International Development (USAID) reports similar findings for its projects.[5]

These failures are rooted in the orientation and characteristics of the vast majority of multilateral and bilateral aid projects. For the most part, donors are less interested in undertaking the slow and sensitive process of building domestic capacity than they are in identifying major needs and fulfilling them quickly. Aid often comes in short-term, large-scale packages. Bilateral agencies also rely largely on 'tied aid', conditioning donations on the use of donor-based firms or technology for implementation.[6]

These approaches can produce results in successful infrastructure and other large-scale projects. The neglect of capacity-building, however, can be fatal even to these kinds of projects. Large-scale aid for individual projects can overwhelm the absorptive capacity of a developing country. When the short-term loans or grants end and donors depart, recipient countries still lack the basic staff, equipment and training to maintain the projects.

When donors attempt capacity-building projects, they seem to retain their preference for a crazy quilt of short-term interventions. The approach is antithetical to capacity-building. Developing the resources and expertise of institutions and NGOs requires a long-term commitment to regular expenditures. The costs of capacity-building are recurrent costs.[7] Reviewing the performance of donors in financing environmental protection, the World Bank has observed that:

> Donors, including development banks and multilateral agencies, are often reluctant to finance what is needed most – improved operation and maintenance of fledgling national environmental administrations ... (M)ost donor-funded projects are relatively short term and small scale. What is needed most is longer-term reliable funding, especially for institution building and research.[8]

In its first years of existence, the Global Environment Facility (GEF) (see Chapter 9), has been criticized for repeating the mistakes of its institutional cousins. Although the GEF has received praise for its development of a Small Grants Window and its willingness to channel funds directly to NGOs, commentators have criticized it for its early bias towards moving large amounts of money quickly for largescale projects. An unpublished UNEP report analysing 23 early GEF projects discovered that 21 had budgets larger than the entire annual budget of the developing country agency working on the project. Ten projects used funds exceeding ten times the agencies' budgets. In one notable case, the GEF disbursed US $8 million for the construction of two tourist reserves in Costa Rica. At the same time, the Costa Rican government was cutting its protected area staffing positions by a third to fulfil the conditions of a loan from the International Monetary Fund.[9]

The GEF also has received criticism for its perpetuation of another defect of traditional approaches to development aid: its persistently top-down character. Critics have long assailed aid as a donor-dominated affair. Donor agencies frequently consult only a few élites within recipient countries when planning and implementing projects. They neglect the broad range of local stakeholders.[10]

The failure to engage the participation of local communities and grass-roots NGOs has several consequences. Neglecting local participation means neglecting local knowledge. Many grass-roots NGOs have developed substantial expertise in identifying conservation needs in their communities. Local peoples often have an extensive understanding of natural resources on which their livelihoods rely. These social groups should be playing a key role in selecting and designing sustainable development projects.

Omitting local participation also has consequences for project implementation. When projects do not engage the support of stakeholders, those stakeholders feel little sense of commitment to the long-term success of those projects. Such projects can not only fall short of their own immediate objectives, but can also fail to generate the secondary benefits of ongoing local concern for environmental protection. Protecting the environment becomes an issue that is important to outsiders only.[11] Reviewing the role of local participation in conserving biodiversity, a Global Environment Facility policy paper observes:

> The success or failure of biodiversity conservation projects will in large measure depend upon the ways in which local people are brought into the protected area management process. No amount of additional funding for protected area management will have a positive effect if local peoples and communities are not convinced, trained and empowered to be the key actors in biodiversity conservation.[12]

The pilot phase of the Global Environment Facility began with high hopes that this newest international financial institution would employ a different approach from its forebears. In 1991, when the Facility was established, a GEF policy paper announced the organization's intention to include NGOs in the 'identification, design, and implementation' of its projects.[13] However, a number of evaluations of the GEF's pilot phase strongly criticized the GEF's performance in consulting local communities and NGOs. In 1992, the GEF's own Scientific and Technical Advisory Panel reported that 'projects take little consideration of the involvement of local people, their expertise, and their priorities' and 'NGOs involvement is regarded as inadequate'.[14] The *Independent Evaluation* of the GEF found that 'the shaping of projects, where local participation and cooperation are essential to successful outcomes, has been particularly problematic during the pilot phase'.[15] The role of NGOs, it also concludes, 'was not systematically or successfully developed in the early planning of the pilot phase, although various attempts at collaboration were made'.[16]

The *Independent Evaluation*'s more specific review of the GEF's Biodiversity Portfolio is a strongly worded criticism of the Facility's neglect of capacity-building and broad participation:

> Appropriate plans and programs for conserving biodiversity and using biological resources sustainably need a balance between international, national, and local activities and close cooperation between a number of institutions. Most GEF work to date has been characterized by a top-down approach rather than responding to the needs of governments. It has not involved local communities in an effective way; it has sparked destructive competition among the implementing agencies and other global organizations working in the field of biodiversity; it has given inadequate consideration to sustainable use of biological resources; it has not meaningfully involved NGOs; and it has been overly dependent on international consulting firms.[17]

The *Independent Evaluation* strongly suggests that the GEF's early experience has been marred by the same defects as historical approaches to development aid. Notably, however, the evaluation underscores the Global Environment Facility's partnerships with national environmental funds as its most promising innovation.[18]

EXISTING AND FUTURE NATIONAL ENVIRONMENTAL FUNDS

National Environmental Funds have evolved as a response to the shortcomings of traditional approaches to environmental aid. They have roots in their experience with debt-for-nature swaps in the late 1980s.[19] Money generated by some debt-for-nature swaps was channelled into trust funds that were variously controlled by governments and/or national NGOs. Money in these trust funds came entirely from the swap.

A breakthrough in the development of National Environmental Funds occurred in 1991 with the establishment of Bhutan's National Environmental Fund.[20] Before 1991, the Royal Government of Bhutan had identified a large menu of needs for its sustainable development programme. These included the hiring and training of additional forest rangers, the establishment of environmental education programmes in its schools, and assessments of its protected areas. Bhutan, however, faced barriers to soliciting external assistance. Having no significant debt, it was not 'eligible' for a debt-for-nature swap.[21] More significantly, Bhutan's capacity-building needs required a stable, long-term source of funding. A large-scale, three- to five-year loan or grant – the traditional approach – would be ineffective.

Confronted with Bhutan's dilemma, Barry Spergel and Bruce Bunting of the World Wildlife Fund (WWF-US) came up with the idea of a free-standing trust fund in the form of a perpetual endowment. Such a fund could receive multiple donations from multiple sources. As a perpetual endowment, it could invest the money received and use the annual income from interest as an annual budget. From this budget, the trustees could make small or large disbursements for various one-off or ongoing projects.

Establishing a board of trustees was an opportunity for additional benefits. While negotiating with potential donors, Spergel insisted that the Bhutanese should have majority representation on the board.[22] Today, the board consists of five members: two representatives from the Royal Government of Bhutan; one representative from the Royal Society for the Preservation of Nature, the tiny country's sole environmental NGO; one representative from the WWF-US; and one representative from the United Nations Development Programme. Selecting a programme of disbursements requires four affirmative votes. This voting scheme has several implications. One is that an international donor-representative acting alone cannot block a disbursement. Another implication is that, if the government of Bhutan desires money from the NEF, usually it will need the support of the country's environmental NGO.

The Bhutanese and the WWF-US were able to persuade the then newly formed Global Environment Facility to collaborate in their innovation. The GEF agreed to contribute US $10 million in two tranches to the principal of Bhutan's NEF in two tranches. It conditioned the release of the second tranche, consisting of US $3 million, on certain institutional reforms in the government's environmental agencies, the funding of certain specific programmes, and solicitation of additional donations from additional donors. The WWF-US, Norway and the Netherlands also made initial contributions. On 6 March 1991, Bhutan's NEF was established with an initial principal of US $9.5 million.[23]

Since 1991, NEFs have started to surface throughout the Southern Hemisphere. According to a March 1996 draft report of the Interagency Planning Group on Environmental Funds (IPG), 25 NEFs are currently operating and 16 are in the process of establishment. Member organizations of the IPG have identified another 28 'Possible New Funds'.[24] NEFs have also entered the arena of international environmental agreements. The international convention on desertification calls upon its Conference of the Parties to 'consider for adoption' mechanisms 'such as National Desertification Funds, including those involving the participation of non-governmental organizations' that 'channel financial resources effectively to local levels in affected countries'.[25] Non-governmental organizations are pressing parties to the Biodiversity Convention to introduce NEF as a favoured financing mechanism for that agreement as well.[26]

Although existing and emerging NEFs are marked by extraordinary diversity, they generally have three elements in common:

(1) The ability to receive money from a variety of sources.
(2) Management by a democratic board consisting of a broad cross-section of stakeholders.
(3) The ability to make appropriately sized grants to a variety of beneficiaries.[27]

Many, if not most, National Environmental Funds are taking the form of trust funds. Examples include Bhutan's NEF and Belize's proposed Protected Areas Conservation Trust (PACT).[28] The trust fund is a time-honoured common law instrument. In its simplest sense, a trust fund is an arrangement in which one party, the trustee(s), manages assets on behalf of another party, the beneficiary(ies), according to a legal charter. The NEFs that are common law trust funds are 'public' or 'charitable' trusts. Such trust funds are chartered to support a public interest; their designated beneficiary is the public in general.[29]

The trust fund has close counterparts in other legal systems, most notably the civil law 'foundation'. NEFs established as foundations include Honduras' National Environmental Protection Fund and the Foundation for the Philippine Environment.[30]

Many NEFs, both trusts and foundations, are established as perpetual endowments. As noted above, these funds have the ability to invest money received and disburse only the income from annual interest. Other funds could be more accurately described as 'channellers'.[31] A broadly representative body manages these NEFs also, but they accept and disburse money continuously rather than use an investment strategy. Belize's proposed Protected Areas Conservation Trust, for example, would be a revolving fund, spending 95 per cent of what the fund collects in a year during that same year or the next.[32]

NEFs are receiving money from a variety of external and internal sources. In its 1991–94 pilot phase, the Global Environment Facility provided support to 11 NEFs, contributing to the principal of 5 and directing technical assistance to another 6.[33] Several international NGOs and foundations are providing direct contributions or technical assistance. Germany, Canada, Switzerland, the Netherlands and Norway have provided direct financial assistance to NEFs or co-financed NEF-funded projects. The United States' bilateral debt relief programme in Latin America, the Enterprise for the Americas Initiative (EIA), has routed US $154 million to seven NEFs through debt-for-nature swaps.[34] Recently USAID, through its parallel co-financing arrangement with the GEF, committed US $19.5 million to the 'endowment core fund' of a new Mexican Nature Conservation Fund. The Mexican government committed US $10 million in matching funds. For the near future, organizers expect to generate an annual budget of US $2 million with which to make grants to grass-roots, national and international NGOs for sustainable development projects.[35]

NEFs will tap both internal and external sources. The Papua New Guinea Trust Fund is considering matching outside contributions with revenues from a levy on domestic extractive industries such as mining and petroleum.[36] Belize's

NEF, as proposed, would receive revenues from a US $8 'conservation fee' charged to tourists.[37]

The variety of legal instruments and funding sources is exceeded only by the diversity in the structures of NEF boards. Unlike Bhutan's board, most of the boards of emerging NEFs give more voting power to local or national NGOs than to government officials. Many consist of some mixture of representatives from governments, NGOs, and international donors and experts. An independent committee of scientists will supplement the board of Peru's Trust Fund for Conservation Units. The board of Uganda's Mghahinga and Bwindi Impenetrable Forest Conservation Trust (MBFICT) will have the support of a Local Community Steering Committee consisting of local residents and local resource professionals. This committee will be the authority to approve small grants.

National Environmental Funds are directing grants to various capacity-building, biodiversity conservation and sustainable development projects. Bhutan's NEF will support institutional strengthening, environmental education, and sustainable activities for communities living near protected areas. Mexico's Nature Conservation Fund will provide money almost exclusively to local, national and international NGOs for a variety of projects. Uganda's MBFICT is being designed to finance conservation efforts in two national forests. The MBFICT will finance park management and research, and the development of alternative economic activities for forest communities.

Although the features of emerging NEFs clearly are tailored to individual circumstances, one recently established NEF – the Indonesian Biodiversity Foundation (IBF) – is being cited as a valuable model. The GEF's Science and Technical Advisory Panel has called the IBF 'a truly innovative project' whose 'potential for success is great'.[38]

A US–Indonesian team designed the IBF with input from 300 Indonesian NGOs, 6 governmental ministries, 8 universities and scientific institutes, and 15 international donors. Although it received the endorsement of the Indonesian President, the IBF is independent of the government. The board of Directors consists of 21 prominent Indonesians, representing the scientific, NGO and business communities. Among the board members is a former Director-General of the World Conservation Union.[39]

The IBF Board of directors will establish three or four advisory panels. Some of the panels will provide scientific and technical support. The other panels will ensure that residents of Indonesia's remote island regions – where most of the country's extraordinary biological wealth is located – will be included in decision-making.[40]

USAID is channelling US $20 million to the IBF. The IBF will use US $16.5 million of the grant as an endowment fund while US $3.5 million will go to institutional development and an initial five-year set of grants.

The responsibilities of the IBF's small professional staff will include soliciting, issuing and monitoring (but not implementing) grants in five theme areas:

- Forest and marine biodiversity protection and management.
- Research on sustainable uses of biological resources.
- Public education and outreach.
- Biodiversity monitoring.
- Interdisciplinary policy analysis.

A significant element of the IBF's mandate is the active solicitation of proposals from, and the channelling of grants to, grass-roots NGOs and local communities.

THE POTENTIAL EFFECTIVENESS OF NATIONAL ENVIRONMENTAL FUNDS

As noted above, the newness and variety of National Environmental Funds militates against a comprehensive assessment of their effectiveness. None the less, evaluating their potential is possible. In making this evaluation, it should be noted that National Environmental Funds represent more than merely conduits for financial transfers. NEFs are also based on international relationships; parties can include official development agencies, international financial institutions, international NGOs, grass-roots NGOs, developing country governments and others. Additionally, NEFs are bureaucracies, establishing environmental priorities and making expenditures on an ongoing basis.

Thus, National Environmental Funds may be better understood as institutions. According to one definition, institutions are:

> persistent and connected sets of rules and practices that prescribe behavioural roles, constrain activity, and shape expectations. They may take the form of bureaucratic organizations, regimes (rule-structures that do not necessarily have organizations attached), or conventions (informal practices).[41]

Peter Haas, Robert Keohane and Marc Levy have developed a framework with which to evaluate the effectiveness of international environmental institutions.[42] They have examined the extent to which these institutions generate certain interrelated conditions that they have determined are necessary for effective environmental protection. These conditions are:

> high levels of governmental *concern*, a hospitable *contractual* environment in which agreements can be made and kept, and sufficient political and administrative *capacity* in national governments.[43]

This framework is applicable to an evaluation of the potential of National Environmental Funds.

Building Capacity

National Environmental Funds are showing promise as institutions that can build the capacity of governments and NGOs to protect the environment. Unlike traditional short-term aid, NEFs can manage money over periods of several years while making regular, appropriately-sized disbursements for salaries, research, monitoring and other items. Even if international donors prefer to make contributions in large blocks, environmental funds can 'retail' these contributions into smaller, better-tailored expenditures for capacity-building needs.[44]

The stability and independence of funding can be important in developing countries that are experiencing rapid changes in governments. For countries in the process of structural adjustment, NEFs may be the only established interim sources of financial support for environmental protection.[45]

Traditionally, developing countries receive project-specific grants from donors and have to develop a separate planning process for each. The World Bank has acknowledged that these 'well-intentioned but unorchestrated offers of assistance' constitute highly inefficient aid.[46] National Environmental Funds can rationalize the aid process. Boards of trustees can tie donor contributions to comprehensive national capacity-building plans.[47]

Donor programmes are directed almost exclusively at governments. National and grass-roots NGOs, however, are quite often more productive investments. National Environmental Funds are flexible enough to channel capacity-building resources to NGOs.

National Environmental Funds can also generate indirect capacity-building. Participating on NEF boards gives government officials, NGOs and community residents the ability to negotiate, plan and manage sustainable development. Board participation can also reinforce values of representative governance, transparency and accountability in societies that may be traditionally authoritarian and closed.[48]

Increasing Concern

Developing countries have scarce resources and many needs. To sustain the priority status of natural resource management in developing countries, institutions must increase concern at all levels of society. Historically, donors have imposed strict conditions on their grants and loans and have often utilized firms from their countries to implement projects. As a result, recipients feel little sense of ownership over these projects and have little interest in sustaining them. National Environmental Funds, on the other hand, can give stakeholders most of the authority over several million dollars for conservation. This authority can focus developing country actors on long-term environmental priorities. Importantly, environmental NGOs – grass-roots, national and often international – are not merely observers but voting members of NEF boards. They can use their leverage as voters to educate government officials and to goad them into higher levels of commitment to the environment.

The presence of representatives from international environmental NGOs on the boards of so many national environmental funds represents opportunities for new kinds of sustainable development partnerships. The combination of the technical expertise of these NGOs and the local knowledge of grass-roots board members may lead to new kinds of projects, initiatives and programmes. National Environmental Funds are likely to become significant catalysts of sustainable development innovation in the developing world.

Enhancing the Contractual Environment

The willingness of donors to dedicate resources to development is limited. When donors make contributions to achieve their objectives of environmental protection in a recipient country, they are eager to ensure that their contributions maximize such protection. Because money is largely fungible, donors face the constant possibility that recipients will divert their financial transfers to other priorities. Thus, if an institution for financing environmental protection is to be effective, it must create an environment in which commitments can be made credible.

In many ways, donors have employed the traditional approaches to aid described above to ensure that aid goes as directly as possible to meet its objective. Top-down planning guarantees that donors have tight control over what kind of projects are set up. Donors prefer short-term rather than long-term aid because the longer money is flowing into a country, the greater are the opportunities to divert it. One reason that donors utilize firms from their own countries is that they have more enforceable legal ties with their domestic businesses.

National Environmental Funds have emerged largely in response to the short-comings of these approaches. Not surprisingly, some donors perceive dangers in the NEF alternative. They fear that entrusting money to environmental fund mechanisms over long periods of time increases the opportunities for corruption. They are reluctant to cede authority over how their money is spent to boards dominated by recipients. Some donors have expressed concerns that NEFs could become entitlements of a sort, discouraging developing countries from establishing and strengthening governmental environmental agencies.[49]

National Environmental Funds can be designed to minimize the risk that money will be shifted to anything other than environmental priorities. Whether it is a common law trust or a civil law foundation, a National Environmental Fund operates against a backdrop of well-developed legal rights, obligations and remedies. The legal instrument that establishes an NEF can set out in significant detail the parameters of its operations: its objectives, criteria for spending decisions, investment strategies, voting rules, etc.

The legal instrument can include conditions that ensure transparency and accountability. Boards can have reporting requirements and be subject to audits. Board meetings can be open to the public and spending criteria and decisions can be well publicized. Such features can make NEFs more accountable than traditional aid mechanisms operating through governments only.

Nervous donors can be represented on NEF boards directly. However less intrusive means of ensuring credible commitments are also available. Mixing grass-roots NGOs and government officials on boards can generate a creative tension and all but eliminate the risk that a fund will become the fiefdom of any particular agency or organization. Positions for grass-roots NGOs can rotate, guaranteeing that no one NGO can dominate the spending decisions. International environmental NGOs can be voting or *ex officio* members of NEF boards, lending expertise and a global perspective.

Funds that have multiple donors with multiple conditions can create subaccounts for each. The board of such an NEF can disburse money from a subaccount only in accordance with the conditions of that account. Bolivia's national environmental fund, FONAMA, is essentially an umbrella account consisting of subaccounts reflecting the priorities of many donors.[50]

Opportunities abound to establish credible partnerships between bilateral and multilateral donors and developing country stakeholders through National Environmental Funds. However, NEF organizers must strike a careful balance between the desire of some donors to place strict boundaries on the authority of NEF boards and the benefits of permitting a significant amount of free rein to those boards. A major part of the promise of National Environmental Funds is their ability to empower developing country stakeholders in the sustainable development process. Although fund designers should continue to explore the various means of reassuring donors by restricting the authority of fund boards, they should also educate donors on the virtues of an alternative to traditional short-term, top-down approaches.

USAID is an example of a donor that seems persuaded of the potential of National Environmental Funds and particularly those that maximize participatory decision-making. Its rationale for supporting the Indonesia Biodiversity Foundation initiative is a concise summary of the advantages of NEFs:

An US–Japanese donor team consulted with Indonesian governmental ministries, NGOs, and scientists to identify possible initiatives that could be launched under a coordinated strategy to help protect the country's biodiversity. One innovative concept quickly took hold: the establishment of an independent, highly-reputed Indonesian foundation capable of funnelling money from the international donor community to local NGOs and communities through small grants. Setting up an endowment fund was viewed as the best way to guarantee long-term financial sustainability for the new organization and, at the same time ensure transparency, accountability, and effective monitoring. Moreover, the endowment grant from USAID would leverage additional contributions from international and Indonesian public and private donors.[51]

EMERGING ISSUES AFFECTING NATIONAL ENVIRONMENTAL FUNDS

Teams of lawyers and financial advisers must help NEF organizers to navigate the complicated questions of where to house the fund on a legal basis and where to locate the assets. These questions encompass issues of stability, financial risk and local versus outsider control. Their complexity underscores the significant transaction costs entailed in developing and managing a National Environmental Fund.

Location Decisions

Locating the fund in the recipient country promotes the country's sense of ownership over the fund and associates it with laws with which the country's residents are familiar. Good reasons may support the decision to house the fund offshore, however. Some developing countries may not have a legal system into which a trust or foundation can be incorporated easily. Also, locating a fund in the country might mean creating stifling links between the NEF and the government. Governments might dominate the NEF to the exclusion of other stakeholders. Instability of the government and the legislative process may also be a concern. For these reasons, some NEF designers are locating the funds on a legal basis under the auspices of another country or, in the case of Bhutan, with a multilateral agency.[52]

Choosing a location for NEF assets involves many of the same factors that exist for choosing a legal location. Domestic asset management can be preferable because it promotes domestic commitment and builds skills of financial management. On the other hand, assets located in the recipient country may be subject to tax liability, inflation or instability. Another risk is attachment by the country's creditors.[53]

Transaction Costs

The Global Environment Facility is considering the development of a new mechanism, the Global Umbrella Fund (GUF), which could provide an answer to the specific problems of asset management and the more general problem of transaction costs. The GUF would be a separate trust fund that would invest the assets of individual NEFs in subaccounts. Each NEF would maintain its individual authority over spending decisions.[54]

Funds housed in the GUF would benefit from the GEF's tax-exempt status and would be protected from attachment. The staff of the World Bank would manage and invest the assets. The staff has a record of outperforming the market.[55] With funds commingled, the GUF could achieve greater diversity in its investments than individual NEFs could and thus could maximize the stability of returns. Moreover, the National Environmental Funds participating in the GUF would not need to bear the transaction costs involved in developing financial strategies and hiring asset managers.[56]

Despite these potential benefits, GEF/Bank officials remain unresolved about a GUF. They loathe forfeiting the opportunity to build the capacity of developing country officials and NGOs to manage national environmental finances.[57] For most of the international environmental NGOs working on NEFs, this aspect of capacity-building is not as much of a concern. They perceive domestic asset management as a risky and resource-consuming burden on fund boards.[58] Thus, some of these NGOs are tentatively supportive of a Global Umbrella Fund.

Notably, when they discussed the GUF proposal at a forum of NEF fund managers, their reaction was quite negative. Despite assurances that fund boards would maintain their full authority over how money would be spent, the managers none the less expressed concern that the GUF would be a mechanism through which the World Bank could dominate NEFs.[59]

Opportunity Costs

Even if the GEF establishes the Global Umbrella Fund, the issue of opportunity costs remains. For NEFs that take the form of perpetual endowments, such costs can be large. To generate an adequate income from annual interest, perpetual endowments require the collection and investment of substantial amounts of capital. The GEF generally recommends that the minimum account size of a perpetual endowment NEF should be US $5–10 million.[60] In countries where biological resources are disappearing rapidly, tying up such large amounts of capital in investments may not be the highest use of funds.[61] These countries may still determine that the ability of NEFs to rationalize funding and to link it to a representative decision-making process is worthwhile. They should establish National Environmental Funds that are 'channellers' rather than perpetual endowments.

The Global Environment Facility and NEFs

Although the GEF was a hesitant collaborator in the breakthrough national environment fund in Bhutan, its staff now seem strongly committed to making such funds viable and effective mechanisms. The Global Umbrella Fund is one means of enhancing support under consideration. International environmental NGOs and others are also advocating that the GEF should establish a Medium Grants Window dedicated to providing technical assistance grants to NEFs.[62] Generally, there are high hopes that Global Environment Facility funding for NEFs will rise considerably in its new phase.

Increased GEF funding, however, faces potential obstacles. To date, GEF money for NEFs has come from its Biodiversity Portfolio. The Facility is the interim financing mechanism for the Biodiversity Convention. Increasingly, the Biodiversity Convention's Conference of the Parties will have the final word on what kinds of projects receive funding out of the Biodiversity Portfolio. As noted above, several international environmental NGOs are working to persuade the Conference of the Parties to commit itself to national environmental funds.

GEF support for national environmental funds may also be imperilled by shifting interpretations of the legal restrictions on Facility funding. According to the Biodiversity Convention, developed country parties shall provide funding to developing country parties to meet the 'agreed full incremental costs to them of implementing measures which fulfil the obligations of this Convention . . .'[63] The concept of incremental costs is complex and currently subject to a variety of interpretations. The incremental cost restriction suggests that the GEF should compensate developing countries for the costs of undertakings whose benefits are primarily global rather than domestic.[64] The restriction implies that projects with significant domestic benefits might have no true incremental costs and thus are ineligible for GEF support. Under strict interpretations of incremental costs, therefore, GEF support for NEFs may be difficult to justify because NEF disbursements for capacity-building not only benefit the global environment, but can also generate significant domestic benefits. To date, NEFs have profited from a degree of operational leniency in the Biodiversity Portfolio.[65] As the Conference of the Parties increases its authority, this leniency may end. The GEF Council and the Biodiversity Conventions Conference of the Parties need rigorous evidence of the global benefits provided by capacity-building generally and by National Environmental Funds specifically.

Another emerging issue regarding Global Environmental Facility support for National Environmental Funds is the GEF's orientation toward NEFs that are perpetual endowments. GEF officials seem to perceive the primary benefits of environmental funds as their ability to fund recurrent costs. The GEF categorizes the 'process-related' benefits of expanded participation of NGOs and local communities as secondary.[66] Because recurrent costs are the emphasis for the GEF, its Working Papers on National Environmental Funds indicate an interest only in NEFs that are perpetual endowments. As noted above, such NEFs are not the best choice for several countries that may otherwise benefit from the coordinated, participatory decision-making processes offered by NEFs. A looming question is whether the GEF will provide assistance to the developing countries which are interested in creating National Environmental Funds that are 'channellers' rather than perpetual endowments.

The Interagency Planning Group on Environmental Funds

A noteworthy development in the emergence of National Environmental Funds has been the establishment of the Interagency Planning Group on Environmental Funds. The Interagency Group is a round-table of fund managers and representatives from the GEF, official development agencies, international environmental NGOs and private foundations. The Interagency Group has been, by all accounts, a successful and, to date, all too rare example of cooperative and collegial planning by stakeholders, multilateral and bilateral donors and NGOs.[67] The Interagency Group organized the first Global Forum on Environmental Funds in May 1994. The Forum attracted 20 managers of NEFs in various stages of operation and design. Principal items on the Interagency Group's future agenda include: providing technical assistance to NEFs; facilitating networks among them: assisting them with financial management; and broadening donor bases.[68]

Regional Environment Funds

Another emerging development is the use of funds in regional settings. A small fund was established to support conservation efforts in a region of the Carpathian Mountains that spans the borders of the Slovak Republic, Poland and the Ukraine.[69] Another regional fund is being discussed for the Caribbean.[70]

Eco-systems do not necessarily respect state boundaries. Problems of collective action hinder efforts to protect eco-systems that span more than one country. States have incentives to free-ride, letting other state(s) do most of the work. *Ad hoc* cooperative action among different governments also involves significant transaction costs.

Regional Environmental Funds can generate better results. They create arenas in which designated representatives from the states can meet and plan on a regular basis. They can reduce, therefore, transaction costs that are associated with the *ad hoc* approach. Also, fund boards can include national or international environmental NGOs that presumably are more interested in protecting the eco-system than furthering the interests of any particular state. Participation by NGOs creates opportunities for creative coalitions that break through the obstacles of collective action.

The board of the Carpathians fund may provide a model. It will consist of 14 members: four representatives from each of the partner states, one from the World Wide Fund for Nature and one from the MacArthur Foundation. Disbursements will require the affirmative votes of nine of the country representatives and one of the two international representatives.

CONCLUSION

Hilary French of the Worldwatch Institute has observed that it is a 'paradox of our time' that 'effective governance requires control being simultaneously passed down to local communities and up to international institutions'.[71] Reversing ecological deterioration and making development sustainable, she observes, involves 'literally millions of small actions and decisions in villages, farms, businesses, and cities around the world'.[72]

> It is through a diversity of responses, suited to local and regional conditions, that the security of the planet will ultimately be assured. The task for international governance is not to micromanage these actions, which depend on the genius, commitment, and ingenuity of individuals worldwide, but to ensure that the climate is favourable for them.[73]

The challenge of sustainable development and its inherent paradoxes suggest the need for new kinds of institutions. Making the 'climate favourable' for the multitude of local initiatives that are necessary for environmental protection requires institutions that can forge new partnerships among international, state and non-state actors. The National Environmental Fund is an example of this new kind of sustainable development institution. Even as the world's policy-makers are focusing on means by which local participation can be brought 'up' into international governance, National Environmental Funds are demonstrating a way to channel resources and authority 'down' to the social groups that must implement initiatives of international importance.[74]

National Environmental Funds face challenges in the near future. They must persuade donors of their credibility and many will suffer through the inevitable slow starts and growing pains. None the less, the potential of National Environmental Funds to transform positively the process of sustainable development is significant. Policy-makers, advocates and scholars should support the maturation of these new institutions.

PART IV

Regional Institutions

11   THE EUROPEAN UNION AND THE OECD

Han Somsen

The terms of reference of both the European Union (EU) and the Organization of Economic Cooperation and Development (OECD) are predominantly inspired by economic considerations. It is not self-evident, therefore, that the OECD and the EU should have evolved into fora for international environmental cooperation. The EU in particular is now one of the key forces determining the national environmental policies of its Member States, while it also increasingly asserts itself at international level. In view of the ever-increasing role of the EU in this area, as well as the fact that the membership of both organizations partly coincide, only relatively little attention will be devoted to the OECD, while the evolution of the environmental policy of the European Union will be subject to a more detailed analysis.

THE ORGANIZATION FOR ECONOMIC COOPERATION AND DEVELOPMENT

The OECD represents a rather unusual cross-continental alliance of states aiming to promote economic growth, to aid developing states, as well as to encourage worldwide trade. Its 27 members include all Western European countries, Australia, Canada, Japan, New Zealand, the United States, Mexico, the Czech Republic and, most recently, Hungary. Not unlike the European Union,[1] the OECD has been able to develop an environmental policy mainly by virtue of Article 2 of its constitution which refers to the promotion of 'the efficient use of economic resources'. In 1970, the OECD created a Committee on the environment which consolidated the environmental activities of some 20 committees which had been active in that field on an *ad hoc* basis and which set itself the task of assisting its member states in the elaboration of their environmental policies.

The institutional structure of the OECD is formed by a Council which consists of the representatives of the member states, an Executive Committee of 14

Member States, a Secretariat and a number of committees. It is important to note that the OECD is primarily intended to work as a 'think-tank', designed to stimulate research and the elaboration of principles. As far as decision-making is concerned, the OECD can only adopt binding decisions in respect of those states which agree to them.

Recommendations addressed to Member States, although not binding, have tended to be of considerable significance to the development of national and international environmental law. In this respect it must be observed that the EC participates in the activities of the OECD. An example of the impact of the OECD on EC environmental law is the polluter pays principle, which was first elaborated by the OECD and was subsequently adopted as one of the key principles of the EC's environmental policy. Other guiding principles of international environmental law developed by the OECD include those of consultation, the precautionary principle,[2] non-discrimination and equal access to justice.[3]

At a more concrete level, reference must be made to the detailed standards that were elaborated under the auspices of the OECD.[4] It has been particularly active in elaborating standards and principles for the management of hazardous waste. A recommendation was issued establishing an overall approach for the management of wastes[5] as well as more specific recommendations relating to beverage containers[6] and the recuperation of paper.[7] In addition, the OECD pioneered a strategy to address the problem of transfrontier air pollution[8] which chiefly is based on a policy of the coordination of national policies, together with a policy of equal access and non-discrimination, based on the polluter pays principle.[9]

The International Energy Agency and the Nuclear Energy Agency were established as specialized agencies under the OECD umbrella to encourage cooperation and harmonization of practice in the field of energy policy and of radioactive waste disposal and management. These Agencies too lack the power to adopt binding decisions. The OECD can also claim credit for having initiated the convention on third-party liability and a multilateral consultation procedure for sea dumping and radioactive waste.[10]

All in all, although the OECD is not equipped with independent institutions that are capable of breaking the monopoly enjoyed by states, the OECD's contribution to the formation of international environmental law has been a significant one. Its strength resides particularly in the elaboration of general principles which serve as a basis for national and regional environmental policy-makers. In this respect, the interaction between the EC and the OECD has been a particularly fruitful one.

ENVIRONMENTAL POLICY IN THE EUROPEAN UNION

It is exactly 20 years ago that the European Economic Community first adopted environmental directives on the disposal of waste oils[11] and the quality of surface water intended for use as drinking water.[12] Whereas earlier manifestations of the harmonization of laws in the sphere of the environment exist,[13] the centre of gravity of these directives usually was the establishment of the Common Market. The desirability of the pursuit of a proper environmental policy was first acknowledged at inter-governmental level in the momentous year of 1972[14] and articulated in greater detail in the first environmental action programme in 1973.[15]

In the course of the two decades of Community activity in this field, a marked change of emphasis and direction has taken place, partly reflecting new insights in environmental management and more generally mirroring changed perceptions as to the desired form and substance of European integration, and running parallel with the elevation of the principle of subsidiarity as a principle of Community law. An attempt will be undertaken here to trace this development and provide indications as to the possible future direction of the Union's environmental policy.

First, it will be necessary to explain the paradox of the rapid growth of a body of Community environmental law in the absence of formal empowering provisions in the 1957 Rome Treaty. Attention will then be paid to changes brought about first by the Single European Act in 1987 and subsequently by the Treaty on European Union in 1993. The next question relates to the reception of secondary environmental law in the legal orders of the Member States or, in other words, the implementation of EU environmental law as well as the enforcement of EU environmental law by the institutions of the Community and individuals before their national courts. Finally, the future direction of the Union's environmental policy will be discussed with specific reference to the principle of subsidiarity. It is, however, beyond the scope of this chapter to focus on the more than 300 legal instruments which have been adopted in this field.[16]

Accommodating an Environmental Policy in the 1957 Rome Treaty

The rude awakening of the world in Stockholm in 1972 to the harsh reality of global environmental decline could hardly leave unaffected an organization whose main objectives were economic growth and the establishment of a common market.[17] It is not a coincidence, therefore, that the Heads of State and Government meeting in Paris in 1972 proclaimed that 'economic growth was not an end in itself' and invited the institutions of the Community to draw up an environmental action programme.[18] Such swift action should only partly be taken as evidence of a genuine reassessment of priorities within the Community. At least as important was the emergence of obstacles to trade posed by environmental legislation adopted in particular by the Federal Republic of Germany[19] combined with the certainty that such obstacles could only increase in importance in the future.

Despite the deep-rooted suspicion with which the rising 'green' movement has traditionally regarded the growth and free trade policies of the Community, this unusual organization possesses qualities which in many ways gave it the potential to be a uniquely effective international environmental organization.[20] Its ambitious and dynamic long-term objectives of integration, solidarity and cohesion opened the prospect for a transnational environmental regime which might overcome the sort of 'North-South divide' problems which other international organizations are still struggling to overcome.[21] In addition, the unique institutional set-up of the Community could serve the environment in a number of different ways. First, the monopoly to initiate secondary legislation independent from Member States enjoyed by the Commission means that the direction and general thrust of the Community's environmental policy is not dominated by states' self-interest, but can be inspired by more objective and scientific criteria. In general, the Community's capacity to adopt secondary legislation which legally binds Member States without prior ratification provides it with more potent instruments to pursue its policies than any other known international organization.[22] As will be seen, more recently member states have also lost the power to veto the adoption of such environmental laws.

Apart from its legislative competencies, the Commission also enjoys a supervisory role and brings instances of breaches of Community environmental law to the attention of the European Court of Justice whose jurisdiction, it should be underlined, is compulsory.[23] In international law, this role of 'watchdog' is traditionally exercised by states rather than by some independent authority. As is well known, the reluctance of states to pursue such cases has led to only a handful of judgments by the International Court of Justice, contrasting sharply with the constant flow of environmental cases emanating from the European Court (see Chapter 13).

It is obvious, therefore, that the European Court of Justice could play a key role in enforcing EC environmental law and hence in ensuring its effectiveness. Moreover, the Court's well-known preparedness to interpret EC law in the context of its wider social and political aspirations (so-called 'teleological interpretation'), exemplified perhaps best by its elaboration of the doctrines of direct effect and supremacy of Community law, further provides the law with a degree of flexibility which is ideally suited to respond speedily and effectively to the continuously changing (environmental) circumstances.

In brief, there were ample reasons to embrace the prospect of a comprehensive environmental policy at Community level. Yet, the fact remained that the 1957 Treaty did not contain any clear environmental objectives and that the so-called *principe d'attribution des compétences* as embodied in Article 4 of the Treaty therefore seemed to pose an insurmountable obstacle to the realization of such a policy.[24] In reality, however, this legal constraint has not been decisive for the development of the Community's environmental policy, nor even does it seem proper to attribute to it the significance that many legal commentators have given it in the past.[25] A number of circumstances may account for this paradox.

First and foremost, the framework nature of the Treaty, in conjunction with the Court's dynamic interpretation of its provisions, leaves considerable scope for gap-filling by interpretative means. Thus, Article 2 could easily be interpreted as implying the need for a Community environmental policy so as to ensure that growth indeed would be 'balanced' and 'harmonious'. This approach was indeed adopted by the Heads of State and Government gathered for the Paris Summit in 1972 and formally sanctioned by the Court in 1985.[26] Evidently, in the age of unanimity, the *sine qua non* for such a reorientation to take place was the existence of political consensus as to its desirability. As has already been observed, in view of the considerable trade implications of unharmonized national environmental laws such consensus was not difficult to achieve. As far as environmental goals that were unrelated to the objective of the establishment of the common market were concerned, public opinion was heavily in favour of strong Community action, a point which was not lost on a European Parliament in the run-up to the first direct elections.[27] The Commission, too, recognized in the elaboration of an environmental policy an opportunity to win public support for the European ideal at large. These circumstances by themselves might not have been sufficient to overcome the constitutional constraints or the scepticism still entertained by France in particular,[28] if it were not for the fact that Member States themselves had developed only the most rudimentary of environmental policies, if at all. Hence, unlike some other policy areas like transport[29] for which an explicit Treaty base did exist, the elaboration of an environmental policy was not hindered by well-established national traditions or policy choices. The three environmental action programmes which were adopted before the formalization of the Community's powers in the sphere of the environment further clarified the objectives of the Community in this field.[30]

Once it had been recognized that environmental protection formed part of the 'tasks' of the Community, the obstacle posed by Article 4 EEC was overcome. It thus became possible to pursue an environmental policy without even the need to resort to Article 236 EEC, the cumbersome procedure used for amending the Treaty. This is because the 1957 Rome Treaty already contained numerous and wide-ranging powers which could be successfully employed to pursue an environmental policy. Apart from such provision as Articles 43 (Common Agricultural Policy), Articles 92 and 93 (State Aids), 113 and 114 (Common Commercial Policy) and Article 238 (Power to enter into association agreements), the most important provisions which came to be used for the advancement of the Community's new environmental ambitions were Articles 100 and 235 of the Treaty.

Article 100 empowers the Commission to 'issue directives for the approximation of such laws, regulations or administrative provisions as directly affect the establishment or functioning of the common market'. Article 235, on the other hand, provided the Community with a residual power providing that 'if action by the Community should prove necessary to attain, in the course of the operation of the common market, one of the objectives of the Community, and this Treaty has not provided the necessary powers, the Council shall, acting unanimously on a proposal from the Commission and after consulting the European Parliament, take the appropriate measures'. Much has been written about the scope of both respective provisions and, as their importance is now largely historical, it suffices to consider some of the possible implications of the use of these powers for the shape of the present Community's environmental policy.

As far as the harmonization of laws under Article 100 is concerned, four questions deserve particular consideration:

(1) What are the implications of the use of directives?
(2) Has the requirement of unanimity been translated in an environmental policy dictated by the lowest common denominator?
(3) Does the technique of harmonization of existing national environmental laws rule out an autonomous Community environmental policy?
(4) To what extent has the Community's scope of action been adversely affected by the required link with the objective of the establishment of a common market?

The issue of the implications of the use of Directives can be approached from at least three different angles. From the perspective of the Community legislature, the question as to any possible formal limitations arises. Member States, on the other hand, are most concerned with the degree of discretion left to them by virtue of Article 189(3) in the implementation of environmental Directives. Finally, from the perspective of the individual Directives can be viewed as sources of enforceable environmental rights.

In this section only the question of the formal limitations inherent in the use of Directives needs briefly to be addressed; the other two questions are dealt with elsewhere in this chapter.

Does the nature of Directives, which impose merely obligations of result rather than obligations of form,[31] limit the Community legislature, in terms of the degree of detail that may be pursued? In practice, and particularly during the first 15 years of Community environmental policy-making, Directives have often employed an extremely high level of detail, approaching the detail expected from Community Regulations. Recently, Member States have criticized this use of Directives, concerned by the difficulties involved in the implementation of the sometimes very detailed definitions and standards. As will be seen, in this respect more recent environmental directives are indeed markedly different from their earlier counterparts. However, the Court has endorsed the practice of Regulation-type environmental Directives in its jurisprudence[32] and, within the boundaries of the principle of proportionality, the institutions of the Community are free to pursue the degree of detail deemed necessary for the achievement of the goal of the Directive in question.

A second striking feature of the Treaty of Rome was Article 100, the requirement of unanimity. It has often been asserted that the need for consensus implies that the level of environmental protection pursued by the Community under Article 100 would necessarily reflect the standards of the lowest common denominator. With the benefit of hindsight, there is little doubt that the requirement of unanimity has not produced such effects and that, in fact, many of the environmental directives adopted prior to the introduction of qualified majority voting in 1987 incorporate environmental standards which, in the present climate, are often judged unduly stringent.[33] Although there are many possible explanations for this phenomenon, it should not be ignored that the power to veto proposed environmental legislation at the same time has allowed 'green' Member States such as Denmark, the Federal Republic of Germany or the Netherlands to ensure that harmonized standards would reflect their existing or desired national standards, often by offering 'compensation' to less enthusiastic Member States in the form of package deals. Indeed, as will be seen, the inclusion of paragraph 4 in Article 100A in many ways was intended to offset the consequences of the loss of this power after the introduction of qualified majority voting by the Single European Act.

A third question deserving consideration is whether the technique of the harmonization of laws, which by definition is a reactive rather than a proactive process, has undermined the development of a coherent and autonomous Community environmental policy. Although it is true that the Community's environmental policy is characterized by its *ad hoc* and piecemeal development, which at the same time is one of its most serious deficits, it would be misconceived to attribute this state of affairs primarily to the reactive nature of Article 100. In practice, the existence of national provisions which could justify Community action has never been a serious obstacle during periods when Member States themselves were increasingly developing appropriate legal responses to threats to their environments. In addition, by virtue of a gentlemen's agreement (which has later been translated into a Directive) the

Commission possessed an 'early warning' system, giving the Commission prior notice of any planned national environmental legislation which could affect the establishment of the common market, allowing it to pre-empt such plans by proposing a Community Directive.[34] In addition, action could also be justified by virtue of Article 235 if this was deemed more appropriate. The lack of coherency in the Community's environmental policy therefore must be attributed to factors which are not unique to the Community, as is also evidenced by the consolidation programmes which are being undertaken in numerous Member States, and which are now also taking place at Community level.[35]

Finally, it might be expected that the requirement that community action should be necessary for the establishment or functioning of the common market has severely limited the possible scope of action under Article 100. Once more, however, there is little evidence suggesting that this legal constraint has produced such effects. Until the late 1980s the political climate still allowed the Commission to adopt an extremely broad interpretation of its powers under Article 100 which, sanctioned by the European Court,[36] allowed it relatively unchallenged[37] to propose such measures as the Directives on the conservation of wild birds[38] and the quality of bathing water[39] based on Article 100. No Member State has ever directly challenged the legality of an environmental action on the basis that it had been erroneously adopted under Article 100 in an action pursuant to Article 173,[40] a fact partly explained by the circumstance that such directives were adopted unanimously.[41]

In October 1972 the Heads of State and Government at the Paris Summit Conference agreed that in order to accomplish the tasks to be laid down in the action programmes, it was advisable to use as widely as possible all the provisions of the Treaties, including Article 235.[42] In cases where Article 100 did not suffice to justify Community action, action could therefore be based on Article 235, often in conjunction with Article 100. Article 235 is sometimes, inappropriately, branded a 'catch-all' provision. In reality, recourse to Article 235 is subject to a number of conditions. Thus, action must be *necessary* to attain one of the objectives of the Treaty and must take place 'in the course of the operation of the common market'. In addition, recourse to Article 235 is only justified if the Treaty has not provided the necessary powers. Although the availability of Article 235 to pursue the Community's environmental objectives was therefore conditional upon the fulfilment of a number of conditions, it cannot be denied that, more important than the nature of these conditions, is the political climate. For the reasons discussed above, at the time these powers were allowed to be employed but since then the climate has changed to a degree that Article 235, although not repealed, now is not much more than a curious legal fossil.[43]

The combined effect of Article 100 and 235 was that even before 1987 the Community had adopted more than 100 environmental Directives, ranging from Directives on the protection of wild birds or shellfish to Directives on the quality of drinking water.

Environmental Law following Single European Act

Thus, while the absence of a clear legal basis in the Treaty in no way proved an insurmountable obstacle to the formation of an environmental policy, when amendments to the Treaty were first negotiated in 1985 it was only logical to address this paradox by including in the Treaty a Title devoted to the Community's environmental policy. A comparison between the four environmental action programmes and the provisions of what came to be Title VII shows that the latter in most respects constitutes a codification of pre-1987 practice rather than a radical reorientation in respect of the relation between the Community's trade and environmental objectives. In many ways more innovative, and controversial, than the provisions in Title VII was the provision primarily intended to accelerate the establishment of the internal market, Article 100A. The latter, like Article 100 previously, could potentially prove a significant legal basis for action in the sphere of the environment. Indeed, one of the most difficult questions which needed to be resolved after the coming into force of the Single European Act was the relationship between Article 100A (qualified majority decision-making in the sphere of the internal market after cooperation of the European Parliament) and Article 130S (unanimous decision-making in the sphere of the environment 'as such' after mere consultation of the European Parliament). Before turning to this question, however, and in particular in view of Article C in the Maastricht Treaty on European Union (TEU) which stipulates that its provisions are intended to build upon the *acquis communautaire*, the most important features of the provisions in Title VII and Article 100A as in force between 1987 and 1993 should be outlined briefly.

Title VII

Ample literature exists regarding the interpretation of the environmental provisions in the Single European Act and it is therefore possible to limit ourselves to some observations of a more general nature.[44]

By way of preliminary observation, it is notable that the Single European Act left Article 2 unchanged and that, as a result, the Community's environmental objectives were not mentioned in (the symbolically important) Part One of the Treaty entitled 'Principles'. Instead, these *objectives* were found in Article 130R(1) and are:

- To preserve, protect and improve the quality of the environment.
- To contribute towards human health.
- To ensure a prudent and rational utilization of resources.[45]

The Commission's initial proposals had been to include a more detailed list of objectives.[46] Although this might have had the advantage of granting the environmental objectives similar weight to the equally detailed economic objectives, at the same time it would have restricted the Community's competencies in this field. In this respect, it is noteworthy that the notion of 'environment' is not in any way circumscribed and therefore can be taken to embrace the urban environment[47] as well as the extra-Communitarian environment. As a result, the Community's environmental objectives were (and still are) extremely wide-ranging and to a large extent reflect those that were previously contained in the three environmental action programmes.[48]

This observation equally applies to the principles on which environmental policy is based and which is spelled out in Article 130R(2). Preventive action deserves priority or, if this is not possible, damage must be rectified at source.[49] This latter principle would seem to imply that the Community's environmental policy should preferably make use of emission standards rather than quality objectives.[50] The Court has interpreted this provision in the light of the principles of 'proximity' and 'self-sufficiency' which in turn allowed Member States to restrict imports of waste in apparent derogation of the general provisions regarding the free movement of goods.[51]

The polluter pays principle remained the main approach in respect of cost allocation.[52] The idea that environmental protection must be a component of other policies[53] was extracted from the fourth programme. As will be seen, in the *Titanium Dioxide* case, the Court used this principle of integration to justify an extensive interpretation of Article 100A.[54]

Article 130R(3) stipulated that a number of factors needed to be *taken into account* during the *preparation stage* of an environmental measure and, as such, appears therefore to be little more than a political instruction. Thus, the Community must take into account 'the available technical data' or the 'environmental conditions in the various regions of the Community'[55] as well as 'the cost of action or lack of action'[56] and 'the economic and social development of the Community as a whole and the balanced development of its regions'.

Article 130(4) incorporated what has gradually become known as 'the principle of subsidiarity', stipulating that 'the Community shall take action relating to the environment to the extent to which the objectives referred to in paragraph 1 can be attained better at Community level than at the level of individual Member States'. No other Community policy was made subject to this principle. Despite the intense academic debate to which the provision has given rise, the principle has been of very little practical significance and has never been subject to a ruling by the European Court.[57] The same paragraph provides that 'without prejudice to certain measures of a Community nature, the Member States shall finance and implement the other measures', a provision which seems largely irrelevant as it merely restates the division of responsibilities within the Community's legal order but which, at the same time, was partly intended to rule out the creation of an 'environmental fund'.[58]

Article 130R(5) stated:

Within their respective spheres of competence, the Community and the Member States shall co-operate with third countries and with the relevant international organizations. The arrangements for Community co-operation may be the subject of agreements between the Community and the third parties concerned, which shall be negotiated and concluded in accordance with Article 228.

Although the drafting of this provision seems to suggest otherwise, a Declaration was attached to the Single European Act to the effect that 'the provisions of Article 130R(5), second subparagraph do not affect the principles resulting from the judgment in the *AETR* case'.[59] This means that the Communities' external environmental competencies are derived either explicitly from the Treaty itself[60] or implicitly from its internal powers,[61] which implies that the Community's external powers, though not exclusive, are extremely extensive.

Article 130S governed the environmental decision-making procedure (evidently leaving unaffected the procedure in respect of Community acts based on Article 100A) and as a general rule required unanimity after mere consultation of the European Parliament. It is noteworthy that environmental policy, after the coming into force of the Single European Act, thereby remained one of the very few policies where unanimity was still required, mirroring the controversial nature the Community's environmental policy had acquired by the mid-1980s.

Although Article 130S does not limit the Community to the use of Directives as had previously been the case under Article 100, Community practice has hardly changed as a result[62] and the Directive continues to be the most widely used instrument for environmental policy-making.

The second paragraph of the same provision stipulates that the Council shall define, under the conditions laid down in the first paragraph (ie unanimity after consultation of the European Parliament) those matters on which decisions are to be taken by a qualified majority. No use has been made of this procedure, even though the Commission has submitted proposals to make use of this procedure in the context of Directive 76/464[63] and the eco-audit scheme.[64] Although the position of the European Parliament remained unclear, from this scarce practice it appears that the European Parliament was merely to be consulted and the cooperation procedure as found in other provisions which provided for qualified majority voting therefore was not to apply.

Environmental Law and the Internal Market
The second important legal basis for environmental policy-making introduced by the Single European Act is found in Article 100A. Much in the way Article 3b (principle of subsidiarity) is currently the focus of critical attention, following the adoption of the Single European Act it was Article 100A(4) which generated most of the controversy.[65] Article 100A, like Article 3b, was drafted by diplomats rather than lawyers resulting in a provision which A G Tesauro in case C 41/93, French Republic v Commission of the European Communities, characterized as 'less than crystal clear'.[66] Both provisions are intended to serve as a safety-valve against an over-expansionist Community. This is probably where the comparison should end because, whereas Article 100a(4) aims to allow Member States to continue to apply more stringent national rules after harmonization, the main objective of the principle of subsidiarity is chiefly to prevent harmonization from taking place in the first place.

Article 100a(4) reads as follows:

> If after the adoption of a harmonization measure by the Council acting by a qualified majority, a Member State deems it necessary to apply national provisions on grounds of major needs referred to in Article 36, or relating to protection of the environment or the working environment, it shall notify the Commission of these provisions.
>
> The Commission shall confirm the provisions involved after having verified that they are not a means of arbitrary discrimination or a disguised restriction on trade between Member States.
>
> By way of derogation from the procedure laid down in Articles 169 and 170, the Commission or any Member State may bring the matter directly before the Court of Justice if it considers that another Member State is making improper use of the powers provided for in this article.

The scope of Article 100a(4) is far from clear. 'Internal marketeers' support a narrow interpretation whereas 'environmentalists' argue for a green reading. Even a superficial reading of the provision gives rise to numerous important questions, such as:

(1) Can Article 100a(4) be invoked in respect of all harmonizing measures adopted by a qualified majority or only those based on Article 100a?

(2) Can the provision be invoked in the case of amendments of earlier Directives previously adopted on the basis of Article 100 (where unanimity applied)?

(3) Can the provision be invoked even if the measure has been unanimously adopted under Article 100a?

(4) Can the provision be invoked by Member States which voted *for* the measure?

(5) Can only existing measures be justified, or can national provisions also be enacted after the adoption of the harmonizing legislation?

(6) What is the relation between Article 36, the Cassis de Dijon jurisprudence and Article 100a(4)?

(7) When should the Commission be notified of the intention to apply national provisions?

(8) What is the legal effect of such notification?

Only some of these questions have been answered in the Court's judgment in case C-41/93 since, in that case, the Court focused on the Commission's role in the verification procedure and, as far as the substance of Article 100a(4) is concerned, limited itself to observations of a general nature, noting merely that: '. . . if the conditions which Article 100a(4) lays down are fulfilled, that provision allows a Member State to apply rules derogating from a harmonisation measure adopted in accordance with Paragraph 1'. This lack of precision is deplorable, since it has perpetuated some of the confusion about the scope of paragraph 4. Yet, even though the Court may not have explicitly addressed many of the substantive issues, by unreservedly stating that the provision must be interpreted in the light of the objective of the creation of the internal market and hence be applied restrictively, it appears that the 'green' interpretation of Article 100a(4) has been rejected.[67]

Determining the Appropriate Legal Basis for EC Environmental Law

As has been seen, EC environmental legislation can be adopted on numerous legal bases, the most important of which are Articles 100A and Article 130S. It is important to acknowledge that the choice of the legal basis for a Community act had (and will continue to have) a number of practical implications.[68]

In the first place, legislation aimed at the establishment of the internal market under Article 100A was adopted by a qualified majority, whereas Article 130S required unanimous approval of the Council. Furthermore, the principle of subsidiarity as pronounced in Article 130R(4) governed the exercise of the Community's environmental competencies under Article 130S, whereas no such restrictions apply under Article 100A. It can also be argued that the quality of EC environmental law was served by increased use of Article 100A. Thus, proposals based on this provision pursued 'a high level of protection' (paragraph 3). The unanimous approval of the Council required under Article 130S, at least in theory, harboured the threat of Community standards reflecting those of 'the lowest common denominator'.[69] This difference is also reflected in the fact that Article 100A(4) arguably only allows member states to *apply* (existing) more stringent national rules whereas, in the case of Article 130T, it was deemed necessary to allow progressive member states to *maintain or introduce* much more stringent national rules. However, in practice Member States have been reluctant to go unilaterally beyond what is required by Community law. Finally, the quality of EC environmental law is also increased by virtue of the more intensive role played by the European Parliament under Article 100A (cooperation procedure). Without exception, the European Parliament pressurizes the Commission and the Council to adopt more stringent environmental standards. Although prior to the adoption of the TEU the differences between the decision-making procedures of Articles 100A and 130S were perhaps more pronounced than they are at present, as will be seen, the differences between Article 100A and 130S are still sufficiently profound to expect future litigation as to the appropriate legal basis for EC environmental legislation.

It is not surprising, therefore, that the Court's ruling in the famous titanium dioxide case to the effect that directive 89/428 should be based on Article 100A, was widely hailed as a significant victory for the Community's environmental policy. The Court arrived at this conclusion employing the following line of reasoning:

(1) The purpose and the contents of directive 89/428 related as much to the protection of the environment as to the elimination of disparities between national environmental laws.

(2) The decision-making procedures under Articles 100A and 130S being fundamentally different, it was not possible to base the directive on both provisions simultaneously.

(3) The present directive had to be based on Article 100A for the following reasons:
  – in view of the 'principle of integration' of Article 130R(2), a Community act is not dependent on Article 130S for the sole reason that it also pursues environmental objectives;
  – Article 100A(3), which obliges the Commission, in its proposal concerning environmental protection, to take as a base a 'high level of protection', indicated that the environmental objectives of Article 130R can be pursued effectively by way of harmonizing legislation based on Article 100A;
  – environmental measures which eliminate distortions of competition contribute to the establishment of the internal market and hence fall within the scope of application of Article 100A.

After the titanium dioxide case, it was widely expected that, at the very least, waste directives, which after all regulate the 'good' waste,[70] would in the future be based on Article 100A. However, in case C-155/91 the Court arrived at the opposite conclusion. Although not denying that certain provisions of the directive in question[71] affected the functioning of the internal market, the Court found that this was not the directive's *principal* aim *(objet principal)*. There can now be little doubt that the theory of 'the centre of gravity' as an indicator for the legal basis of Community acts is embraced by the Court and the ruling implies that the Court's interpretation of the notion of 'internal market' is either not as extensive as has been inferred from the titanium dioxide case or, at the very least, that it does not produce the effects advocated by some commentators.

Thus, in the titanium dioxide case, the Court had raised the strong impression that the mere fact that a directive had the *effect* of eliminating distortions to competition, in conjunction with the fact that environmental action was not dependent on Article 130S (in view of Articles 130R(2) and 100A(3)), sufficed to base such an act on Article 100A. Any such impressions were dispelled by the Court's dictum in ground 19:

> ... the sole fact that the establishment or functioning of the internal market is concerned does not suffice for the application of Article 100A. It follows, in fact, from the jurisprudence of the Court that recourse to Article 100A is not justified if the proposed act only incidentally has effects on the conditions of competition and trade.

Hence, and contrary to what the titanium dioxide ruling seemed to suggest, Article 130S is by no means a 'residual' environmental competence but in fact will serve as the legal basis of perhaps the majority of environmental directives. There is no reason to suggest that the Treaty on European Union (TEU) has in any way changed this state of affairs.

Environmental Law Following the Treaty on European Union

The TEU, or Maastricht Treaty,[72] represents one further step in the process of the evolution of an 'ever closer union'[73] set in motion by the 1957 Rome Treaty. Thus, the *acquis communautaire* is not called into question and the TEU is intended further to build upon past achievements.[74] The provisions regarding the Union's environmental policy therefore must be interpreted in this light and many of the observations made in respect of the provisions in the Single European Act apply equally to the present Treaty.

One of the first striking changes brought about by the TEU is the insertion of environmental goals in Articles 2 and 3, and thereby the elevation of environmental protection to one of the 'principles' of the Community. This change, although not without political significance, would seem to have few practical implications.[75] It is doubtful whether in the future the Court will need to resort to Articles 2 or 3 in order to 'activate' empowering provisions in the way that it sometimes has in the past.[76] At the same time, any added (political) weight that environmental objectives could have acquired in relation to more firmly established economic goals has been completely off-set by the almost random proliferation of other policy areas in these provisions.[77]

As far as provisions specifically relating to the environment are concerned, the most important changes are found in Articles 130R–T which are now found in Title XVI.

Title XVI

Title XVI entitled 'Environment' incorporates a number of changes that deserve particular attention.

As far as the objectives spelled out in Article 130R(1) are concerned, the fact that the verb 'to contribute to' has replaced potentially more definite separate verbs which were previously used for each individual objective should not be regarded as proof that the Union is less committed to these goals. Rather, the Community's competencies in the sphere of the environment have always been concurrent with those of the member states and in that sense the Union only contributes towards the attainment of the environmental goals.

'Promoting measures at international level to deal with regional or worldwide problems' has been added to paragraph 1 as a fourth objective. Although this amendment codifies existing practice,[78] at the same time it reflects the increased importance the Community's international environmental policy has acquired, partly as a result of the principle of subsidiarity.[79]

Two new principles have been added to Article 130R(2):

- Community policy on the environment shall aim at a high level of protection, taking into account the diversity of situations in the various regions of the Community.
- Community policy on the environment 'shall be based on the precautionary principle'.

The principle that Community environmental policy should aim at 'a high level of protection' was previously found in Article 100A(3), while a similar instruction was lacking in Title VII. This inconsistency has now been removed. On the other hand, Article 130R(2) allows geographical diversification of standards, mirroring the situation in the various regions. Environmental measures whose principal aim is the establishment of the internal market and which are based on Article 100A, understandably, do not benefit from this flexibility.

More innovative is the precautionary principle which now precedes the principle that preventive action should be taken. In view of their independent position in Article 130R(2), both principles clearly should be afforded independent significance. As far as the principle of prevention is concerned, although it requires that proven hazards be eliminated,[80] at the same time such action will only be taken if it is scientifically shown that:

(1) The danger the measure intends to address is 'real'.
(2) The measure will (contribute to) addressing the danger.

In practice, these conditions may prove insurmountable obstacles to a proactive environmental policy.

Although no universally or even Community-wide accepted definition of the precautionary principle prevails,[81] it is clear that it is designed to lower this barrier by abandoning the requirement of proof of a causal link. Thus, by way of example, in Article 2(5)(a) of the Convention on the protection and use of transboundary watercourses and international lakes the principle is defined as a principle 'by virtue of which action to avoid the potential transboundary impact of the release of hazardous substances shall not be postponed on the ground that scientific research has not fully proved a causal link between those substances, on the one hand, and the potential transboundary impact, on the other hand'.[82] The legal significance of the principle would seem to reside primarily in its effects on the principle of proportionality in the sphere of the environment and hence indirectly on the Community's powers. In other words, although the exercise of environmental powers by the institutions of the Community evidently remains conditional upon respect of the principle of proportionality, the European Court (for example in an action under Article 173 EC) in the future will interpret this principle in the light of the precautionary principle.

The principle of the integration of environmental objectives in other Community policies has been maintained, albeit in slightly amended form. Once more, the different wording should not be attributed much significance and the central position of this principle has not been weakened.

What is a novelty is the reference in Article 130R(2) to the inclusion in harmonization measures (Directives or Regulations) of 'a safeguard clause allowing Member States to take provisional measures, for non-economic reasons subject to a Community inspection procedure'. Although there exists some uncertainty as to the exact meaning of this provision,[83] and in particular its relationship to Article 130T, reliance on a safeguard clause would seem to be dependent on the following conditions:[84]

- The clause must be found in a Community act based on Article 130S and hence relate to one of the objectives of Article 130R(2).
- The derogation is not made for economic but for environmental reasons.
- The national measure must be designed to offer degrees of environmental protection, exceeding those contained in the harmonizing measure.
- The national measure must be temporary.
- The national measure must first be made subject to a Community inspection procedure.

Article 130R(3) and 130R(4) has remained unchanged although, in view of the elevation of the principle of subsidiarity to a general principle of Community law,[85] the latter now no longer includes a separate reference to this principle.

By far the most important change in Title XVI relates to environmental decision-making in Article 130S, which will be discussed below.

Finally, Article 130T has been amended so as to require notification to the Commission in cases where Member States maintain or introduce more stringent protective measures. Unlike Article 100A(4), it would seem that the legality of those national measures is not conditional upon confirmation of them by the Commission. The Commission may decide, evidently, to initiate proceedings under Article 169 EC if it believes that those measures are incompatible with the Treaty.

Environmental Decision-Making after Maastricht

One of the most important changes brought about by the TEU is in the area of environmental decision-making. A new decision-making procedure has been introduced so that environmental laws may now be adopted on the basis of the so-called 'co-decision' procedure[86] as well as the cooperation and consultation procedures previously contained in Articles 100A and 130S respectively. Although the TEU has extended the areas where qualified majority voting applies, at the same time it has compounded the confusion surrounding the appropriate legal basis for environmental directives.

All measures based on Article 100A will be subject to the co-decision procedure, which institutes a system of up to three readings. The main novelty of the procedure in comparison to the co-operation procedure[87] resides in the introduction of a third reading and a Conciliation committee which is convened if, in the second reading, no agreement is reached between Council and European Parliament. In such cases the Conciliation Committee seeks to agree on a joint text.[88]

The third reading is completed if, after six weeks, the Conciliation Committee approves a joint text, after which it is referred back to the European Parliament and the Council who in turn have six weeks to adopt the text.[89] If they fail to do so, the proposal fails.[90]

If, on the other hand, the Conciliation Committee does not adopt a joint text, the proposal fails unless the Council adopts the common position it reached in the second reading by a qualified majority within six weeks.[91] Yet the European Parliament has the final word in that it may reject the text adopted by the Council by an absolute majority within six weeks. [92]

Article 189(b)(8) provides that the scope of the co-decision procedure may be widened on the basis of a report submitted by the Commission by 1996 at the latest and it can be expected that, ultimately, all environmental measures may become subject to this procedure. It is clear, even from this very brief résumé of the procedure, that the European Parliament's involvement in environmental decision-making under Article 100A has significantly increased, its ultimate power is 'negative' rather than 'positive'.

Whereas environmental decision-making under Article 100A is undoubtedly complicated, the picture offered by Article 130S is one approaching anarchy as it incorporates all three decision-making procedures for different kinds of environmental laws. What *is* clear is that, as a general rule, environmental decision-making is governed by the cooperation procedure of Article 189c, ie the procedure which, prior to the TEU, governed Article 100A. Thus, there are two readings, with the European Parliament's powers residing mainly in the circumstance that where it proposes amendments or rejects the Council's common position of the first reading, in the second reading the latter will either have to abandon the proposal completely,[93] accept the amendments included by the Commission in its revised proposal by a qualified majority,[94] or unanimously adopt a proposal other than the revised proposal within the time limits specified.[95]

Article 130S(2) stipulates the first exception to this general principle by providing that, by way of derogation from the decision-making procedure provided for in paragraph 1 and without prejudice to Article 100A, the Council acts unanimously after mere consultation of the European Parliament in the following areas:

- Provisions primarily of a fiscal nature.
- Measures concerning town and country planning, land use with the exception of waste management and measures of a general nature, and management of water resources.
- Measures significantly affecting a Member State's choice between different energy sources and the general structure of its energy supply.

An analysis of the second paragraph shows that, within one paragraph, three different decision-making procedures may apply. Hence, in general, for the categories set out in Article 130S(2), the consultation procedure applies and the Council decides unanimously in those areas. However, this is without prejudice to Article 100A and it must therefore be presumed that certain measures, for example in the sphere of waste management, can still be based on Article 100A.[96]

Furthermore, waste management and measures of a general nature are in turn exempted from the consultation procedure and it must therefore be presumed that those areas are as a general rule governed by Article 130S(1) and that hence the cooperation procedure applies.[97]

The Council may still unanimously decide that certain decisions that fall within the scope of Article 130R(2) are to be decided by a qualified majority. As has already been noted, the position of the European Parliament in those cases remains unclear.

Article 130S(3) provides that in the future, environmental action programmes are to be subject to the co-decision procedure which has significant implications in at least two respects. In the first place, future environmental action programmes will have to take the form of a formal Community act rather than an act *sui generis* as has been customary until recently.[98] In addition and more importantly, the European Parliament will become, for the first time, a very significant force in determining future priorities in the sphere of the environment.[99] This is particularly true when it is realized that the European Parliament at the same time enjoys very significant powers to determine budgetary allocations. The fact that the deadlines and details for proposed action to implement the environmental action programmes in the future will be contained in a formal Community act also suggests that it will be more difficult for the Commission to ignore those commitments.

The principle that member states finance and implement the environmental policy which was previously found in Article 130R(4) is now found in Article 130S(4). Paragraph 5 finds a derogation of the principle that, if a measure based on Article 130S(1) involves costs that were deemed disproportionate for the public authorities of a member state, the Council shall, in the act that adopts the measure, lay down appropriate provisions in the form of temporary derogations and/or financial support from the Cohesion Fund.[100]

Implementation and Enforcement of EC Environmental Law

Implementation and enforcement processes bridge the gap between the Union and the Member States. The first process is designed to incorporate EC environmental legislation in the national legal orders, popularly termed 'formal implementation'. Under Article 189 EC, in conjunction with Article 5 EC, Member States are under a duty to take all the necessary legal and administrative steps to ensure the fulfilment of the obligations arising out of environmental directives. This means that Member States must not only transpose the provisions of the directive into their national legal orders by way of the adoption of legal or administrative provisions, but that they must also take the necessary *practical* steps, such as the identification of bathing waters under Directive 76/160[101] or the classification of special protection areas for the purpose of Article 4(1) of Directive 79/409 on the conservation of wild birds.[102] This is usually termed 'practical implementation'. Incomplete implementation of EC environmental law by the Member States has long been regarded as the Achilles' heel of the Union's environmental policy. The institutions of the Community[103] have acknowledged the need for improvements in this field, and Member States have attached a separate declaration to the TEU to this effect.[104] Whereas such political commitment is to be applauded, without the appropriate enforcement mechanisms, uniform and faithful compliance with Community environmental law will almost certainly remain illusory. The final link closing the regulatory chain hence consists of the enforcement mechanisms at the disposal of the institutions of the Community and private parties enabling them to secure compliance with EC environmental laws.

There are a number of factors which make the enforcement of EC environmental law the weakest link of the Community's environmental policy. On the one hand, there are various characteristics peculiar to environmental Directives which make their effective enforcement more crucial than any other body of Community law. Thus, once environmental damage has occurred, it is often no longer possible to remedy the situation. Indeed, in case C-236/85[105] the Court stressed that the faithful transposition of Community obligations becomes *especially* important in respect of environmental directives 'as the management of the common heritage is entrusted to Member States as regards their respective territories'. However, as the Commission has rightly observed, the business community has less direct interest than in other spheres in seeing these standards effectively applied. This, evidently, implies that because 'the vigilance of private individuals to protect their rights'[106] is to a large extent absent in the case of EC environmental directives, more of the Commission's already scarce resources should be allocated to monitoring the implementation of environmental directives than to other areas of Community law. There are indications, however, suggesting that the Commission has used instead its resources mainly to secure the successful completion of the internal market programme.[107] The reactive nature of the infringement procedure under Article 169 EC, too, is incompatible with the need to prevent environmental harm, especially since very scarce use has been made of the powers under Article 186 'to prescribe any interim measures'.

The possible direct effect of environmental directives has so far failed to offset the shortcomings of the infringement procedure in the sphere of the environment. As recently illustrated in case C-236/92, even though the Court has significantly lowered the threshold for direct effect, the programmatic nature of much of EC environmental law will still often prove an insurmountable obstacle for individuals seeking to rely on those provisions before their national courts.[108] Even where environmental directives are directly effective, there remain doubts about the extent to which Community law prescribes the national procedures and remedies for the enforcement of those rights.[109] An 'enforcement gap'[110] can therefore be said to exist in the sphere of EC environmental law, which seriously undermines its effectiveness.

One of the most important motivations leading the Court to embrace the doctrine of the direct effect of Community law in 1963 was the introduction of an element of the private enforcement of Community law[111] and the success of this policy almost seems to have caught the Court by surprise.[112] More than 20 years later the same concern inspired the Court in the well-known Francovich case[113] to endorse the principle that Member States can be liable for damages suffered by private individuals as a result of breaches of Community law.

Three characteristics of the Treaty in particular were advanced to justify this conclusion: the autonomous character of the Community legal order,[114] the principle of effectiveness and protection of the rights of individuals, and the principle of solidarity as expressed in Article 5 EC.[115]

An indispensable prerequisite for a Member State's liability was the nature of the infringement of Community law; only breach of a fundamental Community obligation could give rise to such liability.[116] Such a breach of a fundamental Community obligation in itself does not suffice for a Member State to become liable, however. In addition, liability for Member States depends on three conditions:

(1) The result required by the Directive includes the conferring of rights for the benefit of individuals.
(2) The content of those rights is identifiable by reference to the directive.
(3) There exists a causal link between the breach of the state's obligations and the damage suffered by the persons affected.

Importantly, the Court noted that these three conditions are 'sufficient'.[117] Fault or negligence on the part of the Member State is therefore not required. It remains to be seen, however, to what extent state liability for breaches of environmental directives will be a useful additional remedy to that of the direct effect.[118]

THE FUTURE: SUBSIDIARITY AND EC ENVIRONMENTAL LAW

In addition to *principe d'attribution des compétences* of Article 4 EC, which governs the extent to which powers have been attributed to the Community,[119] and generally applicable principles such as proportionality and respect for fundamental human rights which govern the exercise of powers thus attributed, the European Court of Justice must now also ensure respect for the principle of subsidiarity as spelled out in Article 3b of the TEU. Hence, Community acts adopted in breach of Article 3b EC may be held invalid by the Court under Articles 173 or 177 EC. Article 3b expresses the principle as follows:

> In areas which do not fall within its exclusive competence, the Community shall take action, in accordance with the principle of subsidiarity, only if and in so far as the objectives of the proposed action cannot sufficiently be achieved by the Member States and can therefore, by reason of the scale or effects of the proposed action, be better achieved by the Community
> Any action by the Community shall not go beyond what is necessary to achieve the objectives of this Treaty.

Even though there can be little doubt that the principle of subsidiarity is intended to be justiciable, to focus attention exclusively on its impact on the exercise of the Community's legislative powers would be to ignore the wider philosophical and political aspirations the principle embodies.[120] The enquiry regarding the likely impact of Article 3b should therefore ideally comprise the entire 'life-cycle' of EC environmental law. The following phases could be distinguished for this purpose:

(1) Planning,
(2) Allocation of Powers,
(3) Exercise of Powers,
(4) Implementation,
(5) Enforcement,
(6) Termination/Annulment.[121]

The process of environmental policy- and law-making is initiated by planning. In the context of the Union, planning is the task mainly of the Commission, which since 1973 has drawn up five multi-annual environmental action programmes. As has been seen, in the past these action programmes are endorsed by the Council as 'Resolution . . .' etc, that is to say, they are not, as such, legally binding.[122] Does this mean that for the purpose of establishing the practical significance of the principle of subsidiarity, the action programmes cannot result in any legal effects?

The much more established debate regarding the legal basis of EC environmental law may be of assistance in this context. Prior to the coming into force of the Single European Act, one of the central questions regarded the extent to which the protection of the environment was necessary to satisfy 'one of the objectives' of the Community 'in the course of the operation of the common market' within the meaning of Article 235 EC. Even though the action programmes themselves were not legally binding, the fact that the Council unanimously endorsed certain plans for action (which again normally are couched in vague language) provided the strongest possible indication that a certain measure indeed fell within the ambit of Article 235.

In much the same way, the Fifth Environmental Action programme provides indications as to what action 'cannot be sufficiently achieved by the Member States and can therefore, by reason of the scale or effects of the proposed action, be better achieved by the Community'. The Fifth Programme is particularly authoritative in this respect, as its adoption coincided with the Maastricht Agreement. Subsidiarity is, in fact, the real threat running through the programme. Although this is not the place to analyse the Fifth Programme in any detail,[123] it provides relatively detailed indications as to the kinds of actions that are best pursued at Community level.The authoritative value of future environmental action programmes has been reinforced by the TEU in view of the fact that they will be adopted as formal Community acts.

It should be realized from the outset that the principle of subsidiarity has not affected the allocation of environmental powers to the Community.[124] As far as these powers are concerned, they are contained mainly in Articles 100A and 130R-T and, as has been seen, the TEU has extended the Union's powers in this sphere by extending the areas to which qualified majority voting applies. Article 3b therefore does not affect the Union's environmental competencies.

A crucial question bearing upon the impact of Article 3b is whether these powers are 'exclusive' in the sense that Member States no longer have the power to legislate in this field. One of the major difficulties with the principle of subsidiarity is that the Treaty does not distinguish between areas of exclusive and non-exclusive Community competence. There can be little doubt, however, that the Union's environmental policy does not fall within the Union's exclusive competence. This follows not only from the environmental action programmes, but also from Article 130R(4) which explicitly refers to 'respective spheres of competence'. It is not possible to argue credibly from the mere fact that Article 130S(1) authorizes the Council to 'decide what action is to be taken by the Community in order to achieve the objectives in Article 130R', that the Community enjoys exclusive competence in this sphere.

There can therefore be little doubt that the principle will apply to Community legislation to be adopted on the basis of Article 130S or Article 100A, and the principle of subsidiarity applies to almost all aspects of the Union's environmental policy.

Following the inter-institutional agreement on the application of the principle of subsidiarity,[125] the Commission has had to provide some indication as to what criteria will be used to apply the principle of subsidiarity to the Union's environmental policy in practice. According to the Commission, in addition to the proportionality test, three questions need to be answered:[126]

(1) What is the Community's dimension of the problem (Scale and effects test, test of necessity)?
(2) What is the most effective solution, given the means available to the Community and to Member States (effectiveness test)?
(3) What is the real added value of common action compared with isolated action by the Member States (effectiveness test)?

Another aspect of the agreement that needs to be underlined is that the principle of subsidiarity, or at least its proportionality aspect, is not only to govern the content of proposed action, but also the choice of legal instruments by which the action is to be pursued. Evidently, this means that Regulations will only be very rarely used, but this does not constitute a break with tradition: 95 per cent of EC environmental law consists of directives. The use of directives does not necessarily lead to the slackening of the pace of environmental integration, provided that the appropriate enforcement mechanisms are in place.

A possible effect of subsidiarity on the choice of legal instruments may be greater recourse to framework directives and obligations for Member States to elaborate 'national programmes' such as those contained in Directive 76/464 or the surface water directive. It should be noted, however, that Member States have been particularly reluctant to implement these provisions, very few national programmes having been adopted.[127] However, the choice of legal instruments does not involve a simple choice between regulations and directives. In the first place, a particularly potent instrument for the furtherance of the Community's environmental objectives is the accession to international environmental conventions. It is not difficult to argue that the Union is ideally suited to represent Member States on the international plane as it is manifestly more effective than the Member States acting individually, enjoying a block-vote of 15.[128] It is no coincidence that the Fifth Environmental Action programme puts great emphasis on international cooperation. International cooperation has also been elevated to an objective of the Union's environmental policy by the Maastricht Treaty. Brinkhorst, too, argues that Article 3b will lead to greater Community participation in international environmental regimes.[129] As far as the Union's competencies to conclude international environmental agreements is concerned, reference merely needs to be made to the ERTA judgment and the opinion in Krämer.[130]

Secondly, in deciding how best to achieve the Union's environmental objectives, the institutions are not limited to the instruments discussed above. In addition, they should consider the use of tax or economic instruments, which is made abundantly clear by the Fifth Environmental Action programme as well as recent Commission documents. Deregulation in favour of the use of tax instruments evidently complies with the spirit of subsidiarity. On the other hand, such economic instruments by their very nature are unable to discriminate between environments, which in turn would go against the grain of subsidiarity. An example illustrating the difficulties with tax instruments would be Directive 76/464 relating to dangerous substances discharged into the aquatic environment. This Directive allows the UK to apply quality objectives, rather than uniform limit values, a concession for which the UK has had to fight long and hard, and allows it to benefit from its island status. Were the directive replaced by a tax system, it would be difficult, if not impossible, for the UK to retain its special position.

The implementation of EC environmental law traditionally has been the task of the Member States. As far as environmental directives are concerned, this follows from their very nature, being binding merely as to the result to be achieved and leaving Member States 'the choice of form and methods, as well as more generally from Article 5 of the Treaty itself'.[131] In the past, the formal and practical implementation of EC environmental law has indeed been the exclusive preserve of Member States. There would therefore not seem to be a prima facie role for subsidiarity in respect of the implementation of EC environmental law. Yet the choice of tax instruments rather than directives or regulations will evidently have repercussions at national levels as new structures will have to accommodate the change.

In addition, the Fifth Environmental Action programme clearly intends to extend the newly found 'bottom-up' approach to the stage of implementation, too. Paradoxically, this will involve a greater Community participation in the implementation process than is currently the case.

In the enforcement of EC environmental law, direct enforcement mechanisms should be distinguished from indirect enforcement mechanisms. The former are in the hands of the Commission and Member States under Articles 169 and 170 EC. Indirect enforcement, on the other hand, is carried out by individuals invoking EC environmental law in their national courts. The spirit of subsidiarity (as opposed to the literal wording of Article 3b) would appear to favour an extension of the possibility for individuals to uphold EC environmental law in their national courts. In addition, as has been seen, centralized enforcement by the Commission has lacked the required effectiveness.

The vehicles that enable individuals to enforce EC environmental law in their national courts are, chiefly, direct effect and supremacy. More recently, the Court has established that, even in the absence of direct effect, individuals may rely on Community law in their national courts in an action for non-contractual liability for breach of EC law. The conditions for direct effect need not be discussed as they are well known: a provision of a Directive must be sufficiently clear and precise, unconditional and not leave the national authorities any discretion in its implementation. Even though an analysis of EC environmental directives reveals that many, if not most, provisions of EC environmental directives pass this test, the direct effect of environmental directives has not been the source of individual rights one might have expected. The main reasons for this are:

(1) Unlike, for example, equal pay legislation, individuals have no direct financial self-interest in the enforcement of environmental law.

(2) Where individuals having such a self-interest seek to prevent the adoption of more stringent national standards than those contained in EC environmental directives, the fact that the EC normally pursues minimum harmonization will prove an insurmountable obstacle.

(3) Establishing breach of environmental laws very often involves detailed scientific or technical examinations. Individuals will not normally possess the necessary resources to avail themselves of the necessary data.

(4)   Rules relating to access to justice are still to a large extent governed by national law. Hence, in the absence of a direct interest/negative effect, individuals or common interest groups are often barred from seeking redress.

Thus it is that individuals have found it difficult, if not impossible, to rely on Community law directly in their national courts so as to uphold Community environmental law. The question therefore arises whether the principle of subsidiarity can be advanced as an argument for increased involvement by individuals in the enforcement of EC environmental law.

As has already been seen above, the traditional wisdom that the law relating to remedies is within the exclusive preserve of Member States has already been undermined by the case law of the European Court of Justice. In other words, there is a clear Community right for individuals to uphold their Community rights even in the absence of national or EC rules to that effect. Coupled to the principle of subsidiarity, the position would seem to be that it is for Member States to comply with these minimum requirements, while the Commission must supervise the application of these rules under Article 169.

The Commission has always been keen to increase the scope for indirect enforcement, but due to the controversial nature of the harmonization of national remedies, it has been reluctant to take concrete steps. Some individual directives contain provisions relating to the position of individuals and common-interest groups, such as the access to information directive and the draft directive on civil liability for damage caused by waste. The Commission has elaborated a draft directive on access to justice in the sphere of the environment in the past.[132] Although, in the wake of subsidiarity, it is unlikely that this directive will see the light in its present form, the preamble advances the principle of subsidiarity by way of justification. The principle of subsidiarity, it would seem, has provided the Commission with the political ammunition to put pressure on the Council to cooperate in elaborating rules on access to justice which it would otherwise have found difficult to propose.

Exactly what form Community rules *will* take is difficult to predict. Most recently, the Commission has published its green paper on access to justice in consumer affairs. In this document it rules out the adoption of a Regulation, but mentions a Community procedure for minimum harmonization of actions for injunction and mutual recognition of existing national provisions as serious alternatives. Similar ideas in respect of access to justice for environmental interest groups may be viable, the effect of which would be to promote the indirect enforcement of environmental laws, increasing individual rights in the sphere of the environment.

On the basis of the foregoing, it becomes possible to make some more concrete remarks about the application of the principle in the sphere of the environment. For this purpose the current body of EC environmental legislation will be divided into 'internal market directives' and 'environment directives'. All directives which are based on Article 100A have a significant impact on the internal market. It is clear that in all those cases, by virtue of the scale and effect of the proposed measure, the Community must take action rather than the Member States individually. This would mean that all directives relating to noise, vehicles and industrial sectors require Community action.

Directives based on Article 130S will need to undergo the test as outlined above. In respect of transfrontier pollution (water and air) it will normally be clear that the 'scale and effects' test is satisfied. However, as has been noted earlier, there is a strong case for the Community to focus its attention on participation in international regimes, rather than the adoption of internal rules.

Where there are no notable transfrontier effects (as with the drinking and bathing water directives for example), the Community is still under an obligation to safeguard a minimum degree of environmental and health protection in *all* Member States (Article 2, 130R). In view of the principle of cohesion, it may be necessary for the Community to assist the poorer Member States to this effect, using the Cohesion Fund. This would require some Community standards, but not necessarily of a detailed nature. General minimum standards, coupled with national improvement plans, may be sufficient.

12 THE SOUTH PACIFIC REGION

Wayne King and Vanessa C J Goad

INTRODUCTION

The South Pacific Region is vast, so vast that to fly along the equator from Indonesia to Ecuador, a distance of some 14,400 kilometres would take approximately 14 hours in a modern jet. While the countries and territories of the South Pacific constitute only 6 per cent of the earth's land mass, they are responsible for large ocean resources; their Exclusive Economic Zones (EEZs) together occupy more than 30 million sq km of the Pacific Ocean – about one-sixth of the globe's surface. It is worth noting that the South Pacific Region does not consist solely of countries situated in the Southern Hemisphere, as its name might suggest, but stretches north of the Equator, to the Federated States of Micronesia and the Marshall Islands.

The South Pacific countries and territories range from low-lying atolls to towering mountains. Their environments demonstrate considerable physical diversity, resulting from their various geological origins, which include continental islands formed by underlying mountain ranges, and volcanic and raised limestone islands. The volcanic islands tend to be fertile and relatively rich in natural resources and biodiversity, in comparison with the low atolls which have little diversity in topography, soils or terrestrial fauna and flora.

The islands' populations range from only a few thousand to over 3 million. Less than 6 million people, which is about one-tenth of 1 per cent of the world's population, reside in the South Pacific Regional Environment Programme's[1] 22 developing country island members. The people who reside within the region belong to three main ethnic races – Micronesian, Melanesian and Polynesian – some of whom are spread across the entire South Pacific Region, some across groups of islands, and others who are indigenous to one specific area. The ethnic origin of the various peoples of the South Pacific Region, which is evident in their socio-religious history, is naturally reflected in their cultures and their relationship with the environment.

During prehistoric times, much of the Pacific was settled by people whose way of life was largely dependent on the seas and oceans, and who lived in harmony with their environment in order to survive. Colonialism brought with it great and radical changes, from alterations in power structures to changes in the methods of food production.

Today, many Pacific Islands face ever-increasing environmental problems which can be seen to originate from their historical and political progress in the pursuit of economic development. Colonialism brought a greater dependence of the islands' economies on the outside world and a mistaken belief that self-sufficiency and environmental harmony were no longer a necessary precondition for survival. Over the last 15 years, however, environmental concerns have again resurfaced as the pressures associated with economic development highlight the fragility of many island states.

It is the aim of this discussion first briefly to examine the origins and development of the main regional organizations designed to respond to these pressures, which have been established by the islands and the former colonial powers. It is these organizations which, at a regional level, through the pooling of domestic resources and external aid from the international community, are addressing the environmental problems commonly faced today by the Pacific Islands. Together they are seeking to meet the challenge of balancing improvements in living standards and economic growth with the sustainable development and preservation of the region's environmental resources. This first section concentrates on those regional organizations which can be considered to have played the most important role in initiating, promoting and furthering the process of sustainable development in the Pacific Islands.

The next section focuses on the role of the United Nations Conference on Environment and Development (UNCED), and the Global Conference on Sustainable Development of Small Island Developing States (the SIDS Conference), in outlining regional cooperation, coordination and action to be adopted by the Pacific Island States in their attempts to achieve sustainable development.

The extent to which the South Pacific Regional organizations under discussion have to date succeeded in adopting and implementing the provisions of UNCED's Agenda 21 and the SIDS Programme will then be examined with reference to specific examples that highlight the main common environmental issues and concerns facing the Pacific Islands. The work of the South Pacific Regional Environment Programme (SPREP) will be looked at in particular, drawing upon personal involvement and practical experience within that organization. Finally, present inadequacies will be identified and suggestions for improvements made.

THE ORGANIZATIONS, THEIR ORIGINS AND DEVELOPMEMT

The South Pacific Commission

The South Pacific Commission (SPC) was established in 1947 as a response to the desire of the then colonial powers to assure the economic and social stability of the Pacific Islands and as part of the global movement of institution building which was aimed at creating mechanisms for relations among governments.

The SPC is an international organization consisting of 27 members (13 island developing countries, 5 industrialized countries with a presence in the region, and 9 island territories).[2] As a non-political technical assistance agency with an advisory and consultative role, the SPC provides technical advice, assistance and training, and facilitates the dissemination of information in social, economic and cultural fields, on its own initiative or at the request of member countries, to 22 Pacific Island governments and administrations in the region. To this end, it holds regional conferences and technical meetings, training courses, workshops and seminars at regional and national levels.

The SPC's guiding philosophy is that of service to its island member countries, together with cooperation with other regional and international organizations, working to improve the economic, social and environmental qualities of the region. The organization draws up an annual work programme which is then approved by the SPC Annual Intergovernmental Meeting, a process which ensures that it remains responsive to the expressed needs of the island members. This work programme currently covers such diverse activities as agriculture and plant protection, marine resources, environmental management, rural development and technology, community health, statistics, economics, demography, women's programmes and activities, community education and training, media training, youth and adult education, information services, awards and grants and cultural conservation and exchange.

It can be seen, therefore, that while the SPC was not established initially with a specific environmental agenda, its work programme now covers many areas of environmental concern and has great potential to facilitate in the promotion, implementation and achievement of sustainable development.

The South Pacific Forum

The South Pacific Forum (the Forum) was born from a common desire by the leaders of South Pacific countries to develop a collective response to regional issues. Established in 1971, the leaders of the South Pacific Forum Nations[3] gather each year in July in one of the Forum Countries (the host country being determined on a rotational basis in alphabetical order), to discuss regional and international concerns on diverse topics from security matters to environmental and economic issues. A Pre Forum Officials Committee Meeting is generally held in advance, in order to determine the agenda and matters to be discussed at the Forum.

During the two-day negotiations, the heads of all the relevant intergovernmental regional organizations have the opportunity to make representations to the Forum leaders. Recommendations require the endorsement of the leaders, and the discussion and consultation process is designed to ensure that a political mandate is obtained for particular issues, such as sustainable development and the integration of environmental and developmental policies. The Forum's working activities seek to implement environmentally sound policies, programmes and activities over the mid to long term.

The Post Forum Dialogue, held immediately after the Forum, is attended by agencies and dialogue partners, such as, for example in 1995, Canada, China, France, Japan, the United Kingdom and the United States. The result is the Forum Communiqué, which is a statement agreed by all the leaders of the South Pacific Regional States who are present at the Forum, on economic, environmental and security issues, and which, in recent years, has included comments on sustainable development initiatives to enable island states to proceed with their implementation.

The Second South Pacific Forum decided in 1972 to establish a 'Trade Bureau' to provide consultation on trade and economic matters within the region and to prepare specific proposals in areas of special economic concern to the Pacific Island Countries. The South Pacific Bureau for Economic Cooperation (SPEC) was set up with its headquarters in Suva, Fiji, and the formal agreement to establish SPEC was signed in Apia, Western Samoa, the following year by the governments of the seven founding members of the South Pacific Forum.

At the 1988 South Pacific Forum in Tonga, a resolution was passed to rename SPEC the Forum Secretariat and to broaden its mandate. The Forum Secretariat seeks to tackle the practical problems of development which are faced by its island members, with a strong emphasis placed on trade, shipping, civil aviation, telecommunications, energy and economic issues.

Within the Forum Secretariat, the Environment Unit seeks to coordinate sustainable development policies at the regional level in close cooperation with the South Pacific Regional Environment Programme (SPREP, see below), as well as being guided by the leaders of the member governments of the South Pacific Forum.

The Forum Fisheries Agency (FFA)

The South Pacific Forum Fisheries Agency (FFA) was established in 1979 following a directive from the Forum in response to a need for increased regional cooperation in the management and conservation of fisheries across the vast Pacific.

Changes in the management, use and ownership of the ocean's resources proposed by the Third United Nations Law of the Sea Conference, and in particular the introduction of the Exclusive Economic Zone (EEZ) which gave coastal states (and thereby, island states) jurisdiction over areas within a 200 nautical mile limit of their coasts, necessitated the establishment of a regional agency to deal exclusively with matters affecting fisheries.

The FFA Convention reflects the common interest of its 16 independent member states[4] in deriving maximum economic benefit from their marine resources in particular migratory species such as tuna, within the EEZs of member countries and in the high seas of the region. The Agency functions as a consultative and advisory body and takes its direction from the Forum Fisheries Committee (FFC). The FFC consists of representatives from all FFA member countries and is required to meet at least once a year to approve a budget and work programme. FFC's decisions are subsequently reviewed by the Forum.

Recently, the FFA coordinated the participation of its member states at the Preparatory Sessions for the UN Conference on Straddling and Highly Migratory Fish Stocks on the High Seas which adopted a global and legally binding agreement in August 1995. Prior to and during the Preparatory Sessions, the FFA has been assisting in the formulation of fisheries policy on the issue of the sustainable utilization of fish stocks at both international and regional levels. Other tasks undertaken by the FFA on behalf of its member states include maritime surveillance, the monitoring of marine resource utilization, facilitation within member states' EEZs, and capacity-building within member states in relation to fisheries policy.

The South Pacific Regional Environment Programme (SPREP)

Preparations leading to the establishment of the South Pacific Regional Environment Programme commenced in 1974 with the initiation by the SPC of a special project on the conservation of nature. Consultations between the SPC and the United Nations Environment Programme (UNEP) (see Chapter 3) in 1975 led to the formulation of concrete proposals for a comprehensive programme for environmental management, and also promoted the idea of convening a conference on the human environment of the South Pacific. In the same year, consultations were held between other regional organizations with a view to preparing proposals for a coordinated approach to the South Pacific's environmental problems, reflecting the interest of all the countries in the region. Support was gained from the United Nations and subsequently, at the 1977 SPC Annual Conference, a proposal was submitted that led to the inception of SPREP in 1978. Preparations were also made for the Conference on the Human Environment which took place in Rarotonga in the Cook Islands in 1982 where SPREP's First Action Plan for future activities was produced.

The 1982 Conference adopted the Action Plan for Managing the Natural Resources and Environment of the South Pacific Region (the Action Plan). It provides the mandate for the activities of the SPREP Secretariat and a framework for environmentally sound planning and management that is suited to the Region. As a regional strategy, it identifies some 60 aspects of environmental assessment, management and law. These include coastal area management, protected areas and species conservation, management of natural resources, environmental education and training, waste management and pollution control and environmental planning and administration. Since that time, further reviews have been conducted and an updated plan has been drafted that incorporates an emphasis on sustainable development, reflecting the UNCED process and taking into account the region's responsibilities and its situation under the Climate Change and Bio-Diversity Conventions (see Chapter 4).

SPREP is responsible to its member governments and administrations for the overall technical coordination and continuous supervision of the implementation of the Action Plan. Its activities require constant consulation with other regional organizations to ensure that overlapping activities are coordinated. This coordination is achieved in part through the annual intergovernmental general meeting of SPREP which examines SPREP's administrative and management activities in addition to its working programme and activities.

UNCED AND THE GLOBAL CONFERENCE ON THE SUSTAINABLE DEVELOPMENT OF SMALL ISLANDS — DEVELOPING STATES

UNCED

SPREP played an important role in preparations for UNCED, the 'Earth Summit', held in Rio de Janeiro in June 1992. The UNCED's mandate from the UN General Assembly (see Chapter 1) Resolution 44/228 states that the conference was to:

elaborate strategies and measures to halt and reverse the effects of environmental degradation in the context of increased national and international efforts to promote sustainable and environmentally sound development in all countries.

Working with task forces appointed by the governments of over 12 SPREP members and consisting of teams of government officials, consultants and non-governmental organizations (NGOs), SPREP assisted in the production of National Reports[5] analysing the links between environmental challenges and development trends. The National Reports were in turn used as a foundation for the preparation of two further reports.[6] In addition to assisting the island countries in preparing for UNCED, these reports were essential in ensuring that the specific concerns and needs of the South Pacific Region would be fully understood at the Earth Summit.

Agenda 21 and the Rio Declaration

Agenda 21 and the Rio Declaration, adopted at the Earth Summit, established a programme for action on sustainable development for the international community that has general implications for, as well as specific references to, the institutional needs of small islands. Agenda 21 recognizes that the many environmental problems it addresses, such as safeguarding ocean resources and the protection of the atmosphere, are not confined within national boundaries. Consequently, nearly all of the programme proposals in Agenda 21 call for regional action which is to take the form of the establishment of regional research centres, data collection, and information exchange and consultation to harmonize strategies and policies. The Rio Declaration embodies as its first principle, the priority of the human being in the international debate on sustainable development. While governments may often purport to represent their citizens, having been democratically elected, the extent to which governments can be said adequately to represent their citizens in the environmental arena has been called into question, as for example in the Narmada Dam case. UNCED recognizes the important role to be played by NGOs in providing an alternative voice for individuals in the international and regional debate on the environment. UNCED also recognizes the importance of the empowerment of stakeholders – ie those countries, communities and individuals affected, in policy formation and project implementation in the protection of the environment – who must be entitled to participate in the decision-making and policy-formulating processes.

In order to give effect to this principle, UNCED similarly embodies the principle of transparency which requires access to information, and the free flow of information into and out of organizations in relation to, for example, the environmental and social impacts of projects.

Chapter 38: international institutional arrangements

The overall objective of Chapter 38 of Agenda 21 is the integration of environmental and developmental issues at national, subregional and regional levels. The chapter then goes on to set out proposals for international institutional arrangements which should be implemented in order to facilitate achievement of the overall objective. It includes a statement recognizing the importance of regional cooperation and sets out some of the aspects that regional cooperation should involve, namely:

(1) Promoting regional and subregional capacity-building.
(2) Promoting the integration of environmental concerns in regional and subregional development policies.
(3) Promoting regional and subregional cooperation, where appropriate, regarding transboundary issues related to sustainable development.[7]

The importance of cooperation between regional, national, UN and other relevant international organizations, including non-governmental organizations (NGOs) is also recognized.

Chapter 17: protection, rational use and development of oceans, seas, coastal areas and their living resources

In addition to Chapter 38, which applies to institutions generally involved in the implementation of its many and varied areas of operation, Agenda 21 also specifically addresses the issue of the sustainable development of small islands in Chapter 17(G). It recognizes the special case presented by SIDS in having all the environmental problems and challenges of the coastal zone concentrated in a limited land area. The international community has commited itself to:

(1) Adopt and implement plans and programmes to support sustainable development and utilization of marine and coastal resources of SIDS, including meeting essential human needs, maintaining biodiversity and improving the quality of life for the island people.
(2) Adopt measures to enable SIDS to cope with environmental change effectively, creatively and sustainably, and to mitigate the impacts on, and reduce the threats posed to marine and coastal resources.

Chapter 17 calls for the review and modification of existing unsustainable policies and practices and provides for the review of existing institutional arrangements. Institutional reforms that are essential to the effective implementation of sustainable development plans can then be identified and carried out.

The earlier general principles, recognized by UNCED and embodied in the Rio Declaration and Agenda 21, of transparency (requiring the free and open flow of information into and out of organizations) and democracy (recognizing the need for greater community participation in the planning process) are reiterated in this chapter. The need for increased intersectoral coordination, which is of particular importance in the special case of the Small Island Developing States, is similarly stressed.

The above actions were envisaged to be financed from international aid and carried out through:

(1) *Capacity-building*: identified in Agenda 21 as one of the three main forms that regional action should take and is further defined in the SIDS programme (see below) as 'the restructuring of existing capacity to make the most appropriate and efficient use of the limited resources available to SIDs and to meet the most immediate needs for sustainable development and integrated management'.
(2) *Scientific and technical means*: the establishment of centres for the development and diffusion of scientific information and technical strategies developed to combat environmental problems from a SIDS viewpoint.

(3) *Human resource development:* the implementation of appropriate training and education strategies.

The Global Conference on the Sustainable Development of Small Island Developing States

The Global Conference on the Sustainable Development of Small Island Developing States (the SIDS Conference) was held in Bridgetown, Barbados, between 26 April and 6 May 1994 and was the first post-Rio United Nations global conference. UN General Assembly Resolution 47/189 established the SIDS Conference as a follow-up to Agenda 21 which in Chapter 17 had envisaged the holding of the first global conference on the sustainable development of SIDS in 1993.

The participation by 98 NGOs from developed and developing countries, in particular small island developing states (including some related to major groups), is of particular note and demonstrates the valuable role to be played by such organizations in the negotiating process. It is hoped that their participation will provide a role model for the future.

Among the Conference objectives was the review of institutional arrangements at the international level with the aim of determining whether the existing arrangements were sufficient to enable states to give effect to the relevant provisions of Agenda 21.

The SIDS Conference adopted the Declaration of Barbados which was intended to give the SIDS Programme, also adopted at the Conference, its political impetus. The preamble to the SIDS Programme provides a concise summary of the peculiar vulnerabilities and characteristics of small island developing states and the particularly severe and complex difficulties they face as a result in the pursuit of sustainable development.

The SIDS Programme addresses those environmental issues, from climate change and sea-level rise, through the management of wastes, to the protection and sustainable development of coastal and marine, freshwater, land, energy, tourism and biodiversity resources, which are of particular relevance to SIDS. It follows the UNCED by calling for regional and in-country workshops on environmental law subjects, including environmental conventions and treaties, environmental impact assessment, heritage, pollution, civil enforcement, prosecution and environmental mediation which recognizes the imperative for public participation. Community awareness and motivation are prerequisites in the development of 'home-grown' environmental planning and management abilities. The SPREP published report entitled `Environment and Development: A Pacific Island Perspective' noted a general lack of environmental awareness and motivation. Once traditional controls, such as tabu and ra'ui[8] disappear, community awareness becomes difficult to define and re-establish. Close consultation with the island people is absolutely essential to regenerate a commitment to environmental protection, without which the imposition of environmental management plans cannot succeed.

The SIDS Programme also follows Agenda 21 in providing an outline of policies related to environmental and developmental planning, and action to be undertaken at national, regional and international levels in each programme area. Chapter XI of the SIDS Programme which specifically relates to regional institutions and technical cooperation, incorporates the three main forms of regional action identified in Chapter 38 of Agenda 21, together with the recommended actions to be taken in achieving the aims and objectives identified in Chapter 17, while at the same time providing further detail and more specific suggestions for action.

(1) *The integration of environmental concerns in regional and subregional development policies.* The SIDS Programme provides specifically for the drafting of model environmental provisions to act as a guide to countries. The states, under the principle of sovereignty, enshrined in Agenda 21, are left to incorporate their own country-specific provisions at national level, although the harmonization of environmental legislation and policies is encouraged in order to ensure the highest possible level of environmental protection. The preparation of environmental-law training manuals for both lawyers and others working in the environmental field is a further specific suggestion.

(2) *Cooperation and coordination.* Coordination among regional bodies should be improved. In this area it proposes the development of a SIDS technical assistance programme to promote inter- and intraregional coordination of sustainable development. This will clearly also facilitate the integration of environmental policies.

(3) *Human resource development.* The need for the establishment of regional sustainable development centres where appropriate, also recommended by Agenda 21, is confirmed. These centres will aid in the implementation of the sustainable development of SIDS, through the carrying out of research and training, the development and transfer of endogenous technology, and the provision of legal and technical advice.

The joint formulation of regional programmes and strategies between regional and national authorities is recommended.

IMPLEMENTATION OF THE GENERAL PRINCIPLES, AGENDA 21 AND THE SIDS PROGRAMME: DEVELOPMENTS SINCE THE SIDS CONFERENCE

The SIDS Conference, building on the general principles and recommendations of the Rio Declaration and Agenda 21, and with the special circumstances and requirements of the Pacific Island states in mind, established a number of more specific recommendations for action to be taken by SIDS with the assistance of the international community in order to move towards sustainable development. Emphasis was placed on the need to establish a mechanism, preferably at the regional level, to enable SIDS to implement the more specific recommendations set out in the SIDS Programme agreed at the SIDS Conference.

Access to Information

An increasing amount of information is moving in and out of the region, although this has yet to be quantified. Much of the existing data relates to environmental management and protection and sustainable development approaches for reference purposes only.

Two networks are being set up in the Pacific as part of a global effort by the United Nations Development Programme (see Chapter 3), 'SIDSNET' and 'SIDS/TAP', with the aim of collecting and coordinating information to sustainable development and promoting the dissemination of information relating to SIDs in regions around the world.

Stakeholder Participation

The extent to which stakeholders are currently involved in decision-making processes relating to sustainable development has also yet to be quantified. Participation by community and village groups in programmes and activities which have environmental implications and may contribute to the achievement of sustainable development is certainly increasing. The extent to which stakeholders are actively involved in policy formulation in partnership with the government, however, is limited. The importance of such involvement by stakeholders at all levels, from village to national to regional, and recognized in the international environmental treaties which have recently come into force, has already been emphasized above, and can only be reiterated. NGOs play and will continue to play a vital and key role in facilitating the implementation of sustainable development activities through awareness raising and capacity-building, by bringing pressure to bear on decision-makers through their activities, and by assisting in policy implementation at village level through the organization of community meetings and activities which seek acceptance of a particular programme of action.

At the regional level, increased participation in environmental issues together with an open and transparent flow of information, will enable NGOs to assist governments actually to undertake and implement sustainable development programmes and activities. A commitment at governmental level, however, is required in addition to the financial and technical assistance needed to facilitate the development of such partnerships.

Cooperation Between National, Regional and International Organizations

There has been an improvement in cooperation between organizations at all levels, with a greater understanding of each other's various responsibilities and work programmes. While in the past overlapping programme activities and inadequate information collection and dissemination caused difficulties, during the Preparatory Process for UNCED and the Global Conference for SIDS, the Forum Secretariat and SPREP coordinated their efforts in assisting the participation by SIDS, and in offering technical assistance and coordination in the meetings.

However, it can be seen that the impetus for greater cooperation and the potential integration of regional work programmes comes from the pressure brought to bear on the regional organizations by member governments rather than the management stuctures of the regional organizations themselves. As demand for dwindling financial resources increases, there will come a time when the organizations themselves will seek cooperative partnerships to ensure suvival in the first instance, and the development and implementation of effective work programmes in the second instance.

Regional Technical and Scientific Centres

Although the SIDS Conference included deliberation on the establishment of new regional scientific and technical centres for sustainable development in SIDS, none has been established to date. The University of the South Pacific in Fiji and the University of Papua New Guinea are institutions that already serve in this capacity. Without doubt, enhancing the Universities' financial and technical capabilities would see an improvement in their capacity-building capability, while a change in their policy directives could lead to the establishment of an academic institution that could function as a regional technical centre for sustainable development activities, and facilitate information dissemination and storage.

Human Resource Development

Human resource development has been recognized within the region as one of the most important issues at all levels. This recognition has resulted from the increasingly complex issues being dealt with today – for example, integrated coastal management programmes that may be implemented within the working programme of SPREP, yet cover areas of responsibility that form part of the mandates of the Forum Secretariat, SPC and FFA.

At national level, the management of multi-disciplinary teams and involvement in the consultation process require highly trained staff with excellent management skills. Active on-the-job training is becoming an important part of skills acquisition in the field of environmental management training. Although academic institutions aim to provide the participant with a sound basis in research and evaluation skills, they do little to prepare people for managerial roles. This is best achieved at a practical level and through the experience of interacting with organizations, companies and individuals throughout the region. A whole range of human resource training programmes are available, on each of which it would be possible to devote a complete chapter to examining their contribution to essential human resource development at national, regional and international levels.

CONCLUSION

A number of initiatives are taking place at the time of writing this article; among them are the United Nations Economic and Social Council for Asia and the Pacific (ESCAP) assessment of the implentation of the SIDS Programme of Action, undertaken during July 1995 in Vanuatu, as a precursor to the ESCAP Ministers' Meeting.

The UNDP with the assistance of SPREP is also initating a regional-based programme called Capacity 21, which is a capacity-building project focusing at a national and local level on sustainable development objectives, based upon the relevant Chapters of Agenda 21.

SPREP is also facilitating information collection and data analysis on the extent to which states in the region have been able to implement the SIDS Programme of Action, including, at the national level, the National Environment Management Strategies, which are the prioritized national strategies outlined by each state for achieving sustainable development.

Other programme areas focusing on implementation, and facilitated in particular by SPREP, include Integrated Coastal Zone Management, the South Pacific Biodiversity Conservation Programme, and programmes that are being developed with the assistance of the Global Environment Facility (see Chapter 9) on the implementation of the Climate Change and Biodiversity Conventions.

It can be seen that the South Pacific Region provides a unique example of regional cooperation necessitated by limitations on land, resources, population and economic power that is common to many small island countries. Just as these countries have learnt and benefited from cooperation with each other, so other regions can learn and benefit from the South Pacific Region's experience. Neither should it be forgotten that the region depends on continued support from the international community and on increasing understanding of the area's special needs and vulnerability. It is hoped that this chapter may contribute to such increased understanding.

PART V

Avoiding and Settling Disputes

13 THE INTERNATIONAL COURT OF JUSTICE AND THE EUROPEAN COURT OF JUSTICE

Philippe Sands[*]

INTRODUCTION

This Chapter considers the contribution made by the International Court of Justice (ICJ) in The Hague and the European Court of Justice (ECJ, referring to the Court of Justice and the Court of First Instance) in Luxembourg to the development of international environmental law.[1] These and other international courts can properly be treated as international institutions in the traditional sense of the term, having a judicial rather than legislative or executive function.

The ICJ is the principal judicial organ of the United Nations. Its function is to settle contentious disputes between states and to give advisory (non-binding) opinions at the request of authorized bodies. The ECJ is the judicial organ of the European Union, called upon to ensure that in the interpretation and application of the EC Treaty 'the law is observed'.[2] The function of these and other international courts is 'not to develop international law in the abstract'.[3] However, as Professor (now Judge) Higgins goes on to observe:

> the very determination of specific disputes, and the provision of specific advice, *does* develop international law. This is because the judicial function is not simply the application of existing rules to facts. The circumstances in which it will be said to apply, the elaboration of the content of a norm, the expansion upon uncertain matters, all contribute enormously to the development of international law.[4]

This observation is especially pertinent in the case of international environmental law. Whether at the international or EC level, these obligations are often ambiguous and open to a wide degree of latitude in interpretation. The intended ambiguity in much of the language of international environmental law permits a range of views expressed in the negotiating process to be accommodated in the

---

[*] The views expressed are the author's alone. He would like to thank Caroline Blatch for her assistance in the preparation of this chapter.

rule that is finally adopted. It also frequently reflects caution in adopting norms in the face of scientific uncertainty or concern about the effect of certain rules on economic activities, and prudence in the face of limited precedents in this new and fast-expanding field. Thus, in environmental law, the Courts' tasks of 'choosing, explaining, and refining'[5] may be even more onerous than in other contexts.

The focus of this chapter is on the ICJ and the ECJ, although they are not the only international courts or dispute-settlement bodies charged with addressing environmental issues. Others include regional and global human rights courts and commissions (addressing the nexus between human rights and the environment), the WTO Appellate Body and WTO Panels (dealing with environmental issues in the context of international trade obligations – see Chapter 6), the Inspection Panel recently established by the World Bank (to deal with complaints against the World Bank for non-compliance with, *inter alia*, internal environmental standards – see Chapter 8), the newly established International Tribunal for the Law of the Sea (which can be expected to play an important role in marine environment issues), and the non-compliance bodies established within the context of various multilateral environmental agreements.[6]

What distinguishes the ICJ and the ECJ is their long-standing contribution, their authority (respectively at the global and regional level), and their capacity, potentially, to deal with an exceedingly wide range of environmental issues. Their approach can provide useful guidance to these other bodies, both in the interpretation of environmental rules and in establishing the balance between environmental and other competing societal objectives.

In considering whether, and if so to what extent, these two Courts have been 'greened', it is appropriate to define the basic criteria for assessing such a development. For the purposes of this chapter I have found it helpful to ask three pertinent questions. The first is whether the two Courts have addressed environmental issues at all and, if so, whether they have been willing to recognize the place of environmental protection objectives in the legal orders within which they function. The second question is whether either Court has shown any propensity to give real weight to environmental objectives, as compared to other societal objectives which the EC and international legal orders support, such as economic objectives (trade and competition), territorial integrity, and freedom of high-seas fishing.

The third question is possibly the most difficult. It asks whether either Court has recognized and acted upon the particular characteristics of environmental issues. These characteristics include the important role of science and other technical knowledge and related considerations, the difficulty of dealing with uncertainty in that knowledge, and the inherently global nature of certain environmental issues, which means that interests in environmental concerns must necessarily be widely held. This last point is closely related to the fact that environmental resources and the pollution which harms them do not respect, for the most part, national boundaries and are therefore part of a common interest, which will often be shared by the many rather than the few.

INTERNATIONAL COURT OF JUSTICE[7]

The ICJ, which is sometimes referred to as the World Court or The Hague Court, is the principal judicial organ of the United Nations. It was established in 1946 as a successor (although not formally the legal successor) to the Permanent Court of International Justice. This year sees its fiftieth anniversary. The ICJ has a bench of 15 judges, chosen by reference to the UN approach to 'equitable geographic distribution'. Presently, eight of the judges are from developed countries, and seven from developing countries, and by custom each of the five Permanent Members of the Security Council has had a judge. The Court has jurisdiction in contentious cases to settle disputes between two or more states, and to give advisory opinions on questions of law at the request of certain international organizations.[8]

The ICJ is yet to make a really significant contribution to the development of international environmental law, as opposed to simply confirming that environmental obligations exist. Nevertheless, it has recognized the growing role of the environment in international law, as reflected in its decision after UNCED in June 1992 to establish a specialized Chamber for Environmental Matters. This decision followed previous consideration by the Court on the possible formation of such a Chamber. It was taken in view of the developments in the field of environmental law which have taken place in the last few years and the need to be prepared to the fullest possible extent to deal with any environmental case falling within its jurisdiction.[9]

Jurisdiction

The Court has a contentious and an advisory jurisdiction. Contentious cases reach the ICJ in at least two ways. First, under Article 36(1) of its Statute, the ICJ has jurisdiction by agreement between the parties to the dispute, either by a special agreement (compromise) whereby two or more states agree to refer a particular dispute to the ICJ, or by a compromissory clause in a multilateral or bilateral treaty. The treaty might be a general treaty for the peaceful settlement of disputes, a treaty dealing with the general relations between the states, or a treaty regulating a specific topic, such as environmental protection. Indeed, many environmental treaties provide for possible recourse to the ICJ to settle disputes. Very occasionally they provide for the compulsory jurisdiction of the ICJ.[10] More usually the reference of a dispute to the ICJ requires the consent, in each case, of all parties to the dispute.[11] In recent years the practice has developed in environmental treaties of allowing parties at the time of signature, ratification or accession, or at any time thereafter, to accept by express opt-in the compulsory dispute settlement by recourse to arbitration or to the ICJ.[12] In practice very few Parties accept this option. It is not probable, therefore, that many disputes arising under environmental agreements would go to the ICJ.

Another way in which contentious cases get to the ICJ is under Article 36(2) of the Statute (the 'Optional Clause'), under which Parties to the Statute of the Court may declare that they recognize the compulsory jurisdiction of the Court, in relation to other states accepting the same obligation, in all legal disputes concerning the interpretation of a treaty, any question of international law, the existence of any fact which, if established, would constitute a breach of an international obligation; and the nature or extent of the reparation to be made for the breach of an international obligation.[13] Acceptance of the jurisdiction of the Court under Article 36(2) may be made unconditionally, or on condition of reciprocity, or for a limited period of time.[14] Many states include reservations or conditions to declarations made under the Optional Clause, which means that certain categories of disputes can be expressly excluded.

The ICJ's advisory jurisdiction also provides it with an opportunity to address environmental issues. The UN Charter allows the General Assembly or the Security Council to request the International Court of Justice to give an advisory opinion on any legal question;[15] other UN organs and specialized agencies authorized by the General Assembly may request advisory opinions of the Court on legal questions arising within the scope of their activities.[16] Advisory opinions are not binding in law upon the requesting body, although in practice they are accepted and acted upon by that body.

Case-law

Although the ICJ currently has before it a number of important international environmental cases, neither it nor its predecessor, the Permanent Court of International Justice (PCIJ), have dealt to conclusion with a full-blown international environmental dispute. The three major international environmental cases decided over the past century have gone to *ad hoc* arbitration.[17] Nevertheless, some cases before the ICJ and the PCIJ have been concerned with natural resource or other issues which have allowed the Court to give dicta on certain environmental and conservation issues.[18]

These have contributed to the development of international environmental law. In 1949 the ICJ in the *Corfu Channel* Case affirmed 'every State's obligation not to allow knowingly its territory to be used for acts contrary to the rights of other states'.[19] Although the case did not raise any environmental issues, it is often cited in the field of environmental law, since the dicta quoted is especially pertinent to obligations relating to transboundary environmental issues.

In 1974, in the *Fisheries Jurisdiction* Cases brought by the United Kingdom and Germany against Iceland in respect of the latter's 'extraterritorial' application of its fisheries conservation measures, the ICJ set forth basic principles for the conduct of consultations in relation to the conservation of shared natural resources. The ICJ also suggested, in tantalizingly opaque language, that coastal states and the international community as whole had a special interest in the conservation of fisheries:

> both States have an obligation to take full account of each other's rights and of any fishery conservation measures the necessity of which is shown to exist in [waters in the 12-mile to 50-mile zone]. It is one of the advances in maritime law, resulting from the intensification of fishing, that the former *laissez-faire* treatment of the living resources of the sea in the high seas has been replaced by a recognition of a duty to have due regard to the rights of other States and the needs of conservation for the benefit of all.[20]

This might suggest that coastal (or other) States could, in certain circumstances, apply fisheries conservation measures outside their national jurisdiction, limiting the right of States to engage in absolute freedom of the high seas. Whether this is in fact the case remains to be seen.

Later in 1974, in the *Nuclear Tests* Cases, the ICJ declined to give a ruling on the merits of separate Australian and New Zealand applications concerning the legality of French nuclear tests in the South Pacific.[21] The refusal followed France's unilateral declaration of its intention to cease carrying out atmospheric nuclear tests. Nevertheless, during the pleadings comprehensive environmental arguments were put to the Court on the obligation to prevent transboundary fallout of radioactivity,[22] inspiring at least one dissenting opinion on environmental law.[23] It is also noteworthy that in the Nuclear Tests applications, the ICJ indicated interim measures of protection which called on all three states to 'ensure that no action of any kind is taken which might aggravate or extend the dispute submitted to the Court or prejudice the other party in respect of carrying out whatever decision the Court may render in the case', and which specifically called on France to 'avoid nuclear tests causing the deposit of radioactive fall-out on the territory of' Australia, New Zealand, the Cook Islands, Niue or the Tokelau Islands.[24] France did not accept that the Court had jurisdiction, and continued to carry out atmospheric tests pending the coming into effect of its unilateral declaration.

It is only in the very recent past that events have contrived to test further the Court's environmental character. In May 1989 Nauru brought a case against Australia (*Case Concerning Certain Phosphate Lands in Nauru*), concerning Australia's responsibility for breaches of international legal obligations relating to its phosphate mining activities in Nauru. The application raised issues of international environmental law, including the extent of certain legal obligations governing the use of natural resources, the land rights of indigenous peoples, and the extent of entitlement to the costs of rehabilitation. Again, Nauru's application led to environmental arguments being put forward in the pleadings. These were never addressed by the Court: after it had ruled that the case was admissible and that it had jurisdiction[25] the parties settled the case and it was removed from the list.[26] Accordingly, Nauru's pleadings will remain unpublished. Nevertheless, in overruling Australia's preliminary objections, the ICJ put forward principles of some significance for the development of international environmental law. First, it made clear that for a waiver of any claim (including an environmental claim) to be effective, it would need to be made in a clear and effective manner. Secondly, it found that acts of international institutions (in this case a General Assembly resolution) which have definitive legal effects will not discharge rights which might exist with regard to environmental and other claims in the face of clearly expressed differences of opinion which exist between states supporting such an act. Thirdly, it held that, provided that certain minimum steps are taken to maintain a legal position and to promote a legal claim, the passage of time will not necessarily render a claim inadmissible. Fourthly, particularly significant in the field of environmental law, the question of whether states have 'joint and several liability' is to be distinguished from the question of whether one of those states may be sued alone in respect of a claim of a breach of an international legal obligation, and that the possibility of attributing responsibility to one state might have implications for the legal situation of other states concerned does not establish a bar to proceedings being brought against that other state.

Even more recently, in August 1995 New Zealand requested the ICJ to reopen its 1974 nuclear tests case against France. Although the ICJ dismissed the New Zealand request on jurisdictional grounds, its Order of 22 September 1995 is of considerable interest. In its 1974 judgment in the original nuclear tests cases, the ICJ had added a precautionary paragraph 63. This stated that 'if the basis of this Judgment were to be affected, the Applicant could request an examination of the situation'. It was on the basis of paragraph 63, and in response to France's announced intention to resume underground nuclear testing, that New Zealand returned to the ICJ nearly 21 years later (not having any other basis for invoking the Court's jurisdiction). New Zealand's 1995 request was premised on the view that paragraph 63 referred not only to atmospheric testing but also 'to any developments that might reactivate New Zealand's concern that French testing could produce contamination of the Pacific marine environment by any artificial radioactive material'.[27] Relying on arguments based upon treaty and customary international environmental law, in particular the 1986 Noumea Convention for the Protection of the Natural Resources and Environment of the South Pacific region (to which both New Zealand and France are parties), New Zealand asked the ICJ to declare that it would be unlawful for France to conduct underground nuclear tests before it had carried out an environmental impact assessment according to international standards, which assessment must establish that the tests would not give rise to any radioactive contamination of the marine environment. New Zealand also asked the ICJ as a matter of urgency to indicate provisional measures pending the Court's decision, as it had done 21 years earlier. Five States (Australia, Samoa, Solomon Islands, Marshall Islands and the Federated States of Micronesia) sought to intervene in support of New Zealand. France opposed the request on jurisdictional grounds, arguing in particular that paragraph 63 of the 1974 judgment related only to atmospheric nuclear tests.

As widely predicted, a majority of the Court (12 votes to 3) joined to dismiss the New Zealand request. The majority found that 'the basis of the [1974] Judgment . . . was France's undertaking not to conduct any further atmospheric nuclear tests' and that consequently it could not now take into consideration questions relating to underground nuclear tests.[28] A result the other way would have required an expansive reading of paragraph 63 of the 1974 judgment. By treating the original New Zealand application as relating only to atmospheric tests, when in fact its pleadings demonstrated a broader interest in all nuclear tests, the 1995 Court was left with little room for manoeuvre in interpreting and applying paragraph 63 of the 1974 Judgment.

The Court's unwillingness to address the merits of New Zealand's 1995 request does not mean that the 1995 Order and the proceedings leading to it are without interest. Most importantly, the ICJ has contributed, in a limited but nevertheless significant way, to the development of international environmental law. In language which was not necessary to support its finding, by way of *obiter dicta*, the ICJ referred to 'the development of international law in recent decades', referring in particular to the 1986 Noumea Convention, and indicated that its Order was 'without prejudice to the obligations of States to respect and protect the natural environment, obligations to which both New Zealand and France have in the present instance reaffirmed their commitment'.[29] Even if the ICJ was not prepared to go as far as some (including some judges) may have wished, it appears to be assuming and recognizing, for the first time, the existence of general rules of international environmental law. This becomes apparent if the 1995 Order is read in the context of the pleadings, in which France recognized the existence of a general obligation to prevent environmental damage, as well as obligations relating to environmental impact assessment and an approach based on the 'precautionary principle' (the international legal status of which France questioned but did not deny). These substantive issues of international environmental law are explored in greater detail in the three dissenting opinions. The elegantly comprehensive dissenting opinion of Judge Weeramantary, in particular, will surely become a text of first reference, with consequences significant beyond these proceedings.

Pending Cases

The ICJ therefore stands on the edge of addressing environmental issues, a position it has now been in for more than 20 years. Three matters of environmental significance are pending before the ICJ, which might allow it to take a few steps forward. In July 1993 Hungary and Slovakia notified to the ICJ a Special Agreement submitting their differences over the joint construction of a dam on the Danube River (*Case Concerning the Gabcikovo–Nagymaros Project*). By a 1977 Treaty, Hungary and Czechoslovakia had agreed to construct and operate the Gabcikovo–Nagymaros Barrage System. In May 1989, citing environmental concerns, Hungary suspended part of the construction work. It later abandoned some of the works; Czechoslovakia commenced work on an alternative solution to its part of the project and Hungary sought to terminate the 1977 Treaty. The Court is now asked by the two countries (Slovakia as the successor state to Czechoslovakia) to decide whether Hungary was entitled to suspend and then abandon works on the project, whether Czechoslovakia was entitled to proceed to and put into effect a 'provisional solution', and to indicate the legal consequences of Hungary's purported termination, in May 1992, of the 1977 Treaty. The case raises a number of important issues on the relationship between treaty law and environmental law, including the effect of changes on environmental laws or the state of environmental knowledge on pre-existing treaty obligations, as well as broader issues concerning prior notification and consultation on projects which might have transboundary environmental consequences, the nature and scope of the obligation to carry out an environmental impact assessment, and the nature and status of certain principles and rules of international environmental law, such as Principle 2 of the Stockholm Declaration, Principle 2 of the Rio Declaration, and the precautionary principle. The three rounds of written pleadings have been completed and oral arguments are due to be heard in 1997.

Two advisory opinions before the ICJ raise issues concerning the protection of the environment in times of war and armed conflict. In September 1993 the World Health Organization requested an advisory opinion which asked the Court to address the following question:

> In view of the health and environmental effects, would the use of nuclear weapons by a State in war or armed conflict be a breach of its obligations under international law including the WHO Constitution?[30]

In December 1994 the General Assembly similarly requested the ICJ 'urgently to render its advisory opinion on the following question: "Is the threat or use of nuclear weapons in any circumstance permitted under international law?".'[31] The requests raised two environmental issues which were the subject of lively differences of view during the written and oral stages of pleading, which were concluded in November 1995. The first was the applicability of environmental protection rules set forth in two international humanitarian instruments[32] to the use of nuclear weapons. The second was the question of whether certain international environmental agreements continue to apply during war and armed conflict, and if so what are the legal consequences of such agreements for the effects of nuclear weapons. If the Court renders either or both of the Advisory Opinions (the nuclear weapons states have argued that the Court should not render the Opinions), it is expected to do so in mid-1996.

In March 1995 Spain brought a case challenging the legality of the Canadian fisheries conservation legislation and measures taken by Canada on the basis of that legislation outside its territorial jurisdiction, namely the boarding on the high seas of a Spanish fishing boat (the *Estai*) which was flying the Spanish flag.[33] The Canadian measures were intended to supplement fisheries conservation measures within its own exclusive economic zone. The jurisdiction of the ICJ to receive the case has been challenged by Canada. Assuming that it gets to the merits, the ICJ would need to address whether there are any circumstances in which a coastal state may lawfully take conservation measures outside its territorial jurisdiction and if so, whether the Canadian measures were lawful. This would allow the Court, of course, to revisit an issue it addressed in the *Fisheries Jurisdiction* Case in 1974.

The ICJ's Willingness to Recognize the Place of Environmental Objectives in the International Legal Order

At a political level, the Court's awareness of the growing importance of environmental concerns in international relations is reflected in its establishment of an Environmental Chamber in 1993. The fact that this decision may have been motivated by an essentially political desire to prevent the establishment of a separate international environmental court, as some have suggested, and as has occurred in the law of the sea (with the establishment of an International Tribunal for the Law of the Sea), does not diminish from the significance of the decision. It recognizes the place of environmental objectives, the existence of disputes which could be characterized as 'environmental', and the possible existence of a discrete body of obligations of international environmental law which might be applied to those disputes. It indicates that the Court considers the importance of giving proper effect to those obligations.

This political recognition has not yet been translated into a clear legal recognition which is capable of practical application, or even influence. Recognition of the existence of environmental obligations in separate or dissenting opinions is of limited authority. Of greater authority are the majority's generalized recognition of 'the needs of conservation for the benefit of all' (in 1974) or 'the obligations of States to respect and protect the natural environment' (in 1995). These comments indicate that the Court may be receptive to environmental claims, but they provide a less-than-clear indication of what the content of the relevant norms might be, how they might be applied in a practical sense, and whether they could override (or at least compete with) other, more established international norms. The Court may have an opportunity in some of the cases currently before it to address those points. In the meantime, the international community will have to be content with these general statements.

The ICJ's Willingness to Give Environmental Protection Objectives Precedence Over Other Societal Objectives

At this point it is simply not possible to say how far the Court might be willing to go in giving effect to the 'needs of conservation' or 'obligations to protect the natural environment'. Other important societal objectives which might be limited by environmental objectives include the right to use military force in self-defence, the absolute right to fish on the high seas, and the sanctity of treaties (*pacta sunt servanda*), each of which is in issue in the matters currently before the Court. How far the Court is willing to go on these and other matters will depend upon the views of individual judges, but recent judgments suggest that this Court is unlikely to apply or develop the law in an expansive manner. The minimalist tendency which currently prevails would tend to indicate an unwillingness to tamper with established norms or practices, and to give prudent and limited effect to new or emerging norms (such as those in the environmental field). This suggests that the time for an expansive application of environmental norms may be some time away.

The ICJ's Appreciation of the Character of Environmental Issues

It is similarly not possible to know whether the Court does or does not appreciate that environmental cases may raise particular requirements in a judicial forum. No cases before the Court have yet required it to evaluate and assess competing technical or scientific arguments in the environmental domain, and so we cannot know what the applicable burden of proof might be. It is also impossible to know what weight, if any, the Court might give to scientific uncertainty in giving credence to environmental claims, or whether it would be prepared to take into account the inherently global character of certain environmental issues on jurisdictional or substantive matters.

In this regard it is perhaps noteworthy that in the *Case Concerning the Gabcikovo–Nagymaros Project* the Court has asked to make a visit to the site of the dispute, apparently the first time that such a request has been made. Although at the time of writing it had not appointed experts to assist it in the evaluation of competing scientific or environmental arguments, this decision indicates at a minimum a recognition by the Court of the importance of factual elements in the dispute.

EUROPEAN COURT OF JUSTICE[34]

In contrast to the ICJ, the ECJ (Court of Justice and Court of First Instance) has addressed a large and diverse range of environmental issues within the EC context.[35] Since 1976, when the Court first addressed an explicitly environmental issue,[36] more than 150 environmental cases have been decided.[37] The ECJ has recognized the place which environmental protection has in the Community legal order. It has given (on occasion) environmental protection objectives an equal (or occasionally greater) weight over entrenched economic and trade objectives. And it has demonstrated a willingness to recognize and act upon some of the special characteristics of environmental issues.

Jurisdiction

Environmental cases reach the ECJ in a number of ways. The most frequent route is via Article 169 of the EC Treaty. Since 1980 the EC Commission has brought more than 60 cases to the ECJ, alleging the failure of a Member State to comply with its EC environmental obligations. The Commission is almost always successful. Most of these cases are relatively straightforward and do not indicate one way or another how seriously the Court takes environmental obligations. However, its judgments have been useful to determine, *inter alia*, that Member States may not plead provisions, practices or circumstances existing in their internal legal system to justify a failure to comply with an environmental obligation;[38] that administrative practices which may be altered at the whim of the administration do not constitute the proper fulfilment of an environmental obligation under a Directive;[39] and that the legal obligations imposed on a Member State by an environmental Directive are limited to those dangerous substances specifically listed in the Directive and not to other unlisted dangerous substances as well.[40] More recently, the ECJ has considered the legality of national environmental measures by reference to EC free-trade obligations,[41] and the failure of a Member State to execute one of the Court's judgments (under Article 171 of the EC Treaty).[42]

Under Article 170 of the EC Treaty, a Member State which believes that another Member State has breached its obligations has a similar right to bring a matter before the ECJ but, to the best of my knowledge, only one case concerning alleged breaches of environmental obligations has been brought under this provision.[43]

Under Article 171, as amended by the Treaty on European Union, the ECJ may impose a lump sum or penalty payment on a Member State that has failed to comply with one of its judgments. In such circumstances, it will first be for the Commission to specify the amount of the lump sum or payment which it considers appropriate in the circumstances. Although this new provision has not been utilized, as this chapter goes to press, one can well imagine that a failure to comply with a judgment of the ECJ which results in an environmental injury could provide a basis for its being invoked.

Environmental issues can also make it to the ECJ in judicial review applications. Under Article 173 of the EC Treaty, the ECJ is competent to review the legality of certain acts of the EC Council and Commission. The grounds of review are that the body acted beyond its competence, or that it infringed an essential procedural requirement, or that it infringed the EEC Treaty or any rule relating to its application, or that it misused its powers. Actions may be brought by 'privileged' applicants (a Member State, the Council or the Commission) in most cases, by the European Parliament and the European Central Bank for the purposes of protecting their prerogatives, and by 'non-privileged' applicants, namely any natural or legal person provided that the act concerned is a decision addressed to that person or is a discussion which is of 'direct and individual concern' to that person. Under Article 173 the ECJ has considered, *inter alia*, the legality of the treaty basis of EC and EURATOM environmental legislation.[44] As indicated below, the Court of First Instance is now being asked under Article 173 to decide cases brought by environmental groups and individuals alleging violations by the EC Commission of its legal obligations under the EEC Treaty.

The ECJ also has jurisdiction under Article 175, under similar conditions as Article 173, to challenge the failure of the EC Council or Commission to have acted in pursuance of its environmental obligations under the EEC Treaty. To date, no environmental case appears to have been brought under this provision.

The Court of Justice (but not the Court of First Instance) has also considered environmental questions on the basis of its jurisdiction under Article 177, the 'preliminary reference procedure'. Under this provision the national courts of the Member States may, and in some cases must, refer to the ECJ questions concerning, *inter alia*, the interpretation of the EC Treaty and the validity and interpretation of acts of the EC institutions, where a decision on the question is necessary to enable the national court to give a ruling on the question. Preliminary references from national courts to the ECJ are used when a dispute before the national courts raises a complex question or questions of EC law or where the dispute turns on the EC point and no appeal lies against the decision of the national court. The Article 177 procedure has been used on several occasions to allow the EC to rule on matters of an environmental nature, such as questions concerning the disposal of waste from a nuclear power plant,[45] and the compatibility with EEC law of the ban by an Italian municipality on the sale and distribution of plastic bags and other non-biodegradable packaging material.[46]

Interim Measures

The EC Commission can also apply to the ECJ for interim measures under Article 186 of the Treaty – a form of interlocutory relief that is well established in Community jurisprudence and quite often is employed, for example, in competition and anti-trust cases. The Commission has to show a good arguable case that the need for relief is urgent and that irreparable damage to the Community interest will be done if the order is not granted. The Member State can defend itself by establishing that it will suffer irreparable harm if the order is made. The Commission is in the fortunate position of not having to give a cross-undertaking in damages in the event that it ultimately loses the case.

The ECJ has indicated that interim measures may be prescribed in environmental cases. In *EC Commission v Germany*, the European Court considered the circumstances in which it would be prepared to prescribe the necessary interim measures in environmental cases.[47] The case concerned the construction in Germany of a reservoir and related site, and the Commission sought (a) a declaration that the construction violated Article 4(1) of the 1979 Wild Birds Directive and (b) the adoption of interim measures to suspend the work until the Court had given its decision on the main application. The Court held that for a measure of this type to be ordered the application must state the circumstances that gave rise to the urgency, and the factual and legal grounds that established a prima-facie case for the interim measures.[48] The Court rejected the application on the grounds that the Commission had failed to prove urgency: the application had been submitted after the project was well under way and the interim measures had not been sought until 'a large part of the work had already been completed', and it could not be shown that it was 'precisely the next stage in the construction work ... which will cause serious harm to the protection of birds ...'[49]

The ECJ has developed a rich body of case-law on environmental issues, as this brief and non-exhaustive list indicates. Indeed, it is fair to say that the Court is pre-eminent as an international tribunal in dealing with the legal aspects of environmental protection and, as such, its jurisprudence will no doubt provide useful guidance to other international courts and bodies which face legal issues, in particular the delicate and difficult task of balancing environmental concerns with competing social objectives, particularly those of an economic nature.

In the context of the developments outlined in the introduction, the ECJ stands at the forefront of an emerging global trend. In the limited sense that it has in this body of case-law addressed a wide range of legal issues relating to the protection of the environment, there can be little doubt that the Court is an environmental tribunal. However, the question of whether the Court is an environmental tribunal must also be asked at a deeper level.

The ECJ's Willingness to Recognize the Place of Environmental Objectives in the EC Legal Order

There can be little doubt that the ECJ has recognized environmental objectives in the Community legal order, even if the case law is not absolutely consistent (history suggests that the Court's tendencies will depend on the particular facts of each case and who is sitting on the bench). If anything, of all the Community institutions, the Court has played a pre-eminent role in recognizing and further developing environmental objectives in the Community's legal order.

As early as 1985 the ECJ had ruled that environmental protection was 'one of the Community's essential objectives'.[50] That the Court could reach such a conclusion before the Single European Act had amended the EEC Treaty to include specific provisions on environmental protection may have been a welcome finding from an environmental perspective, but it was a surprising one from a more traditional approach to treaty interpretation. It was also surprising in the sense that the Court was willing to recognize that environmental protection measures might also limit the extent of the application of free trade rules. Nevertheless, the ruling followed the Court's general approach to interpretation and application of the EEC Treaty, and was not unexpected in the light of its ruling five years earlier that 'provisions on the environment may be based upon Article 100 of the [EEC] Treaty'.[51]

More recently, the Court has indicated further support for its early commitment to formalizing the place of environmental protection in the Community's legal order. In 1991, the Court relied on a provision of Article 130r2 of the EEC Treaty ('[e]nvironmental protection requirements shall be a component of the Community's other policies') to support its conclusion that environmental protection measures could be adopted under Article 100a of the EEC Treaty rather than Article 130s: 'a Community measure cannot be covered by Article 130s merely because it pursues environmental protection objectives'.[52] In deciding that a Directive could be based on Article 100a where it was concerned both with the protection of the environment and the elimination of disparities in conditions of competition, the Court gave a significant boost to the Commission's legislative Programme for Environmental Protection by bringing much of it within the qualified majority decision-making process.[53]

The ECJ has also frequently affirmed the importance of proper transposition into domestic law of environmental Directives, recognizing also that certain environmental Directives are intended to create rights and obligations for individuals. In 1991, the Court stated that '[i]n order to guarantee complete and effective protection of groundwater it is vital that the prohibitions set out in the directive be expressly embodied in national law'.[54] One of the reasons for this was that 'procedural rules ... are intended to create rights and obligations for individuals [and] they must be incorporated into German law with the precision and clarity necessary to satisfy fully the requirements of legal certainty'.[55] A further justification indicates the Court's appreciation of the particular characteristics of environmental issues: 'a faithful transposition becomes particularly important in a case where the management of the common heritage is entrusted to the Member States in their respective territories'.[56]

On the other hand, there are also indications that the Court on occasion will interpret environmental Directives in such a way as to lead to a result which will not afford absolute protection to environmental resources. By way of example, in the *Gourmetterie Van den Burg* Case, again interpreting the 1979 Birds Directive, the Court held that a Member State had no right to afford a given species, which was neither migratory nor endangered, stricter protection (by way of trade restrictions) than that afforded to it by the legislation of the Member State on whose territory the species occurred, where such legislation is in accordance with the Directive – a conclusion whose justification is hard to understand given that the actual wording of the Directive might allow that conclusion.[57]

Similarly, in Case 252/85, the ECJ upheld the right of France to apply national provisions allowing the use of lines and horizontal nets ('pantoles' or 'matoles') to catch thrushes or skylarks, even though the use of such techniques was expressly prohibited by Article 8(1) in conjunction with Annex IV(a) of the 1979 Birds Directive.[58] The justification for its conclusions (that the technique only captures a small number of birds, that they are captured in a judicious manner, and that France approached the EC Commission to try to reach agreement) is hardly designed to signal the Court's commitment to environmental protection.

The balance of the ECJ's practice over the past two decades is clearly in favour of recognizing the place of the environment in the Community legal order. Indeed, the Court has been at the forefront of the Community institutions' efforts to ensure that the Community's legal order recognizes environmental objectives and gives proper effect and application to them.

The ECJ's Willingness to Give Environmental Protection Objectives Precedence Over Economic Objectives

The ECJ has demonstrated a willingness to recognize that environmental limitations might limit full effect being given to the trade and economic objectives which are enshrined in the EC Treaty. One question which now arises is whether this is slowly being whittled away as the full implications of earlier case-law becomes apparent.

Particularly in relation to the balance between free trade and environmental protection objectives, the Court has developed a jurisprudence which distinguishes it from its counterpart GATT dispute-settlement panels. In relation to environmental protection requirements, the Court first held in 1983 that 'the principle of freedom of trade is not to be viewed in absolute terms but is subject to certain limits justified by the objectives of general interest pursued by the Community provided that the rights in question are not substantively impaired', and that environmental protection requirements could justify limits on free trade.[59]

In the *Danish Bottles* Case, the Court went even further, stating unequivocally that 'the protection of the environment is a mandatory requirement which may limit the application of Article 30 of the Treaty'.[60] The Court reached its conclusion on the basis of the law as it stood before the entry into force of the Single European Act, nevertheless invoking the Act to justify its prior conclusion that the protection of the environment was 'one of the Community's essential objectives'.[61]

By 1993 the ECJ was prepared to go further still, ruling that the principle enunciated in Article 130r that 'environmental damage should as a priority be rectified at source' could be invoked to allow the conclusion that movements of waste could be limited between and even within Member States. In the absence of Community legislation on the waste in question, the Court stated: 'it is for each region, commune or other local entity to take appropriate measures to receive, process and dispose of its own waste'.[62] In reaching this rather dramatic (from an environmental perspective) conclusion, the Court invoked the principles of self-sufficiency and proximity set out in the 1989 Basle Convention on the Control of Transboundary Movements of Hazardous Wastes and their Disposal.[63] This was surprising because the Convention had not been adopted at the time that the dispute originally arose, and had been in force for barely three months even at the time of judgment; because even at that later date the Community was a signatory but not a party to the Convention; and because the Convention only implicitly (and even then subject to important <u>caveats)</u> invokes the principles identified by the Court only in its preamble! Each of these reasons serves to underscore the Court's willingness to give significant weight to environmental principles and objectives, even where they might be considered to be in an emergent state.

In a similar vein (and again in the context of the 1979 Wild Birds Directive), the ECJ has ruled that the power of a Member State to reduce the size of a special protection area can only be justified on exceptional grounds which must 'correspond to a general interest which is superior to the general interest represented by the ecological objective of the directive', and that economic and recreational requirements do not constitute such exceptional grounds.[64]

These cases illustrate the ECJ's willingness to give environmental protection objectives precedence over economic objectives in appropriate circumstances.[65] They also reflect the significant role played by the Court in the development of EC environmental law, to the point that it will place certain limits on free trade rules.

The ECJ's Willingness to Recognize Particular Characteristics of Environmental Issues

Finally, it may be useful to consider whether the ECJ can be considered an environmental tribunal by reference to its willingness to recognize (and act upon) the particular characteristics of environmental issues and problems, as identified in the Introduction to this chapter. At this point in time, it is unclear whether the Court has really grappled with this aspect of environmental issues, although it may be possible to discern some, limited signs that the Court *might* be inclined to recognize the particular nature of environmental interests.

One example is the 1976 judgment in a case concerning the 1968 Brussels Convention on the Recognition and Enforcement of Judgments. The Court upheld the right of victims of transboundary pollution to choose the national court before which they could commence legal proceedings for damages. The Court ruled that Article 5(3) of the 1968 Brussels Convention must be interpreted 'in such a way as to acknowledge that the plaintiff has an option to commence proceedings either at the place where the damage occurred or the place of the event giving rise to it'.[66] The ECJ recognized that environmental harms can be transboundary in nature and that the law should recognize that feature by introducing flexibility into the applicable conflicts rules. And, as indicated earlier, the Court's willingness to invoke the 'common heritage' principle as an aid to interpreting and applying the law illustrates that, on occasion, it will rely upon the underlying rationale of certain EC environmental legislation to allow it to reach a conclusion which it might not otherwise have reached, or to fortify it in reaching that conclusion.[67] A similar willingness might be reflected in the *Wallonian Waste* Case. Having found that waste should be regarded as a product within the meaning of Article 30 of the EEC Treaty and that its movement should not in principle be impeded, the Court found that waste has 'a special characteristic' since its accumulation 'even before it becomes a health hazard, constitutes a threat to the environment'.[68]

However, more recently there may be some indications that there are real limits on how far the ECJ might be prepared to go. In *Greenpeace and Others v EC Commission*, the Court of First Instance (CFI) was asked by the Applicants to recognize that environmental harm raises a new kind of problem in the field of remedies under the Community legal order, in relation to *locus standi*. The Applicants sought to challenge the disbursement by the Commission of some 12 million ECU in structural funds to Spain for the construction of two coal-fired power plants, on the grounds that the Commission had failed to ensure properly that Spain complied with the obligation to carry out an environmental impact assessment. The Applicants had to show a legal interest in bringing their action and argued that the Court's existing Article 173 jurisprudence related solely to economic interests. They argued that in relation to environmental cases, the 'individual concern' required by Article 173 should be construed by the Court to allow individuals whose environmental rights under EC legislation (such as Directive 85/337 on environmental impact assessment) had been violated should have effective access to the Community courts in order to obtain effective protection of those rights and to ensure that 'in the interpretation and application of the treaties the law is observed'.[69] The CFI rejected that approach, ruling that the applicants did not have *locus standi* to bring this case. In relation to the applicants who were private individuals, the Court ruled that their *locus standi* 'should be assessed in the light of criteria ... already set down in the case law', and that 'the circumstances on which the applicants rely are not sufficient to differentiate them from all other persons and thus distinguish them individually in the same way as the addressee of the decision'.[70] Since the three applicant associations were in no different a position from the private individuals as to individual concern, their *locus standi* was rejected.[71] The CFI's approach rejects the particular character of environmental interests and suggests that for all practical purposes there are no circumstances in which the Commission could be reviewed judicially under Article 173 in environmental cases (since it is hard to imagine circumstances in which victims of environmental harms might be considered to be part of a 'fixed and ascertainable' class).[72] The Court's reliance upon a traditionally narrow approach to standing is, in my view, doubly damaging for the Community legal order: it threatens to limit the application of the rule of law and it signals the Court's unwillingness to recognize an appropriate place for environmental values in the Community legal order. The case has been appealed to the Court of Justice, which will have an important opportunity to indicate the extent to which it recognizes the particular character of environmental interests.

CONCLUSIONS

It is, perhaps, not surprising that the European Court of Justice and the International Court of Justice have played differing roles in the development of environmental law within their respective spheres of competence. EC environmental law and international environmental law are at different stages of development. Indeed, the broader legal systems, of which they form a part, are also at different stages of development, as reflected in the respective arrangements for the resolution of disputes, including the willingness of the EC order to give rights of action to the European Commission, compulsory jurisdiction over disputes between all states and a role (potential at least) for non-state actors.

Nevertheless, it emerges from this brief survey that both institutions perceive themselves as having a role to play in the development of environmental law. The ECJ has seized the opportunity to make a practical contribution, its jurisprudence indicating a general readiness to give a considerable degree of support to environmental arguments. While its approach clearly must be considered on a case-by-case basis, it has tended to extend the weight of environmental objectives, sometimes even where none are expressly stated. Occasionally, the ECJ has limited the extent of application of economic objectives. There can be little doubt that without the Court's jurisprudence, environmental law in the Community legal order would be less well developed and there would probably be a lower degree of support for environmental objectives in other Community institutions, and in the Community more generally.

The International Court has not yet made a similar practical contribution in general international law, although there are some indications that it may wish to do so. This is reflected especially in the decision to establish an Environmental Chamber, as well as in the occasional references in judgments that indicate at least some support for environmental objectives (as in the Order in the recent second *Nuclear Tests* Case), and in several separate or dissenting opinions of individual judges. The most notable of these is the elegant dissenting opinion rendered in the second *Nuclear Tests* Case by Judge Weeremantary, stating his regret that:

the Court has not availed itself of the opportunity to enquire more fully into this matter and of making a contribution to some of the seminal principles of the evolving corpus of international environmental law. The Court has for too long been silent on these issues and, in the words of ancient wisdom, one may well ask 'If not now, when?'.[73]

Several pending cases may give the Court an opportunity to take matters further.

14 NEW INSTITUTIONS AND PROCEDURES FOR IMPLEMENTATION CONTROL AND REACTION

Martti Koskenniemi

The massive increase in international legislation during the last quarter of a century, particularly in the environmental field has not created a legal world order. In fact, the gap between law in books and how states act may now appear wider than at any other time in history – the more rules there are, the more occasion there is to break them. After years of active standard-setting, global and regional organizations stand somewhat baffled in front of a reality that has sometimes little in common with the objectives expressed in the inflated language of their major conventions and declarations.

This chapter will address some of the ways in which those organizations and states themselves have sought to attain better compliance with agreed norms, especially environmental norms. Emphasis will be on new, 'softer' methods of implementation control that seek to replace or at least to defer the use of traditional judicial or arbitral processes (see Chapter 13). The chapter also questions the merits of such deferral and asks what role, if any, is left for legal settlement in a new institutional world order.

PERSUASION OR ENFORCEMENT? PROBLEMS IN THE GENERAL LAW

International instruments use a wide variety of technically flavoured terms such as 'assessment',[1] 'monitoring',[2] 'verification',[3] 'verification of compliance',[4] or 'considering progress made in the implementation'[5] of a Convention in order to refer to procedures which aim to secure that states comply with their commitments. Such expressions do not possess neatly delimited meanings. There is no one procedure that would correspond to any one such term. But all of them seek to achieve one or both of two things:

(1) To assess whether states, in fact, do what they have promised.
(2) To persuade states to do what they have promised.

Assessment and persuasion by reference to accepted rules is not identical with 'enforcement', although the terms do overlap. While the core sense of 'enforcement' refers to a formal, legally circumscribed reaction to a breach of an obligation, the very possibility of such a reaction acts (or is hoped to act) as a means of persuasion. Yet the actual triggering of enforcement is a much more radical intervention in a state's freedom of action than 'persuasion' and implies a blameworthiness which is not necessarily present in the latter.[6]

It is widely accepted today that persuasion instead of enforcement is the appropriate cure to the malady of non-compliance. States cannot be coerced into implementation but must be assisted thereto. This view relies on a humble pragmatism about the force of international treaties: if states fail to do what they have promised, it can only be for the worse to try to force them. In case a conflict emerges between the politics of states and the provisions of treaties, the latter will inevitably succumb. So the prudent internationalist should avoid conflict altogether. Instead of insisting on the validity of the standard (and thus condemning it to irrelevance), the diplomat should soften its contours and detach it from the binary logic of the law for which a conduct can only be either legal or illegal.

This view has accepted the post-war 'realist' critiques of international law and institutions. Power and interest of states, not the law, determines outcomes. Instead of abandoning the law, however, it seeks to cunningly transform it. By explaining the law as always *parallel* to state power and interest it hopes to make room for a sophisticated institutional practice within which states are slowly guided or tricked into conforming behaviour.

One target of this new, suave internationalism is the law of state responsibility for breach of an obligation. That law starts from the ('formalistic') insistence that '... refusal to fulfil a treaty obligation involves international responsibility...'.[7] It then aims to realize this responsibility by resort to the judicial or arbitral process. For a number of reasons, however, this approach may not seem satisfactory. The parties may not agree on a procedure for determining what constitutes a 'refusal to fulfil a treaty obligation', ie a formal breach,[8] or there may be no certainty that the losing party will comply with an eventual judgment or award; or the alleged violation may concern a collective interest (environmental or human rights treaties are obvious examples) but there is no state or body which could claim to represent that interest.[9] Also, formal dispute settlement intervenes only after the breach. In the case of environmental or human rights obligations a reparation-oriented approach seems inadequate. Besides, many treaties contain aspirational and open-textured language that makes it difficult to classify behaviour as 'compliance' or 'breach'.[10] To use the traditional procedures of state responsibility in such circumstances may be unhelpful for the attainment of the aims of the treaty. Finally, dispute settlement through arbitration or judicial decision may seem simply too slow, too expensive, too untried or too confrontational to deal with technically complex and politically sensitive questions relative to a party's implementation.[11]

There is no centralized system for surveying how states comply with their commitments – nor for enforcing those commitments. An injured state is entitled to take peaceful measures (countermeasures) against a state which has breached a norm that is valid in their relations *inter se*.[12] This includes the right of a treaty partner which has suffered injury to suspend or terminate the operation of the treaty as a reaction to a material breach of that treaty by another state.[13] In bilateral relations, this is easy to accept. The countermeasure seeks to restore the contractual equilibrium, distorted by the other party's non-performance.[14] But reciprocal non-performance cannot be invoked meaningfully in the context of humanitarian or human rights treaties, treaties that establish rights in favour of third states or that are intended for the protection of collective interests (eg environmental treaties). Unilateral enforcement does not correspond to the public law character of such treaties.[15] It is only available to strong states and is suspect for misuse as a tool for hegemony.

For these reasons, some treaties provide for collective authorization of countermeasures emanating from bilateral disputes. For instance, under Article XXIII (2) of the General Agreement on Tariffs and Trade (GATT), member states may authorize the suspension of a right or a concession in case of violation by a Party of its GATT obligations. This procedure, however, has been used only once while the protective safeguard clause of Article XIX (which is neither subject to collective authorization nor linked to a prior violation) has been used much more frequently.[16] The UN Security Council may also give authorization under Chapter VII of the Charter to Member States to take (military) action for the maintenance or restoration of international peace and security.[17] However, the Council's competence is not linked with the presence of a treaty violation but with a 'breach of the peace, threat to the peace or an act of aggression'.[18] The Council is under no obligation to react, nor to react in any predetermined way. Its reactive powers cannot be seen as a legally circumscribed system of enforcement.

The constitutions of some international organizations empower their organs to expel a non-complying Member State.[19] Such a dramatic measure, however, has almost never been used.[20] It is feasible only against an outlawed state and may make settlement of the underlying dispute more difficult. More common is the provision for the suspension of a violating state's rights or privileges (eg its voting rights).[21] For instance, international commodity agreements often contain such a clause. But these procedures have in practice been substituted by more subtle diplomatic means to persuade compliance.[22]

Available settlement and enforcement procedures have not been used often. Many see them as too undiplomatic or confrontational to be realistically useful to grapple with the everyday phenomenon of non-compliance. For these reasons, new forms of preventive implementation control and 'soft' reaction regimes have been set up. I shall discuss these under the titles of 'Implementation Control' and 'Reactions to Violation'.

IMPLEMENTATION CONTROL

It is up to states themselves to monitor the actions of their treaty partners by visual, electronic or seismic means from their own territory or by reconnaissance satellites from the extra-atmospheric orbit. Such means of information-gathering, however, apply only to a limited range of physically verifiable technologically advanced activities. They cannot be used to detect violations of commercial or political engagements or of human rights, for example, and are only available for states in possession of adequate equipment. Although all states follow each others' actions through their embassies and the mass media, for the purpose of the reliable assembly of data on treaty compliance, this is insufficient.

Therefore, recent treaties establish special procedures for gathering information on activities covered by them. The 1979 *Long-Range Transboundary Air Pollution Convention* sets up a framework for cooperation among North American and European states to control and reduce transboundary fluxes of airborne pollutants.[23] Treaty partners have agreed on the financing of a programme for the monitoring and evaluation of the emissions of such pollutants (the so-called EMEP programme).[24] The data thus collected have formed the basis for assessing the effectiveness of a 1985 agreement on a 30 per cent reduction of sulphur emissions and for agreeing in 1994 on a tightened emissions reduction schedule.[25] Comparable provisions can be found in many environmental treaties.[26]

Reporting

Many treaties require that parties report on their implementation activities.[27] Virtually all environmental treaties call for periodic reports. For example, the 1992 *Convention on Biological Diversity* provides that: 'Each Contracting Party shall, at intervals to be determined by the Conference of the Parties, present to the Conference of the Parties reports on measures which it has taken for the implementation of the provisions of this Convention and their effectiveness in meeting the objectives of this Convention'.[28] However, no specific mechanism is set up for addressing problems. (Alleged) non-implementation becomes a 'dispute between Contracting Parties' to be dealt with under the standard arbitral or judicial procedures for the settlement of disputes.[29]

The Biological Diversity Convention relies on the parties themselves for inspecting national reports. The setting up of a special Implementation Committee to study such reports under the 1987 *Montreal Ozone Protocol* and the 1994 *Protocol to the 1979 Convention on Long-Range Transboundary Air Pollution on further Reduction of Sulphur Emissions* goes a step further. A small panel of governmental experts study national reports and report back to meetings of states parties.[30] The potential for such an approach is also provided for in the 1992 *Framework Convention on Climate Change*. A Subsidiary Body for Implement-ation (SBI), composed of governmental experts, was established by the Convention and began to meet in August 1995. The SBI will receive reports on national greenhouse gas inventories and on steps taken or envisaged to implement the Convention.[31] These reports are at first scrutinized by teams of experts, who are empowered to conduct on-site examinations in the reporting country (with its consent) and to produce an in-depth review of individual reports. Thus, reports and reviews are examined by the subsidiary bodies and then submitted to the Conference of the Parties for further examination and action, if necessary.[32] Further multilateral consultative procedures for the resolution of questions arising from specific incidences of non-compliance are being considered by the Parties.

Despite these provisions, compliance with environmental agreements remains far from satisfactory. In 1992 it was reported of seven environmental agreements that require reporting, that while 80 per cent or more of the parties to three of them (the 1987 Montreal Ozone Protocol, the 1988 Protocol on Nitrogen Oxides to the Transboundary Air Pollution Convention and the 1946 International Whaling Convention) had submitted required reports, close to half of the reports filed with the Montreal Protocol Secretariat were incomplete. For the remaining agreements (the 1972 London Dumping Convention, the 1974/1978 MARPOL Convention, the 1973 Convention on International Trade in Endangered Species (CITES) and the 1983 International Tropical Timber Agreement), fewer than 50 per cent of the Parties reported. In particular, Parties from developing countries had failed to report.[33]

Yet sometimes, states do react. The Implementation Committee under the Montreal Ozone Protocol 'expressed serious concern' in March 1993 that out of 73 Parties required to provide their 1991 data on the use and production of controlled substances by the end of September 1992, only 18 had done so, 56 Parties having failed to report anything at all.[34] After developing countries had received technical and financial assistance, their reporting improved significantly. Also, the European Community and some of its members corrected their initial failures by submitting overdue reports. Perhaps even more significantly, many non-reporting states agreed to come before the Committee to explain the reasons for their difficulties and to promise more adequate reporting in the future.[35]

Parties will have to ensure that the institutions entrusted with monitoring compliance are adequately funded. Environmentalists should be cautioned by experience in the field of human rights. Lack of resources significantly hampers the examination of reports by the Committee on the Rights of the Child, for example.[36] The Committee on the Elimination of Discrimination against Women has, for its part, voiced concern that the current delay of three years from submission to examination will work as a serious disincentive for filing reports.[37] Insufficient resources that are available to the Committees continue to obstruct efficient consideration of the reports.[38]

But even as reports are submitted, their content often leaves much to be desired. Treaty bodies have tried to grapple with this problem by producing reporting guidelines. The problem, however, goes deeper:

> [T]he task of compiling and presenting the reports has tended to be seen almost exclusively as a diplomatic chore. Accordingly, the accepted wisdom has been that it should be carried out with the least possible expenditure of diplomatic staff resources, with little involvement on the part of those in government who are actually concerned with the rights in question and no involvement at all of the broader range of social partners in the community.[39]

The absence of non-governmental participants in the reporting process goes to the heart of the international system and cannot be expected to be corrected overnight. Although limited and unofficial participation of non-governmental interests is increasing, this is perhaps the aspect of treaty surveillance in most urgent need of reform. [40]

Fact-finding, On-site Observation and Direct Contacts

More is involved in fact-finding than the name may suggest. A statement of facts in relation to a treaty clause defining a prohibited form of conduct comes close to a determination of compliance.[41] For example, the international fact-finding commission established under *Additional Protocol I of 1977 to the Geneva Conventions of 12 August 1949* on the protection of victims of armed conflicts is mandated to enquire into whether any facts in an international armed conflict might constitute 'grave breaches' under the Conventions, thus making the Commission's task a quasi-judicial one. The Commission may also use its good offices to facilitate the restoration of 'an attitude of respect' for the Protocol in a manner that goes clearly beyond simple fact-verification.[42] Yet no formal request for an enquiry seems to have been made since the setting up of the Commission in 1992.[43]

Nor has the Consultative Committee of Experts, established under the 1977 *Convention on the Prohibition of Military or Any Other Hostile Uses of Environmental Modification Techniques* (ENMOD) to 'make appropriate findings of fact and provide expert views relevant to any problem' that is related to the Convention's subject matter, ever been convened.[44] There was some discussion about this in connection with the setting on fire of a large number of oil wells by Iraqi military at its retreat from Kuwait in February–March 1991. No action was taken, however, apparently because Iraq had not ratified the Convention and also because the actions may not have fallen within the strictly limited field of the application of the Convention.[45]

Unlike formal fact-finding under international treaties, informal contact by international organizations, relying on confidentiality and the consent of host governments, has become increasingly common. The UN Secretary-General has often used his good offices for this purpose [46] and in 1991 the General Assembly appealed to states to consent to the despatch of missions in their territories.[47]

The Conference (now Organization) on Security and Cooperation in Europe (C/OSCE) has sent missions of long duration to Macedonia, Georgia, Moldova, Estonia, Latvia, Tajikistan and Sarajevo with mandates combining fact-finding, prevention and conciliation.[48] *Ad hoc* missions have visited new participating states and trouble areas with the aim of checking the states' willingness and capability to live up to CSCE commitments.[49]

Such verification activities rely on the cooperation of host governments and on a general sense of common purpose in the organization that undertakes them. It is unclear to what extent it can work as deterrence against violations by states whose good faith cannot be taken for granted. This latter concern accounts for the crucial role of verification in disarmament. States will not disarm unless they are certain that others will disarm, too.[50] The same type of confidence-building will undoubtedly be necessary in the environmental field where compliance can have at least short-term implications for a party's trade competitiveness. A party making cuts in carbon dioxide emissions will want to know its trading partners and competitors are making similar sacrifices.

Still, on-site verification in the disarmament field proved for a long time impossible. The 1972 *Biological and Toxin Weapons Convention*, for instance, contained no provisions on verification.[51] A breakthrough was attained with the adoption of the 1986 CSCE *Stockholm Document* which called for inspections during large-scale military exercises.[52] This opened the way for the inclusion of a developed mechanism on on-site verification in the 1987 *Intermediate Nuclear Forces* (INF) treaty between the US and the USSR.[53] The Parties' right to conduct on-site investigations and continuous ('portal') monitoring (by means of cameras, etc) in enumerated facilities extends to a period of 13 years and applies to the territories of all countries in which they have deployed such forces.[54]

The 1990 *Treaty on Conventional Forces in Europe* (CFE) continues this relative openness.[55] It allows inspections to declared sites, challenge inspections to undeclared sites and inspections to witness reductions and certification. At the time, no agreement was attained on aerial surveys or on inspections of movements of treaty-limited equipment into and from the treaty area.[56]

In 1993, the former were made the object of the *Open Skies Treaty* under which Parties agreed to accept observation flights carried out by each other in accordance with a detailed system of quotas divided between them.[57] The CFE Treaty, however, illustrates a problem that is inherent in a system based on the treaty partners' reciprocal right to inspect each other without the involvement of a supervisory body: in the new climate of 1990 everyone wanted to inspect the Soviet Union! This and intra-block security concerns (Hungary–Romania–Czechoslovakia; Greece–Turkey) made it difficult to agree on a sharing of inspection quotas in such a fashion that the confidence-building aims among the main protagonists (US, NATO and the Soviet Union/Russia) could be attained.[58]

By contrast, in the 1968 *Nuclear Non-proliferation Treaty* (NPT), non-nuclear power parties have accepted wide-reaching inspection powers for the International Atomic Energy Agency (IAEA). The powers are based on a 'safeguards' agreement that each party has undertaken to conclude with the Agency.[59] The agreement lists all fissionable nuclear materials in a state party's control with provisions on their isolation and monitoring. Inspectors are empowered to verify that listed materials and equipment are treated in accordance with the party's safeguards obligations. Investigations take place through agreed means and only in installations agreed with the party.[60]

Even wider inspection powers are granted under the 1992 *Chemical Weapons Convention* (CWC) to the Organization for the Prohibition of Chemical Weapons (OPCW).[61] The Convention prohibits all production and storage of chemical weapons and contains detailed provisions on the destruction of existing stockpiles. To ensure compliance, each party is entitled to request on-site challenge inspection of any area or facility in the territory of another party.[62] Inspections are carried out by teams of the organization in accordance with detailed verification rules.

In the human rights field, the only body with binding powers to conduct on-site verification is the Committee that was established in the 1987 *European Convention on the Prevention of Torture*.[63] The Committee consists of as many individual members as it has Parties who shall 'by means of visits, examine the treatment of persons deprived of their liberty with a view to strengthening, if necessary, the protection of such persons from torture and from inhuman or degrading treatment or punishment'.[64] Parties have pledged to permit periodic and *ad hoc* visits in any place within their jurisdiction and to give the necessary assistance during the visit.[65] After each visit, the Committee transmits a report and recommendations to the relevant state Party. If the latter fails to cooperate or improve the situation, the Committee may publicize its views after a two-thirds vote on the matter.[66] By the end of March 1993, the Committee had carried out 18 periodic and two *ad hoc* visits (both to Turkey). In December 1992 it made its first public statement (on Turkey).[67] A comparable system is presently being negotiated under the *UN Convention Against Torture*.[68] Although it does not seem likely that the provisions of such a protocol would attain the level of constraint in the European Convention, the finalization of the protocol would still be an advance for the UN human rights system.

In the environmental field, the Conference of the Parties to the Climate Change Convention agreed in 1995 to set up a system whereby national communications are submitted to examination by teams of independent experts, convened by the Convention Secretariat to review each national communication from nominees from states and international organizations. The review teams (consisting of four to six members) are empowered to conduct 'paper' reviews of the national communications, but also to visit the relevant country (with its prior approval) in case that might seem helpful. These reviews should be written in 'non-confrontational language' and are submitted through the Convention's subsidiary bodies to the Conference of the Parties.[69]

REACTIONS TO VIOLATION

In principle, disclosed violations are subject to the general regime of state responsibility and countermeasures surveyed on pp 236–238 above. However, many recent treaties have set up special mechanisms for reacting to violations that set aside or at least claim primacy to the general regime. These mechanisms imply rules on who is entitled to claim that a violation exists, a procedure for determining that a violation exists and the appropriate reaction.

Who is Entitled to Make a Claim?

The general rule is that only state parties, moreover only parties which have suffered injury, may make claims based on an alleged violation by a state of a treaty. When the non-compliance procedure under the Montreal Ozone Protocol was being drafted, proposals were made that both the Protocol Secretariat and non-governmental organizations should be able to seize the Committee. The proposal met with strong resistance on the part of developing countries that also opposed giving the Committee the power to make on-site inspections on its own initiative.[70]

Thus, non-compliance matters may be brought to the implementation committee principally by another state Party.[71] As a compromise, it was agreed also that the Secretariat could contact countries and seek information as well as bring matters to the Committee.[72] This is a novelty. It is very rare that an international secretariat is given the right to initiate procedures in the case of alleged violations. Even within the International Labour Organization, the otherwise activist Secretariat does not seem to have the right to initiate enquiries on its own, although the tripartite structure of the organization seems to guarantee that important implementation failures receive a hearing.[73]

The authority to bring up human rights violations also rests predominantly with states themselves. That states are reluctant to use this possibility is clear from the fact that state complaints procedures in the *1996 International Covenant on Civil and Political Rights* and the *Convention on the Elimination of Racial Discrimination* have never been used.[74] By contrast, the less confrontational 1989 C/OSCE *Vienna Mechanism*, which enables rapid exchange of information, meetings between CSCE states and notification of human dimension situations to other CSCE states or bodies was applied over 110 times during the first two years of its existence.[75] It was, however, used mainly by Western countries to raise human rights issues in Eastern Europe, sometimes the other way around, occasionally between Eastern European states but only once in inter-Western relations.[76]

Non-governmental organizations (NGOs) do not play an official role in compliance review in any field of international law. [77] But they may sometimes act as an informal catalyst. In 1990, the UN Committee Against Torture (CAT) decided to examine a report by Amnesty International alleging that systematic torture was being practised in Turkey. A visit by two Committee members in Turkey took place in June 1992, as a result of which the Committee published its conclusions *against* the view of Turkish authorities, concluding that the 'existence of systematic torture in Turkey cannot be denied'.[78] In this way, a body entitled to react on its own initiative could use information provided by an NGO as the basis for taking the initiative.

The individual's standing is limited to those human rights instruments which provide for an individual right of petition.[79] At the global level, this right exists under the *Optional Protocol to the 1966 Covenant on Civil and Political Rights*, under Article 14 of the UN *Convention on the Elimination of Racial Discrimination* and under Article 22 of the UN *Convention against Torture and Other Cruel, Inhuman or Degrading Punishment*. Each of these systems of individual petition is, however, optional. They become operative only against a government's recognition of the respective treaty body's competence to deal with such petitions.[80] The case-law built by the Committees under these procedures, while important, is still not very large. The Human Rights Committee has registered, between 1977 and 1994, 587 petitions, out of which it has given 193 'views' under Article 5 (4) of the Optional Protocol.[81] By 1994, only four communications had been considered on their merits under the Racial Discrimination Convention and one had been declared admissible under the UN Torture Convention. Yet the purpose of the process is probably not so much to address individual violations – after all, thousands of daily violations remain untouched by them – than to deal with individual cases as symptoms of existing needs for legislative amendments or other action by states, in order to make their internal laws and procedures compatible with the Convention.

The most developed system of individual complaints against treaty violations is that embedded in the *European Convention on Human Rights and Fundamental Freedoms*. Petitions are first considered by the European Commission on Human Rights which aims at amicable settlement between the petitioner and the government. If no settlement is reached, the Commission draws up a report and gives its opinion on whether there has been a violation. It may then refer the matter either to a political body – the Committee of Ministers – or to a judicial organ – the European Court of Human Rights. Altogether, 2037 applications were registered with the European Commission in 1993.[82] In 1994, the parties to the European Convention decided on a reform which combines the two supervisory organs, the Commission and the Court, into a single judicial organ, making thus possible direct appeals by individuals to an international tribunal with the power to issue judgments that are formally binding on a state.[83]

Ascertaining a Breach and Determining Consequences

It is often – wrongly – believed that the ascertainment of compliance is essentially a question of establishing the 'facts'. The inference from facts to the presence of a violation is then thought to take place almost automatically. In practice, a number of non-factual considerations intrude: facts have to be interpreted, just as the provision with which they are compared must be interpreted. There might be exonerating circumstances: lack of resources or *force majeure*, for example. To fix the meaning of facts or of a treaty provision with respect to an alleged violation and to establish the well-foundedness of any excuses are original acts of power. It is no wonder that states have been reluctant to allocate such power to international bodies.

Most treaties leave the ascertainment of breaches to the parties themselves. One recent example is the 1994 *International Tropical Timber Agreement*. Complaints about violations may be referred to a Council consisting of all states parties whose decisions 'shall be final and binding'. A member may be excluded if the breach 'impairs the operation of [the] Agreement'.[84] Most disarmament treaties, too, provide for an implementation review by a general meeting of the parties.[85] In practice, reviews have not led to the detection of violations. They rely on information which is available in a very unorganized way and on parties' political willingness to bring up suspected violations. Often such willingness may not exist, and even if it did, the consensual procedure often makes dramatic action impossible.

Within the C/OSCE, an implementation review is allocated to governmental Review Conferences (formerly 'follow-up meetings'). The first such Conference, held in Budapest from 10 October to 2 December 1994, proved a disappointment. Although the need for better implementation of the commitments in the 1990 Paris Charter or the 1992 Helsinki Document ('Challenges of Change') was constantly stressed, the contribution of the Budapest Document was limited to emphasizing the role of the Permanent Council (formerly the Committee of Senior Officials (CSO)) in the human dimension review, with a provision for 'possible action in cases of non-implementation'.[86] Yet political realities compelled the 46-page Budapest Document to remain silent on the worst of such problems – the Yugoslavian tragedy.[87]

Hence, we may wonder about those environmental treaties that provide for a Conference of the Parties to discuss implementation and, sometimes, to decide on action to 'bring about full compliance'.[88] Such meetings are appropriate places to decide on assistance. But even if the will to take coercive action were present, it is uncertain whether a political body is the proper forum for deciding, for example, about the admissibility of the defences that the allegedly defaulting party will inevitably make.

The non-compliance procedure under the Montreal Ozone Protocol enables the Implementation Committee to suggest limited measures to be taken by the Meeting of the Parties against non-complying states.[89] In practice, however, the Committee has taken an advisory role and avoided commenting on the quality of party implementation – apart from occasionally expressing concern at the failure of states to provide their reports.[90] The corresponding body under the Climate Change Treaty will not be entitled, even in theory, to pass legal determinations of party compliance. Its task at the moment is to consider national reports only 'to assess the overall aggregated effect of the steps taken by the Parties' and 'to assist the Conference of the Parties in carrying out the reviews' related to the possible amendment of the commitments laid down in the Convention.[91]

More ambitious procedures exist within the International Labour Organization (ILO). Under Article 26 of the ILO Constitution, complaints of non-compliance with ILO conventions are directed to a Commission of Enquiry. If a member were to fail to carry out the recommendations of the Commission, the International Labour Conference may take any action 'it may deem wise and expedient to secure compliance therewith'.[92] Complaints may also be raised in connection with the examination of the reports that members are called upon to submit under the total of 171 ILO conventions. Reports are examined by a 20-member Committee of Experts, occasionally noting 'with concern' or 'with regret' the status of implementation in a country. At each annual session the International Labour Conference sets up a Committee on Standards which discusses some of the more serious cases of violation or non-implementation. Non-complying governments are singled out in a special paragraph of the Committee's report. It appears that such publicity does have some effect at least on officials of national labour ministries, although it has also occasioned strong reactions by governments.[93]

Most diplomats and human rights activists stress the non-adversarial character of reporting, the aim of achieving a 'constructive dialogue' with the state's representatives or perhaps even a mutual 'learning experience'.[94] Formal determination of breach has been thought as legalistic or even counter-productive.[95] But there is an element of making a virtue out of a necessity in these explanations, as suggested by the constant push by the committees beyond dialogue whenever it has proved fruitless.

Initially, human rights treaty bodies, with very few exceptions,[96] were not expected to give formal (even less, judicial) determinations on compliance. Reports were, and still are, examined in sessions where the state's representatives are present to introduce the report and to respond to questions in a conversational atmosphere. After the examination, the organ is called to make its own report to the General Assembly or to the states parties generally, and in this connection to 'make suggestions and general recommendations'.[97] During the years, those suggestions and recommendations did not contain country-specific appreciations. It was impossible for the Human Rights Committee to agree on collective conclusions. The report of the Committee only stated the views of members using formulae such as 'Many members were of the opinion ... Some members held the view that ...'.[98]

With the events of 1989 and 1990, this practice was transformed and treaty bodies now state their collective conclusions. The Human Rights Committee singles out for each national report it has studied what were its 'positive aspects', its 'principal subjects of concern' and its suggestions and recommendations to the state party. Successive reports are expected to take these as starting-points, thus enabling an organized and continuous review of the state of national implementation.[99] Other Committees have started to follow this example.[100]

The outcome of the process of examining individual petitions in those organs that have this competence is, of course, more geared towards determinations of violation. The European Convention on Human Rights and Fundamental Freedoms follows a judicial review system under which the Strasbourg Court's decisions are formally binding. The Committee of Ministers supervises their implementation. There has been much discussion about the legal status of the 'views' that the UN Human Rights Committee formulates on individual petitions under the Optional Protocol to the International Covenant on Civil and Political Rights. These 'views' may call upon the state to take very definite action (eg release a prisoner) and even to pay compensation. Many states have publicly stated that they will comply with the Committee's decisions. The recent decisions to increase and publish the Committee's follow-up activities with regard to stated views are clearly directed towards increasing their *de facto* persuasiveness.[101]

In general, however, treaty bodies do not have the authority to order states to comply, but are expected to provide technical and economic/financial assistance for a treaty partner falling short of its commitments. For instance, the 1966 Economic Social and Cultural Rights Covenant empowers the ECOSOC to bring to the attention of UN bodies problems in the implementation of the Covenant and to suggest that assistance be given to states for overcoming such problems.[102] Under the Montreal Ozone Protocol, the Implementation Committee has sought to seek a remedy for non-compliance by calling for assistance by international financial and technical institutions including the Multilateral Fund and the UNEP Secretariat.[103]

APPRAISAL: THE PLACE OF LEGAL SETTLEMENT

The extent to which the administration of international treaties relies on self-incriminating information produced through national reports and initiatives by states shows how far modern internationalism has sought to co-opt states in the creation of a rule-governed international order. The technically complicated and treaty-specific character of these various 'regimes' seeks to reassure states that the rules will always constitute only a bureaucratic and coordinative order that will not pose a threat to important state policies.

At the same time, the treaty-specific character of each 'regime' will hold general issues of state responsibility, fault and sanctions at bay. Each treaty is negotiated separately from every other treaty and sets up its own rules and procedures. Functional specialization ensues: human rights treaties are administered by human rights experts separately from, for example, arms control agreements which, in turn, come about exclusively through talks between arms control experts. Environmental treaties are administered and commented upon by experts in environmental matters, while commercial treaties – such as those emerging from the Uruguay Round in 1994 – are the result of prolonged debates between governmental representatives specializing in the GATT/WTO.

The resulting regimes bear a minimal relationship with general international law. 'Compliance control' replaces the classical law of dispute settlement, breach and sanction. Implementation becomes a technical or financial problem, to be dealt with through advice and assistance, instead of a normative problem, raising disputes about blameworthiness and sanction. Although environmental treaties, for example, do contain a standard clause on the settlement of disputes, this is more by way of ritual than any realistic belief that compliance problems should, or could, be dealt with through the doctrines of fault and attributability which characterize the legal doctrine of state responsibility.

Yet it is doubtful if this technical and piecemeal approach to world order will be able to grapple with implementation in a non-political way. An obsession with effectiveness fails to grasp that often the treaty standard itself may not deal effectively with the problem it is supposed to deal with, even if all parties were to fulfil their commitments to the hilt. In such a case, the problem is not with implementation but with the low level of ambition or ambiguity of the standard. In such circumstances, insisting on 'full compliance' is either simply pointless (because the problem really is what counts as 'compliance' in the first place) or will appear as an act of political power under technical disguise: an attempt to overrule one contested interpretation of the standard – or, better, one negotiating position – in favour of another.[104]

Technical bodies are incapable of dealing with such controversies as they appear now in a normative light. Their activity is based on the assumption that treaty partners have a shared goal and an agreed programme to attain it and that both are encapsulated in the constituting instrument. Hence, all problems are (technical) problems of implementation. But if it is precisely the content of the goals or the substance of the programme that are the real subject of controversy, then the expertise and functions of diplomatic or technical treaty bodies will be irrelevant. Now the questions are deeply political ones: what are the right goals; which is the best programme?

There are two ways in which these questions might be tackled: either the treaty body simply takes on the role of the contracting states and uses its position to determine what the situation requires. If the controversy is only slight and the treaty partners' sense of shared purpose is strong, then perhaps this is successful.[105] But if the controversy is fundamental, and the parties' good faith cannot be taken for granted, the need re-emerges for a procedure to weigh the parties' positions in the light of justice and fairness. What position should the body take in the face of a plea of *force majeure*, or in respect of a particular interpretation it invokes to buttress its behaviour?

These latter arguments are already far removed from the technical problems which expert bodies are called to deal with. They also raise questions that transcend special treaty regimes. To deal with them in an acceptable way requires the establishment of procedural safeguards, presumptions, rules of evidence and interpretation which define the legal process, including notions of fault, accountability and blameworthiness. Such genuinely normative problems, if they are of sufficient import, can only be dealt with acceptably through legal argument in a legally circumscribed process. Such settlement may be weak in the sense that there are no police to enforce it. But as it inevitably creates a norm (instead of applying one), that state of affairs should not seem too worrying. There is little to add to what was said about the place of law in the administration of specialized treaties by the then President of the International Court of Justice, Sir Robert Jennings. The position is limited to environmental affairs, but is equally applicable to the special 'regimes' of human rights, arms control or commerce:

> ... there is no legal question or problem concerning the environment over which the ICJ does not have full jurisdiction and competence *ratione materiae* ... This new law ... must be seen as part and parcel of general international law; otherwise it will technically and politically be bereft of that authority, and binding force, which attaches to general international law. A plea that X is depleting the ozone layer may be legally less effective than a plea that, in so doing, X is not only depleting the ozone layer but also, being in breach of the 1985 Vienna Convention on the Ozone Layer, is in breach of the general international law of treaties and of its cardinal principle of *pacta sunt servanda*.[106]

PART VI

Environmental NGOs and International Institutions

15   THE ROLE OF NON-STATE ACTORS

Hilary French

INTRODUCTION

In theory, international treaties and institutions are compacts among sovereign nations. Individual citizens do not have a direct role in the international legal system. They are expected to make their voice heard through the indirect route of influencing the policies of their own national governments, thereby influencing the positions these governments advocate in international foras.[1]

Yet as any recent participant in international environmental negotiations will readily attest to, this theory is increasingly breaking down in practice. Aided by modern information and communications technologies, a range of non-state actors, including environmental groups, scientists and the business community exert a powerful influence in international environmental negotiations and in international institutions. The sessions in which environmental treaties are negotiated are now routinely attended by scores of non-governmental organizations (NGOs) from diverse corners of the globe. International institutions such as the UN Commission on Sustainable Development, the Global Environment Facility and the World Bank are all the subject of intensive NGO interest and scrutiny. Each of them has developed elaborate procedures and processes for interacting with the non-governmental community.

But despite the recent growth in non-governmental interaction with the United Nations system, the relationship between the two is not an easy one. Citizens' groups working at the global level face formidable obstacles. For instance, there are no provisions for public participation comparable to those that are virtually taken for granted at the national level in democracies around the world, nor is there yet anything resembling an elected parliament in the United Nations or any of its agencies. Although the UN has begun to experiment with occasional public hearings on topics of special concern, these continue to be rare events. No formal provisions are made for public review and comment on international treaties, nor is there a mechanism for bringing citizen suits at the World Court. International negotiations are often closed to public participation, and access to documents of critical interest to the public is generally highly restricted. Many NGOs resent their second-rate status within the international system, and have grown frustrated by the seemingly constant battles required to obtain what they see as the rudimentary tools needed to operate effectively.[2]

UN officials and government representatives, for their part, sometimes grow frustrated with NGOs. Some of the more confrontational NGO tactics, such as Greenpeace's showering of paper dollar bills on the 1994 annual meeting of the World Bank, antagonize governmental officials.[3] It also sometimes appears to governmental officials that NGOs devote endless time and energy to questions of process at the expense of issues of substance. In addition, the growing role of NGOs in international fora raises difficult issues of accountability. NGOs, unlike democratic national governments, cannot claim legitimacy conferred by the ballot box. Their sources of legitimacy are more complex, and therefore more open to questioning.

This year's fiftieth anniversary of the founding of the United Nations is an opportune time to reflect on the growing role of a range of non-state actors in the environmental activities of international institutions. The phenomenon is an outgrowth of two of the most fundamental changes in the world since the United Nations was created: the emergence of environmental degradation on a scale that threatens the health of economies and the security of nations, and the development of a burgeoning civil society around the world. Despite the tensions that inevitably arise from changes to the *status quo*, the growing involvement of NGOs in the United Nations system is an encouraging development that is essential both for reversing global ecological decline and for restoring public legitimacy and support for a beleaguered United Nations.

THE SHAPE OF THE INTERNATIONAL NGO MOVEMENT

The international NGO movement is composed of a range of types of organizations that operate at different levels of governance and with a range of styles and approaches. This diversity is one of the movement's greatest strengths.

The most familiar role for NGOs is within national borders. Around the world, there is an encouraging growth in such activities. To cite but a few examples, some 10,000 NGOs are registered in Bangladesh alone, and some 21,000 in the Philippines.[4] NGOs working at this level focus primarily on influencing local and national policies. By so doing, they often indirectly influence the positions that national governments assert in international fora. If proper channels existed for them to do so, such groups could exert a powerful influence on shaping their countries' development priorities. This would profoundly influence the activities of the World Bank (see Chapter 8), the United Nations Development Program (see Chapter 3), and other international development institutions. In addition, a growing number of groups aim to influence international policies more directly by monitoring international negotiations and institutions. Some of the organizations represented at these meetings, such as Friends of the Earth, Greenpeace, the International Planned Parenthood Federation and the World Wide Fund for Nature, are themselves international. They are answerable to constituences which are sizeable enough to rival the populations of some nation-states: WWF has 3 million members and Greenpeace has 4.1 million.[5]

NGOs are also increasingly organizing themselves into international coalitions that position NGOs as representatives of global constituencies rather than parochial national interests. For instance, the Climate Action Network is an international network of groups which are concerned with climate change that has been actively involved with international climate negotiations since they were first set in motion in the early 1990s. Similarly, the Women's Environment and Development Organization is a coalition of women's groups from around the world that initially came together to lobby for the inclusion of gender equity concerns in the Rio documents. Subsequently, the movement succeeded in broadening the agenda of the Cairo conference beyond a focus on population numbers alone, to issues of women's health and empowerment more generally.

Because achieving sustainable development will require the involvement of all sectors of society, a broad range of groups – not just the traditional environmental groups – will need to have a voice in the international process. 'Agenda 21' (the action plan that emerged from Rio) encourages this by devoting a lengthy section to the important role of 'major groups', which are defined to include women, children and youth, indigenous peoples, non-governmental organizations, local authorities, workers and trade unions, business and industry, the scientific and technological community, and farmers.[6]

Scientists have already played a particularly critical role in a number of cases. For instance, international panels of scientists who were convened to study both ozone depletion and climate change helped to forge the scientific consensus needed to push these political processes forward. The treaties on these two problems created scientific advisory groups that will meet regularly and offer advice on whether the agreements need to be updated in the light of new scientific information. Scientists from a broad range of disciplines have expertise that is relevant to the process including social scientists. Indeed, an international panel of economists is currently analysing the economic costs of responding to climate change, and of suffering its effects. Its report will likely exert a considerable influence on the terms of the international debate.

The business community also is influential in the international arena, for both good and ill. For instance, US industry came to support strongly the Montreal Protocol on Ozone Depletion because it saw US legislation as inevitable and did not want to be at a competitive disadvantage as a result. The Business Council for Sustainable Development, some 50 Chief Executives from some of the world's largest corporations, were active in the lead-up to the Earth Summit. Although in Agenda 21 the Council opposed language that would have advocated developing standards to regulate multinational corporations, it argued persuasively in its report *Changing Course* that sound environmental policies and sound business practices had to go hand-in-hand.[7] More recently, the US-based Business Council for a Sustainable Energy Future – a coalition of energy efficiency, renewable energy, and natural gas companies that favour taking action to avert global warming – has begun to participate in international climate negotiations, where it counterbalances the lobbying efforts of oil and coal companies.[8]

Parliamentarians are another potentially powerful player on the global stage. Although they are 'governmental', they often voice opinions at variance with diplomats from their respective executive branches, and can provide a platform for parties in opposition and local authorities. The New York-based Parliamentarians for Global Action works to promote a more active involvement of parliamentarians at the UN. The Global Legislators for a Balanced Global Environment (GLOBE) is composed of parliamentarians from Europe, Japan and the United States. It passes joint statements to increase pressure for action to preserve the global environment.[9] In a similar initiative, in December 1994 an international group of parliamentarians convened in Washington at the invitation of Congressman Barney Frank to consider ways of improving parliamentary oversight of the World Bank and the International Monetary Fund.[10]

THE RIO MODEL

The June 1992 UN Conference on Environment and Development was a watershed for NGO participation in the international policy-making process: the 20,000 concerned citizens and activists who attended from around the world outnumbered official representatives by at least two to one.[11] The widespread participation of NGOs in the preparations and at the conference itself was unprecedented in its scale and in its results

NGOs were involved in the Rio Conference in a number of ways. During the year-and-a-half-long preparatory process, a number of groups with specific expertise took part in working groups on various issues that were convened by the Conference Secretariat to provide input into the process of developing draft documents. At both the preparatory committee meetings and at the Conference itself, many groups participated actively in the negotiations by lobbying delegates directly to make changes to the negotiating texts. Some even served as members of official delegations at these events. Other NGOs made their influence felt outside the official Conference proceedings by interpreting events for the international media or by organizing parallel gatherings. The 'Global Forum' was the *locus* for these activities at Rio itself.

NGOs have also played important roles in more recent UN Conferences. Thousands of NGOs attended both the 1993 Conference on Human Rights in Vienna and the September 1994 UN Conference on Population and Development in Cairo. At both events, they were widely credited with helping to shape the terms of the debate.[12]

In the years since Rio, considerable NGO attention has focused on the UN Commission on Sustainable Development (see Chapter 2), which was given the task of overseeing follow-up action on the Rio accords. In an important precedent, the Commission on Sustainable Development (CSD) has based its rules for NGO participation on the liberal regulations that were in effect for the Rio Conference.[13] As a result, more than 500 groups are accredited to observe CSD deliberations and to make selective interventions.[14] An international NGO Steering Committee has recently been created to help promote collaboration among these groups from diverse corners of the globe, and to facilitate interaction with the Secretariat of the CSD and with governments.[15]

Another way in which NGOs participate in the Rio follow-up process is through national sustainable development commissions. These bodies take different forms in different countries. Some are composed only of government representatives; others are 'multi-stakeholder' forums composed of a range of interested parties, including government, NGOs and the business sector.[16] In 1987, the Canadian Round Tables on the Environment and the Economy pioneered the concept of bringing diverse parties to the table. This has since been widely replicated, including the Philippine Council on Sustainable Development, and by the President's Council on Sustainable Development in the United States.[17] Indeed, 53 countries have now launched such multi-stakeholder initiatives.[18]

The UN Economic and Social Council is currently reviewing the rules for participation of citizens' groups in the UN system at large. Some of those involved in the debate advocate making it easier for groups to be involved, taking the Rio experience as their guide. Among other things, they urge opening up the criteria for UN consultative status to include more national and regional groups, expanding speaking rights and increasing access to documents and meetings.[19] Others resist these suggestions, worrying about the system being overwhelmed by sheer numbers, or about whether the citizens' groups are accountable to the public at large. The outcome of these deliberations on the role of NGOs at the UN remains to be seen, but it seems likely that the UNCED process has set a new standard for participation that the UN will have difficulty backing away from.[20]

PATHWAYS OF INFLUENCE

NGOs derive their influence in the international political arena from a number of factors. One of the most important is the role NGOs play as information brokers. For instance, daily newsletters produced by NGOs often reveal key failures in negotiations and prevent the obscure language of international diplomacy from shielding governments from accountability for their actions. Widely read by official delegates and NGOs alike during international meetings, these publications have become mainstays of the international negotiating process.

Eco is one such publication. Initially prepared for the 1972 Stockholm Conference on the Human Environment, it has since been distributed at many other international negotiations, such as the negotiations on the Climate Change Treaty. Two other influential NGO publications first made their appearance during the preparations for the Earth Summit – the *Earth Summit Times* and the *Earth Negotiations Bulletin*. *Earth Summit Times* was a newspaper independently financed and published during the UNCED preparatory process that provided background reporting on conference proceedings. After Rio, the paper was renamed the *Earth Times*. The *Earth Negotiations Bulletin* provides a more detailed account of the international negotiating process.[21]

Another example of NGOs providing information that governments themselves lack is Earth Summit Watch, a project of the US-based Natural Resources Defence Council and CAPE 21 (a coalition of US environmental groups). This effort has led to two reports based on in-depth surveys of actions taken to put Agenda 21 and other Rio initiatives into practice around the world. *Four in '94*, which was prepared for the 1994 CSD session, asked governments to list concrete actions taken in four of the portions of the agenda up for review that year – health, human settlements, fresh water, and toxic chemicals and hazardous waste. Among its findings were that 38 of 72 countries surveyed had taken steps to reduce lead exposure by moving towards lead-free petrol and through other means; 24 are planning or constructing water treatment projects; 69 of the 178 countries at Rio have ratified the Basel Convention on Trade in Hazardous Wastes, and 74 have imposed national bans on hazardous waste imports; yet only 10 of the 72 countries surveyed have taken steps to protect rivers. For the time being, most countries are simply reporting on actions that they were planning to take anyway. But over time, the 'peer pressure' process may induce them to move forward on new policies. A *Five in '95* report was planned for that year to cover timber certification, follow-up to the Conference in Cairo, protection of marine biodiversity hotspots, reduction of pesticide use and promotion of environmental democracy.[22]

As they operate in the political realm, NGOs benefit from the fact that they are freer than are national governments to represent the global interest, as they are unencumbered by any mandate to promote purely national goals, or to protect sacred political cows. In an effort to capitalize on this advantage, NGOs from around the world prepared 46 alternative NGO treaties as part of the Rio process on issues as diverse as climate change, Third World debt and international waterways.[23] Although NGOs discovered through this process that coming to a consensus is not easy, the end result was a number of documents that, hopefully, will pave the way for governmental action in the years ahead.

THE BRETTON WOODS CHALLENGE

Despite the impressive contributions that NGOs have made in the political realm, the obstacles remain great. The Bretton Woods institutions pose perhaps the greatest challenges when it comes to openness and accountability (see Chapter 8). To an even greater extent than at the UN itself, information and documents at these institutions are a tightly guarded secret, and negotiations between governments are completely closed to observers, with no NGO newsletters offering blow-by-blow accounts of who says what to whom.

GATT has been subject to particularly strong criticism for its secretive procedures. When a national law designed to protect the environment is challenged as a trade barrier under GATT, the issue is heard behind closed doors by a panel of professors and bureaucrats steeped in the intricacies of world trade law, but not in the needs of the planet. Legal briefs and other critical information are generally unavailable to the public, and there is no opportunity for citizens' groups to testify or make submissions.[24] Governments are currently discussing rules on public participation for the Trade and Environment Committee of GATT's successor, the World Trade Organization. Preliminary reports suggest that the fight for public access will be a long and hard one.[25]

Despite a chequered history regarding openness, the World Bank instituted two new policies in 1993 that others would do well to emulate. Under a new information policy, more Bank documents will be publicly available than before, and an information centre has been established to disseminate them.[26] The second change – the creation of an independent inspection panel – will provide an impartial forum where board members or private citizens can raise complaints about projects that violate the Bank's own policies, rules, and procedures.[27] Although both initiatives were watered down in the negotiating process, they none the less represent sizeable chinks in the World Bank's armour.

It will be up to the concerned public to test the limits of these new policies and to press for them to be strengthened, and replicated elsewhere.[28]

Some changes along similar lines are actually afoot at the notoriously secretive IMF. In 1994, a coalition of environment and development groups successfully lobbied the US Congress to withhold $75 million of the Clinton Administration's appropriation request of $100 million for the IMF's Enhanced Structural Adjustment Facility pending changes at the Fund that would increase public access to its documents.[29] And in July 1994, the Fund's directors did take modest steps in this direction.[30]

Besides access to information, the public needs to become a fuller partner in the development process itself. All too often, 'development' has served the purposes of a country's élite, but not its poorest members. A growing body of evidence suggests that for a project to succeed, its planning process must include the people it is supposed to benefit. In other words, aid should be demand-driven rather than imposed from above. Several bilateral aid agencies have developed new ways of fostering widespread participation in the development planning process, and both the United Nations Development Programme and the World Bank have also recently come up with new strategies along these lines. The challenge, as always, will be moving from words to action.[31]

One model for moving towards this more participatory approach to development is the recent growth in the number of 'environmental funds' around the world. Since 1990, at least $850 million has been committed to such entities in more than 20 countries.[32] These small funds to finance conservation investments can take the form of trust funds, endowments, foundations or other grant-making bodies (see Chapter 10). They receive money from diverse sources, including fees for park visits, private foundations, the Global Environment Facility and bilateral donors. Governed by boards on which NGOs are heavily represented, local people play an important role in identifying and carrying out projects. So far, this has led to impressive results.[33]

LOOKING AHEAD

To date, the growing involvement of non-governmental organizations in the making of international environmental policy has been a largely *ad hoc* process. Looking towards the future, a more formalized role for non-state actors in international institutions seems inevitable.

One of the most easily accomplished changes would be to develop a procedure for holding public hearings on issues of current concern. In most countries around the world, parliamentary hearings are an important means of influencing national policies. They could also be influential at the international level. In one important experiment along these lines, in June 1994 the Secretary-General conducted hearings on his Agenda for Development. Among those testifying were UN ambassadors, university professors, parliamentarians, members of advocacy groups and representatives of research institutes.[34] A priority for the future is to develop a more regularized process for such events.

As international organizations are revamped for the future, thought should be given to developing mechanisms for involving non-governmental organizations in a systematic fashion. For instance, there are a number of proposals that have been made to upgrade the United Nations Environment Programme to become a fully-fledged UN environment agency or to create a new Global Environmental Organization.[35] One interesting model for such an organization would be the International Labour Organization (ILO), which constantly modifies and strengthens the hundreds of standards it has issued on concerns such as workplace safety and child labour. The ILO also reviews whether members are complying with its standards. Representatives from both management and labour actually form part of the governing body of the ILO, through a unique tripartite system in which they share equal standing with governments.[36]

Finally, the time may soon be ripe to create a new assembly within the United Nations where the views of the people of the world could be more directly represented than under the current system. One model for such an assembly is the directly-elected European Parliament. A more feasible alternative might be to create an assembly that is composed of representatives of national parliaments – perhaps as a transition to a fully fledged people's assembly. This idea has been endorsed in a number of recent reports.[37]

Although opening up international institutions to the more active involvement of non-governmental organizations will not be an easy process, rapidly changing times leave the world community with little choice. The reality of ecological interdependence means that nations will need to rely more and more on international institutions to confront shared challenges. Yet international institutions as they are currently structured suffer from a 'democratic deficit' which both undermines their legitimacy and impedes sound policy-making. Only when international institutions are suitably reformed to redress this deficit will they be able to address the pressing transnational environmental threats of today and tomorrow.

NOTES AND REFERENCES

1 THE UNITED NATIONS GENERAL ASSEMBLY AND THE SECURITY COUNCIL

1 United Nations Charter Article 1: 'The purposes of the United Nations are:
   (3) To achieve international co-operation in solving international problems of an economic, social, cultural or humanitarian character, and in promoting and encouraging respect for human rights and for fundamental freedoms for all without distinction as to race, sex, language or religion; and
   (4) To be a centre for harmonizing the actions of nations in the attainment of these common ends.
2 The other principal organs are the Economic and Social Council, the International Court of Justice, the Secretariat and the Trusteeship Council.
3 See Chapter 2 for a more detailed discussion of the UNCED process.
4 Agenda 21, Chapter 38.9.
5 P Sands, *Principles of International Environmental Law* (1995) at 70.
6 UN Charter Article 22.
7 UNGA Resolution 2997 (xxvii) (1972).
8 UNGA Resolution 2029 (XX) (1965).
9 UNGA Resolution 47/191 of 22 December 1994.
10 Jim O'Brien, *Yearbook of International Environmental Law* (YIEL) (1991) pp 398–399: 'Its [the GA's] efforts to create and manage the negotiating process, rather than to address substantive matters, may prove to be a valuable example of its role in future environmental initiatives ... The procedural, or facilitating, role of the UNCED, together with the UNGA's successful role in creating the procedures for climate change negotiations, suggest that the UNGA should look closely at procedural initiatives in future environmental initiatives.'
11 UNGA Resolution 49/75/K of 15 December 1994.
12 UN Charter, Articles 9(2) and 18(1).
13 Id Article 18(2–3).
14 Agenda 21, Chapter 8.9.
15 See V Morris 'Protection of the Environment in Wartime: The United Nations General Assembly Considers the Need for a New Convention', 27 *International Lawyer*, 1993, 775.
16 See statement of Sir Crispin Tickell before ECOSOC, 9 May 1989, p 2.

17 UN Charter Articles 10–14. See also articles 55 and 60. The main restriction on this mandate is that the General Assembly may not make recommendations on a matter that is being dealt with by the Security Council.

18 For discussion of the effects of General Assembly resolutions, see O Asamoah, The Legal Effect of Resolutions of the General Assembly, 3 *Columbia Journal of Transnational Law* (1964–65) 210; M Ellis, The New International Economic Order and General Assembly Resolutions, 15 Cal and West *ILJ* (1985) 647; R Falk, The Quasi-Legislative Competence of the General Assembly, 60 *AJIL* (1966) 782; R Higins, The Development of International Law through the Political Organs of the United Nations (1963); Sloan, General Assembly Resolutions Revisited, 69 *British Yb IL* (1989) 39; S Schwebel, The Legal Effect of Resolutions and Codes of Conduct of the United Nations, Forum Internationale paper.

19 UN Charter Article 22.

20 Id Article 4.

21 Id Article 4.

22 Id Article 23.

23 Harrod and Schrijver, *The United Nations Under Attack*, p 43: 'The use of the term "declaration" suggests that the General Assembly is concerned with an act of the confirmation or codification of already existing customary principles of international law rather than the creation of new ones.'

24 Sloan, General Assembly Resolutions Revisited, 66 *Br Ybk IL* (1989) 39 at 68–9; 'In some instances a norm will have been in the process of development through the regular procedures of customary law, and a resolution of the General Assembly may give it the final impetus to crystallize it into a rule of law.'

25 Sloane at p 70 states that 'A resolution whose norms are clearly *de lege ferenda* when adopted may become the basis for state practice, and thus be transformed into customary international law ... By providing a focal point for concordant practice the process of norm generation is greatly accelerated and may even be changed.'

26 International Covenant on Civil and Political Rights 1966 and the International Covenant on Economic, Social and Cultural Rights 1966.The basic principles forming the legal regime governing outer space were elaborated in a series of General Assembly resolutions in the early Sixties, including the Declaration of Legal Principles Governing the Activities of States in the Exploration and Use of Outer Space 1963, UNGA Resolution 1962 (1963), and these formed the basis for the Outer Space Treaty of 1967.

27 Pardo, Whose is the Bed of the Sea? 62 ASIL Proc 225–6 1968.

28 25 UN GAOR Supp (No 28) at 24, UN Document A/Resolution/2749 (1970), adopted with 104 votes in favour, none against, 16 abstentions.

29 UNCLOS 1982 Articles 136–7, in force November 1994; Agreement Governing the Activities of States on the Moon and their Celestial Bodies 1979, in force 11 June 1984; Article 11(1) declared the moon to be the common heritage of mankind.

30 1992 Framework Climate Change Convention, Preamble.

31 1992 Convention on Biological Diversity, Preamble.

32 The unpopularity of the common heritage of mankind principle with many of the industrialized states resulted in the very low ratification rate for the Moon Treaty and the long delay in the coming into force of UNCLOS. Now, with the coming into force of UNCLOS, the General Assembly has been involved in trying to ensure the broadest possible participation with UNCLOS by resolving the outstanding issues relating to the deep sea-bed regime. UNGA Resolution 48/28 of 9 December 1993 'Recognises that political and economic changes including particularly a growing reliance on market principles underscore the need to reevaluate in the light of the issues of concern to some States matters in the regime to be applied to the Area and its resources'.

33 See discussion on p 10 on the evolution of policy in the General Assembly from the New International Economic Order to UNCED.

34   UNGA Resolution 45/197 of 21 December 1990.

35   UNGA Resolution 46/215 of 20 December 1991.

36   Chris Stone in *Greening International Law* (1994), ed P Sands p 39.

37   P Sands, *Principles of International Environmental Law* (1995) 431: 'The resolution is
      not legally binding but the fact that it was adopted by consensus, its clear terms, and
      the subsequent support for it by a very large number of States since its adoption,
      suggest that it may now reflect a rule of customary law.'

38   Greenpeace Fisheries Campaigner, Martin Gianni, said, 'Japan, Korea and Taiwan
      have, by all accounts, acted responsibly and taken the hard steps necessary to halt
      high seas driftnet fishing in the Pacific Ocean since the 1992 moratorium. On the
      other hand, the European Union alone has defied the United Nations by bowing to
      pressure from France and Italy, even though the EU agreed to the UN ban.'
      Greenpeace press release, 7 December 1994, 'UN Puts Pressure on Europe to Toe the
      Line on Driftnets'.

39   UNGA Decision 49/436 of December 1994. See also the Report of the Secretary-
      General on Large-scale pelagic drift-net fishing and its impact on the living marine
      resources of the world's oceans and seas, UN Document A/49/469, 5 October 1994.

40   Greenpeace press release of 26 December 1994, 'No Decision on Driftnets: EU
      Ministers Fuel Further Tuna Wars'.

41   A Boyle, International Law and the Protection of the Global Atmosphere: Concepts,
      Categories and Principles in International Law and Global Climate Change 1991 (eds
      Churchill and Freestone) p 11, said that Resolution 43/53 does not make the global
      atmosphere common property beyond the sovereignty of individual states but it
      does treat it as a global unity in so far as injury in the form of global warming may
      affect the community of states as a whole. Its main effect is that it places the issue on
      the international agenda and makes it the legitimate object of international attention
      overriding the reserved domain of domestic jurisdiction or the possible contention
      that it relates to matters solely within the exclusive sovereignty of individual states.

42   UNGA Resolution 43/53, 6 December 1988, paras 1 and 7.

43   UNGA Resolution 44/207, 22 December 1989, paras 1 and 3.

44   Id at para 5.

45   UNGA Resolution 45/212, 21 December 1990, paras 1 and 7.

46   The initiative was supported by Malaysia, with Antigua and Barbuda.

47   For example, in UNGA Resolution 47/57 of 9 December 1992, paragraph 10, the
      General Assembly 'reiterates its call that any move at drawing up an international
      convention to establish a nature reserve or world park in Antarctica ... must be
      negotiated with the full participation of the international community'.

48   Lee Kimball, in P Sands, *Greening International Law* (1994) p 136.

49   UNGA Resolution 37/7, 28 October 1982.

50   Id at paragraphs 2(a) and 4(a).

51   Id at Article 1.

52   Id at Article 2.

53   Id at Article 3.

54   Id at Article 8.

55   Id at Article 16.

56   Id at Article 11(a).

57   Id at Article 11(c).

58   Id at Article 23.

59   See UNGA Resolution 44/228 of 22 December 1989 and 45/211 of 21 December
      1990.

60   UNGA Resolution 45/212 of 21 December 1990, preamble and paragraph 1.

61   The Charter of Economic Rights and Duties of States, UNGA Resolution 3281, 29 UN
      GAOR Supplement (No 30) at 50, UN Document A/9631 (1974), Article 22.

62   See R L Barsh, 'A Special Session of the UN General Assembly Rethinks the
      Economic Rights and Duties of States', 85 AJIL (1991) 192.

63 Declaration of the Special Session of the UN General Assembly on Economic Cooperation and Development, 1 May 1990, para 29.
64 Rio Declaration 1992, Principle 26.
65 Charter of the United Nations, Article 24.
66 UN Charter, Article 39.
67 V Vinogradov, 'International Environmental Security: The concept and its implementation', in *Perestroika and International Law* (1991) by A Carter and G Dandenko.
68 Note by the President of the Security Council on 'The Responsibility of the Security Council in the Maintenance of International Peace and Security', UN Document S/ 23500 (1992), emphasis added.
69 See Hilary French, 'After the Earth Summit: the Future of Environmental Governance', *Worldwatch Paper* no107, at 35.
70 This development is traced by Joseph J Romm in *Defining National Security: The Non-Military Aspects* (1993), 15–29. See also Jessica Tuchman Mathews, *Redefining Security*, *68 Foreign Affairs* (1989) 162; M Renner, 'National Security: The Economic and Environmental Dimensions', *Worldwatch Paper* no 8 (Worldwatch Institute 1989).
71 See the speeches of Mikhail Gorbachev and the Soviet Foreign Minister Schevardnadze to the 43rd UNGA: A Timoshenko, Ecological Security: Global Change Paradigms, 2 Colorado *Journal of Environmental and International Law and Policy* (1990) 127.
72 For example, see Hilary French supra no 2 at 36; Mark Imber, 'Environment, Security and UN Reform' (1994) at 40; Admiral Sir Julian Oswald, Defense and Environmental Security' in Gwyn Prins, *Threats Without Enemies: Facing Environmental Security* (1993); Philippe Sands, 'Principles of International Environmental Law' (1995) at 80; and Sir Crispin Tickell, 'The Inevitability of Environmental Security', in *Threats Without Enemies* supra.
73 *The Independent*, 'Troubled Waters', 14 November 1993.
74 *The Independent*, 'Troubled Waters', 14 November 1993. The principle of absolute sovereignty over international rivers, commonly known as the Harmonn doctrine, is contrary to the international law on shared rivers, where the fundamental principle is equitable sharing of international rivers. See Birnie and Boyle *International Environmental Law* (1994) 215–249.
75 See J Bulloch and A Darwish *Water Wars: Coming Conflict in the Middle East* (1993).
76 Security Council Resolution 688, April 5 1991, concerned with Iraqi repression of its Kurdish population 'which led to a massive flow of refugees . . . across international frontiers . . . [and] threatens international peace and security in the region'. The Resolution insisted that Iraq allow immediate access by international humanitarian organizations to all those in need of assistance in all parts of Iraq.
77 See Thomas F Homer–Dixon, 'Global Environmental Change and International Security', in *Building a New Global Order: Emerging Trends in International Security* (1993), eds D Dewitt and J Kirton.
78 Myers, *Ultimate Security* (1993) 191.
79 UNEP IUCC fact sheets on climate change 1993, pp 107 and 114.
80 UN Charter Article 33(2).
81 Id, Article 36(1 and 3).
82 Id, Article 37(2). Bowett, 'The Law of International Institutions' (1982) 35, comments that 'this is tantamount to assuming a quasi-judicial function where the dispute affects the legal rights of the parties'.
83 Security Council Resolution 687/1991, para 16, reprinted in 30 *ILM* 846 (1991).
84 For discussion of the UN Compensation Commission, see C Alzamara 'Reflections on the UN Compensation Commission', *9 Arb Int* (1993) 349; N C Ulmer 'The Gulf War Claims Institution', *J of Int Arb* (1993) 85.
85 Security Council Resolution 688, note 76, above. See also Security Council Resolution 794, 3 December 1992, determining that the magnitude of the human suffering

caused by the conflict in Somalia constituted a threat to international peace and security.

86   UN Charter, Article 24(2). The Purposes and Principles are in Articles 1–2.

87   'Question of the Interpretation and Application of the 1971 Convention Arising From the Aerial Incident at Lockerbie (*Libya* v *UK*) (Request for the Indication of Provisional Measures)' (1992) *ICJ* 3; *Libya* v *US* (1992) *ICJ* Rep 114.

88   From D Deudney, 'The Case Against Linking Environmental Degradation and National Security', cited in Mark Imber *Environment, Security and UN Reform* (1994) 11.

89   Philippe Sands, *Principles of International Environmental Law*.

90   General Assembly, Resolution 48/26 (1993).

91   David D Caron, 'The Legitimacy of the Collective Authority of the Security Council', 87 *AJIL* (1993) 552; 'Our Global Neighbourhood, The Report of the Commission on Global Governance' (1995), 233–241; Burns H Weston, 'Security Council Resolution 678 and Persian Gulf Decision Making: Precarious Legitimacy', 85 *AJIL* (1991) 516.

92   Weston, id at 523–525 stated: 'the process by which Security Council Resolution 678 was won, while perhaps legally correct stricto senso, confirms how complete the power of the United States over the United Nations policing mechanism had become in the absence of cold war opposition', and listed the promises made to the other members of the Council to ensure support for the Resolution, including the promise of financial help to Colombia, Côte d'Ivoire, Ethiopia and Zaire; agreement with the Soviet Union to help keep Estonia, Latvia and Lithuania out of the November 1990 Paris summit conference; a pledge to the Soviet Union to persuade Kuwait and Saudi Arabia to provide it with desperately needed hard currency; agreement to lift sanctions in place against China since the Tiananmen Square massacre and to support a World Bank loan of $114.3 million to China. As a result of Yemen's negative vote on Resolution 678, the United States said it would cut off its $70 million in annual aid to that state.

93   Article 23(2) of the UN Charter states that regard should be paid 'in the first instance to the contribution of Members of the United Nations to the maintenance of international peace and security and to the other purposes of the organization, and also to equitable geographical distribution'.

94   See the Statement of the Mission of Indonesia to the UN on behalf of the Non-Aligned Movement, 8 March 1994.

95   See UNGA Document A/48/264, 20 July 1993, p 66.

96   See statement of Indonesia above, note 94.

97   This new procedure was outlined by Michael Reisman in 'The Constitutional Crisis in the United Nations', 87 *AJIL* (1993) 83 at 85–6: 'as the Council has become more powerful, it has become more secretive ... it now contains ever-smaller "mini-councils" each meeting behind closed doors without keeping records, and each taking decisions secretively. Before the plenary Council meets in "consultations" in a special room assigned to it near the Security Council, the P-5 have met in "consultation" in a special room now assigned to them outside the Security Council; and before they meet, the P-3, composed of the United States, the United Kingdom and France, have met in one of their Missions in New York. All of these meetings take place in camera and no common minutes are kept. After the fifteen members of the Council have consulted and reached their decision, they adjourn to the Council's Chamber where they go through the formal motions of voting and announcing their decision. Decisions that appear to go further than at any time in the history of the United Nations are now being taken, it seems, by a small group of States separately meeting in secret'.

98   Jake Werksman, 'Greening Bretton Woods', in P Sands, *Greening International Law* (1994) at 77.

2 THE UNITED NATIONS COMMISSION ON SUSTAINABLE DEVELOPMENT

1 United Nations Framework Convention on Climate Change, adopted in 1992, was launched under the auspices of the United Nations General Assembly.

2 See Chapter 3. UNEP was established after the United Nations Conference on the Human Environment in Stockholm, Sweden, in 1972. In 1985, UNEP provided the forum for the adoption of the Vienna Convention on the Protection of the Ozone Layer. That Convention was later followed by the 1987 Montreal Protocol. More recently, UNEP took the lead in bringing to the attention of the international community the need for a multilateral convention on the preservation of biological diversity, having regard to the work done by the World Conservation Union (IUCN) and leading to the adoption of the 1992 Convention on Biological Diversity.

3 Under UN-ECE auspices the Convention on Long-Range Transboundary Air Pollution (LRTAP) was negotiated and concluded on 13 November 1979.

4 UNESCO also provided the forum for the negotiation of the Convention for the Protection of Cultural Heritage.

5 The IMO continues to play a vital role in the oceans sector.

6 Stockholm Declaration of the United Nations on the Human Environment, 11 ILM 1416 (1972).

7 Adede, A O, *International Environmental Law Digest: Instruments for International Responses to Problems of Environment and Development 1972-1992* (1993) Chapter V.

8 See Chapter 3.

9 Ibid. at p 54.

10 Awoonor, *Africa: The Marginalised Continent*, Accra (1994) p 114.

11 Report of the United Nations Conference on Environment and Development, A/CONF 151/26/Rev 1, vol 1, p 3 (1993).

12 *Our Common Future*, UNGA Doc A/42/427(1987).

13 Ibid.

14 Supra, note 11, vols I, II, and III.

15 UN Docs A/CONF151/PC/L 74, A/CONF 151/PC/128 and A/CONF 151 /2.

16 Article 68 of the Charter provides that the Council '. . . shall set up commissions in the economic and social fields and for the promotion of human rights, and such other commissions as may be required for the performance of its functions', The Charter of the United Nations, Chapter 10, Article 68.

17 The Council has only 54 members at any particular time, whereas the General Assembly is composed of all the members of the United Nations.

18 Article 22 of the Charter provides that ' the General Assembly may establish such subsidiary organs as it deems necessary for the performance of its functions', The Charter of the United Nations, Chapter 4, Article 23.

19 Supra, note 11, Chapter 38.

20 Supra, note 11.

21 Supra, note 11.

22 UNGA, Doc A/47/191 (1992).

23 Ibid.

24 Ibid.

25 Ibid.

26 Ibid.

27 Ibid.

28 Ibid.

29 UNECOSOC, Doc E/5975/Rev 1 (1993).

30 UNECOSOC, Doc E/1993/14 (1993)

31 Supra, note 22.

32 UNECOSOC, Doc E/1993/12 (1993).

33 Ibid.
34 UNGA, Docs A/CONF 151/PC/L 74, A/CONF 151/PC/128, A/CONF 151/2, A/46/897 and PrepCom December 4/8.
35 Ibid and UNGA, Doc A/46/470 (1992).
36 Some sections such as the rule of submission of credentials applied both to the representatives of states and also to the EC; other sections such as the rule on making proposals, applied to representatives without distinguishing among them. Other sections, however, such as those dealing with the holding of office, being counted for quorum purposes and the making of certain procedural motions, were restricted to only the representatives of states.
37 Supra note 22.
38 For a more detailed discussion of the legal competence of the EC in the area of international environmental law, see Chapter 11.
39 Supra note 30.
40 Ibid.
41 Ibid.
42 UNECOSOC, Doc E/1995/201(1995). 'A footnote shall be added to rule 74 of the rules of procedure of the functional commissions of the Council (E/5975/Rev 1), reading: "the participation of the European Community and other regional organization and subregional economic integration organization in the Commission is governed by Economic and Social Council decision 1995/201."
43 UNGA, Docs A/45/211 (1990), A/46/168 (1991).
44 Supra note 22.
45 Supra note 30.
46 UNGA, Doc A/47/190 (1992).

3 THE UNITED NATIONS ENVIRONMENT PROGRAMME AND THE UNITED NATIONS DEVELOPMENT PROGRAMME

1 UNGA, Resolution 44/228.
2 Agenda 21, Chapter 38, para 38.4.
3 Ibid, para 38.24.
4 Ibid, para 38.24.
5 Ibid, para 38.8 (c).
6 For example, UNEP/UNDP Joint Project on Environmental Law and Institutions in Africa.
7 For example, participation in the Committee of International Development Institutions on the Environment (CIDIE) and in the Global Environment Facility (GEF) (see Chapter 9).
8 UN General Assembly Resolution 2997 (XXVII), 15 December 1972, the ninth preambular paragraph. See also Part I, paras 2(1) and 3, and Part III, paras 3 and 4 of the Resolution.
9 UNEP Governing Council decision 1 (1), para 15(d).
10 UNEP Governing Council decision 79 (IV).
11 See Our Common Future, Oxford, NY, 1987.
12 See 'Action and Interaction. The Role and Potential of CIDIE Secretariat', UNEP, Nairobi.
13 Adopted by the UN General Assembly Resolution 42/186 of 11 December 1987.
14 Approved by the UNEP Governing Council in its decision SS1/3 of 18 March 1988.
15 Montevideo Programme for the Development and Periodic Review of Environmental Law. UNEP publication (1982), p 3.

16 Convention for Co-operation in the Protection and Development of the Marine and Coastal Environment of the West and Central Africa Region (1981), preamble.

17 Convention for the Protection of the Marine Environment and Coastal Area of the South-East Pacific (1981), Article 13.

18 Convention for Protection, Management and Development of the Marine Environment of the Wider Caribbean Region (1983), preamble.

19 Convention for Protection, Management and Development for the Marine and Coastal Environment of the Eastern African Region (1986), preamble.

20 Convention for the Protection of the Natural Resources and Environment of the South Pacific Region (1986), Article 5.

21 Agreement on the Action Plan for the Environmentally Sound Management of the Common Zambezi River System (1987), preamble.

22 Ibid, Annex I, para 15.

23 Basel Convention on the Control of Transboundary Movement of Hazardous Wastes and Their Disposal (1989), preamble.

24 UN General Assembly resolution 45.212 on 'Protection of global climate for present and future generations of mankind', 21 December 1990.

25 Shine, C and Kohona, P T B, 'The Convention on Biological Diversity: Bridging the Gap Between Conservation and Development', *Review of European Community and International Environmental Law*, vol 1, issue 3 (1992) pp 178–287.

26 Convention on Biological Diversity (1992), Article 1.

27 United Nations Framework Convention on Climate Change (1992), Article 2.

28 Ibid, Article 3(4).

29 See Agenda 21, Ch 38, para 38.2, in Appendix 1 to this volume.

30 Ibid, para 38.22.

31 According to Agenda 21, Chapter 39 (para 39.2): 'The overall objective of the review and development of international environmental law should be to evaluate and to promote the efficacy of that law and to promote the integration of environment and development policies . . .'

32 Neither Agenda 21 nor the Rio Declaration use identical terms to describe this process. See, for example, 'international law on sustainable development', Agenda 21, 39.1(a), 'international law concerning sustainable development' (Agenda 21, 39, 39.1(f)), 'international law in the field of sustainable development' (Rio Declaration, Principle 27).

33 'Programme for the Development and Periodic Review of Environmental Law for the 1990s', UNEP publication (June 1993), Programme area H.

34 UNEP Governing Council decision 17/25, 21 May 1993, third preambular paragraph, operative paragraph 7.

35 Ibid, operative para 7.

36 See UNEP Doc UNEP/CBD/COP/I/L 7, 6 December 1994.

37 UNEP/CBD/COP/2/19 Add 1, 30 November 1995.

38 Szekely, A and Ponce-Nava, D, 'The Challenge of the 1992 Earth Summit'. Transboundary Resources Report, vol 1, no 1, Spring 1992; Bliss-Guest, P A, 'Proposals for Institutional Reform of the UN System to Promote Sustainable Development Policies', paper presented at the Twentieth Annual American Bar Association Conference on the Environment, Warrenton, Va, 18 May 1991; Riggs, R E and Plano, J C, *The United Nations: International Organization and World Politics*, Chicago, 1988; French, H F, 'After the Earth Summit; the Future of Environmental Governance', Worldwatch Paper 107, March 1992.

39 UN General Assembly resolution 47/191, 22 December 1992.

40 *United Nations Yearbook of International Organizations*, 1992–93, p 1538.

41 *Green Globe Yearbook 1993*, The Fridtjof Nansen Institute, Oxford University Press, p 207 (hereinafter, *Green Globe Yearbook 1993*).

42 'The Follow-Up to UNCED: UNDP's Strategy in Support of Sustainable Development including Capacity 21'. Presented to the Fortieth Session of the Governing Council of the United Nations Development Programme, (1993), p 2.
43 Ibid, p 2.
44 Ibid, p 2.
45 *The Sustainable Development Network*, United Nations Development Programme publication, p 2.
46 *Green Globe Yearbook 1993*, p 207.
47 UNDP's *Handbook and Guidelines for Environmental Management and Sustainable Development*, New York (1992) p 5.
48 See Agenda 21, Chapter 28 in Appendix 1, this volume.
49 'The Follow-Up to UNCED: UNDP's Strategy in Support of Sustainable Development including Capacity 21', presented to the Fortieth Session of the Governing Council of the United Nations Development Programme (1993) (hereafter 'Capacity 21'), p 4.
50 Banuri, Tariq; Hyden, Gordan; Juma, Calestous; Rivera, Marcia, 'Sustainable Human Development From Concept to Operation: A Guide for the Practitioner', UNDP Discussion Paper 16 (1994).
51 Ibid, p 16.
52 Speth, James Gustave, Administrator, 'UNDP, Building a New UNDP: Agenda for Change', presentation to the UNDP Executive Board (1994) (hereinafter Speth, 1994).
53 Ibid.
54 Capacity 21, p 4.
55 Speth (1994).
56 Ibid.
57 'Heading for Change: UNDP 1993 Annual Report' (1993) p 7.
58 Speth (1994).
59 Agenda 21, Chapter 38.24.
60 'Capacity 21' (1993) p 11.
61 Ibid, p 12.
62 Agenda 21, Chapter 38.8 (c).
63 Ibid, p 1.
64 Joint statement by James Gustave Speth, Administrator, United Nations Development Programme, and Elizabeth Dowdeswell, Executive Director, United Nations Environment Programme, May 1994.
65 Agenda 21, Chapter 38.22 (h).
66 'Report of the Commission on Sustainable Development on its Second Session' (1994), p 8.
67 Ibid.
68 Ibid, p 17.
69 Ibid.

4 THE CONFERENCE OF PARTIES TO ENVIRONMENTAL TREATIES

1 Palmer, G 'New Ways to Make International Environmental Law' 86 *AJIL* 259, 262, calling for 'a proper international environmental agency within the United Nations system that has real power and authority' (hereinafter Palmer). See Lang, N 'Negotiation as Diplomatic Rule-Making' in *International Negotiation* (Kluwer, 1996).
2 See, for example, the 1989 Hague Declaration on the Environment, 28 *ILM* 1308, calling for the creation of an institution with the power to 'develop instruments and define standards to enhance or guarantee the protection of the atmosphere and monitor compliance' (hereinafter the Hague Declaration); and Palmer, supra, note 1.

3   Palmer also notes the need for an 'institutional mechanism to provide nations with incentives to comply when they have ratified', Palmer at 263. See discussion of the role of the International Court of Justice and of specialized compliance regimes in Chapters 13 and 14 of this volume.

4   An MEA can create a largely independent international organization, with its own governing body, Secretariat and budget. See memorandum from Carl August Fleischauer, Under-Secretary General for Legal Affairs, United Nations Office of Legal Affairs to Michael Zammit Cutajar, Executive Secretary, Intergovernmental Negotiating Committee for a Framework Convention on Climate Change, on arrangements for the implementation of the provisions of Article 11 of the UN Framework Convention on Climate Change concerning the financial mechanism, 4 November 1993, which concluded that '[o]nce this Convention enters into force it will establish an international entity/organization with its own separate legal personality, statement of principles, organs and a supportive structure in the form of a Secretariat.' The term COP, in this chapter, is used to refer generally to the governing body of an MEA. The Montreal Protocol's governing body was titled a Meeting of Parties to distinguish it from the governing body of its parent treaty, the 1985 Vienna Convention on the Protection of the Ozone Layer (26 ILM 1529, 1987).

5   Sands, P H (1990) *Lessons Learned in Environmental Governance* (hereinafter *Lessons Learned*).

6   *Lessons Learned* at 17; Palmer at 264.

7   The 1987 Montreal Protocol on Substances that Deplete the Ozone Layer, as adjusted and amended, 26 *ILM* 1550 (hereinafter Montreal Protocol).

8   The 1992 United Nations Framework Convention on Climate Change, 31 *ILM* 849 (hereinafter Climate Change Convention). Areas that have been identified as being of global concern in addition to ozone depletion and climate change, include biodiversity loss, (eg the 1973 Convention on International Trade in Endangered Species; the 1992 Convention on Biological Diversity; the transboundary shipment of hazardous waste (the 1989 Basel Convention on the Control of Transboundary Movements of Hazardous Wastes and their Disposal, 28 *ILM* 657 (hereinafter Basel Convention)); air pollution (the 1979 Geneva Convention on Long-Range Transboundary Air Pollution and its Protocols); high-seas living resources (eg the 1982 United Nations Convention on the Law of the Sea and related agreements), and the environment of the Antarctic Continent (eg the 1991 Protocol on Environmental Protection).

9   Even then, some would question whether demonstrable progress towards an MEA's objective is necessarily attributable to the existence of the MEA itself. See, for example, discussion in 'Structural causes and regime consequences: regimes as intervening variables', in Krasner, S (ed) (1982) *International Regimes*.

10   This rhythm is described in detail in Lehring, T 'International Environmental Regimes: Dynamic Sectoral Legal Systems', 1 *YIEL* (1990) (hereinafter Gehring).

11   The Montreal Protocol, for example, was negotiated by the parties to the 1995 Vienna Convention on the Protection of the Ozone Layer, with institutional support from UNEP. The Climate Change Convention was negotiated by an INC set up by the UN General Assembly.

12   Parts of this section are drawn from Werksman, J (1995) 'Consolidating Governance of the Global Commons: Insights from the Global Environment Facility', in the *Yearbook of International Environmental Law* (hereinafter, Werksman, *YIEL* 1995).

13   See, for example, Haas, P M 'Banning Chlorofluorocarbons: Epistemic Community Efforts to Protect the Stratospheric Ozone Layer' International Organizations 46.

14   1985 Convention on the Protection of the Ozone Layer 26 *ILM* 1529 (1987).

15   The Parties to the Protocol have established four such Panels, on Scientific Assessment, Environmental Assessment, Technical Assessment and Economic Assessment. 'Report of the Parties to the Montreal Protocol on the Work of their First Session' UNEP/OzL Pro 1/5, December I/3, Annexes IV and V.

16   Ibid.

17   Article 9 (Subsidiary Body for Scientific and Technological Advice). The Climate Change Convention negotiators will also receive advice from the UNEP/WMO Intergovernmental Panel on Climate Change. For an assessment of how the IPCC has dealt with the politics of climate change, see Boehmer-Christiansen, S 'Global climate protection policy: the limits of scientific advice' 4(2) *Global Environmental Change* (1994) pp 140–159.

18   The Montreal Protocol, preamble, 5th tiret; Climate Change Convention, Article 3.3.

19   For an assessment of the influence of the ozone advisory panels on the decision-making of the Montreal Protocol Parties, and a potential backlash against this, see Parson, E A and Green, O (1995) 'The Complex Chemistry of the International Ozone Agreements', 37 *Environment* 2, at 16 (1995) (hereinafter, Parson and Green).

20   The second meeting of the Parties, London, 1990, adjusted the targets and timetables for eliminating production and use of CFCs and halons, and amended the Protocol to broaden the set of controlled substances to include additional ozone-depleting substances. The fourth meeting of the Parties, held in Copenhagen in 1992, adjusted and advanced the phase-out dates for certain controlled substances and amended the Protocol to include yet additional substances. Parson and Green, at 20. The seventh meeting of the Parties, held in Vienna in 1995, agreed on phase-out dates for substances that had been first regulated at Copenhagen. *International Environment Reporter*, 13 December 1995, at 935.

21   Climate Change Convention, Article 2.

22   Climate Change Convention, Article 4.2(d).

23   The Berlin Mandate, FCCC/CP/1995/7/Add 1, Decision 1 (hereinafter, the Berlin Mandate).

24   *BNA International Environment Reporter*, vol 19, p 3, 10 January 1996.

25   Parts of this section are drawn from Werksman (1995) *YIEL*.

26   Climate Change Convention, preamble, 8th tiret, Biodiversity Convention, Article 3. Parties to the Montreal Protocol recognize Principle 21 in the preamble to the 1985 Vienna Convention for the Protection of the Ozone Layer, 2nd tiret. 1972 Stockholm Declaration on the Human Environment, Principle 21 11 *ILM* 1416 (1972). Principle 2 of the 1992 Rio Declaration on Environment and Development, adopted simultaneously with the Climate Change and Biodiversity Conventions, expresses a similar concept, adding reference to states' 'developmental' policies as well. For a close discussion of the implications of this shift, see M Pallemaerts 'International Environmental Law from Stockholm to Rio: Back to the Future?' 1 *RECIEL* 3 (1992) 254.

27   This approach is also reflected in the 1969 Vienna Convention on the Law of Treaties which provides for a two-thirds majority vote for the adoption of the text of a treaty by international conference (Article 9). Basic Documents in International Law (Brownlie, ed, 3rd edn).

28   Hague Declaration.

29   Montreal Protocol, Article 2.9(c) and (d); Article 11.4(b) and (c). See '1992: The Year In Review, Air and Atmosphere: The Ozone Layer' 3 *YIEL* 225 (1993). For a closer treatment of the complex procedures involved in adjusting and amending the Protocol, see Caron, David 'Protection of the Stratospheric Ozone Layer and the Structure of International Environmental Lawmaking' 14 *Hastings International and Comparative Law Review* 755 (1991). Ott, Hermann (1991) 'The New Montreal Protocol: a small Step for the Protection of the Ozone Layer, a Big Step for International Law and Relations' *Law and Politics in Africa, Asia and Latin America*, p 188.

In Palmer's view, the progressive development of international law and the need to avoid least common denominator solutions will depend on moving away from consensus decision-making to decision-making by majority voting. He points to the amendment and adjustment procedures in the Montreal Protocol and less high-profile decision-making in a number of other international organizations that have the power to adopt new rules which are binding upon their members without unanimous consent. Palmer at 273.

30 1985 Vienna Convention on the Protection of the Ozone Layer, Articles 9 and 10.

31 Amendment to the Montreal Protocol on Substances that Deplete the Ozone Layer, 29 June 1990, London, UN Doc UNEP/OzL Pro 2/3 (hereinafter London Amendment); Amendment to the Montreal Protocol on Substances that Deplete the Ozone Layer, 25 November 1992, Copenhagen, 32 *ILM* 874 (1993) (herinafter Copenhagen Amendment).

32 The original text of the Protocol required a 'two-thirds majority vote of the Parties present and voting and representing at least fifty percent of the total consumption of the controlled substances of the Parties' and was designed to protect the interests of industrialized countries who were to bear the brunt of the obligations. This provision was amended in London in 1990 to reflect the greater role that developing countries were expected to play in reducing production and consumption of ozone-depleting substances, by requiring a 'double majority' representing a two-thirds majority of developing countries, as defined in Article 5.1 *and* a two-thirds majority of industrialized countries.

33 Montreal Protocol, Article 2.9(d).

34 Climate Change Convention, Article 4.10.

35 Climate Change Convention, Article 4.2(d).

36 Climate Change Convention, Annex I. See discussion below about the differentiated structure of the Convention's commitments.

37 The text of the Mandate does not specify that it will result in a legally binding agreement, but it does restrict the method of strengthening industrialized Party commitments to the adoption of a protocol or 'another legal instrument'. The choice of the term 'legal' as opposed to 'legally binding' leaves room for concern that certain negotiators may seek to evade concrete commitments, by concluding the negotiations through soft words or soft instruments enacted through legal processes.

38 Amendments, Articles 15 and 16; Protocols, Article 17. Unratified decisions of the climate change COP (unlike the adjustments provided for under Montreal), though based in law, could not have the same legally binding effect as a protocol or amendment. Article 7.2.

39 The 1985 Vienna Convention provides that amendments to the Montreal Protocol would require ratification by two thirds of the Protocol's Parties to enter into force.

40 Article 17.3.

41 Article 7.2(k); 7.3.

42 Article 7.k.

43 Montreal Protocol, Article 11.4(j); Climate Change Convention, Article 7.2(m).

44 See Gehring, and Decision VI/16 of the Sixth Meeting of the Parties to the Montreal Protocol, UNEP/OzL Pro 6/7, 10 October 1994.

45 See Werksman, J 'Recent Developments: The third meeting of the parties to the Basel Convention', 5 *Review of European Community and International Environmental Law* (*RECIEL*) 1 (1996) (hereinafter Werksman, *RECIEL*).

46 See pp 5–6, Chapter 1 for discussion of the dispute over the 'soft law' character of UNGA resolutions.

47 The Ozone Secretariat begins each session of Parties prepared to count heads should a vote become necessary.

48 Montreal Protocol, Article 5.1 (Special Situation of Developing Countries).

49 Climate Change Convention, Article 4.2(a) and (b).

50 Berlin Mandate, paras 2(a) and (b).

51 As commitments are strengthened, the number of countries, particularly developing countries, that are party to them has diminished.While the various amendments to the Montreal Protocol have enjoyed considerably rapid rates of ratification, substantially fewer than the 150 or so parties to the original Protocol have ratified

the London Amendments adopted in 1990, and even fewer have yet to ratify the Copenhagen Amendments of 1992. Parson and Green, at 36.

52 The UN's five traditional regional groupings are: Africa, Asia, the Group of Latin American and Caribbean countries (GRULAC), Eastern Europe and Russia, and the Western European and Others Group (WEOG). Other than Asia, which occasionally fields a Japanese candidate, the first three groups will nominate candidates from developing countries.

53 Climate Change Convention, Article 17.4.

54 'Parties to Montreal Protocol Agree to Phase out Methyl Bromide by 2010', *BNA International Environment Reporter* 935, 13 December 1995.

55 The Basel Convention, which began without differentiation of responsibilities, has recently adopted an amendment designed to take into account the different positions of developed and developing country parties. At COP-3 the Convention's almost 90 Parties decided to amend the text to ban shipments of hazardous waste from wealthy to developing countries. See Werksman, *RECIEL*.

56 Montreal Protocol, Article 10.1; Climate Change Convention, Article 4.3; Biodiversity Convention, Article 20.

57 Climate Change Convention, Article 4.7; Montreal Protocol, Article 5.5.

5 UNITED NATIONS CONFERENCE ON TRADE AND DEVELOPMENT

1 Mr Ali Alatas, Foreign Minister of Indonesia who was a member of the Commission, later said that he was categorically opposed to the idea of winding up UNCTAD.

2 This part is based on Fortin, C 'The United Nations and the emerging system of governance in international trade', IDS Bulletin, vol 16, no 14, October 1995.

3 Available in the United Nations library in Geneva, Call No UN 338:063 U582 (1974).

4 'International Tropical Timber Agreement, 1983', UNCTAD, TD/TIMBER/11, substantially renegotiated in 1990.

5 'International Agreement on Jute and Jute products', TD/Jute 2/6, United Nations (1989).

6 The UNCTAD work Programme on Environment and Sustainable Development is set out in an annex to this chapter on pp 90–93.

7 Dasgupta, P (1982) *The Control of Resources*, Basil Blackwell, Oxford.

8 Dommen, E (ed) (1993) *Fair Principles for Sustainable Development*, Edward Elgar, Hampshire.

9 Dommen, E 'The four principles for environmental policy and sustainable development: an overview', ibid pp 7–32.

10 UNCTAD/COM/9 to UNCTAD/COM/12.

11 UNCTAD/COM27.

12 These were published later: UNCTAD/RDP/DFP/1.

13 UNCTAD/RDP/LDC/58.

14 UNCTAD/RDP/LDC/58 para 29.

15 'UNCTAD VIII Analytical Report by the UNCTAD secretariat to the Conference', TD/358 (1992).

16 'Proceedings of the United Nations Conference on Trade and Development', Eighth Session, Cartagena de Indias, Colombia TD/364/Rev 1, Annex I (1993).

17 'Proceedings of the United Nations Conference on Trade and Development', eighth session, Cartagena de Indias, Colombia, TD/364/Rev 1 (1993).

18 See Appendix I to this volume for the text of Agenda 21, Chapter 38.

19 United Nations Conference on Trade and Development, Trade and Development Board, thirty-eighth session, second part (21 April – 7 May 1992), official Records Supplement No 1A (Part II), Report TD/B/1323 (Vol II) (1992).

20 Although environmental issues did not appear in their terms of reference, the *ad hoc* working groups on 'comparative experiences with privatization', and the 'interrelationship between investment and technology transfer' took up the issue in their actual work as explained below.

21 Decision 402 (XXXIX), included in 'Report of the Trade and Development Board on the second part of its thirty-ninth session', TD/B/39 (2)/26 Geneva, March 1993. Assembly Resolution 48/55 of 10 December 1993.

22 For a full coverage of these discussions see 'Sustainable development: policy review of UNCTAD's activities on sustainable development', TD/B/41(2)/10, Geneva (10 January 1995).

23 The Board later requested that the Standing Committee on Commodities examine the issue of 'global cooperation on the principle of full cost resource pricing and its implementation in support of sustainable development' in its Agreed conclusion 411 (XL), TD/B/40(2)/24, vol I (1994).

24 Report of the Workshop on the Transfer and Development of Environmentally Sound Technologies (ESTs), UNCTAD/ITD/TEC/13 (1994).

25 TD/B/ITNC/AC 1/3.

26 TD/B/ITNC/AC 1/5.

27 TD/B/ITNC/AC 1/2.

28 TD/B/ITNC/AC 1/4.

29 UNCTAD/DTCI 4.

30 Cartagena Commitment, paragraphs 26 and 50.

6 THE WORLD TRADE ORGANIZATION AND THE GATT

1 By TREMs I mean those international, national or sub-nationally derived policies or regulations concerning environmental protection, natural resource conservation or the promotion of sustainable development.

2 These quotations are extracted from a statement made by Mr Ruggiero and released by the WTO on 29 June 1995. Its purpose was to issue a swift response to US threats of unilateral GATT-inconsistent trade sanctions against Japanese imports in the context of the widely publicized US–Japan car and car parts dispute.

3 See *International Trade and Environmental Protection: A Case Study*, CELA Publications, Toronto, Canada (1993). This document was sponsored by the Government of Ontario.

4 In using the phrase 'environmental protection' I mean to include environmental protection, sustainable development and natural resource conservation law and policy.

5 United States – Restrictions on Imports of Tuna (Tuna/Dolphin No 1), Report of the Panel, 16 August 1991.

6 These issues arose in the context of a press conference organized by Charles Arden-Clarke of WWF at the GATT Marrakesh meetings, 13 April 1995.

7 During the past year UNEP has also created its own Experts Group on Trade and Environment. It has undertaken a programme of solid research resulting in a number of monographs coordinated by Scott Vaughan. See the Environment and Trade Series, 1994. On 27 May 1994, the CSD took a decision encouraging attempts at the integration of trade, environmental protection and sustainable development consistent with Agenda 21 and is now actively monitoring developments in this public policy forum.

8 United States – Taxes on Petroleum and Certain Imported Substances (Superfund), Report of the Panel, adopted on 17 June 1987 (L/6175) GATT, 34th Supp BISD 137 (1988).

9   See the 'Agreement Establishing the World Trade Organization' (WTO Agreement), MTN/FA II, p 1, Art II.1.

10 Article IX.2 of the WTO Agreement.

11 Article IV.1 of the WTO Agreement.

12 Article IV.1 of the WTO Agreement.

13 Article IV.2 of the WTO Agreement.

14 See Articles II.1 and XVI.4 of the Agreement Establishing the World Trade Organization.

15 See Article II.2 of the WTO Agreement. The list of binding Agreements includes those Agreements found in Annexes 1, 2 and 3 of the WTO Agreement. It does not include the Annex 4 Plurilateral Trade Agreements (ie Agreement on Trade in Civil Aircraft, Agreement on Government Procurement, International Dairy Agreement, International Bovine Meat Agreement) whose membership is voluntary, pursuant to Article II.3 of the WTO Agreement.

16 See Articles XVI.4 and XVII.14 of the Understanding on Rules and Procedures Governing the Settlement of Disputes (DS Understanding).

17 This section is based on discussions with members of the WTO Secretariat, WTO Ambassadors, other national representatives and four WTO Documents entitled: 'Sub-Committee completes preparatory work on trade-environment issues' 6 January 1995 (TE 011, 95-0005); 'First meeting of the WTO Committee on Trade and Environment establishes work programme for 1995 and opens discussion on exports of domestically prohibited goods' 22 March 1995 (TE 001, 95-0616); 'GATT/WTO Activities on Trade and Environment 1994–95' 8 May 1995 (TE 002, 95-1198); and, 'The WTO Trade and Environment Committee takes up Transparency and Dispute Settlement' 22 May 1995 (TE 003, 95-1344).

18 The World Commission on Environment and Development (also known as 'The Brundtland Report') 1987; *For the Common Good* (Daly and Cobb) (1989).

19 The main WTO agreements applicable to environmental protection measures include the Agreement on Technical Barriers to Trade (TBT Agreement) and the Agreement on the Application of Sanitary and Phytosanitary Measures (SPS Agreement). Both of these agreements supplement existing GATT rules discussed above. In particular, the Preamble of the SPS Agreement suggests that SPS Agreement provisions are intended to elaborate upon GATT Article XX (b). In effect, they add new disciplines on environmental protection law-making. This section outlines the new concepts which the WTO-TBT (pp 117–137) and SPS Agreements (pp 69–83) introduce *vis-à-vis* the treatment of TREMs. Since these agreements introduce new, untested disciplines for TREMs, any conclusions made about the interpretation of these agreements at this stage are quite speculative in nature. Nevertheless, some preliminary findings may contribute to the further understanding of GATT disciplines and TREMs.

20 The term 'chilling effect' was applied to this situation in 1986 by Stephen Shrybman, an environmental lawyer at the Canadian Environmental Law Association, in the context of the *Canada–United States Free Trade Agreement* negotiations.

21 See WTO Doc PRESS/TE 001, 22 March 1995. The means of integrating international environmental agreements and GATT is more fully discussed in the section below bearing the subject title 'WTO Corrective Measures Concerning MEAs'.

22 International Trade Organization Charter, Article 45.1(a)(x).

23 French, H 'After the Earth Summit: The Future of Environmental Governance', Worldwatch Paper 107 (Washington, DC: Worldwatch Institute, 1992); Kennan, G 'To Prevent a World Wasteland: A Proposal,' Foreign Affairs 48:2 (April 1970); Clark, G 'World Peace Through World Law' (Cambridge, MA: Harvard University Press, 1960.

24 Report of the United International Trade Commission (1991)).

25   Mitchell, R 'Intentional Oil Pollution of the Oceans' in Haas, P *Institutions for the Earth: Sources of Effective International Environmental Protection* (Cambridge, MA: MIT Press, 1993).

26   Martin, Jr, R 'Enforcing the International Convention for the Regulation of Whaling: The Pelly and Packwood-Magnuson Amendments', *Denver Journal of International Law and Policy* 17:2 (Winter 1989); Wilkinson, D 'The Use of Domestic Measures to Enforce International Whaling Agreements: A Critical Perspective,' *Denver Journal of International Law and Policy* 17:2 (Winter 1989).

27   French, H, op cit.

28   The Final Draft of the Agreement was concluded by Canada, the United States and Mexico on 13 September 1993. Article 36 and Annex 36B concern the use of trade sanctions.

29   See discussion in Chapter XX, on the recent decision of the Basel Convention parties to impose such a ban.

30   Basel Convention, Article 4.9.

31   Basel Convention, Article 4.5.

32   'Proposal for a Council Directive Introducing a Tax on Carbon Dioxide Emissions and Energy', Commission of the European Communities. COM (92) 226 Final. Brussels, 30 June 1992, which continues to be revised. See International Environment Reporter 20 March 1996, p 212.

33   Article VI(2) provides in part that: 'In order to offset or prevent dumping, a contracting party may levy on any dumped product an anti-dumping duty not greater in amount than the margin of dumping in respect of such product.' See also Agreement on Subsidies and Countervailing Measures, The Results of the Uruguay Round of Multilateral Trade Negotiations.

34   Such an annex can be found in the appendix to the following document: Z Makuch, *Correcting Potential Conflicts Between Multilateral Environmental Agreements and GATT 1994*, October 1994, Greenpeace International Publications.

35   For a full consideration of potential conflicts between GATT/WTO rules and international environmental agreements see: J Cameron, T Mjolo-Thamage, and J C Robinson 'The Relationship Between Environmental Agreements and Instruments Related to Trade and the Environment' UNCED Research Paper No 35, February 1992; Z Makuch 'Correcting Potential Conflicts Between the GATT/WTO and Multilateral Environmental Agreements' (1994).

36   This list of rules is identified in 'The Relationship Between Environmental Agreements and Instruments Related to Trade and the Environment' (see previous footnote).

37   P Sands, 'GATT 1994 and Sustainable Development: Lessons from the International Legal Order' in Papers presented at the GATT Symposium on Trade, Environment and Sustainable Development, TE 009, 28 July 1994. In a move that was long overdue, the GATT Secretariat coordinated this symposium which was attended by approximately two hundred Southern and Northern NGOs. It is hoped that more such symposia related to WTO–CTE work will be coordinated in the future, though this should take place on a more issue-specific basis so that discussion can be better focused.

38   The argument has often been made that the contractual status of GATT, the absence of an enforcement mechanism and the provisional nature of GATT commitments by GATT Protocol of Provisional Application signatories provide evidence that GATT Contracting Parties did not intend to give the GATT status as an international treaty. Accordingly, GATT dispute settlement panels have tended to focus upon matters of GATT interpretation, not the wider application of international law. For instance, the GATT panel in the Tuna Dolphin No 1 dispute did not properly discuss the protection of dolphins under international law.

39   The exception of course is Ambassador Winfried Lang who sat on the GATT Panel in Tuna Dolphin No 2.

40 Portions of this section are taken from file work conducted by the author for the John Merck Fund, the Rockefeller Brothers Foundation, the Ford Foundation and the German Marshall Fund while engaged in the FIELD Trade and Environment Programme.

41 See the discussion of the SPS and TBT Agreements above.

7 THE NORTH AMERICAN FREE TRADE AGREEMENT

1 The North American Free Trade Agreement Between the Government of the United States, the Government of Canada and the Government of the United Mexican States, 17 December 1992, 32 ILM (1993) (hereinafter 'the NAFTA'). The NAFTA entered into force on 1 January 1994.

2 North American Agreement on Environmental Cooperation, in *NAFTA Supplemental Agreements*, US Government Printing Office, Washington, DC, 1993, ISBN 0-16-041969-7 (hereinafter 'the NAAEC'). The United States, Canada and Mexico are paries to both the NAFTA and the NAAEC.

3 Earth Summit Agenda 21: the United Nations Programme of Action from Rio – the final text of agreements negotiated by governments at the United Nations Conference on Environment and Development (UNCED), 3–14 June 1992, Rio de Janeiro, Brazil (United Nations Publication Sales No E.93.1 11, 1993), (hereinafter the Earth Summit).

4 Agenda 21, para 2.19; Rio Declaration, Principle 12.

5 Principle 11 of the Rio Declaration provides, in part: 'Environmental standards, management objectives and priorities should reflect the environmental and developmental context to which they apply. Standards applied by some countries may be inappropriate and of unwarranted economic and social cost to other countries, in particular developing countries.'

6 At Principle 14, the Rio Declaration provides: 'States should effectively cooperate to discourage or prevent the relocation and transfer to other States of any activities and substances that cause severe environmental degradation or are found to be harmful to human health.'

7 The Rio Declaration provides at Principle 12: 'States should cooperate to promote a supportive and open international economic system that would lead to economic growth and sustainable development in all countries, to better address the problems of environmental degradation. Trade policy measures for environmental purposes should not constitute a means of arbitrary or unjustifiable discrimination or a disguised restriction on international trade. Unilateral actions to deal with environmental challenges outside the jurisdiction of the importing country should be avoided. Environmental measures addressing transboundary or global environmental problems should, as far as possible, be based on an international consensus.' See also Agenda 21 paras 2.22(c)-(f) and (i).

8 The NAFTA, preamble.

9 Done at Washington, 3 March 1973, as amended 22 June, 1979.

10 Done at Montreal, 16 September, 1987. Article 104 of the NAFTA refers specifically only to the London Amendments of 29 June, 1990; the Copenhagen Adjustments of 22 September, 1993 are not specifically mentioned.

11 Done at Basel, 22 March, 1989. The NAFTA at Article 104 specifically provides that the reference to the Basel Convention only applies upon the entry into force of that Convention for all three Parties, 'Canada, Mexico, *and* the United States' (emphasis added). The use of the term 'and' raises a question as to whether a NAFTA party – ie a non-Party to the Basel Convention, eg the United States at the time of publication – could still claim that the Basel Convention's trade obligations are inconsistent with the NAFTA.

12   The NAFTA, Article 104.
13   The NAFTA at Annex 104.1. The agreements contained in this Annex are The Agreement Between the Government of Canada and the Government of the United States of America Concerning the Transboundary Movement of Hazardous Waste, signed at Ottawa, 28 October, 1986; and the Agreement Between the United States of America and the United Mexican States on Cooperation for the Protection and Improvement of the Environment in the Border Area, signed at La Paz, Baja California Sur, 14 August, 1983.
14   Agenda 21, para 2.22(c).
15   United States – Restrictions on Imports of Tuna, Report of the Panel (Mexico–US Tuna Dolphin GATT Panel Report) (1991), (hereinafter 'Mexico tuna–dolphin case').
16   See SPS Article 712.1.
17   Rio Declaration, Principle 14.
18   NAAEC, Article 1.
19   Article 8.1.
20   Article 8.2.
21   Article 9.1.
22   Article 9.3. The Council must hold public meetings in the course of all regular sessions (Article 9.4). The Council Rules and Procedures, Part VI, addresses rules pertaining to public meetings and accreditation of NGOs.
23   Article 9.5(a).
24   Article 45.1 defines a 'non-governmental organization' as any scientific, professional, business, non-profit or public interest organization or association which is neither affiliated with, nor under the direction of, a government.
25   Article 9.5.
26   Article 11.1.
27   Id.
28   Article 11.2.
29   Article 11.4.
30   Article 12.
31   Article 13.
32   Article 14.
33   Article 12.2(a).
34   Article 12.2(b).
35   Article 12.2(d).
36   Article 12.3.
37   Article 12.1.
38   Article 13.1.
39   Id.
40   Article 13.1.
41   Article 13.3. The Council will normally make the report public within 60 days of its submission. Article13.3 provides no reason on which the Council would have to base its decision not to publicize the report.
42   Article 13.2.
43   Article 16.1.
44   Article 16.4.
45   Article 16.5. For the 'factual record' *see infra*.
46   *Memorandum of the JPAC to the Council*, 26 July 1994. Article 16.3 of the NAAEC requires the JPAC to meet once annually at the time of the Council's regular session.
47   *Vision Statement of the JPAC*, 26 July 1994, Washington, DC.
48   Lichtinger, the Executive Director of the Secretariat, has said that although the Council 'doesn't have to listen to [the JPAC], generally they do.' *International Environment Reporter*, vol 17, No 25, 14 December 1994.
49   The NAC to the US government representative is established within the US Environmental Protection Agency (EPA). According to EPA procedures, NAC

meetings must be open and interested parties must be able to file comments before or after meetings, or to make statements as permitted by NAC guidelines.

50 Article 17.
51 Id.
52 Each party may also convene a Governmental Committee to advise on governmental issues related to the implementation and elaboration of the NAAEC. It would be made up of representatives of federal, state and provincial governments (Article 18).
53 Article 45 defines a 'persistent pattern' as a sustained or recurring course of action or inaction beginning after the date of entry into force of this Agreement.
54 Article 22.1.
55 Article 23.1.
56 Article 23.4.
57 Article 24.1.
58 The Council must maintain a roster of up to 45 individuals who can serve as panellists. Roster members shall be appointed by consensus for three-year terms. They 'shall have expertise or experience in environmental law or its enforcement, or in the resolution of disputes arising under international agreements, or other relevant scientific, technical or professional expertise or experience; be chosen strictly on the basis of objectivity, reliability and sound judgment; [and] be independent of and not be affiliated with or take instructions from, any Party, the Secretariat or the Joint Public Advisory Committee . . .' (Article 25).
    The Panel can still seek information and technical advice from any person/body that it deems appropriate, provided that the disputing Parties agree and are subject to any conditions that such Parties agree to.
59 See Article 31. This initial report will be based on the submission and arguments of the Parties and on any advice sought under Article 30 of the NAAEC. Parties have to make available to the panel any information in their possession which is necessary for the compilation of the report, including enforcement and compliance data.
60 Article 31.2.
61 Article 31.4. After considering these comments, the panel, on its own initiative or on the request of any disputing Party, may request the views of any participating Party, reconsider its report or make any further examination that it considers appropriate (Article 31.5).
62 Article 32.
63 Article 33.
64 Article 34.
65 Article 34.5.
66 Article 34.6.
67 Article 36.
68 Article 14.1.
69 Article 14.1 The Secretariat may consider a submission from any non-governmental organization or person asserting that a body is failing to enforce effectively its environmental law, if the Secretariat finds that the submission:
    (1) is in writing in a language designated by that Party in a notification to the Secretariat;
    (2) clearly identifies the person or organization making the submission;
    (3) provides sufficient information to allow the Secretariat to review the submission, including any documentary evidence on which the submission may be based;
    (4) appears to be aimed at promoting enforcement rather than at harassing industry;
    (5) indicates that the matter has been communicated in writing to the relevant authorities of the Party and indicates the Party's response, if any; and

(6) is filed by a person or organization residing or established in the territory of a Party.

70   Article 14.2.
71   Id (a)–(d).
72   Article 14. 3(a).
73   Id (b).
74   Article 15.
75   Article 15.4.
76   Id.
77   Article 15.5.
78   Article 15.6.
79   Article 15.7. The final factual record will be made available to the public within 60 days following its submission to the Council.
80   Article 13.1.
81   *1994 Work Program Activities.*
82   *1994 Work Program Activities.* Authority for these activities: NAAEC Articles 10.3(a)–(b).
83   The study will also compare procedures and regulations on access to publicly available corporate information on hazardous materials and activities in communities.
84   *International Environment Reporter*, vol 17, No 25, 14 December 1994.
85   P95.6 (1995) Work Plan (draft). This section was included to implement Article 10.7 of the NAAEC.
86   Emerson, Peter M, and Gaines, Sanford E, Why Not Trade Pollution Too?, *The New York Times*, Sunday, 1 January 1995.
87   P95.8 (1995) Work Plan (draft).
88   The groups' salvage logging claim may have been undermined by the Commission's rejection on 25 September 1995 of a legally similar petition filed by five environmental groups challenging a new US law suspending listings of threatened and endangered species and designations of such species' critical habitat. The Commission rejected the position, saying that it 'cannot characterise the application of a new legal regime as a failure to enforce the old one'. There is no clear NAAEC requirement that the Commission should proceed to consider subsequent cases on the basis of precedent on any other common law principle. It remains to be seen, nonetheless, whether the Commission will distinguish the salvage logging challenge. See 'CEC Will Not Investigate Claim of US Failure to Enforce ESA', *BNA International Environment Reporter*, 763, 4 October 1995.
89   'Scientists Say Raw Sewage Killed 40,000 Birds', Sam Dillon, *The New York Times*, Friday, 29 September 1995, p A9.
90   The BECC on 28 September 1995, approved a first set of border infrastructure projects, including $31 million water-treatment. Another $62 million in water-treatment projects are currently under consideration. See 'Border Environment Panel Approves First Set of Infrastructure Projects', *BNA International Environment Reporter*, 762–63, October 1995.
91   'Divers, Cruise Ships Battle over Cozumel's Coral Reefs: Mexico Wants New Pier to Draw Tourists', *The Washington Post*, 25 May 1996, PA1.

8   THE WORLD BANK AND THE IMF

1   Thoreau, Henry David (1968) *Walden, or Life in the Woods and On the Duty of Civil Disobedience*, Collier Books, New York, p 63.
2   The World Bank, 'Current Questions and Answers' (for staff use only), Creative Services of the External Affairs Department, September 1994, p 138.

3   Wapenhans, Willi A 'Report of the Portfolio Management Task Force', the World Bank, Washington, DC, 1992.

4   Only the Bank and the IMF were set up following the 1944 conference. The International Trade Organization was finally realized as the World Trade Organization (WTO) in January 1995, providing an institutional home for the General Agreement on Tariffs and Trade (GATT) and is examined in Chapter 6.

5   United States Foreign Operations, Export Financing, and Related Program 1995, Public Law, 103–306, 23 August 1994.

6   The World Bank, Annual Report 1994, Washington, DC, August 1994.

7   These terms are largely related to the rates of economic return and do not include the environmental and social costs of many of the projects, which, if they had been included, would have led to an even higher rate of project failure.

8   Wapenhans, Willi A 'Report of the Portfolio Management Task Force', the World Bank, Washington, DC, 1992.

9   United States Foreign Operations, Export Financing, and Related Programs Appropriations Act 1993, Public Law 102–391, 6 October 1992.

10   The World Bank, Current Questions and Answers, p 7.

11   World Bank staff 'Access to Information: An Alternative View', unpublished manuscript, Washington, DC, 1993.

12   The World Bank, Policy on Disclosure of Information, Washington, DC, March 1994.

13   *Financial Times*, 'World Bank Scales Down Proposals to Become More Open', 16 August 1993.

14   Davis, Gloria 'Office Memorandum on Social Assessment', Washington, DC, 10 May 1994.

15   The World Bank Operations Policy Department, 'The World Bank and Participation', Washington, DC, September 1994.

16   Alexander, Nancy 'Bread for the World', personal communication, January 1995.

17   Wapenhans, Willi A 'Efficiency and Effectiveness: Is the World Bank Group Well Prepared for the Task Ahead?' in the Bretton Woods Commission, *Bretton Woods Looking to the Future*, Washington, DC, 1994.

18   The World Bank Group, *Learning From the Past, Embracing the Future*, Washington, DC, 1994.

19   The World Bank, *Making Development Sustainable*, the World Bank Group and the Environment Fiscal 1994, Washington, DC, 1994.

20   The World Bank, Staff Appraisal Report Malawi, Fisheries Development Project, 25 February 1991.

21   Global Environment Facility, Report by the Chairman to the December 1991 Participants' Meeting, Washington, DC, November 1991.

22   See note 19.

23   Coady, E Patrick, Statement to the Board of Directors, Washington, DC, 3 April 1990.

24   The World Bank, Operational Directive 4.30: Involuntary Resettlement, Washington, DC, 29 June 1990.

25   The World Bank, Environment Department, Resettlement and Development, The Bankwide Review of Projects Involving Involuntary Resettlement 1986–93, Washington, DC, 8 April 1994.

26   Ibid 5/5.

27   The World Bank, Operational Directive 4.00 on Environmental Impact Assessment, Washington, DC, 1989.

28   Hirji, Rafik and Ortolano, Leonard 'EIA Effectiveness and Mechanisms of Control: Case Studies of Water Resources Development in Kenya', abstract accepted for publication in *The International Journal of Water Resources Development*, December 1990.

29   *Ministère de la Planification de l'Economie et de l'Aménagement du Territoire, Rapport d'Evaluation d'Impact Environmental*, Libreville, Gabon, 21 April 1992.

30 Friends of the Earth and Environmental Defense Fund, The World Bank's Forestry and Environment Project for Gabon, Special Briefing Paper, September 1992.
31 Jaycox, Edward V K Vice-President, Africa Region, World Bank, 'Capacity Building: The Missing Link in African Development', transcript of address delivered to the African–American Institute Conference, Reston, Virginia, 20 May 1993.
32 Korten, Francis F 'The High Costs of Environmental Loans', East–West Centre, no 7, September 1993.
33 The World Bank, 'Review of Implementation of the Forest Sector Policy', 9 August 1994, p 14.
34 The World Bank, 'Memorandum and Recommendation of the Director of the Occidental and Central Africa Department to the Regional Vice President', Washington, DC, 26 October 1994.
35 The Ecologist magazine, vol 15, nos 1/2, 5/6 and vol 16, nos 2/3 (1986), England.
36 Beazley, Mitchell The Last Rainforests, IUCN, The World Conservation Union, 1990, p 168.
37 UN Food and Agriculture Organization, Forest Resources Assessment, 1990, Forestry Paper 112, Rome, 1993.
38 Gillis, Malcolm (1988) 'The Logging Industry in Tropical Asia', in People of the Tropical Rainforest, University of California Press, p 180.
39 Hewlett, Sylvia Ann (1979) The Cruel Dilemmas of Development: Twentieth Century Brazil, Basic Books Inc, New York, p 173.
40 Schwartzman, Steven and Horta, Korinna 'The World Bank in the Amazon', in 'International Working Group for Indigenous Affairs', newsletter no 57, May 1989.
41 European Parliament, Environmental Problems, 9, citing a May 1989 resolution on the Carajas iron-ore project, cited in Rich, Bruce (1994) Mortaging the Earth, Beacon Press, Boston, p 32.
42 Conable, Barber B, President, the World Bank, address to the World Resources Institute, 5 May 1987.
43 Rich, Bruce (1994) Mortaging the Earth, Beacon Press, Boston, p 146.
44 Francisco Alves Mendes Filho, letter to Mr Barber Conable of 13 October 1988.
45 Colchester, Marcus and Lohmann, Larry (1990) 'The Tropical Forest Action Plan: What Progress?', Penang, Malaysia and London, UK, World Rainforest Movement.
46 Winterbottom, Robert, Taking Stock: The Tropical Forestry Action Plan after Five Years, World Resources Institute, Washington, DC, 1990.
47 Reed, David and Smith, Jennifer 'IDA Credit for the Republic of Guinea for a Forest and Fisheries Management Project', WWF, November 1989.
48 ASSOANE, Association des Amis de la Nature et de l'Environnement, Problematique de la Conservation des Forêts Denses Tropicales de Diecke et de Ziama par le Progerfor', Conakry, Guinea, July 1992.
49 The World Bank, 'The World Bank and the Environment', First Annual Report, Washington, DC, Fiscal 1990.
50 Environmental Defense Fund and National Wildlife Federation, letter and memorandum regarding Côte d'Ivoire Forestry Project, Washington, DC, 21 March 1990.
51 Bradsher, Keith 'Rain Forest Project in Africa Stirs Debate at World Bank', The New York Times, 14 October 1991.
52 Coady, E Patrick, Statement to the Board of Directors, Washington, DC, 3 April 1990.
53 The World Bank, Policy Paper: 'The Forest Sector', Washington, DC, 1991.
54 The World Bank, 'Review of Implementation of the Forest Sector Policy', 5 December 1994, pp ix, 20.
55 Ibid pp 24, 25.
56 Remarks by Jan Piercy, 'Review of the Implementation of the Forest Sector Policy', 1 December 1994.
57 Sachs, Jeffrey (1989) 'Strengthening IMF Programs in Highly Indebted Countries', in The IMF in a Multipolar World Overseas Development Council, Washington, DC, p 102.

58 IMF Survey, 'The IMF at 50: Entering a New Era', a publication of the International Monetary Fund, Washington, DC, 8 August 1994, p 252.

59 IMF Survey, Seminar Explores Links Between Macro Policy and Environment, a publication of the International Monetary Fund, Washington, DC, 14 June 1993.

60 Munsinghe, Mohan and Cruz, Wilfrido 'Economywide Policies and the Environment', World Bank Environment Paper, no 10, December 1994, p 3.

61 Smith, Patrick 'Bank Moves to Write off African Debt', in *Emerging Markets*, 4 October 1994, p 11.

62 Report of the House/Senate Committee of Conference on HR2295, Report 103–267 of 28 September 1993.

63 Morse, Bradford and Berger, Thomas A 'Sardar Sarovar, The Report of the Independent Review', Resource Futures International, Ottawa, 1992.

64 Independent Review, press release, 18 June 1992.

65 World Bank, Resolution no 93–10 and Resolution no IDA 93–6, 22 September 1993.

66 Hunter, David and Udall, Lori, The World Bank's New Inspection Panel: Will It Increase the World Bank's Accountability?, Centre for International Environmental Law, Brief, no 1, April 1994.

67 The Inspection Panel, Operating Procedures, Washington, DC, August 1994.

68 The Inspection Panel, Notice of Registration, Washington, DC, 3 November 1994.

69 The Inspection Panel, Memorandum to the Executive Directors, 16 December 1994.

70 Letter from Gopal Siwakoti, Arun Concerned Group, on behalf of some of the claimants to the World Bank President, Lewis T Preston, 5 January 1995.

71 Arun III power project press release, 4 August 1995, World Bank Public Information Centre.

72 Letter to James Wolfensohn from concerned NGOs on the interference of Bank Management in the claims process, 7 July 1995, greennet:de.worldbank.

73 Two further claims were never formally registered because they failed prima facie to fall within the Panel's mandate.

74 The World Bank, office memorandum to Regional Vice-Presidents, 1 February 1993.

75 Shihata, Ibrahim F I (1994) *The World Bank Inspection Panel*, published for the World Bank by Oxford University Press, p 119.

76 Friedman, Thomas L 'World Bank at 50, Vows To Do Better', *The New York Times*, 24 July 1994

77 Ibid.

78 Picciotto, Robert and Weaving, Rachel 'A New Project Cycle for the World Bank?', in *Finance and Development*, December 1994.

79 Ibid.

80 Wapenhans, Willi A 'Efficiency and Effectiveness: Is the World Bank Group Well Prepared for the Task Ahead?' in *Bretton Woods Commission, Bretton Woods Looking to the Future*, Washington, DC, 1994.

9 THE GLOBAL ENVIRONMENT FACILITY

1 Robert M MacIver in the Foreword to *The Great Transformation* by Karl Polanyi (Beacon Press Books, Boston, first paperback edition, 1957).

2 This perspective is most clearly articulated in the work by so-called realists and neo-realists. *Theory of International Politics* by Kenneth N Waltz remains a classic in the field (Addison–Wesley, Reading, Massachusetts, 1979).

3 An early and influential account of regime theory is found in *International Regimes*, by Stephen D Krasner (ed) (Cornell University Press, Ithaca and London, 1983). In the introductory chapter, the editor defines regimes as 'sets of implicit and explicit principles, norms, rules and decision-making procedures around which actors' expectations converge in a given area of international relations'.

4　See, for example, 'Territoriality and beyond: problematizing modernity in international relations' by John Gerard Ruggie, in *International Organization*, vol 47, no 1, Winter 1993.

5　See Chapter 4. The paradigmatic case for incremental negotiations is the series of agreements on protection of the ozone layer. The first agreement was a weak framework convention signed in Vienna in 1985. The text round of negotiations led to the Montreal Protocol in 1987, which has since been further developed, notably in London, 1990, and in Copenhagen, 1992.

6　See, for example, 'Improving the Effectiveness of International Environmental Institutions', by Marc A Levy, Robert O Keohane and Peter M Haas. In *Institutions for the Earth: Sources of Effective International Protection* M A Levy, R O Keohane and P M Haas (eds) (The MIT Press, Cambridge, Massachusetts, 1993) pp 401–430.

7　The Interim Multilateral Fund was set up in 1990; in the period covering 1991–93 it was funded at a level of US $160 million, which was increased to US $240 million when India and China joined. The interim fund was converted into a permanent fund in 1992. Funding for 1994–97 is estimated at US $510 million.

8　The two convention funds administered by UNEP are the CITES Trust Fund and the Mediterranean Trust Fund, which each have an annual income of about US $4 million. For an overview of the variety and significance of trust funds in the service of the environment, see 'Trust for the Earth: New Financial Mechanisms for International Environmental Protection', by Peter H Sand. The Josephine Onoh Memorial Lecture, 1994, published by the University of Hull Press, 1994.

9　For a more detailed account of how the Global Environment Facility was created, see 'From Idea to Reality: the Creation of the Global Environment Facility', by Helen Sjöberg, Working Paper no 10, The Global Environment Facility.

10　The Development Committee advises and reports on broad developmental issues to the Governing Boards of the World Bank and the International Monetary Fund. Its members are usually Ministers of Finance. It is formally known as the Joint Ministerial Committeee of the World Bank and the International Monetary Fund on the Transfer of Real Resources to Developing Countries.

11　The amount corresponded to approximately US $100 million.

12　The formal name of the Brundtland Report is *Our Common Future*, World Commission on Environment and Development (Oxford University Press, New York, 1987). The Commission was lead by Norwegian Prime Minister, Gro Harlem Brundtland.

13　The proposal was published in *Natural Endowments: Financing Resource Conservation for Development* (World Resources Institute, Washington, DC, 1989).

14　Prime Minister Gandhi's proposal was made at a summit of the non-aligned countries in Belgrade. He suggested a UN based fund to which all countries should contribute a fixed percentage of their income. The proposal was included in the final Belgrade Declaration.

15　The influence of professional networks on international environmental cooperation has been emphasized by the literature on epistemic communities. See, for example, 'Banning chlorofluorocarbons: epistemic community efforts to protect stratospheric ozone', by Peter M Haas. Published in a special issue on epistemic communities in *International Organization* vol 46, 1992, pp 87–224. Generally, epistemic communities are seen as networks of professionals with an authoritative claim to policy-relevant knowledge within their domain of expertise. They share a set of normative as well as casual beliefs which derive from their analyses. It is argued that the influence of epistemic communities increases in policy areas where information is technical, complex and uncertain.

16　There is no doubt that the developed countries dominated the process. It should be noted, however, that developing countries constituted almost one-third of the original participants. It is relevant that the countries were represented by their Finance Ministries or Executive Directors of the World Bank.

17 Elegibility to recipient countries was made conditional on having a UNDP country programme in place or being eligible to borrow from the World Bank. It corresponded to a per capita income of approximately US $4,000 or less.

18 At the time, less public attention focused on the issue of international waters. It was, however, the classic example of a problem of a commons used by many, but beyond the control of any one nation.

19 The concept of incremental cost was defined as the extra cost incurred in the process of redesigning an activity *vis-à-vis* a baseline plan - which is focused on achieving national benefits – in order to address global environmental problems. See 'The Pilot Phase and Beyond',Working Paper Series, no I, The Global Environment Facility, May 1992.

20 Putting in place a programme with an exploratory strategy without a mechanism for evaluation has been a source of continuous criticism, especially from NGOs. A kind interpretation of this somewhat puzzling deficiency is that it takes a long time before there are projects to evaluate. When an evaluation did take place, in 1993, there were still not many projects up and running. The evaluation focused mainly on the process by which projects and programmes were developed.

21 Miles Kahler has argued that the 'collective action problems posed by multilateral governance were addressed for most of the post-war era by minilateral great power collaboration disguised by multilateral institutions . . .' He believes that in areas such as monetary affairs and economic policy coordination, this pattern will remain. In other issue areas, however, he sees a reduced 'ability of minilateralism to produce satisfactory cooperative outcomes'. (See 'Multilateralism with small and large numbers', *International Organizations*, vol 46, no 3, Summer 1992.) The GEF provides an interesting variant in this context; its creation followed the pattern he identifies for monetary and economic affairs, while over time the pattern shifted to the mulitilateral approach he identifies for other issue areas.

22 Agenda 21 is a non-binding document that sets out a plan for achieving sustainable development. It contains 40 chapters on 115 programme areas that span an enormous range of policy-related activities, including marine resources and pollution, deforestation, desertification and waste management. It discusses the roles played by different actors from women and NGOs to international governmental institutions (see Chapter 13).

23 Costs for implementing Agenda 21 during the period 1993–2000 would be in excess of US $600 billion. While the main portion of this amount would come from developing countries, it was estimated that US $125 billion needed to be transferred from the developed countries annually. These figures were published in the *Financial Times*, 14 February 1992.

24 The Green Fund can be seen as a renewal of the idea put forward by Prime Minister Gandhi in September 1989. The notion of a Green Fund was never specified into a negotiable proposal. Instead, proposals for a Green Fund rather took the form of a wish-list from the South. See, for example. 'Beijing Ministerial Declaration on Environment and Development', 19 June 1991.

25 The different preferences of developed and developing countries were mirrored on an international level by the agencies involved with the GEF. The UN agencies involved have a longstanding tradition of representing the interests of developing countries. The UNEP had close ties to the Conventions and indicated its preference for financial arrangements other than the GEF on a number of occasion. The UNDP was closely involved in the UNCED and used this process to increase its leverage in the GEF. The World Bank clearly preferred the pilot phase system, but found itself on the defensive and recognized the need for some modifications. The new political balance opened opportunities for interagency conflict. Although the agencies influenced the GEF, an analysis of their interaction falls beyond the scope of this chapter. For an account of their influence on the pilot phase, see 'The Making of the

Global Environment Facility: An actor's perspective' by Lin Gan in *Global Environmental Change*, 3, 1993, pp 256–275.

26 Principle 1 in 'The Pilot Phase and Beyond', Working Paper Series, no 1, The Global Environment Facility, May 1992.

27 Ibid.

28 Ibid.

29 Ibid.

30 Richard Mott describes the relations between the Conventions and the GEF in 'The GEF and the Conventions on Climate Change and Biological Diversity', in *International Environmental Affairs*, pp 299–312.

31 The significance of the Preston offer is described in *Negotiating Survival: Four Priorities After Rio* by Richard N Gardner (Council of Foreign Relations Press, New York, 1992).

32 Chapter 33 of Agenda 21 refers to the GEF in language very similar to that used in the Conventions. It called for restructuring to encourage, *inter alia*, universal participation and to ensure 'a governance that is transparant and democratic in nature, including in terms of decision-making and operations, by guaranteeing a balanced and equitable representation of the interests of developing countries, as well as give due weight to the funding efforts of donor countries'.

33 Mr Preston's offer had been conditional on the ability to raise funds for IDA–10 that were over and above the real-term equivalent of IDA–9.

34 Up until this time, a minimum mandatory contribution of SDR 4 million had been required to become a participant in the GEF. (Contributions were unrelated to being a recipient of funding.)

35 Both the Conventions and Agenda 21 had underlined the importance of universal membership in a restructured GEF. The GEF document agreed to in April 1992 had also emphasized that 'The goal of the GEF is universal membership'. See 'The Pilot Phase and Beyond'.

36 See 'Bulletin and Quarterly Operational Summary', no 9, Global Environment Facility, September 1993.

37 This interpretation avoids the issue of whether the essence of the process was about power or principles; instead, these are viewed as interlinked, It is noteworthy, however, how frequently the proponents involved in the process are convinced that their own stance is a matter of principle, while they interpret the views of others as motivated by considerations of influence.

38 The role of the NGO community throughout the evolution of the GEF deserves more attention than it has been given in this chapter. Their influence was exercised both through some of the national governments and directly on the international agencies. Their continous criticism constrained and shaped the process in a number of respects, in particular on issues of transperency and information disclosure. Their role in the GEF has also evolved over time. During the pilot phase, NGOs could propose projects to the agencies and receive funding in a special Small Grants Programme. In the restructuring process, each meeting was preceded by an NGO consultation. After the GEF was restructured, NGOs have been awarded observer status to the Council meetings. This constitutes yet another break with the Bretton Woods system.

39 In personal communication with the author, many delegations have reported they had problems coordinating their position internally. In some countries, however, one branch remained firmly in the lead throughout the process, and in many developing countries, knowledge of the GEF was limited to ministries of foreign affairs.

40 See 'Between nations and the world: welcome to some new ideologies', by Michael Waltzer. In a special issue on World Politics and Current Affairs, *The Economist*, 11 September 1993, pp 51–54.

41 In a personal communication with the author, representatives of the implemention agencies report their own steep learning curve as a primary benefit of the GEF experience.

42 This point is also made by David Fairman in 'Increments for the Earth: The Global Environment Facility and Financial Transfers for Global Environmental Problems' in a draft paper for discussion at Harvard/MIT Joint Research Seminar on International Environmental Affairs, 13 October 1994.

43 See, for example, 'International Aid for the Environment: Lessons from Economic Development Assistance' by David Fairman and Michael Ross, Paper No 94-4, Working Paper Series, Harvard University, 1994.

44 The language of the two Conventions is very similar. In the case of the Biodiversity Conventions, however, the COP decides also on strategy. The Climate Change Convention is constrained to the use of 'existing' institutions. For other differences between the Conventions, see 'The GEF and the Conventions'.

45 For a classic article of organizational theory, see 'Differentiation and Integration in Complex Organizations' by Paul R Lawrence and Jay W Lorsch, *Administrative Science Quarterly*, vol 12, no 1, 1967, pp 1–47.

46 UNCLOS is the acronym of the United Nations Conference on the Law of the Sea. It was an attempt to create a comprehensive new ocean regime. Arguably the 'largest, longest, and most complex formal negotiation in modern times', the negotiations began in 1967 and ended in 1982. It entered into force in 1994, although few analysts expect it to function in the way it was intended. For an account of the negotiations, see *Negotiating the New Ocean Regime* by Robert L Friedheim, University of South Carolina Press, 1993.

47 The UN Commission of Sustainable Development has the mandate to coordinate action on an international level. However, it does not have the capacity to alleviate coordination problems on a national level.

48 'Trusts for the Earth.'

49 'Territoriality and Beyond.'

10   NATIONAL ENVIRONMENTAL FUNDS

1 World Resources Institute, World Conservation Union, World Wide Fund for Nature, *Global Biodiversity Strategy: Guidelines for Action to Save, Study, and Use Earth's Biotic Wealth Sustainably and Equitably*, Washington, DC, 1992, p 7.

2 US Congress, Office of Technology Assessment, 'Changing by Degrees: Steps to Reduce Greenhouse Gases', OTA-O-482, Washington, DC, US Government Printing Office, February 1991, p 274.

3 The World Bank, *World Development Report 1992: Environment and Development*, Oxford University Press, Oxford, 1992, p 92.

4 Three observations about the mechanisms discussed in this chapter are: 1). Some refer to these mechanisms as 'conservation trust funds' or 'environmental trust funds'. This can be somewhat misleading. Trust funds are a specific kind of common law mechanism. Many, but not all, NEFs are trust funds. 2). One of the funds in the category of mechanisms discussed in this chapter is actually a regional fund and other regional funds may soon be established. Thus, 'National Environmental Fund' is not a perfect name for the mechanisms. 3). The funds described in this chapter should be distinguished from the environmental funds established in several Central and Eastern European countries. Those funds are housed within their governments and for the most part are supported by pollution fines only. Almost all of the funds described in this chapter are independent of direct governmental control and almost all are capable of receiving money from multiple sources.

5 Israel Arturo, *Institutional Development*, John Hopkins University Press, Baltimore, 1987, p 3.

6   'The Greening of Giving', *The Economist*, 25 December 1993.

7   Alex Duncan, 'Aid Effectiveness in Raising Adaptive Capacity in the Low-Income Countries', in *Development Strategies Reconsidered*, John P Lewis (ed), Overseas Development Council, Washington, 1986, pp 129–152, 137.

8   The World Bank, *World Development Report 1992: Environment and Development*, Oxford University Press, Oxford, 1992, p 92.

9   'Buying Diversity', *The Economist*, 329, 2 October 1993, p 16.

10 Redclift, Michael, *Sustainable Development: Exploring the Contradictions* (London and New York, 1989), p 80.

11 Fairman, David and Ross, Michael, 'International Aid for the Environment: Lessons from Economic Development Assistance', Paper No 94-4, Working Paper Series, the Center for International Affairs, Harvard University, Cambridge, Massachusetts, June 1994, p 27.

12 'The Social Challenge of Biodiversity Conservation', Shelton H Davis (ed), GEF Working Paper no 1, Global Environment Facility, Washington, DC, 1993, p 1.

13 The World Bank, 'Establishment of the Global Environment Facility', Washington, DC, 1991, p 12.

14 GEF Scientific and Technical Advisory Panel, 'Report by the Chairman to the Fourth Participants' Meeting', Appendix I, Washington, DC, 1992.

15 Global Environment Facility, 'Independent Evaluation of the Global Environment Facility', United Nations Development Programme, United Nations Environment Programme, The World Bank, Washington, DC, May 1994, p 12.

16 Id p 13.

17 Id p 53.

18 Id pp 74–76.

19 Rubin, Steven M, Shatz, Jonathan and Deegan, Colleen, 'International Conservation of Biodiversity', *The Journal of Social, Political, and Economic Studies*, 1994, pp 21–43.

20 For a more detailed study of the development of the Trust Fund for Conservation in Bhutan, please see Danish, Kyle, 'The Promise of National Environmental Funds in Developing Countries', *Journal of International Environment Affairs*, vol 7, no 2, 150–175, spring 1995.

21 Lamenting this 'ineligibility', the Deputy Minister Dasho Paljor 'Benji' Dorji, sardonically observed that, if Bhutan had only elevated a dictator who mismanaged its finances and pillaged the country's natural resources, it would be rewarded by the international community with aid for its conservation programmes. Bruce Bunting, Vice-President of the South and East Asia Programme, the World Wildlife Fund – US, personal communication with the author, 6 May 1994.

22 Barry Spergel, Legal Adviser, Conservation Finance Division, World Wildlife Fund – US, personal communication with the author, 18 April 1994.

23 Global Environment Facility, 'Bhutan Trust Fund for Environmental Conservation', GEF Green Band Project Document, Washington, DC, May 1992.

24 Interagency Planning Group on Environmental Funds, 'Existing or Proposed Environmental Funds' (draft), 13 March 1996.

25 'Elaboration of an International Convention to Combat Desertification in Countries Experiencing Serious Drought and/or Desertification Particularly in Africa', A/ AC.241/27,12, Article 21(d), September 1994.

26 Mark Dillenbeck, Programme Officer, IUCN, personal communication with the author, 6 January 1995.

27 International Union for Conservation of Nature and Natural Resources, The Nature Conservancy, the World Wildlife Fund – US, 'Summary Report: Global Forum on Environmental Funds', Washington, DC, 23 June 1994, p 2.

28 World Wildlife Fund – US, 'Belize: Protected Areas Conservation Trust', Washington, DC, January 1993.

29 Peter Sand has observed the extraordinary proliferation of trust and trustlike arrangements for financing international environmental protection: '(E)ven a

cursory glance at international financial mechanisms for sustainable development shows an amazing – and clearly growing – variety of legal instruments that either call themselves trusts (regardless of what they really are) or could be categorized as trusts (regardless of what they call themselves).' Peter H Sand, 'Trusts for the Earth: New International Financial Mechanisms for Sustainable Development', Symposium on Sustainable Development and International Law, Baden bei Wien, 14–16 April 1994.

30 The World Bank, *Issues and Options in the Design of GEF Supported Trust Funds for Biodiversity Conservation*, Washington, DC, May 1994, pp 86 and 89.
31 International Union for Conservation of Nature and Natural Resources, the Nature Conservancy, and the World Wide Fund for Nature, 'Summary Report: Global Forum on Environmental Funds', Washington, DC, 23 June 1994, p 2.
32 The World Wildlife Fund – US, 'Belize: Protected Areas Conservation Trust'.
33 The World Bank, 'Financing Innovation and Instruments: Contribution of the Investment Portfolio of the Pilot Phase of the Global Environment Facility', paper presented to the Regional Conference on Biodiversity Conservation, Asian Development Bank, 6–8 June 1994, p 2.
34 Barry Spergel, personal communication with the author, 20 January 1995.
35 'USAID Parallel-Financed Projects in the Pilot Phase of the Global Environment Facility', Progress Report, United States Agency for International Development, The Environment and Natural Resources Information Center, February 1995, pp 59–62.
36 World Wildlife Fund – US, 'Papua New Guinea Trust Fund', Washington , DC, January 1993.
37 World Wildlife Fund – US, 'Belize: Protected Areas Conservation Trust'.
38 'USAID Parallel-Financed Projects', p 10.
39 Id p 10.
40 Id p 11.
41 Haas, Peter M, Keohane, Robert O and Levy, Marc A (1993) *Institutions for the Earth: Sources of Effective International Environment Protection*, the MIT Press, Cambridge, Massachusetts, p 5.
42 Haas, Keohane, Levy and Clarke, William C are employing this framework to analyse the effectiveness of financial transfer mechanisms in a forthcoming book. Clark, William C, Keohane, Robert O and Levy, Marc A 'The Effectiveness of Financial Transfers for Solving International Environmental Problems: Analytical Framework and Research Design', second draft, 16 December 1993, unpublished manuscript.
43 Haas et al, *Institutions for the Earth*, p 11. Emphasis is from text.
44 Spergel, Barry, 'Trust Funds for Conservation', World Wildlife Fund – US, Washington, DC, 19 January 1993, p 6.
45 IUCN, TNC, WWF, 'Summary Report', p 3.
46 The World Bank, *World Development Report 1992*, p 92.
47 Id p 3.
48 Id p 3.
49 Spergel, 'Trust Funds for Conservation', p 6.
50 The World Bank, *Issues and Options*, p 45.
51 USAID, 'Parallel-Financed Projects', p 61.
52 The World Bank, *Issues and Options*, pp 47–48.
53 Id pp 47–48.
54 The World Bank, 'Financing Innovation', p 11.
55 Spergel, personal communication with the author, 20 January 1995.
56 The World Bank, 'Financing Innovation', p 11.
57 Mikitin, Kathleen, Operations Officer, Global Environment Coordination Division, Environment Department, The World Bank, personal communication with the author, 5 January 1995.
58 Spergel, personal communication with the author, 20 January 1995.

59   Id.
60   The World Bank, 'Financing Innovation and Instruments', p 8.
61   The World Bank, *Issues and Options*, p 7.
62   Mikitin, personal communication with the author, 5 January 1995.
63   'Convention on Biological Diversity', in Guruswamy, Lakshman D, Palmer, Sir Geoffrey W, and Weston, Burns H, *International Environmental Law and World Order*, Supplement of Basic Documents, St Paul, West Publishing Co, Minnesota, 1994.
64   King, Ken, 'Incremental Costs of Global Environment Benefits', GEF Working Paper No 5, 1993.
65   Mikitin, personal communication with the author, 8 February 1995.
66   The World Bank, *Issues and Options*, p 6.
67   Dillenbeck, personal communication with the author, 6 January 1995; Mikitin, personal communication with the author, 5 January 1995; Spergel, personal communications with the author, 20 January 1995.
68   United Nations Development Programme – Global Environment Facility, 'Inter-agency Group on Environmental Funds: Programme of Action', draft, 2 August 1994.
69   The World Bank, *Issues and Options*, p 8.
70   Dillenbeck, personal communication with the author, 6 January 1995.
71   French, Hilary, 'Forging a New Global Partnership', in *State of the World 1995*, W W Norton, New York, London, 1995, pp 170–189, 179.
72   Id p 188.
73   Id.
74   I credit Jacob Werksman for this conceptualization. Werksman, Jacob, Foundation for International Environmental Law and Development, personal communication with the author via the Internet, 10 January 1995.

11   THE EUROPEAN UNION AND THE OECD

1   See Article 2 EC.
2   The precautionary principle was first pronounced by the OECD in the context of the 1987 Ministerial Declaration of the Second Conference on the Protection of the North Sea (London, 1987).
3   OECD Council Recommendations C(74) 224, C(76) 55, C(77) 28. See generally OECD, *Legal Aspects of Transfrontier Pollution* (Paris, 1977).
4   See, for example, OECD Recommendation C(74) 215 on ecotoxicity, OECD Recommendation C(77) 79 on procedural guidelines and requirements for antici-pating the potential effects of chemical products on the environment.
5   OECD Recommendation C(76) 155.
6   OECD Recommendation C(78) 8.
7   OECD Recommendation C(79) 218.
8   OECD Recommendation C(74) 16, C(74) 219 and C(85) 101.
9   See Birnie, P B, and Boyle, A E (1992) *International Law and the Environment*, Oxford, p 396.
10   1960 Convention on Third Party Liability in the Field of Nuclear Energy (Paris Convention) as amended (1964). See *IAEA Conventions on Civil Liability or Nuclear Damage* (Vienna, 1976).
11   Directive 75/439 OJ 1975 No L 194/23.
12   Directive 75/440 OJ 1975 No L 194/26.
13   See, for example, Directive 67/548 on the approximation of the laws, regulations and administrative provisions relating to the classification, packaging and labelling of dangerous substances, OJ 1967 No L 196/1.
14   Bull EC 10-1972.
15   OJ 1973 No C 112/1.

16 For an analysis of these instruments, see Haigh, N, *Manual of EC Environmental Policy.*

17 Article 2 EEC provided:
'The Community shall have as its task, by establishing a common market and progressively approximating the economic policies of Member States, to promote throughout the Community a harmonious development of economic activities, a continuous and balanced expansion, an increase in stability, an accelerated raising of the standard of living and closer relations between the States belonging to it.'

18 Note 4 supra.

19 A prime example is provided by German legislation regulating the lead content in petrol which was adopted, despite threats by the Commission to challenge those provisions, on the grounds of their incompatibility with Article 30 under Article 169 EC and which led to the adoption of Directive 78/611 concerning lead in petrol, OJ 1978 No L 197/1.

20 All references in this section refer to the 1957 Treaty unless stated otherwise.

21 The Cohesion Fund payments made to Ireland, Greece, Spain and Portugal which, between 1993 and 1999 may total 15.150 million Ecus (see Regulation 1164/94 Article 4), may be viewed partly as a manifestation of the principle of solidarity in the sphere of the environment.

22 Article 189 provides:
In order to carry out their task and in accordance with the provisions of this Treaty, the European Parliament acting jointly with the Council, the Council and the Commission shall make regulations and issue directives, take decisions, make recommendations or deliver opinions.
A regulation shall have general application. It shall be binding in its entirety and directly applicable in all Member States.
A directive shall be binding as to the result to be achieved, upon each Member State to which it is addressed, but shall leave to the national authorities the choice of form and methods.
A decision shall be binding in its entirety upon those to whom it is addressed.
... Recommendations and opinions shall have no binding force.

23 Article 169 provides:
If the Commission considers that a Member State has failed to fulfil an obligation under this Treaty, it shall deliver a reasoned opinion on the matter after giving the State concerned the opportunity to submit its observations.
If the State concerned does not comply with the opinion within the period laid down by the Commission the latter may bring the matter before the Court of Justice.

24 Article 4 provides:
The tasks entrusted to the Community shall be carried out by the following institutions:
–   an Assembly,
–   a Council,
–   a Commission,
–   a Court of Justice.
Each institution shall act within the limits conferred upon it by this Treaty (emphasis added).

25 Behrens, F, *Rechtsgrundlagen der Umweltpolitik der Europäischen Gemeinschaften* (1976); Bradley, Kst C, 'The European Court and the Legal Basis of Community Legislation', *European Law Review* (1992) 18 pp 379–402; Grabitz, E, *Competence of the European Communities for Environmental Policy* (1977); Krämer, L, *EEC Treaty and Environmental Protection* (1990); von Moltke, K. 'The Legal Basis for Environmental Policy', *Environmental Policy and Law* (1977) 3 pp 136–140; Saggio, 'Le basi giuridiche della politica ambientale nell'ordinamento comunitario dopo d'entrata in vigore dell'Atto Unico Europeo', *Rivista di Diritto Europeo* (1993) 33 pp 39–50; Scheuning, 'Umwelt-schutz auf der Grundlage der Einheitlichen Europäischen Akte', *Europarecht* (1989)

pp 153–192; Scheuer, H, 'Aspects Juridiques de la Protection de l'Environnement dans le Marché Commun', *Revue du Marché Commun* (1975) 109 pp 441–456; Vorwerk, *Die Umweltpolitischen Kompetenzen der Europäischen Gemeinschaft und ihrer Mitgliedstaaten nach Inkrafttreten der EEA* (1990).

26 In case 240/83, Procureur de la République v Association de 'Défense de Brûleurs' ECR (1985) 531, the Court ruled that environmental protection belonged to the Community's 'fundamental objectives'.

27 For the role of the European Parliament in the early years see Hannequart, J-P, 'Le Parlement Européen et l'Environnement', *Res Publica* (1979) 21 pp 127–143.

28 France argued that the Community lacked the powers to pursue an environmental policy and insisted that the environmental action programme would take the form of an instrument other than those listed in Article 189 so as to ensure that the environmental policy would remain 'inter-governmental'. The first action programme therefore has the somewhat curious title of a 'Declaration of the Council of the European Communities, and of the representatives of the Governments of the Member States meeting in the Council'.

29 Article 75 EC. The European Parliament eventually challenged the Council for its failure to take the necessary steps to establish a common transport policy.

30 OJ 1977 No C 139/1 (second), OJ 1983 No C 46/1 (third), OJ 1987 No C 328/1 (fourth), OJ 1993 No C 138/1 (fifth). Note that the EC's environmental policy is the only policy which, from the beginning has been based on multi-annual action programmes with clear deadlines for their implementation (see Krämer, L, note 20 infra).

31 See Article 189 note 10, supra.

32 In the sphere of the environment, see case C-405/92, Mondiet v Armement Solaris, ECR (1993) I-6133.

33 Prime examples are the parameter concerning pesticides of Directive 80/778 on the quality of drinking water, and many of the parameters in Directive 76/160 on the quality of drinking water. Both directives are in the process of revision and, although some unnecessary parameters have indeed been removed, first indications are that the principle of prevention alongside the principle of precaution have had the effect of maintaining the most controversial parameters.

34 Agreement of the representatives of the governments of the Member States meeting in the Council on information for the Commission and for the Member States with a view to possible harmonization throughout the Communities of urgent measures concerning the protection of the environment, OJ 1973 No C 9/1. See also Directive 88/182 laying down a procedure for the provision of information in the field of technical standards and regulations (OJ 1988 No. L 109/8).

35 See in particular the proposal on Integrated Pollution Prevention and Control, COM(93) 423 fin.

36 Case 91/79, Commission v Italy ECR (1980) 1099.

37 See, however, the House of Lords Select Committee on the European Communities 22nd Report Session 1977–78 *Approximation of Laws under Article 100 EC Treaty*, which was critical of the Communities' use of this provision in the sphere of the environment.

38 OJ 1979 No L 103/1.

39 OJ 1976 No L 313/1.

40 In case 91/79, Italy, by way of a defence in a case pursuant to Article 169 for failure to implement Directive 73/404 on detergents, in its defence questioned the Communities' powers to adopt the directive.

41 It should be noted, however, that the mere fact that a Member State has voted for a proposal does not affect its right to challenge the legality of that directive in a subsequent action pursuant to Article 173. See generally St Bradley, Kieran, 'The European Court and the Legal Basis of Community Legislation', 13 *European Law Review* 1988, pp 379–402.

42   Bull, EC 10-1972 p 24.

43   Since the coming into force of the Treaty on European Union, no Community act has been adopted, wholly or in part, on Article 235. The provision is particularly difficult to reconcile with the principle of subsidiarity.

44   See note 13 supra. In addition see Krämer, L (1978) 'The Single European Act and Environmental Protection: Reflections on Several New Provisions in Community Law', *Common Market Law Review* 24, pp 225–231; Krämer, L (1990) *EC Treaty and Environmental Protection*, Krämer, L, (1993) *Focus on European Environmental Law*; Roelants du Vivier, F (1988) 'Une Nouvelle Stratégy Européenne pour l'Environnement dans le cadre de l'Acte Unique Européenne', *Revue du Marché Commun*, 25, pp 225–231; Sevenster, H (1992) *Milieubeleid en Gemeenschapsrecht*.

45   See the Declaration in the Final Act reading: 'the conference confirms that the Community's activities in the sphere of the environment may not interfere with national policies regarding the exploitation of energy resources'.

46   Originally the Commission's list contained:
- the protection of the atmosphere and the improvement of water quality;
- water protection;
- the fight against noise;
- the protection of national sites, soils and landscapes;
- conservation of fauna, flora and the protection of animals;
- the fight against squandering natural resources;
- the reutilization, recycling and disposal of waste;
- measures which would stimulate responses to the needs of environmental protection;
- prevention and repair of damage to persons or goods who are endangered through the carrying out of industrial activities or by the use or, or the contact with, poisonous or dangerous substances or products, especially if more than one member state is concerned by the risk of the necessity of redress;
- research in the field of the environment in techniques for environmental protection.

This proposal was dropped after insistence from Greece and the Netherlands that the proposal should be less detailed. See Jacqué, J-P (1986) 'The Single European Act and Environmental Policy', *Environmental Policy and Law* 16/3/4 at p 123.
See Ehlremann, C G, 'The Internal Market Following the Single European Act', *Common Market Law Review*, 24, 1987, pp 361–409.

47   This interpretation is borne out by the Green Paper on the urban environment (Resolution 11/1191 OJ 1992 No C 59/1). Excluded from the notion 'environment' is the working environment which is subject to separate Community provisions.

48   Meanwhile, a comparison between the action programmes and Article 130R shows, for example, that the principle that activities on the territory of one Member State should not have detrimental environmental effects on the territory of another Member State is not found in the Treaty. However, this principle of customary international law (see also Principle 21 of the Stockholm Declaration) equally binds the Community.

49   Examples of practical manifestations of this principle are Directive 85/337 on environmental impact assessment (OJ 1985 No L 175/40) and the more recent Community's waste policy as expressed in particular in SEC(89)394 and OJ 1990 No C 122/2).

50   On the controversies surrounding the choice between quality objectives and emission standards in the context of Directive 76/464 (OJ 1976 No L 129/93) see Somsen, H 'EC Water Directives' *Water Law* (1990).

51   Case C-2/90, Commission v Belgium (1992) ECR I-4431.

52   See also Recommendation 75/436 OJ (1975) No L 194/1.

53   However, this so-called 'integration-principle' that arguably already forms part of the preventive principle.

54 See also House of Lords Select Committee on the European Communities Report 8, Session 1992–93, *Fifth Environmental Action Programme: Integration of Community Policies*.

55 These first two principles were included after insistence from Britain that (at the time) there was not sufficient scientific proof to hold that British emissions of CO_2 were responsible for the destruction of forests elsewhere in Europe and which was arguing that Community action was therefore not necessary. Its insistence on the taking into account of the differing conditions existing in the various regions of the Community is a reflection of its determination to take as much benefit as possible from its island status.

56 Again, this principle was included after UK pressure. It is agreed with Krämer and Sevenster (p 129) that this principle should not be interpreted as requiring a 'cost-benefit analysis' or as codifying a preference for 'best practical means' rather than 'best available technology not exceeding excessive cost'.

57 See Sevenster, H, op cit, pp 131–144.

58 This provision failed to have this effect; Regulation 1973/92 established a financial instrument for the environment (LIFE) OJ 1992 No L 206/1.

59 Case 22/70, Commission v Council (1971) ECR 263.

60 See Articles 113, 238 and 130R(5).

61 See cases 3, 4 and 6/76, Krämer, ECR (1976) 1270 and Opinion 1/76 ECR (1977) 741. On the Community's external environmental powers, see generally Bargero, J V (1991) 'La CEE y el Convenio sobre Derecho de Mar de 1982. Consderaciones sobre la Relacion entre el Derecho Comunitario y el Derecho Internacional' *Revista de Instituciones Europeas* 18 551–583; Leenen, Ath S, (1984) 'Participation of the EC in International Environmental Agreements' *Legal Issues of European Integration*, pp 93–111; Haigh, N (1992) 'The European Community and International Environmental Policy' in *International Environmental Policy*; Nollkaemper, A, (1987) 'The European Community and International Environmental Cooperation – Legal Aspects of External Community Powers' *Legal Issues of European Integration*, pp 55–91.

62 This observation applies equally to acts adopted pursuant to Article 100A. Note, however, that in respect of this provision, the Final Act contains a Declaration Article 100A urging the Commission to 'give precedence to the use of the instrument of a directive if harmonisation involves the amendment of legislative provisions in one or more Member States'.

63 OJ 1990 No C 55.

64 OJ 1992 No C 76.

65 See Flynn, 'How will Article 100a(4) work? a comparison with Article 93', *CMLR* 1987, p 689 *et seq*; Ehlremann, 'The internal market following the Single European Act' *CMLR* 1987, p 361 *et seq*; Gulman 'The Single European Act; some remarks from a Danish perspective' *CMLR* 1987, p 31 *et seq*; Langeheine, 'Le rapprochement des législations nationales selon l'article 100A du Traité CEE: l'harmonisation communautaire face aux exigences de protection nationale' *RMC* 1989, p 347 *et seq*; Sevenster, *Milieubeleid en Gemeenschapsrecht*, 1992.

66 Case C-41/93, France v Commission, 17 May 1994 (not yet reported).

67 For such a 'green' interpretation, see in particular Gulman, op cit, note 49.

68 The question has given rise to intensive scholarly debate, eg Barents, R 'The Internal Market Unlimited: Some Observations on the Legal Basis of Community Legislation', 30 CML Rev 85. Everling, U, 'Abgrenzung der Rechtsangleichung zur Verwirklichung des Binnenmarktes nach Art 100A EWGV durch den Gerichtshof' (1991) EuR, 179 and Schröer, T 'Mehr Demokratie statt umweltpolitischer Subsidiarität? (1991) Eur 356. Somsen, H in 29 CML Rev 140.

69 Contra, Sewandono, 'Beginsel van democratie versus milieu', (1992) NJB, 63.

70 The Court ruled in case C-2/90, Commission v Belgium that waste – even non-recyclable waste – must be regarded as good for the purposes of EC law.

71 Directive 91/156 amending directive 75/442 on waste.

72   The Treaty is printed in (1992) 31 *International Legal Materials* 247 (1993) ILM 1693.
73   See first recital of the preamble.
74   See Articles B and C(1) of the Common Provisions.
75   Contra Epiney von, A and Gallen, A R 'Umweltschutz nach Maastricht' Europarecht 1992, vol 4, pp 369–408 at pp 373–374.
76   For example, Article 235 at present very much presents a dead letter.
77   Article 3 now mentions:
     –   a common commercial policy;
     –   an internal market characterized by the abolition, as between Member States, of obstacles to the free movement of goods, persons, services and capital;
     –   measures concerning the entry and movement of persons in the internal market as provided by Article 100c;
     –   a common policy in the sphere of agriculture and fisheries;
     –   a common policy in the sphere of transport;
     –   a system ensuring that competition in the internal market is not distorted;
     –   a policy in the social sphere comprising a European Social Fund;
     –   the approximation of the laws of the member states to the extent required for the functioning of the internal market;
     –   the strengthening of economic and social cohesion;
     –   a policy in the sphere of the environment;
     –   the strengthening of the competitiveness of Community industry;
     –   the promotion of research and development;
     –   the encouragement of the establishment and development of trans-European networks;
     –   a contribution to the attainment of a high level of health protection;
     –   a contribution to education and training of quality and the flowering of the cultures of the Member States;
     –   a policy in the sphere of development cooperation;
     –   the association of the overseas countries and territories in order to increase trade and promote jointly economic and social development;
     –   a contribution to the strengthening of consumer protection;
     –   measures in the sphere of energy, civil protection and tourism.
78   See note 45 supra.
79   The Commission recently indicated that, as regards the application of the principle of subsidiarity in the sphere of the environment, the absence of internal measures can only be justified if the Community can play a full part in the elaboration of international rules (WQ E-2933/93, OJ 1994 No C310/43).
80   See Freestone and Ryland, 'EC Environmental Law after Maastricht' *Northern Ireland Law Quarterly* (1994) 45, pp 152–176 at p 156.
81   Definitions are found in 'virtually every recent environmental Treaty' (Freestone and Ryland, ibid, at p 156). See, for example, 1992 Paris Convention for the protection of the marine environment of the North East Atlantic, 1992 Helsinki Convention on the protection of the marine environment of the Baltic Sea area, 1992 Framework Convention on Climate Change, 1992 Convention on Biological Diversity.
82   OJ 1993 No C 212/60, COM(93) 271 final. Principle 15 of the Rio Declaration incorporates the precautionary principle thus:
     'In order to protect the environment, the precautionary *approach* shall be widely applied by States according to their capabilities. Where there are threats of serious or irreversible damage, lack of full scientific certainty shall not be used as a reason for postponing cost-effective measures to prevent environmental degradation' (emphasis added).
83   See Epiney, A and Furrer, A, 'Umweltschutz nach Maastricht', *Europarecht* (1992) pp 369–408.
84   Cf Epinay and Furrer, ibid p 388 *et seq.*.
85   See further infra.

86 Cf Article 189b EC.
87 A very brief description of the cooperation procedure is provided below.
88 By qualified majority of the Council and a simple majority of the European Parliament (Article 189b(4)).
89 The European Parliament may adapt it by absolute majority, the Council by a qualified majority (Article 189b(5)).
90 Article 189b(5).
91 Article 189b(6).
92 Article 189b(6).
93 Article 189c(f).
94 Article 189c(e).
95 Article 189c(e).
96 Fiscal measures will not fall within the ambit of Article 100A in view of the exceptions in Article 100A(2).
97 This is without prejudice to Article 100A. Note that this provision may be interpreted in various ways and it is not entirely clear whether only waste management or also measures of a general nature and possibly even management of water resources are subject to Article 130S(1).
98 The evolution of the perception as regards the Community character of the action programmes is reflected in the evolution of the legal form of the action programmes themselves. The first action programme was adopted as a 'Declaration of the Council and of the representatives of the governments of the Member States, meeting in the Council', the second and third programme had the status of a 'Resolution of the Council and of the representative of the governments of the Member States in the Council', the fourth and fifths programmes were a 'Resolution of the Council'.
99 See generally Krämer, L (1994) 'Um eine Umweltpolitik von innen Bittend', *Zeitschrift für Umweltrecht*, vol 4, pp 172–177.
100 See Ryland, D 'The Cohesion Fund: A Question of Balance', *European Environmental Law Review* (1994) 3 p 263 *et seq.*
101 OJ 1976 No L 31.
102 OJ 1979 No L 103.
103 See Bekkers, V J J M, Bonnes, J A, Moor–Van Vugt de, A and Voermans, W (1994) 'The Process and Problems of Implementation of EC Regulations in the Netherlands', *COST Conference on 'The Evolution of Rules for a Single European Market'*, Exeter, Collins, K and Earnshaw, D (1992) 'The Implementation and Enforcement of European Community Environmental Legislation', *Environmental Politics* 1:213–249; Crockett, T R and Schultz, C B (1991) 'The Integration of Environmental Policy and the European Community: Recent Problems of Implementation and Enforcement' *Colombia Journal of Transnational Law* 29:169–171; Haigh, N (1987) *EC Environmental Policy & Britain*; Jans, J H (1989) 'Legal Problems Concerning the Implementation of EEC Environmental Directives Regarding Dangerous Substances and the Netherlands Chemical Substance Act' *Leiden Journal of International Law*; Krämer, L (1991) 'The Implementation of Community Environmental Directives within Member States: Some Implications of the Direct Effect Doctrine', *Journal of Environmental Law*; Laffan, B (1987) 'Putting European Law into Practice: the Irish Experience'. *Administration* 37:201–217; Siedentopf, H and Ziller, J (1989) *Making European Policies Work.*
104 The Declaration provides, *inter alia:*
      'The Conference stresses that it is central to the coherence and unity of the process of European construction that each Member State should fully and accurately transpose into national law the Community Directives addressed to it within the deadlines laid down therein (. . .) The Confrence calls on the Commission to ensure, in exercising its powers under Article 155 of the Treaty, that Member States fulfil their obligations. It asks the Commission to publish periodically a full report for the Member States and the European Parliament.'

105   Case 236/85, Commission v Netherlands (1987) ECR 3989 (in respect of Directive 79/409 on the conservation of wild birds).

106   Case 2/62, Van Gend and Loos, ECR (1963) 1.

107   In its fifth supervision report, for example, the Commission states:
'In this respect, Article 169 of the EEC Treaty is now an instrument for the achievement of a policy, and not solely an essential legal instrument. The objective of Article 8a of the Treaty, namely to achieve by 1992 an area without frontiers, is now the Commission's priority objective and requires a strict application of existing Community law.' (Fifth Annual Report to the European Parliament on Commission monitoring of the application of Community Law (1987) COM(88) 425 fin.'
See in similar vein the most recent 11th report (OJ 1994 No C 154 6 June 1994) at p 8.

108   Case C-236/92, Comitato di Coordinamento per la Difesa della Cava and Others and Regione Lombardia and Others, ECR (1994) I-483. The case revolved around the question whether Article 4 of Directive 75/442 could produce direct effect. Krämer had earlier argued that such would be the case – Krämer (1992) *Focus on European Environmental Law*, 163. The Court, however, now seems to have rejected this interpretation.

109   On this question, see Jakobs, F 'Remedies in national courts for the enforcement of Community rights', *Hacia un Nuevo Orden Internacional y Europeo* (1993).

110   The term 'enforcement gap' is used as a paraphrase of the notion of an 'implementation gap' used by Rehbinder and Stewart in *Environmental Protection Policy* (1986).

111   Case 26/62, Van Gend and Loos (1963) ECR 1.
'The vigilance of private individuals to protect their rights amounts to an effective supervision in addition to the supervision entrusted by Articles 169 and 170 to the diligence of the Commission and the Member States.'

112   Thus, in its judgment in cases C-267 and C-268/91, Bernard Keck and Daniel Mithouard of 24 November 1993 the Court remarked:
'In view of the increasing tendency of traders to invoke Article 30 of the Treaty as a means of challenging rules whose effect is to limit their commercial freedom even where such rules are not aimed at products from other Member States, the Court considers it necessary to re-examine and clarify its case-law on this matter' (para 14).

113   Reference Francovich.

114   The Court in particular invoked Van Gend and Loos, case 2/62 (1963) ECR 1 and Costa, case 6/64 (1964) ECR 585.

115   For the constitutional importance of this provision on the role of Article 5 see Mancini, F (1989) 'The Making of a Constitution for Europe', *Common Market Law Review* 26:595-614; Temple Lang, J (1991) 'The Sphere in which Member States are Obliged to Comply with the General Principles of Law and Community Fundamental Rights Principles', *Legal Issues of European Integration* 23-35; Temple-Lang, J (1990) 'Community Constitutional Law: Article 5 EEC Treaty' *Common Market Law Review* 27:645-681.

116   See Bebr, G, Joined Cases C-6/90 and C-9/90, *Francovich v Italy, Bonifaci v Italy*, CMLR 29, pp 557–585 at p 570.

117   Para 41.

118   See Somsen, H 'Francovich and its Application to EC Environmental Law' in Somsen, H (ed) *Protecting the European Environment: the Enforcement of EC Environmental Law*, Edward Elgar (forthcoming).

119   Note 12 supra.

120   See in particular: Geelhoed (1991) 'Het subsidiariteitsbeginsel: enn communautair principe?' *Tijdschrift voor Sociaal en Economisch Recht* pp 422–435; House of Lords Select Committee Report on Economic and Monetary Union and Political Union, 30 October 1990, HMSO, HL Paper 88, 1; Toth (1992) 'The Principle of Subsidiarity in

the Maastricht Treaty' *Common Market Law Review* 29 pp 1079–1105. Brinkhorst (1993) 'Subsidiarity and European Community Environmental Policy: A Panacea or a Pandora's Box?' *European Environmental Law Review* 2 p 8 *et seq.* Brinkhorst, 'Subsidiarity in European Environmental Policy', Schaefer, 'The Subsidiarity Principle and European Environmental Policy'; Pappas, 'The Legal Basis for Action to be Taken by the European Community in the Field of Environment', all in *Subsidiarity, the Challenge of Change* (1989).

121   This question relates to the justifiability of the principle of subsidiarity, which will not be discussed here. See Toth, op cit, note 120.

122   As for the legal significance of future action programmes, see supra.

123   For a detailed analysis of the Fifth Environmental Action Programme, see Grado, V (1993) 'Tendenze Evolutive della Politica Comunitaria dell' Ambiente in Relazione al Quintro Programma d'Azione' *Revista di Diritto Europeo* pp 17–60.

124   This is acknowledged in Part I, The Inter-institutional Declaration on Democracy, Transparency and Subsidiarity which provides that the principle of subsidiarity is designed to govern the exercise of Community powers and that the procedures will not call into question the *acquis communautaire*, the powers conferred on the institutions or the institutional balance (*Europe* Documents No 1857).

125   Note 113 supra.

126   COM(93) 545, 24 November 1993.

127   See also Krämer, L 'Um eine Umweltpolitik von innen Bittend', op cit, note 80 at p 174.

128   Cf note 120 supra.

129   Note 120 supra.

130   Case 22/70 Commission v Council (ERTA), [1971] 1 ECR 263, Cases 3, 4 and 6/76; Kramer, [1976] ECR 1279.

131   See note 115 supra.

132   Unpublished draft directive.

12   THE SOUTH PACIFIC REGION

1   See below, p 209.

2   The Cook Islands, Federated States of Micronesia, Fiji, Kiribati, Marshall Islands, Nauru, Niue, Papua New Guinea, Solomon Islands, Tonga, Tuvalu, Vanuatu and Western Samoa; the United States of America and its territories of American Samoa, Guam, Northern Mariana Islands and Palau; France and its territories of French Polynesia, New Caledonia, and Wallis and Futuna; The United Kingdom and its territory of Pitcairn Island; New Zealand and its territory of Tokelau Islands; Australia.

3   The seven founding members of the South Pacific Forum were Australia, the Cook Islands, Fiji, Nauru, New Zealand, Tonga, and Western Samoa. Today the membership has increased to 15, the additional members being the Federated States of Micronesia, Kiribati, the Marshall Islands, Niue, Papua New Guinea, the Solomon Islands, Tuvalu and Vanuatu.

4   Forum members, excluding territories and metropolitan states.

5   SPREP received the support of the Asian Development Bank (ADB) and the United Nations Development Programme (UNDP) in its preparation of the National Reports which highlight the importance of international financial assistance for the Pacific Islands.

6   'Environment and Development: A Pacific Island Perspective' and 'The Pacific Way: Pacific Island Developing Countries' Report to UNCED' respectively. The former analyses the National Reports together with other information available relating to sustainable development in the South Pacific region, and identifies the issues and constraints to sustainable development. The latter summarizes the findings of the first report and presents the regional consensus on the priorities for further action.

7 Chapter 38, Section I. Regional and subregional cooperation and implementation.

8 In the Cook Islands, the traditional conservation practice known as ra'ui (prohibition), is applied by village leaders and enforced by the Island Council. It may be used to restrict access to land, lagoons and reef areas in order to allow a resource to recover or to increase yields, thereby aiding the conservation of foods, coconuts and marine resources. Ra'ui is, however, now more often breached than complied with as a result of changing attitudes, the erosion of traditional practices and the development of consumer society.

13 THE INTERNATIONAL COURT OF JUSTICE AND THE EUROPEAN COURT OF JUSTIC

1 On the subject of international environmental law, including its historical development, see generally P Sands (1995) *Principles of International Environmental Law* (Manchester University Press), (hereafter 'Principles').

2 EC Treaty, Article 164. The ECJ also has competence in relation to the interpretation and application of the 1950 ECSC Treaty and the 1957 Euratom Treaty.

3 Rosalyn Higgins (1994) *Problems and Process: International Law and How We Use It*, Clarendon Press, Oxford, p 202.

4 Ibid.

5 Ibid.

6 See Principles, Chapter 5.

7 See generally H Lauterpacht (1958) *The development of international law by the International Court*; S Rosenne, *The Law and Practise of the International Court* (2nd rev edn, 1985); T Franck (1986) *Judging the World Court*; Sir G Fitzmaurice (1986) *The Law and Procedure of the International Court of Justice*; L F Damrosch (ed) (1987) *The International Court of Justice at a Crossroads*; S Rosenne, *The World Court: what it is and how it works* (5th rev edn, 1994).

8 In relation to contentious cases it is important to recall that 'only states may be parties in cases before the Court', United Nations Charter, Article 34(1).

9 International Court of Justice, Communiqué 93/20, 19 July 1993. The Chamber was established under Article 26(1) of its Statute and comprises seven judges.

10 See eg 1963 Vienna Convention, Optional Protocol Concerning the Compulsory Settlement of Disputes, Article I (not in force).

11 See eg 1959 Antarctic Treaty, Article XI(2); 1974 Baltic Convention, Article 18(2).

12 See eg 1985 Vienna Convention, Article 11(3); 1989 Basle Convention, Article 20(3); 1992 Climate Change Convention, Article 14(2); 1992 Biodiversity Convention, Article 27(3); 1992 Industrial Accidents Convention, Article 21; 1992 Watercourses Convention, Article 22.

13 Statute ICJ, Article 36(2). As of 1 January 1992, 51 states had accepted the Optional Clause.

14 Article 36(3).

15 Charter of the United Nations, Article 96(1).

16 Article 96(2). ECOSOC, the Trusteeship Council and 15 of the specialized agencies have been authorized by the General Assembly, as have three other entities. The two principal environmental bodies in the UN system, the UN Environment Programme and the Commission on Sustainable Development, have not been so authorized by the General Assembly.

17 Bering Sea Fur Seals Fisheries Arbitration (*Great Britain v United States*), *Moore's International Arbitrations*, 755 (1893); Trail Smelter Arbitration (*United States v Canada*), 3 *RIAA* 1907; Lac Lanoux Arbitration (*France v Spain*), 24 *ILR* 101 (1957).

18 See *The Territorial Jurisdiction of the International Commission of the River Oder*, 1929 PCIJ, Ser A No 23, 27; *Diversion of the Waters of the River Meuse*, 1937 PCIJ Ser A/B, No 70.

19 *Corfu Channel* Case (*UK v Albania*) (1949) ICJ Rep 1, at p 22.

20 *Fisheries Jurisdiction* Case (*UK v Iceland*) (1974), ICJ *Rep* 3, at p 31 (para 72); *Fisheries Jurisdiction* Case (*Federal Republic of Germany v Iceland*), ICJ Reps 1974, p 175, at p 200 (para 64).

21 *Nuclear Tests* Case (*Australia v France*) (Jurisdiction) ICJ Rep 1974, p 253; (*New Zealand v France*) (Jurisdiction) ICJ Rep 1974, p 457.

22 See eg *Nuclear Tests* Case (*Australia v France*), Pleadings, pp 525–526.

23 See Dissenting Opinion of Judge de Castro, ICJ Rep 1974, p 253, pp 388–390.

24 *Nuclear Tests* Cases (*Australia v France*) (Interim Measures) ICJ Rep 1973, p 99, p 106; (*New Zealand v France*) (Interim Measures) ICJ Rep 1973, p 135, p 142.

25 Case concerning *Certain Phosphate Lands in Nauru* (*Nauru v Australia*), Preliminary Objections, Judgment, ICJ Reps 1992, p 240. Judge Oda, one of the dissenting opinions on admissibility, was at pains to point out that by saying that 'the present case should be rejected as inadmissible, I am not denying the importance of the preservation of an environment from any damage that may be caused by the development or exploitation of resources, particularly in the developing regions of the world': ibid, pp 324–325.

26 4 *YbkIEL* 485 (1993).

27 Request for an Examination of the Situation in Accordance with Paragraph 63 of the Court's Judgment of 20 December 1974 in the *Nuclear Tests* (*New Zealand v France*) Case, ICJ Reports 1995, p 288 at 293 (para 18).

28 Ibid, 305 (para 62).

29 Ibid, 306 (para 64).

30 *Legality of the Use by a State of Nuclear Weapons in Armed Conflict (Request for Advisory Opinion by the World Health Organization)*. The request was made pursuant to World Health Assembly Resolution 46.40 of 14 May 1993.

31 *Legality of the Threat or Use of Nuclear Weapons (Request for an Advisory Opinion by the General Assembly of the United Nations)*. The request was made pursuant to Resolution 49/75K of 15 December 1994.

32 1977 Convention for the Prohibition of Military or Any Other Hostile Use of Environmental Modification Techniques, 1108 UNTS 151; 1977 Protocol I (Additional to the 1949 Geneva Conventions) relating to the Protection of Victims of International Armed Conflicts, 16 ILM 1391 (1977).

33 ICJ Communiqué 95/8, 29 March 1995.

34 H G Schermers (1992) *Judicial Protection in the European Communities* (5th edn,); K P E Lasok et al (1993) *Butterworths European Court Practice*; K P E Lasok (1994) *The European Court of Justice: Practise and Procedure*; L N Brown (1994) *The Court of Justice of the European Communities* (4th edn); D W Anderson (1995) *References to the European Court*.

35 The Court of First Instance was established in October 1988 (Decision 88/591, OJ C 215/1) on the basis of Article 168a of the 1986 Single European Act. Its competence has expanded beyond staff and competition cases, although it cannot have jurisdiction over preliminary rulings under Article 177. See generally T Hartley (1994) *Foundations of European Community Law* (2nd rev edn), Clarendon, Oxford, pp 57–93.

36 See Case 21/76, *Handelskwekerij Bier v Mines de Potasse d'Alsace* (1976) ECR 1735. See supra note 38.

37 For a partial list to 1992 see L Krämer, *European Environmental Law Casebook* (1993), Appendix I.

38 Cases 30 to 41/81, *EC Commission v Italian Republic* (1981) ECR 3379; Case 134/86, *EC Commission v Belgium* (1987) ECR 2415.

39 Cases 96 and 97/81, *Commission of the European Communities v Netherlands* (1982) ECR 1791 and 1819.

40 Case 291/84 *Commission of the European Communities v Netherlands* (1989) 1 CMLR 479 (concerning the failure to implement into national law Directive 80/68/EEC on the protection of groundwater against pollution by certain dangerous substances).

41 Case 182/89, *Commission of the European Communities* v *France* (ECR) 1990 I-4337 where the ECJ held that France had infringed Article 10(1)(b) of Council Regulation 3626/82/EEC (on the implementation of CITES) by granting import licences for skins of certain feline animals originating in Bolivia.

42 Case C-75/91, *Commission* v *Netherlands* (1992) 1 ECR 549 (wild birds).

43 Case 141/78 *France* v *United Kingdom* (1979) ECR 2923, where France successfully brought proceedings against the United Kingdom for unlawfully having enforced domestic legislation setting a minimum mesh size for prawn fisheries.

44 Case C-62/88, *Greece* v *Council* (1990) ECR 1527; Case C-300/89, *Commission* v *Council* (1991) IECR 2867; Case C-70/88, *European Parliament* v *EC Council* (1991) IECR 4335.

45 Case 187/87, *Saarland and Others* v *Minister for Industry, Post and Telecommunications and Tourism and others* (1988) ECR 5013.

46 Case 380/87, *Enichem Base et al* v *Commune of Cinisello Balsamo* (1989) ECR 2491.

47 Case 57/89R, *EC Commission* v *Germany* (1989) ECR 2849.

48 Id, para 15.

49 Id, paras 17 and 18.

50 Case 240/83, *Procureur de la République* v *Association de Défence des Bruleurs de l'Huiles Usagées* (1985) ECR 531, para 13.

51 Case 92/79, *EC Commission* v *Italy* (1980) ECR 1099, para 8. Article 100 allows the Council to issue Directives for the approximation of such laws in Member States as 'directly affect the establishment or functioning of the common market'.

52 Case C-300/89, *EC Commission* v *EC Council* (1991) IECR 2867, para 22. Article 100a allows the Council, acting by qualified majority, to adopt measures for the approximation of the laws in Member States which 'have as their object the establishment or functioning of the internal market'; Article 130s allows the Council, acting unanimously, to decide what action is to taken by the Community relating to the environment.

53 But cf Case C-155/91, *EC Commission* v *EC Council*, judgment of 17 March 1993, where the Court held that Article 130s and not Article 100a was the appropriate legal basis 'where harmonization of the conditions of the market within the Community are only ancillary to the act to be adopted', para 17. By the time of this second judgment the point was, in a practical sense at least, somewhat moot, since the Treaty of European Union had amended Article 130s to introduce qualified majority decision-making by the Council on most environmental issues. The importance of the legal basis, and the proper characterization of a Community measure, nevertheless remains since Article 130s retains unanimity voting (without prejudice to Article 100a) on certain types of environmental measures, including those which are primarily of a fiscal nature, or concerning town and country planning, or significantly affecting a Member State's choice between different energy sources.

54 Case C-131/88, *EC Commission* v *Germany* (1991) ECR 825, para 19 (groundwater protection).

55 Ibid, para 61.

56 Case C-339/87, *EC Commission* v *Netherlands* (1990) IECR 851, para 28.

57 Case C-169/89, *Criminal proceedings against Gourmetterie van Den Burg* (1990) IECR 2143.

58 Case 252/85, *EC Commission* v *France* (1988) ECR 2243.

59 Case 240/83, supra note 50, para 12.

60 Case 302/86, *EC Commission* v *Denmark* (1988) ECR 4607, para 9. Article 30 provides, *inter alia*, that 'measures having equivalent effect [to quantitative restrictions] shall, without prejudice to the following provisions, be prohibited between Member States'. Article 36, which sets forth exceptions to Article 36, does not list environmental protection.

61 Supra note 50.

62 Case C-2/90, *EC Commission* v *Belgium* (1993) 1 CMLR 365, para 34.

63   Basle, 22 March 1989, in force 5 May 1992, 28 ILM 649 (1989).
64   Case C-57/89, *EC Commission v Germany* (1991) ECR 883 (paras 21 and 23–4).
65   Cf Case 252/85, supra note 30.
66   See Case 21/76, supra note 4.
67   Case C-339/87, supra note 28.
68   Case C-2/90, supra note 34, para 30.
69   Case C-70/88, *European Parliament v EC Council* (1990) 1 ECR 2041, para 23.
70   Case T-585/93, *Stichting Greenpeace Council and Others v Commission*, Order of 9 August 1995, paras 52 and 57.
71   Id, para 60.
72   See eg Cases 106–107/1963, *Alfred Topfer and Getreide-Import Gesellschaft v Commission* (1965) ECR 405.
73   Supra note 28, 362.

14   IMPLEMENTATION CONTROL AND REACTION

1   Cf *Montreal Protocol on Substances that Deplete the Ozone Layer*, 16 September 1987, XXVI ILM (1987), p 1550, Article 6.
2   *Convention on Long-Range Transboundary Air Pollution*, 13 November 1979, XVIII ILM (1979) p 1442, Article 9 and *Protocol to the 1979 Convention on Long-Term Financing of the Co-operative Programme for Monitoring and Evaluation of the Long-Range Transmission of Air Pollutants in Europe* (EMEP), XXVII ILM (1988), p 701.
3   *The Basel Convention on the Control of Transboundary Movements of Hazardous Wastes and their Disposal*, 22 March 1989, XXVIII ILM (1989), p 657, Article 19.
4   *Treaty between the United States of America and the Union of Soviet Socialist Republics on the Elimination of their Intermediate-Range and Shorter Range Missiles*, 8 December 1987, XVII ILM (1988), p 90, Article XI (1).
5   *Convention on the Elimination of All Forms of Discrimination against Women*, 18 December 1979, XIX ILM (1980), p 34, Article 17 (1).
6   This distinction is sometimes reflected in the varying use of the expressions 'breach', 'violation', 'non-compliance' and 'non-implementation'. All such words convey the meaning that a state has not acted in a way it should have, at least on first impression. Yet 'breach' and 'violation' connote a blameworthiness in the state that is absent if the failure resulted from an excusable lack of technical or economic resources, for instance, and for which, in diplomatic jargon, 'non-compliance' or 'non-implementation' (or even 'problem of implementation') seems a more appropriate expression.
7   ICJ, *Peace Treaties* case, Reports 1950, p 228.
8   This is, in fact, the normal case. The parties are not bound, in their relations *inter se* with any compulsory third-party mechanism, and negotiations lead nowhere.
9   Action by an individual state seems indefensible under normal rules concerning *locus standi*. On this problem in respect of environmental treaties, cf Martti Koskenniemi, *Breach of Treaty or Non-Compliance? Reflections on the Enforcement of the Montreal Protocol*, 3, *Yearbook of International Environmental Law* (1992), pp 123, 127, 147–149.
10   For instance, the general obligation of parties to the 1985 Vienna Convention on the Ozone Layer (Article 2) is formulated as follows: '1. The Parties shall take appropriate measures ... against adverse effects resulting or likely to result from human activities which modify or are likely to modify the ozone layer ... 2. To this end the Parties shall, in accordance with the means at their disposal and their capabilities ...', XXVI ILM (1987), p 1529.
11   Cf eg Thomas Gehring (1990) *International Environmental Regimes: Dynamic Sectoral Legal Systems*, 1 YbIEL, pp 50–51.

12 Present discussion on 'countermeasures' is based on statements by the International Court of Justice in the *Namibia* (1971), *Hostages* (1980) and *US Military and Paramilitary Activities* (1986) cases, on the *Air Services Agreement* (France – United States) Arbitration (1978). For two recent works in a large literature, cf. Laurence Boisson de Chazournes, *Les contre-mesures dans les rélations internationales économiques* (1992) and Denis Alland, *Justice privée et ordre juridique international* (1994). Cf also draft article 30 of Part I of the International Law Commission's project on state responsibility. YbILC 1979-II/2, pp 115–122.

13 *Vienna Convention on the Law of Treaties*, 23 May 1969. A 'material breach' is defined as '(a) a repudiation of the treaty not sanctioned by the present Convention; or (b) the violation of a provision essential to the accomplishment of the object and purpose of the treaty', Article 60 (3).

14 'One of the fundamental principles governing the international relationship thus [ie through treaty] established is that a party which disowns or does not fulfil its own obligations cannot be recognized as retaining the rights which it claims to derive from the relationship.' ICJ, *Namibia* case, Reports 1971, p 46 (para 91).

15 Cf Bruno Simma, *Does the UN Charter provide an Adequate Legal Basis for Individual or Collective Responses to Violations of Obligations Erga Omnes?*, In Jost Delbrück (ed) (1992) *The Future of International Law Enforcement, New Scenarios – New Law?* p 125.

16 That is, 130 times until 1992. Cf Boisson de Chazournes, supra note 12 pp 71–76, 124–126.

17 Cf SCR 678 (1990) (authorization to use force to compel Iraq to retreat from Kuwait); SCR 836 (1993) (authorization of NATO air support in the territory of former Yugoslavia); SCR 929 (1994) (authorization for states to use force for the fulfilment of humanitarian aims in Rwanda); SCR 940 (1994) (authorization to use force to oust the military government of Haiti).

18 Article 39 of the UN Charter.

19 Eg Article 6 of the UN Charter.

20 Cf Derek Bowett (1982) *The Law of International Institutions*, pp 392–394.

21 Cf Articles 5 and 19 of the UN Charter and Bowett, supra note 20, pp 386–389.

22 Boisson de Chazournes, supra note 12, pp 78–79.

23 Supra note 2.

24 Cf supra note 2.

25 Cf *Protocol to the 1979 Convention on Long-Range Transboundary Air Pollution on the Reduction of Sulphur Emissions or Their Transboundary Fluxes by at least 30 per cent*, XXVII ILM (1988), p 707 and for the new protocol of 1994, cf XXX ILM (1994), p 1540.

26 For a review, cf Kamen Sachariew (1991) *Promoting Compliance with International Environmental Standards: Reflections on Monitoring and Reporting Mechanisms*, 2 YbIEL, pp 34–39 and Patrick Szell (1995) *The Development of Multilateral Mechanisms for Monitoring Compliance* in Lang (ed) *Substainable Development and International Law*, pp 97–113.

27 For instance, the 1959 *Antarctic Treaty* partners are obliged to inform each other of all expeditions conducted and stations established, as well as of all military personnel or equipment introduced in the Antarctica. Text in eg US Arms Control and Disarmament Agency, *Arms Control and Disarmament Agreements* (1990), p 23, Article VII 5. In a 1991 Protocol to the Antarctic Treaty, parties agreed to increase the transparency of their actions by setting up an environmental impact statement procedure whose results are forwarded to a Committee for Environmental Protection and 'made publicly available'. *Protocol on Environment Protection to the Antarctic Treaty*, Article 8 and Annex I, XXX ILM (1991), pp 1461–1486.

28 *Convention on Biological Diversity*, 5 June 1992, text in 3 YbIEL (1992), p 664, Article 26.

29 Ibid, Article 27.

30   Cf note 1 above and generally Koskenniemi, supra note 9, pp 123–162. For the text of the 'Second Sulphur Protocol', cf XXX ILM (1994), p 1540, especially Article 7, (pp 1545–1546).

31   *United Nations Framework Convention on Climate Change*, New York, 9 May 1992, text in 3 YbIEL (1992), p 684, Articles 10 and 12. For the system of review of national communications, cf Report of the Conference of the Parties on its First Session, Berlin 22 March – 7 April 1995, FCCC/CP/1995/7/Add 7, pp 7–11 (Decision 2/CP.1).

32   Article 7(2)(e, f, g), 10.

33   *International Environment. International Agreements are not Well Monitored*, United States General Accounting Office, Report to Congressional Requesters, GAO-RCED-92-43 (January 1992).

34   *Report of the Fifth Meeting of the Implementation Committee Under the Non-Compliance Protocol for the Montreal Protocol*, UNEP OzL.Pro/ImpCom/5/3 (9 March 1993), para 9.

35   Cf *Reports of the Implementation Committee under the Non-Compliance Procedure of the Montreal Protocol on the Work of its Seventh Meeting*, UNEP/OzL.Pro/ImpCom/7/2 (16 November 1993) and its Ninth Meeting, UNEP/Ozl.Pro/ImpCom/9/2 (5 October 1994).

36   *The Convention on the Rights of the Child* was adopted on 20 November 1989 and entered into force on 2 September 1990. As of 30 June 1994, it had 160 parties, the largest number in any international treaty. At its fifth meeting in 1994, the Committee repeated its earlier request to have, aside from more secretarial resources, three annual meetings plus a resource room containing country files at its disposal in order to be able to deal systematically with the massive flow of incoming reports. Cf *Report of the Committee on the Rights of the Child*, A/49/41 (1994), pp 1–3, 5–6, 17, 62–63.

37   *Report of the 13th Session of the Committee on the Elimination of Discrimination against Women*, A/49/38 (1994).

38   Cf *Report of the Human Rights Committee*, GAOR A/49/40 (1994), pp 3, 5 (paras 14–15, 27); *Report of the Fourth Meeting of Persons Chairing the Human Rights Treaty Bodies*, 12–16 October 1992, A/47/628 (10 October 1992), pp 7, 14–16 (paras 19–20, 47–55).

39   Philip Alston (1992) *The Committee on Economic, Social and Cultural Rights*, in Alston (ed) *The United Nations and Human Rights. A Critical Appraisal*, p 491.

40   One attempt to give legal standing to individuals and non-governmental entities is contained in the 1992 *Convention on the Protection of the Marine Environment of North-East Atlantic* which obliges national authorities to make available all information on all their activities that are likely to have an impact on the state of their maritime areas to 'any natural or legal person', Article 9 ('Access to Information'), text in 3 YbIEL (1992), pp 759, 769.

41   Cf discussion below, pp 244–247.

42   Article 90.

43   Cf generally Yves Sandoz, Christophe Swiniarski, Bruno Zimmermann (1987) *Commentary to the Additional protocols of 8 June 1977 to the Geneva Conventions of 12 August 1949*, pp 1037–1052 and Allan Rosas, *International Monitoring Mechanisms in Situations of Armed Conflict*, in Bloed et al (eds) (1993) *Monitoring Human Rights in Europe*, pp 221–246.

44   *Convention on the Prohibition of Military or Any Other Hostile Uses of Environmental Modification Techniques*, 18 May 1977, Article V.2 and Annex; for text, cf XVIILM (1977), p 90.

45   At the 1992 ENMOD Review Conference certain Western states notified that they were considering requesting the convening of this group 'not later than 1995'. Nonetheless, reporting remains seriously deficient, if Patrick Szêll, *Implementation Control: Non-Compliance Procedure and Dispute Settlement in the Ozone Regime*, in Österreichische aussen politische dokumentation, special issue: The Ozone Treaties and their Influence in Building International Environmental Regimes (1996) p 47.

However, other states objected to this and no action has so far been undertaken. UNIDIR Newsletter 21 (1993), pp 60–61.

46 Cf Christiane Burloyannis, *Fact-Finding by the Secretary-General of the United Nations*, 22 NYJ Int'l L and Pol'y (1991), pp 641–669. For a comprehensive review, Thomas M Franck, *Fairness in the International Legal and Institutional System. General Course in Public International Law*, 240 Recueil des cours (1993-III) pp 151–188.

47 *Declaration on Fact-Finding by the United Nations in the Field of Maintenance of International Peace and Security*, UNGA Res 46/59 (9 December 1991), adopted without a vote.

48 Four missions (Belgrade, Kosovo, Sandjak, Vojvodina) were set up in 1992–93 in the territory of the Republic of Yugoslavia (Serbia–Montenegro), but these had to be withdrawn due to a controversy regarding the representation of former Yugoslavia in the CSCE.

49 These have been sent at least to Yugoslavia, Georgia, Moldova (Trans-Dniestria) and Nagorno-Karabakh. Cf Arie Bloed, *Monitoring the CSCE Human Dimension: In Search of its Effectiveness*, in Bloed et al, supra note 43, pp 65–66, 83.

50 Cf Pascal Boniface (1989) *Les sources du désarmement*, pp 108–110.

51 In the case of alleged breaches, states were only entitled to consult or turn to the UN Security Council. *Convention on the Prohibition of the Development, Production and Stockpiling of Bacteriological (Biological) and Toxin Weapons and on their Destruction*, 1972, Articles V-VII. For text, cf XI ILM (1972), p 309.

52 Conference on Confidence- and Security-Building Measures and Disarmament in Europe, 17 January 1984 – 19 September 1986.

53 *Treaty between the United States and the Union of Soviet Socialist Republics on the Elimination of their Intermediate-Range and Shorter-Range Missiles*, Washington, 8 December 1987, and the *Protocol regarding inspections* of the same date, texts in XXVII ILM (1988), pp 90–97 and 190–198.

54 Article X.2. Each party assured the other that it had received the 'basing country's' consent for such inspections, Inspections Protocol, Article II.2. For numbers of annual inspections, cf Article XI.5.

55 *Treaty on Conventional Armed Forces in Europe* plus *Protocol on Inspections*, XXX ILM (1991), pp 6, 52.

56 The absence of entry and exit inspections remains a gaping hole in the system, dictated by the unwillingness of the parties to submit to continuous monitoring entailed by it and its cost. Cf Patricia Lewis, *Verifying the CFE Agreement*, in Stuart Croft (ed) (1994) *The Conventional Armed Forces in Europe Treaty*, pp 184–187.

57 For the text of the Open Skies Treaty, cf SIPRI, SIPRI yearbook 1993: World Armaments and Disarmament (1993), appendix 12c, pp 653–671.

58 Lewis supra note 56, pp 189–193, 196–198.

59 *Treaty on the Non-Proliferation of Nuclear Weapons* (1967). VII ILM (1968), p 809.

60 The expansion of the system to all installations in a state party's territory was under discussion in connection with the Conference that was held in April–May 1995 to consider the 'unlimited and unconditional extension' of the NPT.

61 *Convention on the Prohibition of the Development, Production, Stockpiling and Use of Chemical Weapons and on their Destruction*, 13 January 1993. Text in XXXII ILM (1993), pp 800–873. Cf especially Article VIII (establishment of OPCW).

62 Ibid, Article IX.8.

63 Text in XXVII ILM (1988), pp 1154–1159.

64 Article 1.

65 Articles 2 and 8. In strictly limited 'exceptional circumstances', however, parties may object to particular visits. Article 9.

66 Article 10 (2).

67 Public statement on Turkey, CPT/Inf (93). For a general review of the Committee's activity, cf Jim Murdoch, *The Work of the Council of Europe's Torture Committee*, 5 EJIL (1994), pp 220–248. For commentary, cf Manfred Nowak, Walter Suntinger, *Inter-*

national Mechanisms for the Prevention of Torture, in Bloed et al, supra note 43, pp 149–153.

68   Report of the Working Group on the Draft Optional Protocol to the Convention against Torture and other Cruel, Inhuman or Degrading Treatment or Punishment, E/CN.4/1994/WG.11/WP.3 (28 October 1994).

69   Cf Report of the Conference of the Parties to the Framework Convention on Climate Change on its First Session, Berlin 28 March – 7 April 1995, FCCC/CP/1995/7/Add 1 pp 7–11 (Decision 2/CP.1). The national communications of developed states are to be submitted to review within one year of their receipt by the Secretariat.

70   Cf Koskenniemi, supra note 9, pp 131–132.

71   Non-compliance procedure, 3 YbIEL (1992), p 819 (para 2).

72   Ibid, paras 3 and 7(b).

73   Also, the ILO Secretariat appears to be an indispensable resource in the analysis of country reports and the preparation of draft comments for the members of the Committee of Experts. Virginia A Leary, *Lessons from the Experience of the International Labour Organization*, in Alston supra, note 39, pp 595–602.

74   CERD Articles 11–13, CCPR Articles 41–43.

75   Bloed, supra note 43 p 72. There are six such 'mechanisms': 1. the Berlin emergency mechanism (June 1991); 2. the Vienna mechanism for unusual military activities (November 1990); 3. the Valletta mechanism for the peaceful settlement of disputes (January 1991, amended in October/December 1992); 4. the Helsinki provisions on early warning and preventive action mechanisms; 5. the Vienna Human Dimension mechanism (1989); 6. the Moscow Human Dimension mechanism (1991). Cf CSCE, *Mechanisms and Procedures, A Consolidated Text* (1994). By May 1994, the first two mechanisms had been used three times. The Valletta mechanism has never been used and it seems unlikely that it will be used. Nor have the 1992 Helsinki provisions on early warning and preventive action been formally utilized.

76   The one situation being an Austrian complaint against Turkey. Bloed, supra, note 43 pp 725. Cf also A Bloed and P van Dijk, *The Human Dimension of the Helsinki Process* (1991), pp 77–88 and *passim*.

77   In the C/OSCE, they have been integrated into those parts of its review conferences which deal with human rights. Cf CSCE *Helsinki Document: The Challenges of Change*, Part IV (1992) and CSCE *Budapest Document: Towards a Genuine Partnership in a New Era* (1994), Chapter VIII (The Human Dimension), para 17.

78   Summary results of the Proceeding Concerning the Inquiry on Turkey, Report of the Committee against Torture, A/48/44/Add 1 (1994), p 7 (para 38).

79   Outside treaty procedures, the UN Commission on Human Rights has, since 1979, developed the procedure embedded in resolution 1503 (1972) into a mechanism of response to complaints by individuals about the behaviour of governments in situations forming 'a consistent pattern of gross and reliably attested violations of human rights'. Despite the confidentiality of this procedure, the names of the countries under review are nowadays published and the relevant documents and other information regularly leaked to outsiders and the press. Cf generally Philip Alston, *The Commission on Human Rights*, in Alston, supra, note 39, pp 138–181.

80   There is a very large literature on the individual complaints systems under these three Conventions. For a brief, general comparison and assessment, cf Rein Müllerson, *The Efficiency of Individual Complaint Procedures: The Experience of CCPR, CERD, CAT and ECHR*, in Bloed supra, note 43, pp 25–43. Out of 127 parties to the CCPR in 1994, 77 had accepted the Optional Protocol. The figures at the end of 1992 for the CERD and the CAT were, respectively, 132/16 and 66/28.

81   Altogether 201 communications were declared inadmissible, 94 were discontinued or withdrawn, 31 were pending and 68 were at the pre-admissibility stage. Report of the Human Rights Committee, Vol I A/49/40 (1994), p 63 (para 377).

82   European Commission of Human Rights, Survey of Activities and Statistics (1993) p 21.

83 Protocol 11 to the European Convention on Human Rights and Fundamental Freedoms. For text and commentary, cf XXXIII ILM (1994) pp 943–967. As the Protocol will enter into force only after *all* the parties to the ECHR have ratified it, it is not expected that this will be before the year 2000.

84 *International Tropical Timber Agreement*, XXXIII ILM (1994), pp 1014–1041, Articles 31 and 44.

85 Cf eg *Treaty on the Non-Proliferation of Nuclear Weapons*, supra note 59, Article VIII.3. *Convention on the Prohibition of the Development, Production or Stockpiling of Bacteriological (Biological) and Toxin Weapons and their Destruction*, supra note 51, Article XII.

86 The Budapest Document ('Towards Genuine Partnership in a New Era'), Chapter VIII, para 5. The OSCE human rights commitments are submitted to a regular 'human dimension review' that takes place in specialized Human Dimension Meetings (actually Seminars) in accordance with the decision of the OSCE Follow-Up Meeting in Helsinki 1992 and Budapest 1994. Ten such seminars have been held, the latest in Warsaw on 28 Nov–1 Dec 1995. For the results, if OSCE, *Human Dimension Seminar on the Rule of Law, Consolidated Summary*, OD/65/95 (20 December 1995).

87 The otherwise applicable consensus principle can be set aside by a 'consensus-minus-one' procedure in the CSCE Council or the CSO (now Permanent Council) in cases of 'clear, gross and uncorrected violations' of human dimension commitments. Cf *Prague Document on Further Development of CSCE Institutions and Structures, Prague Meeting of CSCE Council*, January 1992 (Helsinki Monitor 1992–1992, pp 71–77). Its use against great powers is, however, politically problematic.

88 Cf *Convention for the Protection of the Marine Environment of the North-East Atlantic*, 3 YbIEL (1992) Article 23 ('Compliance') p 779; cf also *Convention on Climate Change*, supra note 31, Article 7(2).

89 Such action may include 'Suspension, in accordance with the applicable rules of international law concerning the suspension of the operation of a Treaty, of specific rights and privileges under the Protocol . . .', cf Montreal non-compliance procedure, supra note 71, p 820.

90 Cf generally Koskenniemi, supra note 9. In 1995, five countries from former Eastern Europe (Belarus, Bulgaria, Poland, Russia and Ukraine) invoked the non-compliance procedure for the first time and in respect of themselves asking for a five-year grace period to enable them to comply with their reduction commitments. The Committee dealt with each request separately and produced recommendations thereon to the 7th meeting of the Parties held in Vienna on 5–7 December 1995. Cf UNEP/OzL.Pro.7/Decision VII/13–17. For a recent analysis, cf David G Victor, *The Montreal Protocol's Non-Compliance Procedure: Lessons for Making Other International Environmental Agreements More Effective*, a paper distributed at a workshop held in connection with the above meeting. The Workshop Report is distributed as UNEP/OzL.Pro.7/INF.1 (6 December 1995).

91 Article 10 (2) (a, b). According to the preparatory works for the first Conference of the Parties (COP) to the Climate Treaty, the SBI's function in the examination of reports would be to 'advise the COP on matters related to the consideration of information in national communications', INC, A/AC 237/WG 1/L 21, p 9. Cf also comments in Daniel Bodansky, *Managing Climate Change*, 3 YbIEL (1992), p 72. For the decisions of the COP in 1995, cf at note 69 above.

92 ILO Constitution, Article 33.

93 Cf Virginia A Leary, *Lessons from the Experience of the International Labour Organization* in Alston, supra note 39, pp 595–602.

94 Vojin Dimitrijevic, *The Monitoring of Human Rights and the Prevention of Human Rights Violations through Reporting Procedures*, in Bloed et al, supra note 43, p 22.

95 Eg Thomas Gehring, *International Environmental Regimes: Dynamic Sectoral Systems*, 1 YbIEL (1990), pp 50–54.

96 Under its Rules of Procedure, the Convention on the Elimination of Racial Discrimination (CERD) may make a determination that a state party has not discharged its obligations and relate its suggestions and comments directly to that failure. The Committee has so far refrained from making such determinations.

97 CERD Article 9 (2). To the same effect, CAT Article 19 (4). Cf also CCPR Article 40 (4) which reads 'It [i.e. the Human Rights Committee] shall transmit its reports, and such general comments as it may consider appropriate, to the States Parties'. CEDAW remains silent on what the Committee may do with the reports, Article 18.

98 Cf Torkel Opsahl, *The Human Rights Committee* in Alston, supra note 39, pp 407–410, 416–417.

99 Cf *Report of the Human Rights Committee*, Vol I, A/49/40 (1994), pp 19–61.

100 Cf *Report of the Fifth Session of the Committee on the Rights of the Child*, A/49/41 (1994), pp 20–61; CEDAW, *Report of the 13th Session*, A/49/38 (1994), p 144 (paras 812–817).

101 Report of the Human Rights Committee, A/49/40 (1994), pp 84–87.

102 Article 22 of the CESCR, cf also General Comment No 2 of the ESCR Committee, adopted at its fourth session in 1990, on international technical assistance measures in HRI/GEN/1/Rev 1, pp 45–48. Cf further Bruno Simma, *Die internationale Kontrolle des VN-Paktes über wirtschaftliche, soziale und kulturelle Rechte: neue Entwicklungen* in Beyerlin, Boethe, Hoffman, Petersmann (eds), *Recht zwischen Umbruch und Bewahrung. Festschrift für Rudolf Bernhardt* (1995), pp 579–593.

103 Cf Report of the Implementation Committee under the Non-Compliance Procedure for the Montreal Protocol on the Work of its Ninth Meeting, UNEP/Ozl.Pro/ImpCom/9/2 (5 October 1994), paras 5–17.

104 Cf also Martti Koskenniemi, in Lang, supra note 26, pp 91–6.

105 Some of this strategy is visible in the human rights treaty bodies' practice of adopting 'general comments', or interpretative statements on the provisions of their constitutive treaties. Up to 1994, the Human Rights Committee had adopted 23 General Comments, while the respective numbers of such statements by the Economic, Social and Cultural Rights Committee, the Racial Discrimination Committee and the Committee on Discrimination against Women was 4, 18 and 20. Cf *Compilation of General Comments and General Recommendations Adopted by Human Rights Treaty Bodies*, UN Document HRI/GEN/1/Rev 1 (29 July 1994).

106 Judge Sir Robert Jennings (1992) *The Role of the International Court of Justice in the Development of International Environment Protection Law*, 1, Review of European Community & International Environmental Law, p 242.

15 THE ROLE OF NON-STATE ACTORS

1 Levi, Warner (1991) *Contemporary International Law: A Concise Introduction* Westview Press, Boulder at pp 72–74.

2 Wirth, David (Winter 1992) 'A Matchmaker's Challenge: Marrying International Law and American Environmental Law' *Virginia Journal of International Law*; Shepard, Daniel (1994) 'UN Seeks Experts' Testimony in Series of Extraordinary Hearings on Development' *Earth Times*, 15 June; Leonard, Paula and Hoffman, Walter (1990) *Effective Global Environmental Protection: World Federalist Proposals to Strengthen the Role of the United Nations*, pp 16–17.

3 'The Annual Meeting of the IMF and World Bank' *News and Notices*, International Financial Institutions Accountability Project, Bread for the World Institute, Silver Spring, Md, 14 November 1994.

4 Salamon, Lester M 'The Rise of the Nonprofit Sector' *Foreign Affairs*, July/August 1994 at 109:111. See also, Fisher, Julie *The Road from Rio: Sustainable Development and the Nongovernmental Movement in the Third World* (Westport, Connecticut, Praeger, 1993).

5   Spiro, Peter J (1995) 'New Global Communities: Nongovernmental Organizations in International Decisionmaking Institutions' *The Washington Quarterly*, Winter 1995, p 47.

6   Section III (Chapters 23–32) Agenda 21. UN Conference on Environmental Development (UNCED) at Rio de Janeiro, UN Doc A/C 151/26 (1992).

7   Benedick, Richard E (1991) *Ozone Diplomacy* 6; Greenpeace International, *Beyond UNCED* (Amsterdam, 1992); Zarocostas, John 'Earth Summit at Odds Over Issue of Multinationals' *Journal of Commerce*, 6 April 1992; Schmidheiny, Stephan with the Business Council for Sustainable Development (1992) *Changing Course* (Cambridge, Massachusetts, The MIT Press).

8   'Constructive Industry Hits INC 10' *ECO*, Climate Negotiations, Geneva, 26 August 1994.

9   'Parliamentarians for Global Action' brochure; 'Global Legislators Organization for a Balanced Environment', Activity Report, 103rd Congress.

10 'Meeting of Multinational Group of Parliamentarians Involved in Oversight of the IMF and the World Bank' *News and Notices*, International Financial Institution Accountability Project, Bread for the World Institute, Silver Spring, Md, 19 December 1994.

11 Hinrichsen, Don (1992) 'The Earth Summit' in Amicus, J, Winter 1992 at p 15.

12 Randolph, Kate, Coordinator, NGO Planning Committee for ICPD, private communication, 18 October 1994; Clough, Michael (1994) 'Grass-Roots Policy-making: Say Good-Bye to the "Wise Men"' *Foreign Affairs*, January/February.

13 Sessions, Kathryn G 'Options for NGO Participation in the Commission on Sustainable Development' UNA-USA Background Paper, Washington, DC, May 1993.

14 Ayoub, Ferita, Chief of NGO Section, Department of Policy Coordination and Sustainable Development, United Nations, New York, private communication, 24 August 1994.

15 'The NGO Steering Committee to the Commission on Sustainable Development', memorandum, New York, 5 June 1994.

16 Earth Council, NRDC, and WRI, 'Directory of National Commissions on Sustainable Development', Washington, DC, May 1994; Earth Summit Watch (1994) *Four in '94. Assessing National Actions to Implement Agenda 21: A Country-by-Country Report* (Washington, DC).

17 Earth Council, Natural Resources Defence Council (NRDC) and World Resources Institute, supra note 16.

18 Silveira, Diomar, Earth Council, San José, Costa Rica, private communication, 29 June 1995.

19 'Key Issues for the Open-Ended Working Group on the Review of Arrangements for Consultation with Non-Governmental Organizations', submitted by an *ad hoc* committee of NGOs, 23 June 1994.

20 Kakabadse Ni, Yolanda with Burns, Sarah 'Movers and Shapers: NGOs in International Affairs' *International Perspectives on Sustainability*, WRI, Washington, DC, May 1994; Stanley Foundation, 'The UN System and NGOs: New Relationships for a New Era?' Report of the Twenty-Fifth United Nations Issues Conference, Harriman, NY, 18–20 February 1994; Wiseberg, Laurie S 'Consultative Status Review Stalled', *Tribune des Droits Humains*, June–July 1995.

21 *Eco* is produced regularly by NGOs at major international negotiations. The *Earth Times* is published by the Earth Times Foundation of New York, NY. The *Earth Negotiations Bulletin* is published by the International Institute for Sustainable Development of Winnipeg, Manitoba.

22 Earth Summit Watch, *One Year After Rio: Special First Edition* (New York, NRDC, June 1993); Earth Summit Watch, supra note 16; '1995 Earth Summit Watch Survey', unpublished memorandum.

23 Commonwealth Sustainable Futures Group (February 1994) *The People's Treaties from the Earth Summit* (2nd edn) (Bolinas, California, Common Knowledge Press).

24 For a discussion of the GATT dispute resolution procedure, see Steve Charnovitz 'Dolphins and Tuna: An Analysis of the Second GATT Panel Report' *Environmental Law Reporter*, October 1994.

25 Zarocostas, John (1994) 'Environmental Proposal for WTO Met Coolly' *Journal of Commerce*, 19 September 1994; James Cameron and Ross Ramsay, 'Participation by Non-Governmental Organizations in the World Trade Organization', Global Environment and Trade Study, undated.

26 World Bank, Operational Manual Section BP 17.50 – Disclosure of Operational Information (September 1993).

27 World Bank (1993) *Operations Inspection Function: Objectives, Mandate and Operating Procedures for an Independent Inspection Panel.*

28 Bramble, Barbara 'World Bank Reforms: The Beginnings of Accountability' in *Citizens Network for Sustainable Development Newsletter*, October–November 1993 at p 31.

29 Friends of the Earth 'The IMF: Why the Secrecy?', unpublished statement.

30 Conference Report to Accompany HR 4426, Making Appropriations for the Foreign Operations, Export Financing, and Related Programmes for the Fiscal Year Ending 30 September 1995, 103rd Congress, US House of Representatives, 1 August 1994.

31 The importance of participatory approaches to project success from Operations Evaluation Department, *Evaluation Results for 1991* (Washington, DC, World Bank, 1993), and from Bhuvan Bhatnagar and Aubrey C Williams (eds) *Participatory Development and the World Bank: Potential Directions for Change* (Washington, DC, World Bank Discussion Papers, 1992); Nancy Alexander, Bread for the World Institute, private communication, 20 October 1994; Jo Marie Griesgraber (ed) *Rethinking Bretton Woods: Toward Equitable, Sustainable, and Participatory Development* (Washington, DC, Center of Concern, 1994); UNDP 'UNDP and Organizations of Civil Society', prepared for the public events marking the 50th anniversary of the UN Charter, San Francisco, June 1995; 'The World Bank and Participation', Report to the Board of the World Bank, 25 August 1994, including NGO Addendum.

32 UNDP/GEF 'Environmental Funds: The First Five Years', A Preliminary Analysis for the OECD/DAC Working Party on Development Assistance and the Environment, April 1995.

33 Dillenbeck, Mark IUCN-US, Washington, DC, 'National Environmental Funds: A New Mechanism for Conservation Finance', 20 May 1994.

34 Frederich Ebert Foundation, *United Nations: World Hearings on Development: Expressing a Need for Change and Reform*, UN Document No A/49/320, 22 August 1994, Reprinted with the permission of the United Nations.

35 French, Hilary F *Partnership for the Planet: An Environmental Agenda for the United Nations*, Worldwatch Paper 126 (Washington, DC, Worldwatch Institute, July 1995); Esty, Daniel C 'GATTing the Greens' *Foreign Affairs*, November/December 1993; Esty, Daniel C 'The Case for a Global Environmental Organization', in Kenen, Peter B (ed) *Managing the World Economy: Fifty Years After Bretton Woods* (Washington, DC, Institute for International Economics, 1994).

36 Joyce, James Avery (1980) *World Labor Rights and Their Protection* (Croom Helm, London); Charnovitz, Steve 'Improving Environmental and Trade Governance', *International Environmental Affairs*, Winter 1995.

37 Commission on Global Governance, *Our Global Neighbourhood* (Oxford University Press, Oxford, 1995); Erskine Childers with Brian Urquhart, (1994) *Renewing the United Nations System* (Uppsala, Sweden, Dag Hammarkjöld Foundation).

APPENDIX 1: AGENDA 21 (EXTRACT)

Distr. GENERAL

A/CONF.151/26 (Vol. III)
14 August 1992

ORIGINAL: ENGLISH

REPORT OF THE UNITED NATIONS CONFERENCE
ON ENVIRONMENT AND DEVELOPMENT

(Rio de Janeiro, 3–14 June 1992)

SECTION IV. MEANS OF IMPLEMENTATION

Chapter 33

FINANCIAL RESOURCES AND MECHANISMS

INTRODUCTION

33.1.   The General Assembly, in resolution 44/228 of 22 December 1989, inter alia, decided that the United Nations Conference on Environment and Development should:

Identify ways and means of providing new and additional financial resources, particularly to developing countries, for environmentally sound development programmes and projects in accordance with national development objectives, priorities and plans and to consider ways of effectively monitoring the provision of such new and additional financial resources, particularly to developing countries, so as to enable the international community to take further appropriate action on the basis of accurate and reliable data;

Identify ways and means of providing additional financial resources for measures directed towards solving major environmental problems of global concern and especially of supporting those countries, in particular developing countries, for which the implementation of such measures would entail a special or abnormal burden, owing, in particular, to their lack of financial resources, expertise or technical capacity;

Consider various funding mechanisms, including voluntary ones, and examine the possibility of a special international fund and other innovative approaches, with a view to ensuring, on a favourable basis, the most effective and expeditious transfer of environmentally sound technologies to developing countries;

Quantify the financial requirements for the successful implementation of Conference decisions and recommendations and identify possible sources, including innovative ones, of additional resources.

33.2. This chapter deals with the financing of the implementation of Agenda 21, which reflects a global consensus integrating environmental considerations into an accelerated development process. For each of the other chapters, the secretariat of the Conference has provided indicative estimates of the total costs of implementation for developing countries and the requirements for grant or other concessional financing needed from the international community. These reflect the need for a substantially increased effort, both by countries themselves and by the international community.

BASIS FOR ACTION

33.3. Economic growth, social development and poverty eradication are the first and overriding priorities in developing countries and are themselves essential to meeting national and global sustainability objectives. In the light of the global benefits to be realized by the implementation of Agenda 21 as a whole, the provision to developing countries of effective means, inter alia, financial resources and technology, without which it will be difficult for them to fully implement their commitments, will serve the common interests of developed and developing countries and of humankind in general, including future generations.

33.4. The cost of inaction could outweigh the financial costs of implementing Agenda 21. Inaction will narrow the choices of future generations.

33.5. For dealing with environmental issues, special efforts will be required. Global and local environmental issues are interrelated. The United Nations Framework Convention on Climate Change and the Convention on Biological Diversity address two of the most important global issues.

33.6. Economic conditions, both domestic and international, that encourage free trade and access to markets will help make economic growth and environmental protection mutually supportive for all countries, particularly for developing countries and countries undergoing the process of transition to a market economy (see chapter 2 for a fuller discussion of these issues).

33.7. International cooperation for sustainable development should also be strengthened in order to support and complement the efforts of developing countries, particularly the least developed countries.

33.8. All countries should assess how to translate Agenda 21 into national policies and programmes through a process that will integrate environment and development considerations. National and local priorities should be established by means that include public participation and community involvement, promoting equal opportunity for men and women.

33.9. For an evolving partnership among all countries of the world, including, in particular, between developed and developing countries, sustainable development strategies and enhanced and predictable levels of funding in support of longer term objectives are required. For that purpose, developing countries should articulate their own priority actions and needs for support and developed countries should commit themselves to addressing these priorities. In this respect, consultative groups and round tables and other nationally based mechanisms can play a facilitative role.

33.10. The implementation of the huge sustainable development programmes of Agenda 21 will require the provision to developing countries of substantial new and additional financial resources. Grant or concessional financing should be provided according to sound and equitable criteria and indicators. The progressive implementation of Agenda 21 should be matched by the provision of such necessary financial resources. The initial phase will be accelerated by substantial early commitments of concessional funding.

OBJECTIVES

33.11. The objectives are as follows:

(a) To establish measures concerning financial resources and mechanisms for the implementation of Agenda 21;

(b) To provide new and additional financial resources that are both adequate and predictable;

(c) To seek full use and continuing qualitative improvement of funding mechanisms to be utilized for the implementation of Agenda 21.

ACTIVITIES

33.12. Fundamentally, the activities of this chapter are related to the implementation of all the other chapters of Agenda 21.

MEANS OF IMPLEMENTATION

33.13. In general, the financing for the implementation of Agenda 21 will come from a country's own public and private sectors. For developing countries, particularly the least developed countries, ODA is a main source of external funding, and substantial new and additional funding for sustainable development and implementation of Agenda 21 will be required. Developed countries reaffirm their commitments to reach the accepted United Nations target of 0.7 per cent of GNP for ODA and, to the extent that they have not yet achieved that target, agree to augment their aid programmes in order to reach that target as soon as possible and to ensure prompt and effective implementation of Agenda 21. Some countries have agreed to reach the target by the year 2000. It was decided that the Commission on Sustainable Development would regularly review and monitor progress towards this target. This review process should systematically combine the monitoring of the implementation of Agenda 21 with a review of the financial resources available. Those countries that have already reached the target are to be commended and encouraged to continue to contribute to the common effort to make available the substantial additional resources that have to be mobilized. Other developed countries, in line with their support for reform efforts in developing countries, agree to make their best efforts to increase their level of ODA. In this context, the importance of equitable burden-sharing among developed countries is recognized. Other countries, including those undergoing the process of transition to a market economy, may voluntarily augment the contributions of the developed countries.

33.14. Funding for Agenda 21 and other outcomes of the Conference should be provided in a way that maximizes the availability of new and additional resources and uses all available funding sources and mechanisms. These include, among others:

(a)   The multilateral development banks and funds:

(i)   The International Development Association (IDA). Among the various issues and options that IDA deputies will examine in connection with the forthcoming tenth replenishment of IDA, the statement made by the President of the World Bank at the United Nations Conference on Environment and Development should be given special consideration in order to help the poorest countries meet their sustainable development objectives as contained in Agenda 21;

(ii)   Regional and subregional development banks. The regional and subregional development banks and funds should play an increased and more effective role in providing resources on concessional or other favourable terms needed to implement Agenda 21;

(iii)   The Global Environment Facility, managed jointly by the World Bank, UNDP and UNEP, whose additional grant and concessional funding is designed to achieve global environmental benefits, should cover the agreed incremental costs of relevant activities under Agenda 21, in particular for developing countries. Therefore, it should be restructured so as to, inter alia:

Encourage universal participation;

Have sufficient flexibility to expand its scope and coverage to relevant programme areas of Agenda 21, with global environmental benefits, as agreed;

Ensure a governance that is transparent and democratic in nature, including in terms of decision-making and operations, by guaranteeing a balanced and equitable representation of the interests of developing countries and giving due weight to the funding efforts of donor countries;

Ensure new and additional financial resources on grant and concessional terms, in particular to developing countries;

Ensure predictability in the flow of funds by contributions from developed countries, taking into account the importance of equitable burden-sharing;

Ensure access to and disbursement of the funds under mutually agreed criteria without introducing new forms of conditionality;

(b) The relevant specialized agencies, other United Nations bodies and other international organizations, which have designated roles to play in supporting national Governments in implementing Agenda 21;

(c) Multilateral institutions for capacity-building and technical cooperation. Necessary financial resources should be provided to UNDP to use its network of field offices and its broad mandate and experience in the field of technical cooperation for facilitating capacity-building at the country level, making full use of the expertise of the specialized agencies and other United Nations bodies within their respective areas of competence, in particular UNEP and including the multilateral and regional development banks;

(d) Bilateral assistance programmes. These programmes will need to be strengthened in order to promote sustainable development;

(e) Debt relief. It is important to achieve durable solutions to the debt problems of low- and middle-income developing countries in order to provide them with the needed means for sustainable development. Measures to address the continuing debt problems of low- and middle-income countries should be kept under review. All creditors in the Paris Club should promptly implement the agreement of December 1991 to provide debt relief for the poorest heavily indebted countries pursuing structural adjustment; debt relief measures should be kept under review so as to address the continuing difficulties of those countries;

(f) Private funding. Voluntary contributions through non-governmental channels, which have been running at about 10 per cent of ODA, might be increased.

33.15. Investment. Mobilization of higher levels of foreign direct investment and technology transfers should be encouraged through national policies that promote investment and through joint ventures and other modalities.

33.16. Innovative financing. New ways of generating new public and private financial resources should be explored, in particular:

(a) Various forms of debt relief, apart from official or Paris Club debt, including greater use of debt swaps;

(b) The use of economic and fiscal incentives and mechanisms;

(c) The feasibility of tradeable permits;

(d) New schemes for fund-raising and voluntary contributions through private channels, including non-governmental organizations;

(e) The reallocation of resources at present committed to military purposes.

33.17. A supportive international and domestic economic climate conducive to sustained economic growth and development is important, particularly for developing countries, in order to achieve sustainability.

33.18. The secretariat of the Conference has estimated the average annual costs (1993-2000) of implementing in developing countries the activities in Agenda 21 to be over $600 billion, including about $125 billion on grant or concessional terms from the international community. These are indicative and order-of-magnitude estimates only, and have not been reviewed by Governments. Actual costs will depend upon, inter alia, the specific strategies and programmes Governments decide upon for implementation.

33.19. Developed countries and others in a position to do so should make initial financial commitments to give effect to the decisions of the Conference. They should report on such plans and commitments to the United Nations General Assembly at its forty-seventh session, in 1992.

33.20. Developing countries should also begin to draw up national plans for sustainable development to give effect to the decisions of the Conference.

33.21. Review and monitoring of the financing of Agenda 21 is essential. Questions related to the effective follow-up of the Conference are discussed in chapter 38 (International institutional arrangements). It will be important to review on a regular basis the adequacy of funding and mechanisms, including efforts to reach agreed objectives of the present chapter, including targets where applicable.

Chapter 38

INTERNATIONAL INSTITUTIONAL ARRANGEMENTS

BASIS FOR ACTION

38.1. The mandate of the United Nations Conference on Environment and Development emanates from General Assembly resolution 44/228, in which the Assembly, inter alia, affirmed that the Conference should elaborate strategies and measures to halt and reverse the effects of environmental degradation in the context of increased national and international efforts to promote sustainable and environmentally sound development in all countries and that the promotion of economic growth in developing countries is essential to address problems of environmental degradation. The intergovernmental follow-up to the Conference process shall be within the framework of the United Nations system, with the General Assembly being the supreme policy-making forum that would provide overall guidance to Governments, the United Nations system and relevant treaty bodies. At the same time, Governments, as well as regional economic and technical cooperation organizations, have a responsibility to play an important role in the follow-up to the Conference. Their commitments and actions should be adequately supported by the United Nations system and multilateral financial institutions. Thus, national and international efforts would mutually benefit from one another.

38.2. In fulfilling the mandate of the Conference, there is a need for institutional arrangements within the United Nations system in conformity with, and providing input into, the restructuring and revitalization of the United Nations in the economic, social and related fields, and the overall reform of the United Nations, including ongoing changes in the Secretariat. In the spirit of reform and revitalization of the United Nations system, implementation of Agenda 21 and other conclusions of the Conference shall be based on an action- and result-oriented approach and consistent with the principles of universality, democracy, transparency, cost-effectiveness and accountability.

38.3. The United Nations system, with its multisectoral capacity and the extensive experience of a number of specialized agencies in various spheres of international cooperation in the field of environment and development, is uniquely positioned to assist Governments to establish more effective patterns of economic and social development with a view to achieving the objectives of Agenda 21 and sustainable development.

38.4. All agencies of the United Nations system have a key role to play in the implementation of Agenda 21 within their respective competence. To ensure proper coordination and avoid duplication in the implementation of Agenda 21, there should be an effective division of labour between various parts of the United Nations system based on their terms of reference and comparative advantages. Member States, through relevant governing bodies, are in a position to ensure that these tasks are carried out properly. In order to facilitate evaluation of agencies' performance and promote knowledge of their activities, all bodies of the United Nations system should be required to elaborate and publish reports of their activities concerning the implementation of Agenda 21 on a regular basis. Serious and continuous reviews of their policies, programmes, budgets and activities will also be required.

38.5. The continued active and effective participation of non-governmental organizations, the scientific community and the private sector, as well as local groups and communities, are important in the implementation of Agenda 21.

38.6. The institutional structure envisaged below will be based on agreement on financial resources and mechanisms, technology transfer, the Rio Declaration and Agenda 21. In addition, there has to be an effective link between substantive action and financial support, and this requires close and effective cooperation and exchange of information between the United Nations system and the multilateral financial institutions for the follow-up of Agenda 21 within the institutional arrangement.

OBJECTIVES

38.7. The overall objective is the integration of environment and development issues at national, subregional, regional and international levels, including in the United Nations system institutional arrangements.

38.8. Specific objectives shall be:

(a) To ensure and review the implementation of Agenda 21 so as to achieve sustainable development in all countries;

(b) To enhance the role and functioning of the United Nations system in the field of environment and development. All relevant agencies, organizations and programmes of the United Nations system should adopt concrete programmes for the implementation of Agenda 21 and also provide policy guidance for United Nations activities or advice to Governments, upon request, within their areas of competence;

(c) To strengthen cooperation and coordination on environment and development in the United Nations system;

(d)   To encourage interaction and cooperation between the United Nations system and other intergovernmental and non-governmental subregional, regional and global institutions and non-governmental organizations in the field of environment and development;

(e)   To strengthen institutional capabilities and arrangements required for the effective implementation, follow-up and review of Agenda 21;

(f)   To assist in the strengthening and coordination of national, subregional and regional capacities and actions in the areas of environment and development;

(g)   To establish effective cooperation and exchange of information between United Nations organs, organizations, programmes and the multilateral financial bodies, within the institutional arrangements for the follow-up of Agenda 21;

(h)   To respond to continuing and emerging issues relating to environment and development;

(i)   To ensure that any new institutional arrangements would support revitalization, clear division of responsibilities and the avoidance of duplication in the United Nations system and depend to the maximum extent possible upon existing resources.

INSTITUTIONAL STRUCTURE

A.   *General Assembly*

38.9.   The General Assembly, as the highest intergovernmental mechanism, is the principal policy-making and appraisal organ on matters relating to the follow-up of the Conference. The Assembly would organize a regular review of the implementation of Agenda 21. In fulfilling this task, the Assembly could consider the timing, format and organizational aspects of such a review. In particular, the Assembly could consider holding a special session not later than 1997 for the overall review and appraisal of Agenda 21, with adequate preparations at a high level.

B.   *Economic and Social Council*

38.10.   The Economic and Social Council, in the context of its role under the Charter vis-a-vis the General Assembly and the ongoing restructuring and revitalization of the United Nations in the economic, social and related fields, would assist the General Assembly by overseeing system-wide coordination in the implementation of Agenda 21 and making recommendations in this regard. In addition, the Council would undertake the task of directing system-wide coordination and integration of environmental and developmental aspects of United Nations policies and programmes and would make appropriate recommendations to the General Assembly, specialized agencies concerned and Member States. Appropriate steps should be taken to obtain regular reports from specialized agencies on their plans and programmes related to the implementation of Agenda 21, pursuant to Article 64 of the Charter of the United Nations. The Economic and Social Council should organize a periodic review of the work of the Commission on Sustainable Development envisaged in paragraph 38.11, as well as of system-wide activities to integrate environment and development, making full use of its high-level and coordination segments.

C. *Commission on Sustainable Development*

38.11. In order to ensure the effective follow-up of the Conference, as well as to enhance international cooperation and rationalize the intergovernmental decision-making capacity for the integration of environment and development issues and to examine the progress in the implementation of Agenda 21 at the national, regional and international levels, a high-level Commission on Sustainable Development should be established in accordance with Article 68 of the Charter of the United Nations. This Commission would report to the Economic and Social Council in the context of the Council's role under the Charter vis-à-vis the General Assembly. It would consist of representatives of States elected as members with due regard to equitable geographical distribution. Representatives of non-member States of the Commission would have observer status. The Commission should provide for the active involvement of organs, programmes and organizations of the United Nations system, international financial institutions and other relevant intergovernmental organizations, and encourage the participation of non-governmental organizations, including industry and the business and scientific communities. The first meeting of the Commission should be convened no later than 1993. The Commission should be supported by the secretariat envisaged in paragraph 38.19. Meanwhile the Secretary-General of the United Nations is requested to ensure adequate interim administrative secretariat arrangements.

38.12. The General Assembly, at its forty-seventh session, should determine specific organizational modalities for the work of this Commission, such as its membership, its relationship with other intergovernmental United Nations bodies dealing with matters related to environment and development, and the frequency, duration and venue of its meetings. These modalities should take into account the ongoing process of revitalization and restructuring of the work of the United Nations in the economic, social and related fields, in particular measures recommended by the General Assembly in resolutions 45/264 of 13 May 1991 and 46/235 of 13 April 1992 and other relevant Assembly resolutions. In this respect, the Secretary-General of the United Nations, with the assistance of the Secretary-General of the United Nations Conference on Environment and Development, is requested to prepare for the Assembly a report with appropriate recommendations and proposals.

38.13. The Commission on Sustainable Development should have the following functions:

(a) To monitor progress in the implementation of Agenda 21 and activities related to the integration of environmental and developmental goals throughout the United Nations system through analysis and evaluation of reports from all relevant organs, organizations, programmes and institutions of the United Nations system dealing with various issues of environment and development, including those related to finance;

(b) To consider information provided by Governments, including, for example, information in the form of periodic communications or national reports regarding the activities they undertake to implement Agenda 21, the problems they face, such as problems related to financial resources and technology transfer, and other environment and development issues they find relevant;

(c) To review the progress in the implementation of the commitments contained in Agenda 21, including those related to provision of financial resources and transfer of technology;

(d)   To receive and analyse relevant input from competent non-governmental organizations, including the scientific and private sectors, in the context of the overall implementation of Agenda 21;

(e)   To enhance the dialogue, within the framework of the United Nations, with non-governmental organizations and the independent sector, as well as other entities outside the United Nations system;

(f)   To consider, where appropriate, information regarding the progress made in the implementation of environmental conventions, which could be made available by the relevant Conferences of Parties;

(g)   To provide appropriate recommendations to the General Assembly through the Economic and Social Council on the basis of an integrated consideration of the reports and issues related to the implementation of Agenda 21;

(h)   To consider, at an appropriate time, the results of the review to be conducted expeditiously by the Secretary-General of all recommendations of the Conference for capacity-building programmes, information networks, task forces and other mechanisms to support the integration of environment and development at regional and subregional levels.

38.14.   Within the intergovernmental framework, consideration should be given to allowing non-governmental organizations, including those related to major groups, particularly women's groups, committed to the implementation of Agenda 21 to have relevant information available to them, including information, reports and other data produced within the United Nations system.

D.   *The Secretary-General*

38.15.   Strong and effective leadership on the part of the Secretary-General is crucial, since he/she would be the focal point of the institutional arrangements within the United Nations system for the successful follow-up to the Conference and for the implementation of Agenda 21.

E.   *High-level inter-agency coordination mechanism*

38.16.   Agenda 21, as the basis for action by the international community to integrate environment and development, should provide the principal framework for coordination of relevant activities within the United Nations system. To ensure effective monitoring, coordination and supervision of the involvement of the United Nations system in the follow-up to the Conference, there is a need for a coordination mechanism under the direct leadership of the Secretary-General.

38.17.   This task should be given to the   Administrative Committee on Coordination (ACC), headed by the Secretary-General. ACC would thus provide a vital link and interface between the multilateral financial institutions and other United Nations bodies at the highest administrative level. The Secretary-General should continue to revitalize the functioning of the Committee. All heads of agencies and institutions of the United Nations system shall be expected to cooperate with the Secretary-General fully in order to make ACC work effectively in fulfilling its crucial role and ensure successful implementation of Agenda 21. ACC should consider establishing a special task force, subcommittee or sustainable development board, taking into account the experience of the Designated Officials for Environmental Matters (DOEM) and the Committee of International

Development Institutions on Environment (CIDIE), as well as the respective roles of UNEP and UNDP. Its report should be submitted to the relevant intergovernmental bodies.

F. *High-level advisory body*

38.18. Intergovernmental bodies, the Secretary-General and the United Nations system as a whole may also benefit from the expertise of a high-level advisory board consisting of eminent persons knowledgeable about environment and development, including relevant sciences, appointed by the Secretary-General in their personal capacity. In this regard, the Secretary-General should make appropriate recommendations to the General Assembly at its forty-seventh session.

G. *Secretariat support structure*

38.19. A highly qualified and competent secretariat support structure within the United Nations Secretariat, drawing, inter alia, on the expertise gained in the Conference preparatory process is essential for the follow-up to the Conference and the implementation of Agenda 21. This secretariat support structure should provide support to the work of both intergovernmental and inter-agency coordination mechanisms. Concrete organizational decisions fall within the competence of the Secretary-General as the chief administrative officer of the Organization, who is requested to report on the provisions to be made, covering staffing implications, as soon as practicable, taking into account gender balance as defined in Article 8 of the Charter of the United Nations and the need for the best use of existing resources in the context of the current and ongoing restructuring of the United Nations Secretariat.

H. *Organs, programmes and organizations of the United Nations system*

38.20. In the follow-up to the Conference, in particular the implementation of Agenda 21, all relevant organs, programmes and organizations of the United Nations system will have an important role within their respective areas of expertise and mandates in supporting and supplementing national efforts. Coordination and mutual complementarity of their efforts to promote integration of environment and development can be enhanced by encouraging countries to maintain consistent positions in the various governing bodies.

1. United Nations Environment Programme

38.21. In the follow-up to the Conference, there will be a need for an enhanced and strengthened role for UNEP and its Governing Council. The Governing Council should, within its mandate, continue to play its role with regard to policy guidance and coordination in the field of the environment, taking into account the development perspective.

38.22. Priority areas on which UNEP should concentrate include the following:

   (a) Strengthening its catalytic role in stimulating and promoting environmental activities and considerations throughout the United Nations system;

   (b) Promoting international cooperation in the field of environment and recommending, as appropriate, policies to this end;

(c) Developing and promoting the use of such techniques as natural resource accounting and environmental economics;

(d) Environmental monitoring and assessment, both through improved participation by the United Nations system agencies in the Earthwatch programme and expanded relations with private scientific and non-governmental research institutes; strengthening and making operational its early-warning function;

(e) Coordination and promotion of relevant scientific research with a view to providing a consolidated basis for decision-making;

(f) Dissemination of environmental information and data to Governments and to organs, programmes and organizations of the United Nations system;

(g) Raising general awareness and action in the area of environmental protection through collaboration with the general public, non-governmental entities and intergovernmental institutions;

(h) Further development of international environmental law, in particular conventions and guidelines, promotion of its implementation, and coordinating functions arising from an increasing number of international legal agreements, inter alia, the functioning of the secretariats of the Conventions, taking into account the need for the most efficient use of resources, including possible co-location of secretariats established in the future;

(i) Further development and promotion of the widest possible use of environmental impact assessments, including activities carried out under the auspices of specialized agencies of the United Nations system, and in connection with every significant economic development project or activity;

(j) Facilitation of information exchange on environmentally sound technologies, including legal aspects, and provision of training;

(k) Promotion of subregional and regional cooperation and support to relevant initiatives and programmes for environmental protection, including playing a major contributing and coordinating role in the regional mechanisms in the field of environment identified for the follow-up to the Conference;

(l) Provision of technical, legal and institutional advice to Governments, upon request, in establishing and enhancing their national legal and institutional frameworks, in particular, in cooperation with UNDP capacity-building efforts;

(m) Support to Governments, upon request, and development agencies and organs in the integration of environmental aspects into their development policies and programmes, in particular through provision of environmental, technical and policy advice during programme formulation and implementation;

(n) Further developing assessment and assistance in cases of environmental emergencies.

38.23. In order to perform all of these functions, while retaining its role as the principal body within the United Nations system in the field of environment and taking into account the development aspects of environmental questions, UNEP would require access to greater expertise and provision of adequate financial resources and it would require closer cooperation and collaboration with development organs and other relevant organs of the United Nations system. Furthermore, the regional offices of UNEP should be strengthened without weakening its headquarters in Nairobi, and UNEP should take steps to reinforce and intensify its liaison and interaction with UNDP and the World Bank.

2. United Nations Development Programme

38.24. UNDP, like UNEP, also has a crucial role in the follow-up to the United Nations Conference on Environment and Development. Through its network of field offices it would foster the United Nations system's collective thrust in support of the implementation of Agenda 21, at the country, regional, interregional and global levels, drawing on the expertise of the specialized agencies and other United Nations organizations and bodies involved in operational activities. The role of the resident representative/resident coordinator of UNDP needs to be strengthened in order to coordinate the field-level activities of the United Nations operational activities.

38.25. Its role should include the following:

(a) Acting as the lead agency in organizing United Nations system efforts towards capacity-building at the local, national and regional levels;

(b) Mobilizing donor resources on behalf of Governments for capacity-building in recipient countries and, where appropriate, through the use of the UNDP donor round-table mechanisms;

(c) Strengthening its own programmes in support of follow-up to the Conference without prejudice to the fifth programming cycle;

(d) Assisting recipient countries, upon request, in the establishment and strengthening of national coordination mechanisms and networks related to activities for the follow-up to the Conference;

(e) Assisting recipient countries, upon request, in coordinating the mobilization of domestic financial resources;

(f) Promoting and strengthening the role and involvement of women, youth and other major groups in recipient countries in the implementation of Agenda 21.

3. United Nations Conference on Trade and Development

38.26. UNCTAD should play an important role in the implementation of Agenda 21 as extended at its eighth session, taking into account the importance of the interrelationships between development, international trade and the environment and in accordance with its mandate in the area of sustainable development.

4. United Nations Sudano-Sahelian Office

38.27. The role of the United Nations Sudano-Sahelian Office (UNSO), with added resources that may become available, operating under the umbrella of UNDP and with the support of UNEP, should be strengthened so that it can assume an appropriate major advisory role and participate effectively in the implementation of Agenda 21 provisions related to combating drought and desertification and to land resource management. In this context, the experience gained could be used by all other countries affected by drought and desertification, in particular those in Africa, with special attention to countries most affected or classified as least developed countries.

5. Specialized agencies of the United Nations system and related organizations and other relevant intergovernmental organizations

38.28. All specialized agencies of the United Nations system, related organizations and other relevant intergovernmental organizations within their respective fields of competence have an important role to play in the implementation of relevant parts of Agenda 21 and other decisions of the Conference. Their governing bodies may consider ways of strengthening and adjusting activities and programmes in line with Agenda 21, in particular, regarding projects for promoting sustainable development. Furthermore, they may consider establishing special arrangements with donors and financial institutions for project implementation that may require additional resources.

I. *Regional and subregional cooperation and implementation*

38.29. Regional and subregional cooperation will be an important part of the outcome of the Conference. The regional commissions, regional development banks and regional economic and technical cooperation organizations, within their respective agreed mandates, can contribute to this process by:

(a) Promoting regional and subregional capacity-building;

(b) Promoting the integration of environmental concerns in regional and subregional development policies;

(c) Promoting regional and subregional cooperation, where appropriate, regarding transboundary issues related to sustainable development.

38.30. The regional commissions, as appropriate, should play a leading role in coordinating regional and subregional activities by sectoral and other United Nations bodies and shall assist countries in achieving sustainable development. The commissions and regional programmes within the United Nations system, as well as other regional organizations, should review the need for modification of ongoing activities, as appropriate, in light of Agenda 21.

38.31. There must be active cooperation and collaboration among the regional commissions and other relevant organizations, regional development banks, non-governmental organizations and other institutions at the regional level. UNEP and UNDP, together with the regional commissions, would have a crucial role to play, especially in providing the necessary assistance, with particular emphasis on building and strengthening the national capacity of Member States.

38.32. There is a need for closer cooperation between UNEP and UNDP, together with other relevant institutions, in the implementation of projects to halt environmental degradation or its impact and to support training programmes in environmental planning and management for sustainable development at the regional level.

38.33. Regional intergovernmental technical and economic organizations have an important role to play in helping Governments to take coordinated action in solving environment issues of regional significance.

38.34. Regional and subregional organizations should play a major role in the implementation of the provisions of Agenda 21 related to combating drought and desertification. UNEP, UNDP and UNSO should assist and cooperate with those relevant organizations.

38.35. Cooperation between regional and subregional organizations and relevant organizations of the United Nations system should be encouraged, where appropriate, in other sectoral areas.

J. *National implementation*

38.36. States have an important role to play in the follow-up of the Conference and the implementation of Agenda 21. National level efforts should be undertaken by all countries in an integrated manner so that both environment and development concerns can be dealt with in a coherent manner.

38.37. Policy decisions and activities at the national level, tailored to support and implement Agenda 21, should be supported by the United Nations system upon request.

38.38. Furthermore, States could consider the preparation of national reports. In this context, the organs of the United Nations system should, upon request, assist countries, in particular developing countries. Countries could also consider the preparation of national action plans for the implementation of Agenda 21.

38.39. Existing assistance consortia, consultative groups and round tables should make greater efforts to integrate environmental considerations and related development objectives into their development assistance strategies and should consider reorienting and appropriately adjusting their memberships and operations to facilitate this process and better support national efforts to integrate environment and development.

38.40. States may wish to consider setting up a national coordination structure responsible for the follow-up of Agenda 21. Within this structure, which would benefit from the expertise of non-governmental organizations, submissions and other relevant information could be made to the United Nations.

K. *Cooperation between United Nations bodies and international financial organizations*

38.41. The success of the follow-up to the Conference is dependent upon an effective link between substantive action and financial support, and this requires close and effective cooperation between United Nations bodies and the multilateral financial organizations. The Secretary-General and heads of United Nations programmes, organizations and the multilateral financial organizations have a special responsibility in forging such cooperation, not only through the United Nations high-level coordination mechanism (Administrative Committee on Coordination) but also at regional and national levels. In particular, representatives of multilateral financial institutions and mechanisms, as well as IFAD, should actively be associated with deliberations of the intergovernmental structure responsible for the follow-up to Agenda 21.

L. *Non-governmental organizations*

38.42. Non-governmental organizations and major groups are important partners in the implementation of Agenda 21. Relevant non-governmental organizations, including the scientific community, the private sector and women's groups, should be given opportunities to make their contributions and establish appropriate relationships with the United Nations system. Support should be provided for developing countries' non-governmental organizations and their self-organized networks.

38.43. The United Nations system, including international finance and development agencies, and all intergovernmental organizations and forums should, in consultation with non-governmental organizations, take measures to:

(a) Design open and effective means to achieve the participation of non-governmental organizations, including those related to major groups, in the process established to review and evaluate the implementation of Agenda 21 at all levels and promote their contribution to it;

(b) Take into account the findings of review systems and evaluation processes of non-governmental organizations in relevant reports of the Secretary-General to the General Assembly and all pertinent United Nations agencies and intergovernmental organizations and forums concerning implementation of Agenda 21 in accordance with the review process.

38.44. Procedures should be established for an expanded role for non-governmental organizations, including those related to major groups, with accreditation based on the procedures used in the Conference. Such organizations should have access to reports and other information produced by the United Nations system. The General Assembly, at an early stage, should examine ways of enhancing the involvement of non-governmental organizations within the United Nations system in relation to the follow-up process of the Conference.

38.45. The Conference takes note of other institutional initiatives for the implementation of Agenda 21, such as the proposal to establish a non-governmental Earth Council and the proposal to appoint a guardian for future generations, as well as other initiatives taken by local governments and business sectors.

APPENDIX 2: A GUIDE TO INTERNATIONAL INSTITUTIONS ON THE INTERNET

ORGANIZATION	WORLD WIDE WEB SITE
UN SYSTEM	http://www.unsystem.org
UNCSD	http://www.mbnet.mb.ca/linkages/csd
UNEP	http://unep.unep.no
UNDP	http://www.undp.org
SELECTED INTERNATIONAL ENVIRONMENTAL TREATIES	
CBD	http://www.unep.ch./biodiv.html
UNFCCC	http://www.unep.ch/unfccc/html
MONTREAL PROTOCOL	http://www.unep.org/unep/secretar/ozon
UNCTAD	http://gatekeeper.unicc.org/unctad
WTO	http://www.unicc.org.wto/Welcome.html
NAFTA	
COMMISSION FOR ENVIRONMENTAL DEVELOPMENT	http://www.cec.org
WORLD BANK	http://www.worldbank.org
	http://www.esd.worldbank.org
IMF	gopher://gopher.imf.org
GEF	http://www.worldbank.org/html/gef/Welcome.html
EU	http://www.cec.lu
OECD	http://www.oecd.org
SMALL ISLANDS	www.upei.ca/~meinke/sidsnet.html

INDEX

acid rain 22
AETR case 189
Agenda 21: call for international dialogue
111; cooperation 21, 51, 54;
coordinating legal agreements 42–3;
and CSD 29; division of labour 38–9;
and GEF 153, 155; implementation
36–7, 42; international workshops
34–5; and NAFTA 116–17; response to
48–50; and the South Pacific 210–13;
sustainable development cornerstone
policy 24, 26; UNCTAD work
programme 90–3; UNDP's role 47–8
agriculture 47
aid *see* finances
Alliance of Small Island States (AOSIS)
29–30
Amnesty International 244
animals: EC Wild Birds Directive 231, 232
Antarctica: General Assembly resolutions
8–9; treaty of 1959 8
Australia: *Nuclear Tests* cases 223, 224;
phosphate mining case 223
Austria 35

Bangladesh 13
Barbados Declaration 212
Basel Convention of the Transboundary
Shipment of Hazardous Wastes 41, 63,
232; inconsistencies with GATT 103;
and NAFTA 118; reporting 255
Basel Convention on the Transboundary
Shipment of Hazardous Wastes: trade
regulations 100
Belize 168
Berlin Mandate 60, 62, 63, 65, 67

Bhutan 167, 168
biodiversity 22; funding 175; Lake Malawi
135
Biological and Toxin Weapons Convention
241
Bolivia 172
Boutros-Ghali, Boutros 30
Brazil 139, 145
Bretton Woods institutions 131–2, 146;
non-governmental organizations and
accountability 256–7; voting system
157–8
Brundtland Commission *see* World
Commission on Environment and
Development
Brussels Convention 233
Budapest Document 245
Bunting, Bruce 167
business: and non-governmental
organizations 253; private versus
public 85–6, 92; transnational
corporations 86, 89

Camdessus, Michael 143
Cameroon 137, 142
Canada 226 *see also* North American Free
Trade Agreement; trade agreements
94–5
Capacity 21 50–1
capacity-building: failures of developing
aid 164–6; National Environmental
Funds 170–1; neglect 164; small island
states 211
CAPE-21 255
Carabias Lillo, Julia 127
Caribbean 176

For Product Safety Concerns and Information please contact our EU
representative GPSR@taylorandfrancis.com
Taylor & Francis Verlag GmbH, Kaufingerstraße 24, 80331 München, Germany